HITLER'S LAST GENERAL

Also by Ian Sayer & Douglas Botting:
Nazi Gold
America's Secret Army

Also by Douglas Botting:
One Chilly Siberian Morning
Wilderness Europe
Humboldt and the Cosmos
The Second Front
The Aftermath: Europe
In the Ruins of the Reich

HITLER'S
LAST GENERAL
—— IAN SAYER ——
and DOUGLAS BOTTING

BANTAM PRESS
LONDON · NEW YORK · TORONTO · SYDNEY · AUCKLAND

TRANSWORLD PUBLISHERS LTD
61–63 Uxbridge Road, London W5 5SA

TRANSWORLD PUBLISHERS (AUSTRALIA) PTY LTD
15-23 Helles Avenue, Moorebank, NSW 2170

TRANSWORLD PUBLISHERS (NZ) LTD
Cnr Moselle and Waipareira Aves,
Henderson, Auckland

Published 1989 by Bantam Press,
a division of Transworld Publishers Ltd
Copyright © Ian Sayer & Douglas Botting 1989

British Library Cataloguing in Publication Data

Sayer, Ian, *1945–*
  Hitler's last general: the case against
  Wilhelm Mohnke.
  1. German war criminals. Mohnke, Wilhelm
  I. Title   II. Botting, Douglas
  364.1'38'0924

  ISBN 0-593-01709-9

This book is set in Ehrhardt by
Phoenix Photosetting, Chatham.
Printed and bound in Great Britain by
Mackays of Chatham PLC, Chatham, Kent.

This book is for the victims, who never came back; and for the survivors, in the interests of justice.

PHOTO CREDITS

Photographs are reproduced by permission of the following:

ACKNOWLEDGEMENTS

The authors are profoundly grateful to many people and institutions in a number of countries throughout the world who unstintingly gave up a great deal of their time and energy to answering – by letter, telephone and personal interview – a remorseless stream of questions about complicated events of many years ago. To all of these people – and especially to those who on occasion ungrudgingly allowed their privacy to be invaded – the authors extend their very genuinely felt gratitude and appreciation.

Wormhoudt survivors: Charles Daley, Albert Evans, Brian Fahey, Alfred Tombs, Reg West. Also Albert Montague.

Other individuals: Reverend Leslie Aitken, George Amos, Arthur Baxter, Carrie Beeks, Steve Borland, J.A. Borland, Clive Bourne, Alastair Brett, Earl Browning (Fairfax, Virginia), David Burnside, Phil Buss, John Creed, Gerd Cuppens (Belgium), A.S. Davies, Sharon Dixon, I.R. English, Mike Farback, David Foster, Tony Harris, Patrick Harrison, Prett Houston, Pat Howes, J. Hughes, P.J. Jeffreys, Miss P.M. Jennings, W. Jone, Linda Jones, T.H. Nicholls, Anthony Marreco, Rob McLoughlin, James H. Ratcliff (Cincinatti, Ohio), Jost W. Schneider (West Germany), Andy Smith, Hugh Page Taylor, Anthony Terry (New Zealand), Roger Underhay, Mrs Kathleen West.

Institutions:
Will Mahoney, Military Division, National Archives, Washington DC, USA.
Robert Stanogle, National Adjutant, The American Legion.
Robert J. Walsh, Chief, Freedom of Information/Privacy Office, Maryland, USA.
Eli M. Rosenbaum, Office of Special Investigations, Washington DC.

W.J.A. Hobson, Senior General Counsel, Department of Justice, Canada.
Research Library, Imperial War Museum, London.
Wiener Library, London.
James J. Weingartner, Southern Illinois University.
Elizabeth Holtzman, District Attorney, Brooklyn, New York.

Special thanks are due to:
Jeff Rooker, MP, for championing the Wormhoudt survivors' cause in the
House of Commons; Janet Pickering for her interest and support; Tom
Agoston in Hamburg; Richard Richter and Bunny Pantcheff for providing
invaluable information; Richard Lane for his assistance, general encouragement and providing important doumentary evidence; Sir David Napley
for providing free legal advice to the Wormhoudt survivors; Robert Kaplan,
MP, for bringing the matter to the attention of the House of Commons in
Ottawa; Gary Curtis for his general involvement and assistance in tracing a
crucial eyewitness; Philip Rubenstein, Secretary of the All Party Parliamentary War Crimes Group, for his commitment to pursuing the interests
of justice; Sally Slaney for her energetic support at a critical period;
Charles Messenger for his diligence in checking the manuscript and for
locating important judicial papers; Tom Field-Fisher, QC, for his expert
comments as a former war crimes prosecutor; Doug Cordrey, a key figure
in establishing Mohnke's involvement in the Wormhoudt massacre; and
finally Ursula Mackenzie and Jim Cochrane of Bantam Press for their
encouragement and patience.

PREFACE

This is a book about a series of war crimes committed on the orders of one man. That man is former SS-General Wilhelm Mohnke, now living in comfortable and harmless retirement near Hamburg, in West Germany.

The crimes in question do not make pretty reading; to any emotionally balanced person no crimes involving cold-blooded murder can – especially when set against the battlefield traumas of total war and the close-quarter combat ethics of the Waffen-SS. But these crimes do pose some intriguing investigative conundrums, and it was to try and unravel these and thus bring about some prospect of belated justice for the many victims and the dwindling ranks of the survivors and the bereaved that this book was written.

The book is not the result of a vengeful personal witch-hunt, nor has it been written in any spirit of jingoistic and outmoded anti-German feeling. It is well known that many Britons are still reliving the Second World War, while most Germans have spent the best part of forty-five years trying to forget it. As one West German reader wrote to a British national newspaper recently:

'It sometimes seems that for the "average decent Briton" the war happened about six months ago and that every German who today is over eighteen years of age took an active part in it. For the British the Continent is still full of Huns.'

But there are some wartime events, we believe, which common justice demands should be neither forgotten nor forgiven. This book is about some of them. And though it was written by Britons, it is not a purely British book. For the Mohnke case is an international affair, involving war crimes against the citizens of America, Canada, Belgium, even Germany itself, and very possibly Poland, as well as Britain. The fact that Mohnke is still on the wanted list of the United Nations War Crimes Commission, and actually has a file and case number assigned to him by that organization, is indicative of the international scope of his case.

xiii

The book also makes every possible attempt to present an objective account of the tortuous and bloody events it describes. This has led the authors into some strange, uncharted bends in the river. We have discovered that war crimes were not the sole preserve of the Nazis, for example, and that justice was not always the Allies' strongest suit. Thus we have found ourselves arguing, on the one hand, that one of Mohnke's subordinate SS commanders, who was hanged by the British for murdering Canadian POWs in Normandy, was the victim of a miscarriage of justice; and, on the other, that one of the United States' most revered field commanders of World War II, General Patton, may – if the same laws that were applied to German senior commanders had also been applied to Allied ones – have been a star-spangled war criminal in his own right.

Wilhelm Mohnke, it must be said, was not any ordinary, common or garden Nazi or SS henchman. He was, in more senses than one, a distinguished functionary of the diabolical machine of which he himself formed a significant part. Mohnke's career, in the ascendant until the very end, cut a swathe through the history of the Third Reich from the very first to the very last days of Hitler's tyrannic rule – from the bloody episode of the Night of the Long Knives to the final days in the Berlin Bunker. A founder-member of Hitler's élite SS bodyguard, the Leibstandarte, Mohnke was for much of his career very close to the centre of things, whether as a ruthless Waffen-SS commander in the historic campaigns in the East and the West, or as Hitler's last general in charge of the Bunker in those final, surreal *Götterdämmerung* days, when it was his duty first to protect the Führer and then to propose his demise.

It was the Russians who saved Mohnke's life by locking him up in their many camps for ten years. If it had not been for the Red Army and the Secret Political Police, the Western Allies would assuredly have vied for his custody so that he could answer questions about his complicity in the worst atrocities suffered by prisoners of war in modern American, Canadian and British history. But by the time the quarry had slunk back into West Germany, the hunt was over and the hounds had departed. More than thirty years passed before the matter was raised at any official level. Then, in April 1988, a British Member of Parliament, Jeff Rooker, put a question on the subject to the Home Secretary in the House of Commons. In an eloquent and moving statement to the British Parliament a few months later, the Parliamentary Under-Secretary of State for Defence revealed the full extent of the tragedy that had overtaken British troops when they fell into Mohnke's hands at Wormhoudt during the retreat to Dunkirk in 1940. The hounds were back on the scent; the hunt was on again.

This present book constitutes one of the most detailed and comprehensive dossiers about a single war criminal ever compiled outside a court and the official investigative system. Based on our own intensive investigations using original documents and other sources, it presents for the first time the complete case about one of the most senior Waffen-SS generals still alive, a crucial figure in the death throes of the Third Reich. It shows beyond all reasonable doubt that a prima facie case exists against Wilhelm Mohnke on a number of counts; and it urges that the American, Canadian, British and Belgian governments should take action now, or prevail upon the West German authorities to pursue the case with the utmost vigour, in order that justice might take its proper course before it is too late.

'The evil that men do,' it is written, 'lives after them.' Many years have now passed, but there are still men alive today who bear the physical scars and mental anguish of the events described in these pages. We have shown the way. It is up to others to redress the balance of justice – or give up all pretence that a war criminal should not, in all honesty, be allowed to get away with his crimes.

Ian Sayer
Douglas Botting
London
28 June 1989

HITLER'S LAST GENERAL

PART I

—

Hitler's Last General

BERLIN 30 APRIL 1945

The field telephone in the sepulchral Reich Chancellery cellar was ringing. Somewhere deep down in the dark recesses of his dreams, SS General Wilhelm Mohnke heard the shrill, insistent call and struggled to surface from his death-like sleep. He half sat up and looked at his watch. Six o'clock on the morning of 30 April 1945. Springtime in Berlin, a city ringed with steel and wreathed in fire; the beginning of another bloody day of which he might never live to see the end.

The Red Army guns had not yet loosed off the devastating artillery barrage with which they heralded each new dawn, so at least some semblance of peace still reigned in the subterranean warren in which General Mohnke and all the other last-ditch defenders of the Nazi capital now skulked like moles. Mohnke heaved his large frame on to the edge of the bed and grabbed the handset.

'Brigadeführer Mohnke,' he barked brusquely. *'Was möchten Sie?'*

He recognized the voice on the other end of the line before the caller even had time to identify himself, Sergeant Rochus Misch. Another of the Bunker dwellers who lived like troglodytes in the warren of the Führer's concrete catacomb deep beneath the Reich Chancellery garden, Sergeant Misch was the switchboard operator in the Führerbunker. A steady, reliable man and an old SS-Leibstandarte veteran, Misch had been a trooper in Mohnke's infantry company in those distant days of thunder and glory when the Leibstandarte, Hitler's élite SS bodyguard regiment, had cut a swathe through Poland at the very start of Germany's conquest of the East. Heady days! The Nazi dream of a Greater German Reich had seemed within their grasp then, all those years of blood and sacrifice ago.

Mohnke sighed. 'Yes, Misch?'

'Sorry to disturb you, General,' Misch's voice crackled over the field line. 'But it's very urgent. The Führer wants to see you alone in his

3

quarters. Just a moment ago he said he'd like to have a chat with his old friend Mohnke. He told me to ring you.'

Hitler was in a relaxed mood, Misch reported, even though he had not slept a wink all night. He was expecting the General at once.

Mohnke did not take long to make himself presentable. As commander of the inner defensive ring in the German capital – the central government area known as the Citadel which included the Reich Chancellery and the Führerbunker – he was dressed and on call at all times of the day and night. Not that day and night were easily distinguishable in the unnatural underground existence to which the last hard-core of survivors of the Thousand Year Reich were now subjected. Mohnke eased a jackboot over his specially moulded wooden foot – the most spectacular of his many war wounds, a souvenir of the Balkan war – and adjusted the Knight's Cross round his neck, a supreme award for valour which he had won in the killing fields of Normandy. Then he buttoned up his SS general officer's tunic, buckled on his belt and pistol in its holster, strapped his coalscuttle steel helmet on his balding head, pulled himself up to his full SS guardsman's six-foot height, clicked his heels, cleared his throat, gathered his thoughts, then strode purposefully off, unshaven and unbreakfasted, through the dark tunnel system that connected his command post with the Führer's underground lair.

On that fateful morning of the Reich's *Götterdämmerung* and Berlin's apocalypse, SS Brigadeführer Mohnke – at thirty-four the youngest general still on active duty in the Waffen-SS, the last army general over whom Hitler had any direct control, the last commander of the last shrinking patch of the capital of the erstwhile Nazi Empire – looked every inch the war lord he was. A died-in-the-wool career SS man, an unswerving and unrepentant acolyte of the National Socialist faith, a most loyal and faithful-unto-death myrmidon of his revered, doomed, and damned leader, Adolf Hitler.

Mohnke had trod these wretched tunnels through the catacombs so often in the last weeks since he had assumed command of the Reich Chancellery troops that he was now inured to the dank building-site miasma of damp, half-dried cement, the monotonous background whirr of the ventilator systen, the muffled voices that issued confusingly, like the counterfeit utterances of some invisible ventriloquist, from the dark recesses and inner rooms of the maze, the pallid young soldiers with dusty faces slumped down in sleep in the concrete corridors, or standing with vacant, hopeless faces, knowing they had only sudden death to look forward to in the embattled streets above, or at best a not-so-sudden death in some bleak Soviet slave camp in Siberia or the Urals. All this Mohnke was resigned to as he strode to meet his Führer that historic morning. He had been a front-line soldier for five years on five fronts. There was little that could shock him now – except perhaps the sight of the Führer himself.

At this early hour there were few people about in the Führerbunker, only Misch at the switchboard, a couple of guards who had dozed off, and Hitler's secretary, Gerda Christian, stretched out in a bed roll on the floor of the Führer's study. The study was the room where Hitler normally discussed Mohnke's daily situation reports. But not this morning. Misch ushered the general into Hitler's tiny functional bedroom, then closed the door. In this unusual, highly informal setting, Wilhelm Mohnke embarked on what was to prove the single most historically important episode in his life – one which would not only help bring about the death knell of the Third Reich but change for ever the course of the twentieth century.

Hitler was sitting on the edge of his bed, which looked as though it had not been slept in. He was wearing a black satin dressing-gown over his white pyjamas, and patent-leather slippers on his feet. The Führer rose when Mohnke entered, and sat down again in the only chair in the room, gesturing to Mohnke to sit on the bed. Hitler's left arm was trembling, Mohnke noticed, and his gaze was fixed on the wall behind Mohnke's head. Hitler looked a nervous wreck, with a deathly, sepulchral pallor, and the frail, unsteady movements of a prematurely aged man. What Mohnke had to tell his Führer was not very pleasant, but it had to be done; it was Hitler's own wish and command.

Mohnke outlined the up-to-the-minute tactical situation in the streets up top. The Russians now occupied the Tiergarten and had taken the Adlon Hotel and reached the Wilhelmstrasse, four blocks from the Bunker. Russian troops now ringed his positions in the Potsdamer Platz and had got down into the underground railway tunnels under the Friedrichstrasse and the Voss-strasse, just outside the Chancellery itself. Hitler listened to the news that in effect spelt out his death sentence. He said nothing; asked no questions.

'My Führer,' Mohnke told the taciturn man in the chair opposite him, 'as soldier to soldier, true to my oath to you, I no longer can guarantee that my exhausted, battle-weary troops can hold for more than one more day. I now expect a frontal, massed-tank attack at dawn, 1 May. You know what 1 May means to Russians.'

The news Mohnke brought amounted to his Führer's death sentence. For Hitler did indeed know the significance that Stalin would attach to storming the Reichstag and the Reich Chancellery and seizing the Nazi capital on May Day. Hitler now seemed fully aware that his life was at an end. He had hoped to last until 5 May, he told Mohnke, the date Napoleon died on St Helena. After that, he had no desire to live. 'We were both men born before our times. So much the worse for Europe.' It dawned on Mohnke that the only reason Hitler had summoned him to his bedroom at this hour was to chat, to empty his mind to someone he felt he could trust. Wilhelm Mohnke was not a close friend of Adolf Hitler, but he was an outstanding SS officer of the only SS formation that bore his own name in full; he was a front-line veteran; he was, moreover, a fresh set of ears, and though Mohnke might never say very much, he was clearly a good listener to whatever his Führer felt compelled to say to him. After the first ten minutes all conversation ceased and Hitler lapsed into a continuous monologue. For an hour the doomed leader of the Third Reich that had barely more than a week to run sat twitching in his dressing-gown and pouring out whatever was uppermost inside his head.

General Mohnke had many important matters to attend to that morning; he had troops to command, positions to defend, escape plans to formulate for the mass break-out from the Bunker, for which he was responsible. But in the entire length of his long SS career, those twelve hard years of steely discipline and cast-iron orders, there was no greater duty he could perform than this – his last audience with his Führer, whom he had faithfully served from the first day of the Third Reich to the last, and whom he knew he would never see alive again.

Mohnke recalled: 'He reviewed his whole career, what he called the dream of National Socialism and why and how it failed. The German people had, in the end, proved unworthy, just not up to the supreme challenge. His spirit lifted when he reminded me of his old triumphs, like the tumultuous receptions in 1938 in Linz and Vienna. I, too, had participated as a member of the FBK [the SS honour bodyguard]. Then he spoke of the many exultant victory parades in which I had marched with the LAH.* He was, so to speak, cheering himself up.'

At length Hitler came to an end of it and Mohnke rose to leave. Hitler thanked him for his loyalty. 'Your troops have fought splendidly, I have no complaints,' he told Mohnke. 'Would that all the others had fought as tenaciously.' But there was no medal for Mohnke, no parting present. Instead, Hitler handed Mohnke typed copies of his last will and testament, which he hoped Mohnke might carry safely out of the Russian encirclement. Then, as Mohnke returned to his command post to try and hold the Russians one last time, the Führer began to put in order the last day of his life.

Up in the streets Mohnke made one last round of his embattled positions. It was an unreal situation, in an unreal city. The air was thick with fumes and smoke and a fine ash that sifted down like a dry drizzle; and the sky was the colour of sulphur, with here and there a lurid red glow as great fires gutted what was left of this capital of all their dreams. Mohnke stared about him. Were these listless, bedraggled, soot-spattered soldiers the

* This was a new Chancellery guard, set up in 1933 at Hitler's request, of totally loyal SS men which soon became known as SS-Leibstandarte Adolf Hitler, or LAH for short.

remnants of the finest regiment that had ever marched, the warrior knights who had conquered a continent, his old Leibstandarte? Were these piles of rubble, these gaunt, burnt-out ruins, all there was of the capital of a Reich that would last a thousand years? He had marched, once, at the head of his troops through these same shattered streets in the days of the great parades, the victory processions, the crowds cheering, flags flying, bands playing, boots gleaming. '*Die Fahne hoch, die Reihe standen zusammen. . . .*' Days of hope, days of glory, days dizzy with fervour and expectation, a nation resurrected from ruin by the National Socialist revolution, and he, Wilhelm Mohnke, ex-warehouse clerk, ex-unemployed drifter, marching at the head of his men, the cream of the revolution, the élite of a reborn Germany, past his revered, his beloved Führer. '*Meine Ehre heisst Treue.*' My Loyalty is my Honour. They had all sworn the SS oath of loyalty to the palsied old man who now lurked below ground, grimly waiting for the end. Where were they now, those comrades of the early struggle, of the days of smoke and battle, the gallop across Poland, the chase to Dunkirk, the battle for Normandy, the last throw in the Ardennes – and now this final, lingering, inglorious death-rattle in Berlin? Hitler's last general turned his back on the ruins and limped back to his command post in the cellars. His future was as blank as the grey walls of the empty shells of the buildings outside. Only his past still lived – those twelve fantastic years that bridged the entire span of this great adventure, the rise and fall of Adolf Hitler.

7

PART II

—

With the SS Bodyguard

1933–1940

Wilhelm Mohnke was one of those men of history who – like Hitler – rose to eminence from obscure and even humble origins. Born in the Hanseatic city of Lübeck on 15 March 1911, the son of a master joiner of the same name, the young Mohnke was seven when the Great War ended so catastrophically for his Fatherland and in his late teens when the Depression and the Great Inflation all but destroyed the health, wealth and happiness of his family, and that of most of his fellow burgers of Lübeck, and for that matter much of the respectable, hard-working, God-fearing and fervently patriotic middle and lower-middle classes of Germany.

The pain and tumult of those chaotic years were made even more traumatic for the Mohnke boy by the tragic death of his father, which resulted in the abrupt termination of his formal schooling at the Middle School for Boys in Lübeck, which he left with an Upper Fifth Form Certificate at the age of fifteen. The young Mohnke was now precipitated into a harsh and violent world where jobs were few, poverty was rife and political gang warfare endemic in the streets. Mohnke was a diligent and intelligent youngster, however, and succeeded in finding a job where others failed. After a period of training in the State Business School, he rapidly worked his way up the lower rungs of a firm dealing in glass- and porcelain-ware, first as a warehouse clerk, then as a commercial traveller, and finally as manager of a branch in the town of Güstrow. But he was swimming against the rising tide of economic chaos and unemployment, and in March 1932, shortly after his twenty-first birthday, he finally lost his job and joined the ranks of the millions of others for whom only something as drastic as a national revolution could solve the catastrophe which had overwhelmed them.

All this made Wilhelm Mohnke a natural recruit for a political party then sweeping the country like a storm, a party which rallied the jobless, disaffected and disinherited middle classes and gave them purpose for the

11

present and hope for the future – a party called the National Socialist German Workers' Party, led by a rising demagogic leader by the name of Adolf Hitler. Mohnke threw in his lot with Hitler's Nazis as early as September 1931, when he was only twenty, and three months later, for good measure, he joined the SS – specifically the Lübeck SS Troop of the 4th SS-Standarte [Regiment], from which he later transferred to the Lübeck 22nd SS-Standarte. From the outset Mohnke proved an ardent Nazi and an enthusiastic and dedicated SS man. He had, indeed, found his rightful milieu at last. A stern, highly disciplined, rather solemn and aloof personality, with a natural sense of authority marred by a fierce and sudden temper, the new recruit rose rapidly through the ranks – from Corporal in March 1932, to Sergeant in March 1933, to Second-Lieutenant in June of that year, and to Captain (Hauptsturmführer) only four months later.

But the greatest step Wilhelm Mohnke ever took in his life was made in March 1933, when he joined an organization then being set up by a remarkable man with whom his career was to be inextricably linked for many years to come. This man was a forty-year-old Bavarian meat packer's son by the name of Sepp Dietrich, a coarse, stocky ex-Sergeant Major of the Great War, and one of Adolf Hitler's oldest companions in the struggle to power. A man of little education, crude speech, and rough-hewn country manners, Dietrich was described by Hitler as 'cunning, energetic and brutal', and by one eminent German Field Marshal (von Rundstedt) as 'decent but stupid'. But there was no doubting Sepp Dietrich's courage, his charisma, and the intense affection with which he was regarded by the men he led. One of these men was destined to be Wilhelm Mohnke.

On 17 March 1933 Hitler personally ordered Sepp Dietrich to form a special SS guard for his protection in the Reich Chancellery. 120 totally loyal and dedicated SS men were hand-picked to make up the initial hard-core of this new Chancellery guard, which was soon to bear the Führer's own name as the SS-Leibstandarte [SS Bodyguard] 'Adolf Hitler', or LAH for short. Among the founding fathers of this Praetorian Guard, so to speak, which was to become the élite formation of the wartime Waffen-SS, was Wilhelm Mohnke. Others who joined at the same time as Mohnke, or a little later, and were to become famous in the annals of the Leibstandarte's wartime exploits, were Theodor Wisch, Fritz Witt, Max Wünsche, Kurt Meyer, Jochen Peiper, Gerhard Bremer and Bernhard Siebken, all formidable SS warriors who rose to command the Leibstandarte at battalion, regiment or division level.

Recruits to the Leibstandarte were required to be perfect specimens of Nordic manhood – at least five feet eleven inches tall, with an athletic build and no physical defects of any kind, not even a single filled tooth. They also had to be of impeccable Aryan stock, with a spotless, Jew-free record of

12

pedigree dating back to the year 1750 (in the case of officers) or 1800 (in the case of enlisted men). Before the war, all members of the LAH were volunteers, and there was never any shortage of recruits for what many young Germans perceived as an ideological and military élite. Moreover, for able and ambitious young Nazi ideologues like Wilhelm Mohnke, whose lack of acceptable background and education debarred them from gaining an officer's commission in the regular German Army, the Leibstandarte offered a unique opportunity to embark on a military career with officer rank.

In the early pre-war years, however, the Leibstandarte was envisaged not so much as a military combat unit to defend the Reich against its *external* enemies – that was still the Army's job – but as a political para-military formation which in addition to its guard and ceremonial duties could be used as an armed police force to protect the security of the Reich against its *internal* enemies. The original Leibstandarte, in other words, was seen as the armed fist of the Führer and of the Nazi movement and the Nazi State. From this small acorn a great oak would grow.

First introduced to the German public by Hitler at the 1933 Nuremberg rally, the SS Bodyguard Regiment 'Adolf Hitler' moved into its permanent home at the prestigious Lichterfelde Barracks in the southern suburbs of Berlin at the end of the year and there proceeded to grow in numbers and status throughout the peacetime period. As an SS unit the Leibstandarte was nominally under the control of the chief of the SS, Reichsführer Heinrich Himmler. But as Hitler's own personal guard the Leibstandarte in practice was answerable to Hitler himself, as Hitler stressed in a letter to Himmler in 1938: 'Dietrich is master in his own house, which, I would remind you, is my house.' This gave Dietrich in particular and the Leibstandarte in general an unusual independence and prestige within the SS as a whole. 'The Leibstandarte is a complete law to itself,' Himmler was to complain to Dietrich. 'It does, and allows, anything it likes without taking the slightest orders from above.'

The Leibstandarte, in short, was the most élite formation of the most élite order of the Third Reich – a true National Socialist aristocracy. It was not only the Führer's personal bodyguard, the smart, jackbooted formation in raven-black uniforms that mounted the highly drilled, goose-stepping, heel-clicking ceremonial guard on great State occasions, and provided the adjutants, drivers, servants and waiters* who ministered to the Führer in his inner court in the Reich Chancellery in Berlin and at his Bavarian mountain retreat near Berchtesgaden; the Leibstandarte was also the

---

* Hitler's chauffeur, Eric Kempka, and his pilot, Hans Baur – both of them survivors of the last days in the Berlin Bunker – were also on the LAH roster.

armed expression of the will of Adolf Hitler, the disciplined, trained, obedient, para-military instrument of the Führer's pathological urge to violence. In the summer of 1934 this instrument was called upon to prove itself in one of the bloodiest episodes of those formative pre-war years. This was the affair of the Roehm purge – the so-called Night of the Long Knives.

In the spring of 1934 the Leibstandarte was entrusted with its first major task – the purge of the Brown Shirts of Ernst Roehm's SA (*Sturm Abteilung* or Storm Troopers), in a treacherous spasm of Nazi blood-letting known as the Night of the Long Knives.

During the period of the Nazis' rise to power, the thugs of the SA had served as Hitler's principal instrument of internal terror and coercion, and their leader, the burly, scar-faced, homosexual Roehm, had been Hitler's closest comrade in the days of the Party's struggle and one of the founders of the Third Reich. But once the Nazis had achieved power, the random acts of violence committed by the SA, and the swollen ambitions of its leader, were seen as an embarrassment and a potential danger to Hitler, who by now was looking to stabilize the Nazi revolution and achieve respectability in the eyes of a wider section of the German public. Persuaded by Goering and Himmler that Roehm was planning a putsch against the Hitler government – almost certainly a groundless charge – the Führer decided that the power of the SA should be smashed once and for all by the summary liquidation of its leadership. Himmler was given the task of destroying the SA in Bavaria, Goering the same task in Prussia and Berlin. Lists of victims were drawn up by Himmler, Goering and Reinhard Heydrich, the chief of the Prussian Gestapo and head of the security service (SD) of the SS; while Sepp Dietrich's Leibstandarte, the best-trained and best-equipped of the armed SS formations, was chosen to carry out the majority of the executions as part of a meticulously planned and co-ordinated lightning strike against Roehm and the SA leadership.

Preparations for this ruthless and cynical act of treachery against some of Hitler's oldest and most loyal supporters began towards the end of June 1934. Extra arms for a 'secret and very important assignment' were indented for by the Leibstandarte, leave was cancelled, and the regiment placed on alert. On 28 June Dietrich was ordered to report to Adolf Hitler at Bad Godesberg and await instructions. The next day, Friday, 29 June 1934, two companies of the LAH under the command of Obersturmbannführer Reich, the regiment's second-in-command, and Sturmbannführer Jürgen Wagner, commander of the 2nd Battalion – in which Mohnke was a company commander – were despatched from Berlin to Bavaria, where Roehm and his associates were on holiday. Hitler in the meantime flew to Munich, then drove in a long column of cars to the lakeside resort of Bad Wiessee, where he surprised the bewildered Roehm and his cronies still in bed, and at gunpoint had them carried off to the Stadelheim Prison in Munich on a charge of high treason. Dietrich, who unavoidably had been held up, now joined Hitler and was ordered to form a firing squad from his Leibstandarte troopers and carry out the executions of the SA men in Stadelheim as soon as possible. That evening six of Roehm's comrades were gunned down one after the other in the prison courtyard by the Leibstandarte firing squad. Roehm himself was murdered in his cell next day by Theodor Eicke, commandant of Dachau concentration camp, and his adjutant, Michael Lippert.

Meanwhile the Leibstandarte companies which had remained at the Lichterfelde Barracks in Berlin under the command of SS-Sturmbann-führer Martin Kohlroser were busily employed in liquidating the SA leadership in Prussia under the direction of Hermann Goering. According to some accounts, LAH *Einsatzkommandos* roamed the streets of the capital with other SS units, arresting or murdering all the listed 'enemies of the State' they could lay their hands on, while LAH firing squads in the Lichterfelde Barracks continued to carry out executions of some 150 key SA members. This included the leader of the Berlin SA, Karl Ernst, who was apprehended, knocked senseless, and dragged back to Lichterfelde as he was about to depart the Fatherland for a honeymoon in the Canary Islands with his young bride. All through Saturday, 30 June, the local residents in the vicinity of the barracks were disturbed by shouts and screams and orders, and by bursts of gunfire followed after a few seconds by the *coups de grâce*. The shooting went on almost until midnight, then resumed again next morning and continued into the early hours of 2 July, when the gangster-like killings were brought to an end on Hitler's orders.

It is not known exactly how many people were killed in that ghoulish summer weekend, the so-called Night of the Long Knives. The total ran into hundreds, and included not only key SA members but leading perso-nalities of the Weimar years, personal enemies of Himmler, Goering and Bormann, and anyone considered a threat of any kind to the life of Adolf Hitler. Nor was the precise number or identities of the LAH men who took part in the killings ever made known. A heavy cloak of secrecy was drawn over the details of the Roehm purge. Any documents relating to it were destroyed and all LAH members were pledged to secrecy and threatened with dire punishments for any indiscreet disclosures. Sepp Dietrich, though shocked and confused at the brutal slaughter of so many old Party comrades, had had little option but to see the bloodletting through to the end, and was personally promoted by Hitler to the rank of Obergruppenführer for his pains. On 5 July 1934, twenty-four other members of the LAH were also advanced in rank for their part in the Night of the Long Knives.

Wilhelm Mohnke does not appear to have been one of those so honoured at that time – though as a Hauptsturmführer in command of the 5th Company of the LAH it is doubtful if he could have remained unaware of what was going on, even if there was no evidence to indicate whether he did or did not play a personal part in this bloody affair. Throughout the entire Leibstandarte Regiment the horrific events of that violent weekend would have been a sensation without precedent, deeply impacting on the individual consciences of each and every one of the officers and men who were present, whether they were participants in the murders or simply accessories before and after the event. In the sealed-off barracks where so much of the killing was done no one could have escaped the ambience of blood – an ambience even more reeking than that prevailing at the Air Ministry in Berlin, where Goering and Himmler were busy selecting the names of those who were to die. 'I breathed in an air of hate and tension . . . above all, blood – lots of blood,' wrote one visitor to Goering's headquarters, an official in the Prussian Ministry of the Interior by the name of Hans Gisevius. 'On every face, from the sentries' to the humbler orderlies', one perceived the knowledge of terrible things.'

In 1957 Sepp Dietrich and Michael Lippert were tried for manslaughter by the West German authorities for their part in the Roehm purge and sentenced to eighteen months' imprisonment. At their trial the total of victims of the purge was put at 'more than a thousand'. But the names of the others involved in the killings did not emerge. However, the Roehm purge had the effect of making Dietrich and his Leibstandarte members of a criminal organization whose later crimes would make the Roehm affair look like a mere bagatelle in comparison.

———

Following the destruction of the SA, the Leibstandarte, like the other armed SS units, underwent considerable expansion and reorganization. The LAH was enlarged to army regimental strength and then motorized. By 1935 its total strength had grown to 2,660 men, and by the outbreak of the war to 3,700. Along with the other armed SS units it was combined collectively under a new organizational umbrella – the SS Verfügungstruppe, or Special Purpose Troops, later re-named with a title that was to reverberate across Europe and down through history: the Waffen-SS (or Armed SS, as opposed to the Allgemeine or General SS).

For the LAH these changes meant a steady evolution from a political

16

armed police force to a more strictly military formation which could, when the time came and the need arose, be sent into battle against the nation's foes under the operational control of the German Army rather than Heinrich Himmler's SS. General Ludwig Beck, Chief of the Army General Staff, perceived this trend and remarked: 'It was interesting to note that an organization which Hitler had categorically stated would never bear arms in military operations was now taking part in every coup the Führer pulled off. Not only were they taking part, but they were, by 1938, wearing Army uniform instead of their own, except on ceremonial occasions.'

The Leibstandarte was the first German unit to enter the Saar district when Hitler clawed back the demilitarized Rhineland in March 1935. Three years later a battalion of the LAH, with Wilhelm Mohnke commanding one of the companies, moved into Austria with the German Army, providing a guard of honour for the Führer (of which Mohnke was a member) when he returned in triumph to his boyhood town of Linz, and marching through the streets of Vienna in vainglorious procession upon completion of Germany's historic *Anschluss* with the Führer's native land. In October of that same year, 1938, the LAH crossed Germany's frontier again in another ominous act of German external aggression – this time to take part in the occupation of the largely German-speaking Sudetenland area of Czechoslovakia. Germany was now on a war footing and a major conflict in Europe seemed but a step away.

———

On 25 August 1939 the Leibstandarte left its barracks at Lichterfelde, which had been its base throughout its brief history, and took up new positions not far from the Polish border north of Breslau. The Leibstandarte would never return to Berlin again as a unit. Though no one knew it then, ahead lay six years of total war, an Armageddon without parallel in which the Leibstandarte was to fight bravely, bloodily and brutally, in the east and in the west, from the very first to the very last day of hostilities in Europe.

What sort of fighting man was the Leibstandarte SS trooper who was now poised to hurl himself so remarkably upon an unsuspecting world? The answer to this question is profoundly relevant to all that follows. We have seen that in the pre-war and early war years the Waffen-SS soldier was a volunteer of impeccable Aryan credentials and superlative physical fitness and build. But he was much more besides.

More than his physical attributes it was the SS man's state of mind that was to make him such a formidable opponent in war. To the usual soldierly virtues of discipline, courage, regimental pride and patriotic fervour was added a new and powerful quality which the SS men themselves termed

17

'*Härte*' or harshness. '*Härte*' meant many things. It meant toughness in adversity, recklessness under fire, fearlessness in the face of death, ruthlessness in the execution of orders, total dedication to victory in battle. '*Härte*' also meant contempt for the enemy, callousness towards prisoners, brutality towards all who stood in their way. When war came the men of the Waffen-SS proved themselves to be not just soldiers but fighters who fought as often as not for the sake of fighting. A US Army officer who came up against the Leibstandarte during the Battle of the Bulge in the later stages of the war reported: 'These men revealed a form of fighting that is new to me. They are obviously soldiers but they fight as if military ways were of no consequence. They actually seem to enjoy combat for no other reason than that it is combat.' An SS-Hauptsturmführer, recalling the 'sheer beauty' of the winter fighting in Russia in 1941–2, gave an insider's insight into the mind of the SS warrior. 'It was well worth all the dreadful suffering and danger,' he wrote. 'After a time we got to a point where we were concerned not for ourselves, or even for Germany, but lived entirely for the next clash, the next engagement with the enemy. There was a tremendous sense of "being", an exhilarated feeling that every reserve in the body was alive to the fight.'

The SS fighter was a pure belligerent who went into battle with little regard for his own life, which he was prepared to sacrifice with a readiness bordering on madness.* This macho recklessness and soldier-of-fortune spirit was reinforced by a number of other highly-developed characteristics. Loyalty and obedience to the Führer, to the National Socialist ideology, and to any superior authority were *de rigueur*. The SS motto – 'My Loyalty is my Honour' – was the basis of the SS's actions. An order from a superior was regarded as an order emanating from the Führer himself and had to be carried out without hesitation, regardless of the consequences or the sacrifices involved. Camaraderie was total, and in the case of the LAH the *esprit de corps* was developed to a point where its members saw themselves as part of a tightly knit aristocracy of manhood, an exclusive brotherhood which was above and apart from all other formations.

This self-regard, which others saw as incorrigible arrogance, was reinforced, at least in the pre-war and early war years, by the Leibstandarte's ideological indoctrination. In the Waffen-SS as a whole the political and military were united. In the LAH, in particular in the early years, the Nazi

---

* Glorification of death in battle was not, of course, the prerogative of the Waffen-SS alone. In the Second World War the Russians and the Japanese were also notable exponents of the noble art of military self-sacrifice. A more recent and infinitely more lunatic example has been provided by Ayatollah Khomeini's 'army of martyrs' in the slaughterous river war against Iraq.

18

ideological training was considered as important as combat training as a means of hardening the unit into a highly motivated and irresistible force led by dedicated Nazi idealists. Though in practice many men joined the Waffen-SS and LAH for reasons that had little to do with Nazi idealism – the élitism, the glamour, the black uniform, the career opportunities – there is little doubt that the Waffen-SS was imbued with Nazi fanaticism to a far greater degree than any average Wehrmacht unit.

The final sum of all these various parts was an organization of fighting men such as the world had not seen since the distant days of Attila the Hun; an organization which would show short shrift for the enemy on the battlefield and on occasion small mercy to the enemy off it. From its origins as a political police force at Hitler's beck and call the armed SS grew to number thirty-nine wartime Waffen-SS divisions within the Germany Army – seven of them élite panzer divisions with a legendary reputation of reckless bravery and fearsome aggression in battle. As the future commander of perhaps the most élite of these élite divisions, Wilhelm Mohnke was destined to stand at the pinnacle of the Germany fighting hierarchy.

———

On 1 September 1939, Hitler invaded Poland and in a lightning campaign lasting barely more than a month overwhelmed the courageous but poorly equipped and outnumbered Polish army. This was the first Blitzkrieg campaign in history and it was over almost as soon as it began. The spirited charges of the Polish horse cavalry were no match for the mechanized speed and power of the Nazi juggernaut – the ranks of tanks and self-propelled guns, the fighters and bombers, the huge army of one and a half million men. Within forty-eight hours of the beginning of the German invasion, the Polish Air Force had been destroyed on the ground, and Poland's second city, Cracow, had fallen. Within a week the bulk of the Polish army had been trapped in a huge pincer movement round Warsaw. By 17 September all except a few defiant pockets of the Polish army had been surrounded or wiped out.

In this one-sided act of massive criminal aggression, which was to enslave the Poles and turn the world to war and ruin, Sepp Dietrich's Leibstandarte Regiment had a significant part to play. In the advance of the German right flank towards the Polish capital, the LAH took part in a number of crucial engagements, including the 'battle of annihilation' on the Bzura River in which a major part of the Polish forces were encircled and then systematically destroyed. But though the regiment had fought the first battles in its brief history with bravado and élan, it did not emerge from the campaign without criticism from the higher echelons of command in

19

the Wehrmacht. Like other Waffen-SS units, the Leibstandarte had suffered relatively heavy casualties – more than 400 dead and wounded all told – and was judged to have displayed deficiencies of leadership and training and to have conducted its operations with needless recklessness. In the battle for the town of Pabjanice, for example, the Leibstandarte's attacks were not only repulsed but reversed, so that the attackers were surrounded by the defenders and only extricated from their potentially catastrophic predicament by the intervention of a Wehrmacht infantry regiment. It was at Pabjanice that Wilhelm Mohnke, then commanding 5 Company of the 2nd Battalion Leibstandarte, sustained the first to his numerous war wounds, though it does not seem to have kept him out of the line for any length of time, for he was still in command of his troops at the siege of the Modlin fortress towards the end of the month.

More alarming than straightforward tactical deficiencies were the early signs of the Leibstandarte's ominous predilection for violence and brutality over and above the call of duty and the exigencies of battle. During the march on the Warta River, for example, the Leibstandarte had responded to the mounting number of casualties in their ranks by rounding on the Polish populace, setting fire to the villages and wildly shooting up their civilian inhabitants.

More alarming still, it was one of the Leibstandarte's ancillary sections, the regimental band, which notched up one of the earliest recorded war crimes committed by the German military when at Burzeum on 25 September 1939 it randomly machine-gunned to death some fifty Polish civilians whom the bandmaster had judged to be 'Jewish criminals'.

Some perfunctory effort was made by the German authorities to investigate the massacre and punish the accused, but it was not until after the war that a number of other criminal incidents committed by the Leibstandarte in Poland were listed by the United Nations war crimes commission. All of these crimes were committed by the 2nd Battalion of the Leibstandarte, and included the torture of civilians at Lodz and Zdunska Wola in September 1939 and the pillage and confiscation of German property at Grojec and the massacre of civilians at Czestochowa in the following month.

At the time these crimes were carried out, the 2nd Battalion Leibstandarte was commanded by Obersturmbannführer Ritter von Oberkamp, and its three infantry companies were commanded by Hauptsturmführer Wilhelm Mohnke, Hauptsturmführer Otto Baum, and Hauptsturmführer Seppel Lange (who was killed some 12 miles west of Warsaw on the night of 12–13 September).

It is not clear whether the Polish authorities ever completed their investigations into these crimes; certainly no one was ever brought to book for participating in them. In any case, they paled against the broader picture of Nazi barbarism unleashed in occupied Poland – the so-called 'housecleaning' of Polish Jews, intelligentsia, clergy and nobility which began almost as soon as the fighting was over and was carried through in a wave of terror and brutality on a scale without precedent in modern times.

———

With the surrender of the Polish fortress at Modlin on 25 September 1939, the last major episode of the German conquest of Poland came to an end. Early in October the Leibstandarte Regiment was transferred to Prague, where the press reported that tens of thousands of spectators – most of them from the German-speaking section of the Czech population – gathered to watch the victorious regiment march into Wenceslas Square in parade order, with Wilhelm Mohnke among them at the head of his troops, to be greeted by the Reich Protector, Konstantin von Neurath. After two months of guard duties in the Czech capital, the Leibstandarte was transferred again, this time to new quarters near Koblenz on Germany's western borders. Here the regiment began intensive training for Hitler's next exercise in Blitzkrieg conquest – the invasion of the West.

———

In spite of the criticisms of the military standards and criminal activities levelled against the Leibstandarte in the Polish campaign, the reputation of the regiment stood high in the eyes of its mentor, Adolf Hitler. During the fighting in Poland the Führer had intervened personally, as he was to intervene in subsequent campaigns, to ensure that 'his' Leibstandarte were posted to those parts of the front where resounding victories were certain – victories of great propaganda value at home because of his close personal association with the Leibstandarte in name and role. At Christmas he honoured the Leibstandarte with his presence, gave every man the present of a Christmas cake, a bottle of wine, a pouch of tobacco and a ladle of punch, and in his Christmas speech in the nearby spa hotel at Bad Ems told them: 'As long as I have the honour to stand at the spearhead of this fight, it is for you, the men of my Leibstandarte, the honour to be the spearhead of this fight.' But the Führer brought the Leibstandarte more than mere words and gifts. On his personal orders the regiment was also reinforced by the addition of heavy weapons, an additional infantry battalion, and an entire artillery battalion. Though still providing guard details as Hitler's security force in Berlin and Berchtesgaden, the Leibstandarte was now seen as an élite combat formation of the newly designated Waffen-SS – a formation

21

closely linked with Hitler not only by name but as the symbolic military embodiment of the will of the Führer himself.

At daybreak on 10 May 1940 this force was to let its fury loose on the West. As the Luftwaffe swooped on airfields in Belgium, Holland and France, and German paratroopers seized key bridges and strongpoints, the newly reinforced Leibstandarte thrust rapidly across the Dutch border, and within five hours Hauptsturmführer Kurt Meyer's motorcycle company had penetrated nearly fifty miles into the Dutch interior. It took German forces only five days to overrun Holland. On 14 May Rotterdam was bombed into submission. On 15 May Holland capitulated. By then German armour under Guderian and Rommel in the southern pincer of the invasion front had crossed the Meuse and in a brilliant *coup de main* had sliced through Northern France to reach the Channel coast at Abbeville on 20 May.

In just over a week the Germans had driven the Allied armies in the West into a hole from which there was no easy prospect of escape. The British Expeditionary Force, the Belgian army and a substantial part of the French army were now cut off from the main force of the French army south of the Somme and in imminent danger of encirclement and destruction. British efforts to break out and join up with the French to the south came to nothing. By 24 May the German spearhead had become a firm defensive line through which it was no longer possible to break. The Allied armies in the north were now trapped. The only way out was by sea.

At this critical juncture on 24 May, the day the Leibstandarte was transferred south to join Guderian's XIX Panzer Corps in its advance on Dunkirk, the Germans halted. Controversy has always surrounded this astonishing decision, which was to enable a large part of the British Expeditionary Force and a smaller part of the French army to escape the trap and live to fight another day. Devious and subtle explanations have been put forward to explain the German decision, and it has even been suggested that Hitler deliberately spared the British Expeditionary Force from certain annihilation in the hope of coming to a gentlemanly peace which would keep the British out of the rest of the war. But in a handwritten note sent by Hitler's Chief of Staff, General Jodl, to the Reich Labour Leader, Robert Ley, which has come into the hands of the present authors and is published here for the first time, it is clear that the Germans' intentions were less than conciliatory. Sent from the Führer Headquarters on 28 May 1940, the note reads:

> Most esteemed Labour Leader of the Reich!
> Everything that has happened since 10 May seems even to us, who have indestructible faith in our success, like a dream. In a few days four-fifths of the British Expeditionary Force and a

22

great part of the best French mobile troops will be destroyed or captured. The next blow is ready to strike, and we can execute it with a ratio of supremacy of 2:1, which has never before been granted to a field commander. . . .

I can imagine how your thoughts, Herr Labour Leader of the Reich, are with the operations. . . . You too, Herr Labour Leader of the Reich, have contributed significantly to this greatest victory in history.

Heil Hitler!

Your, Herr Labour Leader of the Reich,

always devoted

Jodl

The British, meanwhile, decided the only course of action left to them was to save themselves as best they could. A defensive line was thrown round the Channel town of Dunkirk and the British forces and some of the French proceeded to withdraw to the open beaches to await a seaborne evacuation across the sea to England. To protect the routes of retreat, rearguard units were posed on the perimeter of the defensive cordon. One of these rearguard units was the 2nd Battalion of the Royal Warwickshire Regiment, a regular country infantry regiment for which fate held a cruel trick in store. For it was the Royal Warwicks who were shortly to be called upon to stand in the way of the SS Leibstandarte Adolf Hitler Regiment's triumphal progress to the sea – with consequences of great and awful moment for this story.

PART III

—

The Wormhoudt Massacre

28 MAY 1940

I

RETREAT

It was at Tournai that the killing really began. In this small, historic Belgian market town, retreating British soldiers began to understand in their hearts what they had always known in their minds, but never truly believed – that war is about death, maiming and fear. Above all about fear. Death was for the dead and dying; but after Tournai fear gnawed at the living all the way to Dunkirk. Like hunger, it was the constant companion of their waking hours, the demonic tormentor of their sleep.

Sometimes they moved at night, the trucks feeling their way down the country roads in the dark without lights, and rested during the day. This way at least they avoided the streams of Belgian civilian refugees who now began to clog the roads as they fled from the fighting to the rear – old people, women and children, many of them in tears, pushing farm-carts laden high with their most treasured belongings. It saddened the soldiers to see this flotsam of humanity wandering fearful and homeless across the countryside under the hot early summer sun, but they were forbidden to help them or have anything to do with them, for fear that Fifth Columnists might be mixed up with them.

In these early stages of the retreat there were few other signs of war or impending calamity. Occasionally a German spotter aircraft would fly over the road, checking their movements; but no shots were fired and at first the fighting front still seemed half a world away. But then Belgian soldiers began to straggle back from the front, to swell the ranks of people fleeing west. Weary and downcast, these soldiers brought news of an irresistible German advance and of heavy casualties suffered by their comrades in the Belgian army. The war suddenly seemed much closer.

The 2nd Royal Warwicks – an infantry component of the 48th Division in I Corps of the British Expeditionary Force – were now skirting the edge in the battlefield of Waterloo, where the British, with German support, had won a famous victory over Napoleon's Grande Armée in 1815. This time

27

the Germans were on the opposing side, and nobody in May 1940 entertained any hope that history might repeat itself. Holed up in a house next to the Waterloo Golf Club, Battalion HQ pieced together items of news from the front and saw that the situation was grave indeed. The Germans stood at the very gates of Brussels. A German tank army had broken through the French positions and was racing for the Channel. At Sedan, in the Ardennes, the Germans had already crossed the Meuse and were heading west. The fighting was getting closer. Across the placid green swath of the golf links the sound of heavy gunfire drifted on the wind from the direction of Charleroi. A British fighter pilot, shot down over the links by German anti-aircraft fire, was brought into Battalion HQ to recuperate from the shock, and told of the dire situation in the air over northern France, where the RAF was now heavily outnumbered and stretched to the very limit.

As night came on, the 2nd Royal Warwicks were ordered to move up to help hold a defensive position on the River Dyle. Under the pressure of impending catastrophe, order began to break down into chaos. The night was pitch black and the maps out of date and useless and the road impeded here and there with the scattered detritus of shellfire – a dead horse, an overturned truck, a few smashed carts. The Battalion found itself in a dark wood, where forest tracks led in all directions, so that some trucks wandered off and got lost. When day broke on the 16th – another beautiful warm blue summer's day – the ration truck was still missing and nobody could have any breakfast. At Battalion HQ, now installed in a gamekeeper's house at the edge of the wood, a senior officer managed to net a few rabbits, and another officer contrived to milk a goat in the yard, while overhead fighter aircraft weaved and swooped in fierce aerial combat. The shortage of rations became an increasingly urgent matter and the men began to take the matter into their own hands, looting the abandoned farmhouses, and stealing eggs from the chicken coops.

At noon the Battalion was ordered to withdraw to a ridge a mile to the rear. At midnight it was ordered to withdraw yet again. Though few of the troops could know it, this was part of a general withdrawal along the whole of the Allied line. 'Remember this day,' the CO remarked to his Adjutant. 'It will go down in history as the day on which another classic withdrawal of the British Army began.' The withdrawal to Dunkirk was to last the best part of a fortnight. For the 2nd Royal Warwicks it was to take them steadily westward amid circumstances of mounting confusion and anxiety. They moved by day and by night, eating and sleeping when opportunity allowed, their long march frequently impeded by solid traffic jams of refugees' vehicles or entangled with the columns of other brigades or with the many stragglers who had become separated from their regiments.

Though the 2nd Royal Warwicks had not yet set eyes on the enemy or been under enemy fire, they grew increasingly dismayed by the news they

28

heard and the sights they saw on that long, dusty retreat to the sea. News came that Holland had capitulated and that Belgium would not last much longer. Large fires, started by German air raids, could be seen burning in the north, in the vicinity of Brussels. Along the side of the road lay the bodies of elderly refugees who had not had the strength to carry on. At the wayside shrines women knelt in fervent prayer. Though none of the soldiers fell out of line, they no longer marched in step or kept formation. When they came to a traffic jam they took to the fields and their transport hunted about for an alternative route. Within the Brigade as a whole, six companies became lost or mislaid.

At the River Dendre, a major defensive line to the west of Brussels, the Warwicks had expected to stand and fight, but after unloading trucks and digging positions, they were given the order to withdraw once again. The Battalion's transport was sent off ahead under Major P.H.W. Hicks, the second-in-command, while the rest marched. Heavily burdened with greatcoats, weapons and weapons' tripods, the men were exhausted before they even started and kept going only by a supreme effort of will. Asleep on their feet, they began to straggle. Some discarded the greatcoats and tripods which weighed them down. All semblance of good military order was lost as they trudged through the night, dazed, confused, and weary to death. At dawn there was no sign of the promised transport; but with the Germans so close behind now, it was impossible to rest up, and the agony of the march continued through the morning. The Adjutant wrote of their plight: 'The Battalion was a pitiful sight. We got mixed up with other units and refugees. Long halts could not be made and even on short halts we were all apt to fall asleep immediately we sat down.'

At two in the afternoon the trucks finally caught up with them and the Battalion embussed for the short journey to Hollain, some four miles south of Calonne. The route took them to Tournai, which was jammed solid on its eastern outskirts with vehicles of every description, military and civilian, packed four deep on the road. So dense was the crush of trucks, cars and half-tracks that all traffic movement had ceased, and thousands of soldiers and civilians milled about the streets of the little town in seemingly aimless confusion.

It was at this point, with British troops and Belgian civilians concentrated in a pocket from which there was no easy egress, that the Germans struck. Out of the summer sky from the east came the roar of aircraft rapidly approaching. For the people swarming about on the ground below there was no time to take cover, nowhere to hide as the formation of Stuka dive-bombers pounced on the town. The planes circled over their prey, angrily buzzed round and round the town taking stock of their targets, then with a terrifying howl from their sirens, so characteristic of Stukas, they aimed themselves, one after the other, at the mass of vehicles and humanity trapped below them. Horror overwhelmed the assemblage in and around Tournai.

For the 2nd Royal Warwicks it was their first experience of the reality of war since the campaign began. The slaughter was considerable. Most of C Company's vehicles were destroyed in the attack, and a number of their drivers killed or wounded; one of them was so unhinged by the experience that he shot himself later that day. A driver attached to the Battalion remained unscathed when his truck was straddled by incendiary bombs which struck the trucks immediately in front and behind his own, but some of the men in the truck behind were incinerated in the blaze. All around were scenes both awful and surreal. When a bomb landed on a travelling circus that happened to be in the town, some of the animals broke free from their cages, including a wounded elephant that was seen to lumber off, screeching and trumpeting, through the rubble and leaping flames and choking dust of what had once been a quiet country town. The Battalion tough guy, a hard soldier and a born killer, was seen to lift a small, unconscious child out of the rubble and cradle her in his arms. Weeping, he turned his face towards the heavens and said aloud: 'Please God, tell me what to do with this.' Then he laid the child on the ground and turned back in tears towards the smoking town.

The Germans had not yet finished with Tournai, however. After dropping their bombs, the planes swooped low over the town to machine-gun the streets. It was then that Major Hicks, in command of the Warwicks transport, was struck by a machine-gun bullet which shattered the corner of a cigarette-case in his left breast pocket and then glanced off. Though the Warwicks had escaped relatively lightly, other units in the division had suffered heavy casualties. The Glosters, caught in their trucks, lost 194 men dead and wounded; the Oxford and Buckinghamshire Light Infantry, 48. Captain A. Crook, RAMC, the 2nd Royal Warwicks Medical Officer, had to deal with over 200 cases on the spot – men, women and children, soldiers and civilians, British and Belgians.

For the men of the Battalion it was the most appalling thing they had experienced since landing in France, and it affected them in a way which was to have some relevance in the days to come. Despondency and apprehension now gave way to anger and a stern resolve. Blooded and baptized by fire, the 2nd Royal Warwicks would repay Tournai with interest when they finally came to grips with the Germans on the field of battle. That night, dug in along the west bank of the River Escaut, a few miles from the French border, they slept like babes in the fields. It was their first undisturbed rest for five nights. They would need every minute of rest they could find. For the worst was yet to come.

The 2nd Royal Warwicks awoke the next morning to find the German Army on the far side of the river. From their observation post in the town of Hollain they could see concentrations of enemy soldiers along the bank. When the Germans tried to cross the river a violent fire-fight ensued in which some of the Warwicks were wounded. The Germans were repulsed for the moment, but in the afternoon their guns opened on Battalion HQ and the shelling was so intense that more casualties resulted, the telephone lines were cut and the forward observation post was hit.

All along the River Escaut other regiments of the British Expeditionary Force were joined in battle against superior German forces driving towards France. All of them were now engaged in the first bloody fighting that most of them had ever experienced. *Force majeure*, they were turned virtually overnight into veterans, inured – as far as that was possible – to the sight of brains, bowels, bone and blood, the shattering noise of high explosives, the sudden extinction of comrades and friends.

All next day the battle raged. Against the 2nd Battalion of the Royal Warwicks the Germans concentrated on D Company's front, which was well forward and spread thin. Supported by heavy artillery fire directed from overhead by a spotter plane with Allied markings, the Germans pressed hard, and as the situation deteriorated cooks and clerks were sent forward to help prevent D Company from being overrun. Casualties mounted steeply. The Company Commander was killed leading a counter-attack, and the rest of the Company officers were killed or wounded during the course of the day, along with 80 other ranks out of the 110 that had drawn breath that morning. The other Companies had also taken heavy punishment, and by the end of the day half the entire Battalion were dead or wounded. To make matters worse the CO had suffered a ruptured stomach ulcer and been shipped out to the rear. His place was taken by the second-in-command, Major Hicks, still marvelling at his narrow escape from death in Tournai, even as he continued to narrowly escape death in Hollain.

Such was the situation of the 2nd Battalion, The Royal Warwickshire Regiment at the beginning of one of the most traumatic weeks in its long and battle-scarred history.

————

The 2nd Royal Warwicks were withdrawing, heading towards the sea. Relieved at the Escaut River by another battalion, they were pulled out of the fighting line on 22 May – to lick their wounds and count their dead and recuperate from the shock of battle. They had fully expected to be sent back to the river within forty-eight hours, and they were greatly surprised and

31

filled with a sense of foreboding when they were ordered to move back across the French frontier that night.

Next day disquieting rumours reached them. The situation was ominous. The Channel port of Boulogne was under attack. At Arras the British garrison was encircled and fighting desperately to break out. With its supply lines severed the British Expeditionary Force was on half-rations. Elsewhere the French were under attack along a forty-mile arc. Squeezed into a pocket which contracted day by day, every village, road and footpath became increasingly congested with soldiers and civilians alike. In the bright sun these great crowds of humanity on the move presented a brilliant and gaudy spectacle, like the throng converging on Epsom Downs, some said, to watch the Derby Day races. But the grim faces, the burning towns, the German bombers ranging freely unopposed in the skies above the pocket, all told a different story. A dour struggle for survival was now in progress, and at the perimeter of the pocket the fighting was intense.

For three days the 2nd Royal Warwicks moved steadily westward in circumstances of mounting confusion, complication and maddening delays. Then, on 25 May, the Battalion War Diary noted: '0100 hours. At Seclin, orders received for Battalion to proceed direct to Dunkirk. This was a shock.' A long, hot and harassing march took them through the Great War battle-sites of Armentières and Ypres to Poperinghe. Here they rested and ate a hot meal while they waited for further orders.

These orders, when they came, contained a modification of their original instructions. Instead of retreating all the way to Dunkirk, they were to take part in a rearguard action designed to hold off the Germans and enable the rest of the British Expeditionary Force to reach the coast. The 2nd Warwicks were to dig in on a perimeter around a place called Wormhoudt, some twelve miles to the north-west. A signal received from the C-in-C of the British Expeditionary Force, Lord Gort, VC, demanded: 'You will hold your present position at all costs, to the last man and the last round. This is essential in order that a vitally important operation may take place.' For many members of this already severely depleted battalion these orders were to prove tantamount to a death sentence. Shortly after these orders were received, as if to underscore the gravity of the new turn of events, the weather broke at least and the first rain for weeks began to fall out of a sullen sky.

———

Wormhoudt was a small, unpretentious, north French country town, or village, with a church, a square, a *mairie* and not much else, lying some twelve miles to the south-east of Dunkirk. In the final stages of the BEF's retreat, Wormhoudt was to assume a tactical importance infinitely greater than its physical dimensions would suggest, for the town was the node or junction of no less than seven roads, and straddled one of the main arteries of the Allied retreat to the sea. A long, straight road ran north across the flat agricultural landscape so typical of this part of France and connected the town with Dunkirk, where there was already a large build-up of troops waiting for embarkation across the Channel to England. Another road, no less long and straight, led south to Cassel, from which direction major elements of the Allied forces were pouring north in a desperate bid to extricate themselves from the tightening German noose; while a mile and a half to the west lay the tiny hamlet of Esquelbecq, nestling beneath the walls of an ancient château.

This was the stage on which a terrible drama was soon to be enacted. Here the weary men of the 2nd Royal Warwicks arrived in the misty dawn of 26 May after a sultry night march and snatched a brief rest in the town centre before moving out to their defensive positions on the outskirts. War had not yet greatly troubled this country town and at this late stage in the campaign it was still populated and undamaged. But when the inhabitants awoke that Sunday morning and peered out of their bedroom windows, the harbingers of war were everywhere plain to see in the streets below.

Exhausted British Tommies lay sprawled asleep amidst their packs and guns along the pavements, oblivious of the rain that now began to fall. In the roads stood columns of army trucks, dirty and travel-worn and forlorn. As the church bells began to summon the townsfolk to Mass, the troops began to dig slit trenches for the coming battle, working with intense, unabated energy, as if time was short. But all was quiet on this sector of the western front. No distant sound of gunfire disturbed the tranquillity of this Sabbath morning. A few German planes buzzed lazily and distantly about the sky. Otherwise there was no sign of the approaching enemy and after a day of frantic toil the Warwicks passed an uneventful night in their new positions.

These positions were as follows. Battalion HQ, where the CO, Major Hicks, was based, was initially located in a big house near the western end of the town, with transport parked under the cover of trees in the park behind the house and the Regimental Aid Post under Captain Crook in a redbrick building on the park drive. Around the town the various companies were distributed along an exceptionally extensive perimeter covering the westward side of the town through a 180 degree arc of fire. For the present C Company occupied Esquelbecq to the west; B Company covered the Esquelbecq road and the western and north-western approaches; A Company, commanded by Major C. Chichester-Constable, MC, was sited around Le Fort Rose Farm and covered the western and south-western approaches; while D Company, commanded by Captain John Frazer Lynne-Allen, covered the roads leading to Wormhoudt from the south.

The 2nd Royal Warwicks were not along in the area. The 8th Worcesters guarded the eastern approaches to the town and the 5th Gloucesters held the small town of Ledringhem, two miles to the south-east.

———

May 27 dawned wet and wretched. All morning convoys of troops, some French, some British, kept pouring through the little town, heading north towards Dunkirk. It was evident that some sort of mass evacuation of such Allied forces as could be extricated from the cauldron would be attempted at Dunkirk, though the men in the field knew little of the general tactical situation or higher planning beyond what they could pick up with their own eyes and ears. Some of the troops pouring through Wormhoudt dumped their equipment there and immobilized their vehicles. Before they made off on foot they imparted alarming rumours among the men who had to stay and stand their ground here. The Germans were everywhere, they told them, in overwhelming numbers. Soon Wormhoudt would be cut off, a tiny island in a Wehrmacht ocean. The chances did not look good.

As if to emphasize the atmosphere of Armageddon and the overriding sense of impending calamity, squadrons of German bombers began to drone overhead in the direction of Dunkirk, one wave followed at an interval by another. Though they were some twelve miles away from the bombing, the Warwicks could plainly see across the fields the black pall of smoke that now rose above the port. Then it was Wormhoudt's turn. In the early afternoon, another squadron of German bombers appeared out of the east, but unlike the others they did not press on to the sea but wheeled over Wormhoudt and, having taken the measure of their target, came in low and steady, dropping their bombs on the very heart of the town. Captain Tomes, the Adjutant, was to write in his diary:

> I think this was the worst experience I have ever had. One could do little but wait for the next bomb and listen to them falling with their high-pitched scream. One felt sickened and exhausted with the clamour and violence and the knowledge that there were none of our planes to take on the enemy bombers. I tried to collect some men for concerted small-arms fire, but that was hopeless.
>
> Several old women and children were crouching under a wall, and I herded them into the cellar. One old woman was hit by a piece of falling debris and all the children were too scared almost to move at all.
>
> A few men were able to get into slit-trenches in the park.

34

[Major] Harborne, myself, Corporal Cunningham, Lance-Corporal Garrish and Private Herbert merely stood in the hall and waited. We all tried to remain cool and I think Private Herbert succeeded better than anyone else, making some comical remark after each explosion which shook the house and showered plaster, bricks and glass on us.

When the bombers at last growled off, they left behind a smoking town in ruins. Few buildings had escaped damage, and debris choked the streets. Though the Warwicks only suffered four casualties, many civilians lay dead or injured, and the MO attended to them as best he could. But if fortune had not smiled on Wormhoudt that day, it had at least managed the flicker of a grimace, for a 500-pound bomb had plopped down beside a petrol tanker only fifty yards from Battalion HQ, but instead of blowing it up and starting an inferno, it merely blew it sideways, flinging it ten yards through the air as if with a giant hand.

Following the raid, Battalion HQ prudently moved out of the house and into slit trenches at the east of the park which backed on to it. Brigade HQ and other towns and villages in the surrounding area had also been bombed, and leaflets had been dropped on the British positions which read:

> British soldiers, Germans surround! You are encircled! German troops invade Courtrai, Tournai, Valenciennes. Lillers, Aire, St Omer are occupied. Calais will be taken immediately. Why do you fight further? Do you really believe the nonsense that Germans kill their prisoners? Come and see yourselves the contrary! The match is finished! A fair enemy will be fairly treated.

In the light of the events that had befallen the Royal Norfolk Regiment not far away at Le Paradis that same day, and were to befall the Warwicks on the morrow, there is a black and desperate irony about that poorly worded exhortation.

And so the last evening came. Though there was no enemy activity in the Warwicks' sector, there was little complacency either. A captured enemy order brought to Battalion HQ indicated that the Germans were preparing for a major attack the next day, and already had their troops deployed to the west of the town, waiting for the order to advance. It was not comforting to know that C Company had been withdrawn from the village of Esquelbecq to guard Divisional HQ, though the arrival of reinforcements in the shape of two platoons of a machine-gun regiment, the 4th Cheshire Regiment, equipped with Vickers medium machine-guns, brought some solace.

Placed under the command of the 2nd Warwicks, the Cheshires' two platoons (No 8 Platoon of B Company and No 15 of D Company) took up good fire positions covering the western approaches to Wormhoudt, along with a ring of guns manned by the 53rd Anti-Tank Regiment RA (Worcestershire Yeomanry).

As evening closed in, sounds of gunfire could be heard from the south in the direction of Ledringhem, where the Glosters were heavily engaged with German tanks, mortars and infantry. But as dusk settled over the fields the shooting died away and the night was still, though pregnant with apprehension, each man alone with his thoughts in the brooding dark.

II

BATTLE

It was a short night. The British troops were roused at 0330 and stood to until 0430. Half an hour later the first German shells landed on the British positions, hitting the château and the neighbouring wood. At 0600 the Germans' small spotter plane, a captured Lysander with Allied markings, which seemed to have attached itself to the Battalion ever since Hollain, made its usual appearance. Ten minutes later fifteen Stukas roared out of the grey dawn sky and screamed down on to A Company's positions, dive-bombing them with precision and inflicting numerous casualties. Meanwhile the relentless German artillery barrage continued to soften up the British defences, and the air was rent by the screeching and crashing of high-explosive shells.

The German ground attack was launched at 0745. With the 1st Battalion of the SS Leibstandarte Regiment to the north of Wormhoudt and the 3rd Battalion in reserve on the right, the brunt of the attack was to be borne by the 2nd Battalion under forty-one-year-old Sturmbannführer Ernst Schützeck, attacking from the south and west. Two companies of the 2nd Battalion were primarily involved – No 5 Company under Hauptsturmführer Wilhelm Mohnke in the centre, and No 7 Company under Hauptsturmführer Otto Baum on the right, with No 6 Company held mostly in reserve.

At 0900 the first German ground troops were spotted making for the Dunkirk road by the Warwicks' Adjutant, Captain Tomes, and artillery fire was directed on to them and a few reinforcements sent up the road from Battalion HQ. Half an hour later the machine guns of the 8 Platoon of the Cheshires opened fire on German infantry crossing their front to the north-west of the town, and German vehicles on the Esquelbecq road were fired on and put out of action with the help of the Warwicks' anti-tank guns.

The fire-fight began to spread along the entire Wormhoudt front, and soon the surrounding fields were alive with the crackle of rifle fire, laced

37

with the rat-tat of machine guns and the crump of mortars. Throughout the morning the 2nd Leibstandarte slowly worked their way round to the north and south of Wormhoudt, fighting their way forward yard by yard against heavy shellfire from the British artillery and intense opposition from the Cheshires and Warwicks on the ground. The Warwicks, though opposed by numerically superior forces, hung on grimly and at noon their positions were still intact. For the Leibstandarte, who had grown accustomed to quick and decisive victories against a confused and demoralized enemy that was always retreating and always off-balance, the unexpected resistance put up by the British at Wormhoudt was both surprising and vexing. The Leibstandarte were taking casualties and they did not like it. The British had been dive-bombed, shelled, mortared, outflanked and outgunned and still they would not budge. British artillery fire continued to pummel the German positions. If the Germans broke from cover they drew withering small-arms fire from the British lines. Otto Baum, commanding No 7 Company, considered the British resistance to be 'very fierce', while Eric Maas, one of the Leibstandarte Regiment's Assistant Adjutants, described the fighting round Wormhoudt as 'extremely severe'.

The German infantry tried every stratagem to unnerve their opponents. They would rush forward with rallying cries of 'Heil Hitler!' – only to run into the murderous fire of the Cheshires' medium machine guns. Or they would try First World War tactics and advance *en masse* shoulder to shoulder in an extended line along a broad front; or, when that failed, attack in small groups under their own covering fire. Sometimes they would charge forward with fixed bayonets. Sometimes they would contravene the laws of war and approach the British lines dressed in British, French or Belgian uniforms, or disguised as French refugees in civilian clothes, like an irregular unit, or some wild bunch of colonial dogs of war. Thus disguised they would come up to the British positions shouting, 'Hello, boys! We're here – don't fire!'

But apart from hedges and a few dips in the ground there was little cover for infantrymen on this flat, agricultural battlefield. The moment a soldier stood up to charge forward he was as clear to see as a cut-out target on a rifle range. Anything that moved and was German drew the withering fire of the Warwicks' rifles and Bren light machine-guns. But what was bad for the goose was also bad for the gander. The British had their slit trenches, which offered protection enough except against mortar fire, which was often intense. But they found, like the Germans, that once they left the security of the trenches they immediately drew an angry snicker of enemy fire.

Sepp Dietrich was to blame the failure of the Leibstandarte's initial attack on the 'very strong resistance' put up by the British at Wormhoudt. Greatly concerned, at mid-morning Dietrich decided to find out what was going wrong for himself. In the company of Hauptsturmführer Max Wünsche, formerly Hitler's SS ADC, who was commanding No 15 Company at this time, he set out in his car from 1st Battalion HQ at the western edge of Esquelbecq to find Sturmbannführer Schützeck, commanding the 2nd Battalion, who was directing the main thrust of the attack on Wormhoudt. A small convoy of six trucks joined them on the way. Dietrich had travelled about halfway along the road from Esquelbecq to Wormhoudt and had just reached a road block about fifty yards from the British positions when the convoy was hit by British machine-gun and anti-tank fire. All six lorries were set on fire and many of their occupants killed. Dietrich's car was also hit (by an anti-tank shell fired by the gun of Bombardier Rawlinson of the Worcestershire Yeomanry) and his driver killed. Max Wünsche has given his own version of this dire turn of events.

When we drove along we noticed neither battle noises nor contacts. That's why we approached a road barrier in an unsuspecting and inoffensive way and wanted to remove it. Suddenly we received machine-gun fire from several machine-guns and anti-tank gun fire, so we had to take cover (in a ditch beside the road).

Fortunately the ditch was deep, but they literally shot the edge of the ditch away with machine-guns. We tried to escape to the rear. That was unsuccessful as a path from a field joined the road and we would have to go through a drainage pipe. Meanwhile, our car (Kfz 15, Mercedes cross-country) had been shot out of action; the petrol tanks leaked and a tracer round set light to the lot. I finally tried to go through the drainage pipe, but got stuck in it. I lost consciousness through what happened next. Behind me and in front of me was the burning ditch; artillery fire from friend and foe; attacks by our own troops, sorties by the enemy.

Dietrich, meanwhile, had smeared himself from head to foot in mud in an attempt to protect himself from the flames, and even tried to bury his head in the mire. The exact position of the luckless pair was clearly marked by the thick clouds of smoke rising from the roadside ditch, and British sharpshooters had a clear field of fire and could spot their slightest movement.

It was about 1150 when Dietrich's car was hit. All efforts to extricate him from his dangerous position broke down. No 2 Company ran into heavy British machine-gun and artillery fire. An infantry attack by 15 Company was caught in the defensive fire and a follow-up tank attack fared little better, losing four tanks and the tank unit commander. Later five tanks and a column of armoured cars pushed forward as far as the eastern edge of Esquelbecq, meeting staff resistance from British troops dug in in the grounds of the château. Possibly this is the same armoured column which the Cheshire Regiment reported as bearing down on their own 15 Platoon's positions during the morning. According to the British, the armoured cars were driven off and all six tanks knocked out by two anti-tank guns brought up by a party of Warwicks; and as the tank crews tried to escape they were gunned down by the Cheshires. According to the Germans, when the British finally withdrew they poured gasoline over the roads and ignited it, preventing the German tanks from proceeding further.

With rescue impossible, the two SS officers lay uncomfortably spread-eagled in the mud and mire of their makeshift slit-trench for the rest of the morning and a large part of the afternoon, listening to the pounding of British artillery over the Leibstandarte's entire sector and to the increasingly urgent din of violent combat across the neighbouring fields. In this dangerous and humiliating predicament Sepp Dietrich thus passed the greater part of his forty-eighth birthday, while a subordinate commander, Sturmbannführer Wilhelm Trabandt, commanding the 3rd Battalion, took over temporary direction of the Leibstandarte Regiment.

———

As the morning progressed the Germans increased their pressure on the British defences at Wormhoudt and began to commit more and more tanks and armoured cars to the fray. They also began to take their first British prisoners. Gunner Arthur Baxter was in one of the most forward and exposed positions in the south-west sector of the British perimeter around Wormhoudt, just off the road out to Dunkirk, when the German attack began – an anti-tank gunner in the unenviable predicament of having lost his anti-tank gun. Baxter and his comrades were among the first British prisoners to fall into SS hands that day, and even so early in the battle their experience was ominous, as his own graphic and moving account makes clear:

> I was serving at the time with the 53rd Anti-Tank Regiment (Worcestershire Yeomanry), holding a position on the edge of Wormhoudt village. Our anti-tank gun had been smashed up a few days before and we were tagging along with another gun team – that's Bombardier J.S. Edkins, Gunner Ball (a new lad who'd only joined us the day before), and myself. As the three of us were spare it was decided we should take our Bren gun and rifles and go across to a small coppice in the middle of a ploughed field and use it as an observation post.

40

About ten a.m. all hell let loose, machine-gun and rifle fire coming from the wood on our right, the bullets cutting the twigs off the branches above our heads. We tried twice to get out of our position but the Germans had us pinned down. Then the firing suddenly stopped for a short time and we crawled flat on our stomachs across the field to a ditch, dragging our Bren behind us. The ditch was so narrow we found it impossible to drag the gun with us, and in any case it was plastered up with black stinking slime – we were all plastered with it too, but it was a great help as camouflage. Finally we reached the main road and took the opportunity of a lull in the firing to dash across the road and down into another ditch, when Bombardier Edkins was wounded by a shot in the right arm.

As we lay in the ditch we saw the enemy for the first time – and what a shock they were. They were just the other side of the road, about forty of them – German SS troops, as tall as our own Guardsmen, black uniforms under camouflage smocks, carrying light machine-guns, rifles and bayonets, stick hand grenades, two lightning-strike SS flashes on their helmets and tunic collars.*

They had a couple of half-track light tanks with them and covered us from across the road with rifles and machine-guns. Then a small swine of a chap, who seemed to be an interpreter [and was probably the platoon commander], spoke a word of command to the chap in charge of one of the light tanks. I'd know him today if only I could cross his bloody path again – Alf Garnett reminds me of him in some way. He was middle-aged, with a short row of medal ribbons on his chest, and his nose was pushed back level with his face. Anyway, the light tank started up and drove straight towards us, firing as it came. It seemed as though the bullets were bouncing off the top of our steel helmets and at one frightening stage we all thought they were going to put one of the tracks of the tank into the ditch and crush us to death.

The commander of the tank drew a revolver and ordered me to get out of the ditch, with Ball and Edkins following. Then five or six SS men surrounded us. They stripped us of our jackets,

* Gunner Baxter's position to the south-west of Wormhoudt would have placed him and his comrades in the line of advance of Wilhelm Mohnke's No 5 Company. We must assume that it was one of the platoons of this company which took Baxter and his comrades captive.

steel helmets, webbing, even our dog tags – we had just our trousers, vest, socks and boots left. Then it started. This swine with the flat nose wanted to know what unit we were with, where our HQ was, what other troops were in the area, how many guns and their positions, what tanks – all this in perfect English from Flatnose. Edkins replied that we were only allowed to state our name, rank and number. At this remark the SS chaps around us went mad, and without any order from Flatnose we were all three kicked, belted in the face, rifles jammed into our sides. Ball and myself were knocked to the ground and the boot was put in again, and then they grabbed us by the hair and pulled us to our feet. I got belted in the right ear and then one big sod gave me a full mouthful of snot straight into my face and said in broken English, 'You English bastard!' Then he made motion to throw a stick grenade and I remember thinking at that moment, 'Yes, you cow, you do and you'll go with me.'

Suddenly there was a hell of a commotion and a British army 15 cwt truck came belting straight down the road towards the lot of us. It came to a stop about eight feet from where we were standing, with the SS chaps covering it from the front, one of them armed with a light machine-gun. I saw the passenger, who was an officer, raise his arms above his head, and the driver too, and they both started to edge their way out of the truck to surrender. I could hardly believe my eyes when I saw what happened next.

Without any order given, the SS trooper with the light machine-gun blasted the officer and the driver back into their seats. They must have had a full magazine blasted into their bodies. I stood rooted to the spot, but all the SS men cheered and clapped their hands. Then one chap went to the back of the truck and pulled out a jerrycan full of petrol. He splashed the petrol over the bodies of the officer and the driver, and inside the cab, and over the canvas roof of the cab and over the wheels, and then he put a match to it. They cremated them on the spot, and to this day I can still see those chaps' faces disappearing behind the flames and smoke, and smell their flesh burning. It was as if I was back home in my mother's kitchen and she had a piece of pork roasting in the oven. I shall never forget that smell or the sight of it.

But that wasn't all. While the 15 cwt was burning, another truck, a 30 cwt Bedford, came tearing down the road from the same direction. Again bullets began to fly and the truck came to rest just behind the 15 cwt, with one wheel in the ditch. Whoever was in the front of the cab must have been killed or badly wounded and down in the well of the cab, because I couldn't see anyone. Then about five SS men went to the back of the truck and pulled out a tommy. This chap must have had a watch chain hanging from his tunic pocket, because I saw one SS man reach out to his tunic pocket and the Tommy automatically brush his hand away. A that the SS man simply placed a pistol to the Tommy's heart and pulled the trigger at point blank range. The Tommy went down flat on his face – he fell to the ground like a straight piece of timber, not a word from the poor chap's lips. The SS man turned him over on his side, took out the watch from his pocket and put it to his ear, and when he found it was still ticking he starting laughing and doing a little dance round the body, with the rest of his mates slapping him on the back, clapping and laughing their heads off.*

The SS men then searched the back of the truck and brought two more young chaps out. They stripped them and then made them join us three. These lads told me they were from the Warwick Regiment, and I would say that the officer and the driver of the 15 cwt had been with the Warwicks as well.

We were kept standing in the road for quite some time when I suddenly realized the SS had missed my cigarette case which I kept in my back pocket. It was a flat thin cheap case but inside it was a picture of my mother and father. I gently eased it out of the pocket, opened it, and looked at their photo for what I felt was going to be the last time. And I said to myself, 'Well, I guess this is goodbye, Mother . . . but if there is a Lord God I'm sure he will try to get us out of this mess.' I slipped the case gently back into my pocket. No one had seen me do it.

A short while later, Flatnose in perfect English ordered Bombardier Edkins and the rest of us to form up across the road in line abreast facing the village. As we started to march off I made up my mind to make a last desperate dash for freedom. We came opposite a gap in the hedge along the side of the road and I

---

* Douglas Botting writes: 'When I first read Arthur Baxter's account of this incident I thought I had read it somewhere before. Not so. What I in fact remembered was Captain William Snelgrave's account (in his *New Account of Guinea and of the Slave Trade*) of being boarded by English pirates off the coast of West Africa in 1719. In their monstrous fecklessness, their callousness, and their wild and erratic brutality the pirates and the SS men had a lot in common – and both sported the skull and crossbones and had a thing about watches.'

made one mad dash for it, shouting to the others to follow. I went through the gap and straight down the side of a garden fence. There was a shot from behind me and I saw sparks and chips of stone fly up from the concrete curb of the fence. I kept running till I was nearly at the end of the garden when I heard an explosion and I felt a burning sensation in my right leg and fell down to the ground. I think they had tried to stop me with one of their stick grenades. My trouser leg was ripped open and soaked with blood, but there seemed to be no pain at that stage, only a tight sensation in the leg.

I managed to get to my feet again and turned left into a paddock with a few trees and a six-foot-high fence stretching across the end of it. My luck ran out with the fence. I tried throwing my weight against it but it was no use. Then I made a dash for a wall but before I reached it I heard shouting and someone running and I threw myself down in a patch of weeds and stinging nettles. A second or two later one of the SS chaps was standing there with his rifle, bending forward and looking hard to see if he could spot me, but thank God he didn't and he went off back to the road.

I got up and made two attempts to get to the top of the wall. But this time my leg felt as though it had a diver's boot strapped to it, but I finally made it and dropped down into a back garden. I managed to get out of this garden onto a road. I made my way a short distance down the road and came face to face with a British infantry officer and ten Tommies beside a stationary truck. I told the officer what had happened and warned him that the SS were only a road away. He told us to climb on to the truck and we started to drive off, but unfortunately the driver turned up the side road I had just come out of, slap in the direction of a group of SS who had appeared round the corner. As the SS opened up on the truck, the driver tried to turn round in one swoop. He nearly made it, but ended up on the pavement right against the wall. I heard the officer yell, 'Every man for himself!' and in no time at all the truck seemed to be empty. What happened to the infantry chaps, God knows. I lowered myself over the side of the truck and managed to get across the road and round the corner of the last house. Then I made my way across the fields.

I can't remember how long I travelled. I kept looking round and was cheered by the fact that no one was following me. I was crawling along the ground, dragging my right leg, when I came to a stream. I started to cross and managed to pull myself out of the deep mud by grabbing the exposed roots of a tree on the bank.

At this point I knew I could go no further. I was getting weaker and my leg was in a bad way. How long I stayed there I can't remember, but suddenly in the distance I saw a tommy. I didn't know then he was one of our own boys until he heard my call for help and came over. How he managed to stick with me I don't know. He tried to stop the bleeding by tying a handkerchief round my leg, and all the time he had to support me, sometimes even carry me – I must have felt a dead weight indeed. I asked him to leave me and look after himself, as I would only increase his chances of getting caught, but he refused to leave me.

Eventually we came across an RA Battery of 25-pounders who were just about to pull out. The MO was there treating their wounded and he gave me morphine. I was put in the back of one of their trucks and the Battery moved out. Later I was transferred to one of two ambulances making their way to Dunkirk.

I was the only one who managed to escape from the SS out of the five of us who were lined up on the road to Wormhoudt. My two pals are buried in Wormhoudt cemetery, and I think the two Royal Warwickshire lads are there too, in unnamed graves. Bombardier Edkins' grave is marked and I can only assume the SS never took his dog tag away. He was a fine soldier who carried out his duties to the book, a real gentleman in every sense of the word, and one who upheld the highest standard of 210 Battery and the 53rd Anti-Tank Regiment, RA.

At midday the British positions were still intact and by the early afternoon it became clear to the embattled British that the Germans, far from backing off, were beginning to intensify their efforts. German troops had crossed the road to Dunkirk to the north of the town and the road to Cassel to the south of it. The little spotter plane with Allied marking reappeared and flew blithely to and fro above the battlefield like an angel of death, directing the shells and the mortar fire with deadly precision. Much of the German fire fell round the main square of Wormhoudt, setting the house ablaze and inflicting casualties on HQ personnel and troops passing through the town *en route* to Dunkirk. But the Warwickshires' slit-trenches and anti-tank guns were also badly hit, and the fire grew so intense that it severed communications between Battalion HQ and the Brigade HQ and the companies and made it increasingly difficult to keep the companies supplied with ammunition in the one remaining Bren carrier.

Other things being equal, the battle for Wormhoudt might have reached a stalemate. But they were not equal. The British were surrounded and cut off and could not be reinforced. By 1300 hours they were suffering from an acute shortage of ammunition, especially for small arms and mortars, so that they could now only fire when a good target presented itself, and for the most part had to hold their fire rather than trade fusillade with fusillade, which left the men feeling frustrated and apprehensive about the outcome. The British also lacked tanks, a disadvantage not shared by their well-supported adversaries.

By now the battle was beginning to reach its climax. Wormhoudt itself was in flames and the killing fields around it littered with the dead and wounded. The British, outnumbered and outgunned, took every advantage of the open terrain to trick the Germans into trap areas where they could concentrate their severely rationed fire power. Shortly after 1300 hours 15 Platoon of the Cheshires under Lieutenant J.D. Ravenscroft was withdrawn into Wormhoudt and at 1330 took up positions in the town square, with one section firing up the Dunkirk road to the north and another section firing down the Cassel road to the south.

There is, perhaps not surprisingly, some confusion in eye-witness accounts of the bitter battle for Wormhoudt town centre. What is clear is that even by this time at least one German unit had succeeded in reaching the town square. Lance-Corporal T.A. Oxley was a member of 15 platoon when he entered the square on one of two trucks carrying a mixed party of Cheshires and Warwicks from the direction of Wormhoudt church and the Cassel road. In the light of subsequent events that day, Corporal Oxley's experience of a close encounter with Leibstandarte troops was ominously similar to that experienced by Gunner Baxter a few hours previously:

We entered the square in Wormhoudt and were surprised to see a large party of Germans at the other end of the square. I observed the time on the Church clock and it was 1.50 p.m. They appeared to be resting but immediately they observed us they opened fire. Most of the men on our trucks were either killed or wounded. My truck gave a sudden turn and I was thrown off and the truck went on.

I found that three other men had been thrown off our truck. I said to the other three that it looked as if there was nothing but to be taken prisoner. We therefore stood with our hands up. In fact they were fanatical and some were dancing around us pointing

46

their tommy guns at us. The Germans appeared to me to be very young, no more than seventeen or eighteen years of age. After a matter of minutes they fired on us. Whether they all fired I cannot say, but definitely one of them who I had been watching let go a burst on his tommy gun at the four of us. I was hit twice on the arm and leg and was knocked out immediately.

Corporal Oxley's three comrades were dead and Oxley himself lay seriously wounded and unconscious – the second group of British prisoners-of-war known to have been murdered at Wormhoudt by SS soldiers of the 2nd Battalion Leibstandarte on 28 May 1940. There is no certain evidence as to which company the teenage thugs who perpetrated this deed belonged – Wilhelm Mohnke's No 5 Company entering the town from the south-west or Otto Baum's No 7 Company coming in from the south. Whoever they were, they seem – if Oxley correctly remembered the time on the church clock as 1.50 p.m. – to have been a probing party, the vanguard of the German force rather than the main body, for the Leibstandarte's official historian claims it was not until over an hour later that the 2nd Battalion succeeded in breaking into the town in force, and this conforms with the tactical chronology of the battle.

Though Oxley himself regained consciousness later in the afternoon, he seems to have been oblivious of the heavy fighting that took place in the streets of Wormhoudt during the main battle for control of the town – during which his platoon was split in two and overrun, and his Platoon Commander, Lieutenant Ravenscroft, was wounded and captured – and three hours were to pass before he next noticed the time on the church clock.

———

Shortly after Oxley's party had been shot up in the main square, the German attack assumed a new dimension. This was first detected some minutes earlier by the look-out of a forward section of B Company, guarding Wormhoudt's western approaches, as the 2nd Royal Warwicks' diarist noted in the Battalion War Diary: 'Tanks reported advancing down road from Esquelbecq.' In fact there had been sporadic German tank movements all morning, but this was different – a co-ordinated mass tank attack by the 3rd Panzer Regiment (2nd Panzer Division) with infantry of the 2nd Leibstandarte SS in close support. The tanks advanced at a slow pace, clattering and squealing and whining across the fields, firing long bursts of tracer from their machine-guns and small-calibre shells from their cannons as they lumbered irresistibly forward. Corporal Bill Cordrey,

47

of B Company, who had the good fortune to survive this day, later recounted his section's experience at the sharp end of a Panzer assault:

> Sure enough, there they were, about 700 yards away and making towards us in an extended line. I made a dive for the Boys anti-tank rifle. Ten bloody rounds! What the hell good was that?
>
> Everybody was opening up now. Sticking the barrel of the Boys over the parapet, I picked out the most central tank and decided to let him have the full ten rounds. What a joke! The bloody tank never faltered, and I knew I was hitting it.
>
> The situation was getting really hot. We were being plastered with shells and automatic fire. What to do? Get out, while there was still a chance? Or keep on with our pea-shooter of a Bren, and get massacred?
>
> Every nerve in me was screaming, 'Get out! Don't be a bloody fool, you've done your share.' But I was more scared of running than of staying put! I could hear Ginger, cussing like hell. The Bren had jammed. This was it! Time to go!
>
> Suddenly, Clancy said: 'Quick, Bill! Look! They're turning!' I took a quick look, and sure enough, the whole line had made a half-left incline – and the extreme right flank was going to miss us by at least a couple of hundred yards.
>
> I couldn't believe my eyes. Another few minutes, and it would have been curtains for us. As the tanks moved away, I expected to see the infantry following up behind them. But it was all clear. Except for a few bursts of gunfire to our left, everything had gone quiet. In my own mind, I was certain we were in a pretty bad fix . . . and I wanted to get out as soon as possible.

Though Corporal Cordrey and his section were spared, others in B Company were not so fortunate. One tank drove right over the next trench, killing all its occupants except one, who lost both his legs. In the next line to the right there were no survivors at all. A platoon commanded by Lieutenant Dunwell fought valiantly against the German armour but was in turn overwhelmed, losing many men, including the platoon commander.

In the midst of the catastrophe that was engulfing B Company, certain individuals rose to heights of heroism. Lance-Corporal Handyside, wounded and isolated, kept firing away with his Bren until he had no ammunition left and was forced to withdraw, taking a number of wounded soldiers back to HQ Company with him. (He was killed at a later stage of the fighting.) On B Company's right flank the fighting grew even more desperate. 2nd Lieutenant Gunnell and his platoon fought back stubbornly, knocking out one German tank before being overrun by others. Gunnel was taken prisoner – and correctly treated by his captors. He was subsequently recommended for the VC, but given the MC instead when it was found that the three mandatory witnesses required for this supreme decoration for valour could not be produced.

So desperate was the British resistance that at 1430 the German XIX Corps War Diary noted: 'The Corps Commander is not counting on any success from the attack and is of the opinion that further useless sacrifice must be avoided after the severe casualties which the 3rd Panzer Regiment has suffered.' But one by one the 2nd Royal Warwicks' anti-tank guns were knocked out and the German tanks grew bolder. After sweeping through B Company's positions, they charged on into the sector held by A Company, driving all before them as they swung round the outskirts of Wormhoudt to the south. There was little that lightly armed infantry in shallow slit-trenches could do to resist the onslaught of the German armour. As the Adjutant was to record later:

> It became obvious that we could not stop a tank attack, and would be merely over-run. After all, we were but a few scattered infantry posts, without our mortars, both of which had been destroyed, and no carriers, very inadequate artillery support – and no air, or armoured support whatsoever. But the Battalion had at any rate delayed the advance.

III

CAPTURE

Faced with this kind of attack, the infantrymen of the 2nd Royal Warwicks
had only three options – to die, to surrender, or to run for their lives. Which
option they chose depended on their frame of mind and the vagaries of
battle; but each and every one spelled defeat. A Company broke under the
impact of the Panzers. Many men died, many were captured, a few
doubtless made good their escape. The mood of the German troops was
angry and many of them seemed trigger-happy. When Captain D. Padfield
of A Company and Private Reginald West from HQ Signals section were
surrounded while trying to lay a telephone cable to A Company HQ,
Captain Padfield pulled out his pistol – whether to surrender it or fire it is
not clear – and was immediately gunned to the ground by fire from half a
dozen weapons. After Private Charles Daley had put his hands up in
surrender, a German armed with a pistol screamed at him, '*Engländer
Schwein!* (English pig!)' and shot him straight through the shoulder. At the
end, when all seemed lost, the Company Commander, Major C.
Chichester-Constable, MC, a brave and much-respected veteran of the
First World War, was seen to walk towards the German tanks, alone and
with a pistol in his hand. This brave but hopeless gesture was the form *his*
anger in battle took, and he died in the arms of an SS soldier, who was
himself killed in combat the very next day.

The tanks had turned the tide of battle and the end could not be far away
now. The Warwicks' Battalion HQ sent a brief hint of impending defeat to
Brigade HQ – 'Tanks shelling and mortaring' – but the message never got
through and no further help could be expected from that direction now. By
this time the German tanks had crossed the Ledringhem road and were
bearing down on D Company's positions, due south of the town. As the
tanks rumbled towards the D Company slit-trenches the following infantry
(Baum's No 7 Company) fanned out so as to cover the widest possible
front.

Though much reduced in numbers, D Company had beaten off two German attacks, thanks in part to the personal valour and powers of leadership of the Company Commander, Captain John Frazer Lynn-Allen. But now the company was surrounded and overrun. Private Alfred Tombs was with Captain Lynn-Allen and a few other men when a tank bore down on them and came to a halt right in front of their position. 'Out came a German,' Tombs testified later, 'who told us to put down our weapons. We were then handed over to the SS infantry.' Captain Lynn-Allen was heard to say to his men, 'You've no need to be ashamed. You have fought well.' Then they were marched away.

When nineteen-year-old Private Bert Evans – who had only joined the Battalion in the last few days – saw the tanks bouncing over the bumpy field towards him he made an instant decision and took to his heels. He had not run far, however, when he found his escape route barred by a small river, the Peene Becque, which marked the rear perimeter of D Company's sector. Other like-minded D Company soldiers had fled to the river and jumped in in the hope of swimming to the far bank. But Bert Evans could not swim and he turned in horror in time to see that some eight or nine German soldiers were almost upon him. There was no room for manoeuvre, no time even to think. His hands shot up in surrender. The soldiers were SS men, he noticed, with the words 'Adolf Hitler' on the cuffs of their tunics. 'Not just Germans,' he told himself, dismayed at his luck. 'Bloody Nazis!'

Evans was marched to the main body of D Company prisoners, about fifty men in all, including the Company Commander, Captain Lynn-Allen, and Private Alf Tombs. Shortly after he was captured Alf Tombs had a good opportunity to judge the Germans' mood when he saw a guard despatch one of Tombs' wounded comrades, Private Gould, with a rifle shot fired point-blank through the head.

Not all the men captured at the height of the battle were men from units which had been involved in the rearguard action at Wormhoudt. Gunner Richard Parry, for example, had the misfortune to belong to a Royal Artillery battery (242 Battery, 69th Medium Regiment) that was making for Dunkirk when it ran headlong into the German tank attack near the Peene Becque just south of Wormhoudt. Parry was in the back of one of the trucks in the convoy when it came under fire from an advancing tank. Eighteen officers and men were killed in this ambush, but along with other surviving occupants from the trucks, Parry was able to leap out and run for cover. He found temporary refuge in a warehouse on the river bank, but he knew the

Germans would soon find him there, so he decided to take to the river in the hope of making his way to the sea. So he took off his boots and hung them round his neck, and then he slid quietly into the water, and swam off under the cover of the river bank.

For a mile and a half he swam, and then he began to have doubts about the wisdom of what he was doing. The Peene Becque flowed from south to north, and to reach the sea, therefore, he would have to swim with the current. But this would take him almost into Wormhoudt and all the fighting – and heaven knows where else after that. What he needed was a local map. As he bobbed along he saw a group of houses, so he clambered out of the river and went through the back door of the first house, which was deserted, to see what he could turn up. His hopes rose when he found a map in a bookcase, but were instantly dashed again when he saw that it was a map of Southern France. He decided to try his luck by the front door, but was in such a state that he failed to check whether the coast was clear, and when he opened the door he found himself staring at a group of SS soldiers barely fifty yards down the road. They spotted him at once and two of them ran up to him, motioning with their rifles for him to raise his arms. He was searched, and his helmet, pay book and other belongings were taken from him. Then he was marched a short distance down the road, where he joined a group of prisoners from the 2nd Warwicks, which included Bert Evans.

Battalion HQ, meanwhile, had very rapidly become isolated and embattled. Communications with the companies faltered as the lines were repeatedly severed by shell fire, and then failed entirely as the Company HQs were over-run and one by one fell silent. The Battalion War Diary dutifully recorded the course of the débâcle as perceived at HQ:

> Remainder of Battalion HQ and Headquarters Company, Majors Hicks and Harborne, Adjutant and Intelligence Officer, now joined by 2nd Lieutenant J.W. Tomes,* with signallers, intelligence, MT drivers and others, returned in single file towards Château, with the exception of Orderly Room clerks,

* There were two officers called Tomes in the 2nd Royal Warwicks at Wormhoudt – the Adjutant, Captain L.T. Tomes, and a young subaltern from D Company, 2nd Lieutenant J.W. Tomes. Just to add to the confusion, there was also a Private Alfred Tombs, who features prominently later in this story.

two or three Intelligence Section, who remained behind in slit trench and fired at an advancing tank. Tank passed down towards village. Battle raging furiously. Many casualties. RSM presumed killed [in fact he was wounded]. Party with CO take up positions in slit trenches in garden near Battalion HQ. The air was full of bullets. Tank on Esquelbecq road, and tanks advancing across country, all firing vigorously.

———

A lull in the fighting followed. No firing could be heard from either side. At Battalion HQ this temporary but uncanny silence was taken as a sure sign that all resistance from the rifle companies had ended. Corporal Bill Cordrey of B Company came to much the same conclusion. After the Panzers had veered away from Cordrey's position everything had gone very quiet and he had sent Clancy to try and locate Company HQ and find out what was going on. He feared the worst and Clancy confirmed it when he returned. Company HQ was wiped out, with dead bodies and shot-up trucks all over the place and Platoon Sergeant-Major Agutter in a bad way and needing urgent medical attention. Cordrey decided the only thing that could be done with the Sergeant-Major was to get him to the First Aid Post in Wormhoudt as fast as possible. He laid the badly-wounded man in a Bren gun carrier, mounted his Bren on the carrier, and with Clancy and the two men of the carrier's crew set off post-haste for the town. But even before they got there they could see it was a hopeless prospect. Wormhoudt was in flames. Cordrey made a snap decision. He would go flat out for Dunkirk instead.

Too late he remembered the road block the Warwicks had erected on the Dunkirk road before the German attack. The carrier bore down on it at top speed, hoping to break through the barrier, but at the last moment Cordrey saw that the barrier had been reinforced and was now in German hands.

'Slow down and spin round!' he yelled at Clancy.

At that moment the Germans brought all their machine-guns to bear and sprayed the carrier from one end to the other. As the carrier span round, Cordrey could see that the Germans had levelled an anti-tank gun at the carrier and looking back he saw the red muzzle flash of the gun as it fired. But the shot missed and they sped on back to the burning town and when they got as far as the church lurched hard left, still heading north in the direction of Dunkirk. There were Germans everywhere, moving into Wormhoudt, and the carrier had passed several score of them when they suddenly hit a shell hole, span out of control, veered across the road and crashed into the ditch.

It was, in every sense, the end of the road. The Sergeant Major was already dead. Escape was out of the question. The carrier, riddled with holes, was surrounded by German soldiers. One look at their faces was sufficient to convince Corporal Cordrey that they were not in the best of tempers – one false move and they would open fire. As Cordrey was later to relate:

> We were told to get out of the carrier by a German who spoke a little English. I got out, and as soon as I had put my feet on the ground, another German came running up. Sticking a big revolver in my stomach, he started screaming at me in German.
>
> I could feel the tension building up around us. There seemed to be hundreds of them surrounding us but this one was blowing his top. Looking down at the revolver, I saw that his hand was shaking.
>
> 'Any second now,' I thought, 'and he's going to pull the trigger.'
>
> Suddenly, he turned away from me and shouted an order to the others – and about thirty of them doubled off down the road in the direction we had come from. I then realized that he was trying to find out if there were any more of us.
>
> He seemed to be a senior NCO, and was certainly looking trigger-happy, so I was very relieved when, after shouting a few more orders, he put his revolver away and made off down the road.
>
> I asked the Germans if we could bury Platoon Sergeant-Major Agutter, but they said that it would be attended to. They added that all information concerning us would be sent to the Red Cross.

———

Now only Battalion HQ and scattered pockets of reistance manned by remnants of the Warwicks and Cheshires were left to carry on the grim job of blocking the German road to Dunkirk. To this weary collection of signallers, clerks and headquarters personnel it was unclear which would be expended first – the last man, or the last bullet. The 2nd Leibstandarte, meanwhile, continued to press forward. At about 1500 hours they succeeded in breaking through into the south-west corner of Wormhoudt and began to battle their way house by house towards the market square. At Battalion HQ the silence was broken by a sudden immense explosion as HQ's positions were targetted by the German guns. A firestorm swept

HQ's position and when it died down armoured cars were seen to approach within 200 yards, then pause to take aim before firing. At this critical juncture the Adjutant, Captain Tomes, decided something needed to be done very fast. He wrote later:

> I saw a man with an anti-tank rifle. I don't know where he came from. I told him to follow me, and started off up the road towards the armoured cars, which were behind the hedge. He couldn't see where they were, so I took the anti-tank rifle from him and lay down in the middle of the road, covered by a derelict truck.
>
> I fired two of the remaining three rounds. I couldn't see whether they had any effect. I was feeling curiously exhilarated now, and still had a rifle and fifty rounds which I had taken off a carrier. It had belonged to one of the crew, who had been killed.
>
> After placing the man with the anti-tank rifle in position, I got behind a hedge and fired practically the whole bandolierful at the turrets of the armoured cars and at various vehicles and motorcycles coming along the road.
>
> Hicks sent up Private Fahy [not to be confused with Gunner Fahey of the Royal Artillery, who features later in this narrative] and we fired at these for several minutes. My rifle became almost too hot to hold, and I heard Hicks shouting at me to come back. Fahy and I ran back along the road, which seemed alive with splattering bullets and tracer. The direction of these made me look left, and I saw two tanks coming towards us across the field. They must have wiped out the Intelligence Section, who were at that corner.

It was possibly as a result of Captain Tomes' and Private Fahy's last-ditch stand with their anti-tank rifle that the 2nd Leibstandarte suffered a serious setback, for at some point in this fray their commander, Schützeck, suffered grievous head wounds when his car was struck by an armour-piercing shell in or near the main square.

The wounding of the Leibstandarte's CO is an important factor in this case, though the exact circumstances are not entirely clear. The loss of their Commanding Officer, whose dash and courage had been a tremendous inspiration to his men, plunged the Leibstandarte's 2nd Battalion into considerable disarray. Lacking coherent orders, the attack began to falter. There was some confusion over where to move Battalion Battle HQ. Most importantly, a frantic effort had to be made to locate the man who was designated to take over command of the 2nd Battalion – the commander of No 5 Company, Wilhelm Mohnke. In spite of the confusion, however, it is fairly clear that by about 1600 hours Mohnke had taken over command of the 2nd Leibstandarte Battalion, while Obersturmführer Kraemer had been put in charge of Mohnke's previous command, No 5 Company. The change of command was to have a dramatic effect on the course of events.

Men in the heat of battle often fight in a kind of rage – a compound of intense tension, adrenalin and fear. But the Leibstandarte at Wormhoudt were doubly enraged. The disappearance of their Regimental Commander, the nearly fatal wounding of a popular Battalion Commander, the heavy casualties inflicted by the British defenders, and the loss of so many of their comrades – all these factors greatly stoked up the anger of the trigger-happy men of the Leibstandarte, who began to mutter darkly of revenge. This state in mind was common to many men in combat, and not necessarily peculiar to the SS, or to German soldiers in general. What *was* peculiar to the SS was the form this revenge was to take under the leadership of the Leibstandarte's new commander, Wilhelm Mohnke.

———

From the British point of view the change of command made little difference to the course of the battle. The Germans advanced relentlessly from house to house down streets which presented an archetypal image of the European war – burning buildings, smashed vehicles, soldiers' corpses, staccato gunfire, shouts of command and cries of wounded men amid the litter of battle.

Realizing that it was impossible to hold out much longer, Major Hicks, the Warwicks' CO, cast about for a way out of the German encirclement. The second-in-command, Major Harborne, had already tried to find a route but had been shot through the head while stalking a tank with a rifle (he was later taken prisoner). The commander of HQ Company led a break-out group of nine men off in the direction of the Esquelbecq road, but he too was killed *en route* and the rest of the group were never seen again. At about 1700 hours there was a tremendous thunderstorm and the rain came beating down. Shortly afterwards the Battalion's Intelligence Officer managed to bring a group of eighteen men out on to the Dunkirk road, where he joined up with Captain Sir John Nicholson of the 4th Cheshires, who had also managed to escape with a small group of his men. Together they made their way back to Brigade HQ at Wylder, where they were relieved to find Major Hicks, 2nd Lieutenant Tomes and some sixty-five NCOs and men who had also found a way out of the German trap. Later, after a fighting retreat through the German lines in the dark, the commander of B Company and nine of his men joined what was left of the 2nd Battalion, the Royal Warwickshire Regiment.

Though the Warwicks had pulled out of Wormhoudt, the Germans were not yet in full control of this hotly contested little town. But for the moment their tanks were in the market square and their troops were diverting themselves in various ways after the rigours of combat. It was at about this point that Private Oxley, left for dead in the street, opened his eyes again and found himself alive in the midst of the enemy soldiery – and witness to a surreal nightmare:

After coming to I saw some Germans around the shop fronts; others were eating and drinking and others were going down the streets throwing grenades through bedroom windows. Whilst all this was going on I had the presence of mind to keep perfectly still and watched them. Whilst doing so three Germans brought an English sergeant, who was not known to me, out of a house. He appeared to be badly wounded and a German officer immediately shot him down with his revolver. In fact, he emptied his revolver into the Sergeant whilst he lay on the ground.

Directly opposite where I lay, there was an air raid shelter which appeared to me to be under the railway embankment. A party of men came to the top of the shelter steps. The Germans were calling them out but the men would not come out. After a short while two Germans went along and threw grenades down the shelter. After that I saw no sign of life around the shelter.

As I still lay on the ground I saw three German tanks and two armoured cars parked right in front of me. In fact they were so close I watched one of the crew oiling his tank. I still lay on the ground till 4.50 p.m., still observing the time on the Church clock which was in view. At this time there was very heavy fire from mortars and all kinds of small arms fire. The Germans immediately boarded their tanks and armoured cars and they, including some infantrymen, some 150 in all, moved off together, leaving me and the three Warwicks on the ground. When I saw that they had all gone I sat up. I found that I could not stand up. I then crawled along the ground to the shop fronts and pulled myself to my feet with the aid of the window ledges and then started to hobble down the street.

After proceeding no more than a few yards I saw a British soldier coming out of a house. I hailed him and he told me that he had been hiding in a wardrobe. He also was wounded in the leg but not seriously. I suggested to him that we should make for the British Dressing Station, a big red brick building, where I had noticed that morning several of our lads and many

57

Warwicks had been taken. On arrival there we found the drive littered with corpses, some stripped naked, their bodies patterned with bullet holes, and others in uniform, and there seemed no sign of any life.

No explanation has ever been produced as to exactly what happened at the dressing station. At the time of its capture it would have contained the British soldiers wounded during the day's fighting, along with the Medical Officer, Captain A. Crook, RAMC, and his staff. These are known to have been taken prisoner by the Germans and to have been correctly treated, although there is abundant evidence of Leibstandarte brutality towards British wounded elsewhere on the battlefield in and around Wormhoudt that day. So whose were the corpses that Private Oxley saw strewn over the driveway to the silent, empty dressing station, some in uniform, some naked? Were the naked ones those who had already died and were awaiting burial (stripped prior to medical treatment for their wounds, perhaps?) But if so, why where they strewn along the drive, their bodies 'patterned with bullet holes'? Were those in uniform wounded soldiers who were too far gone to be moved and had been given the *coup de grâce* by their SS captors? Or had a ghastly massacre been perpetrated, of the sort that was to become all too familiar in Wormhoudt by the end of the day, of which no witnesses survived?

One explanation is offered by Lance-Bombardier Tom H. Nicholls, of the 53rd (Worcestershire Yeomanry) Anti-Tank Regiment, who was one of the last British soldiers to get out of Wormhoudt alive, and who also saw the naked bodies in the town. Bombardier Nicholls had been commanding one of the guns positioned just off the Dunkirk road leading out of Wormhoudt. Nicholls was to relate:

> I did not abandon my gun until 1730 hours, when with my three remaining soldiers we withdrew very hurriedly under threat of attack by a considerable number of enemy. I found a British Army truck and started to drive into Wormhoudt with Gunners Marsh, Mathews and Williams. As we drove into the town we were fired upon by a machine-gun immediately to our front. Truly, I prayed to God as to what to do and I was told to take my foot off the accelerator. The Germans stopped firing, possibly because they thought we were Germans in a British truck, and as we drew level with them I threw a grenade at them and accelerated away. But evidently I didn't knock them all out, because they fired into the back of the truck as we sped away, killing Gunner Marsh.
>
> Wormhoudt was full of Germans but my prayer was

answered, because it began to rain heavens hard and the rain saved us. I saw three or four German motorcycles and sidecars with machine-guns mounted but they had taken shelter from the rain and I was able to stop the truck and run across the far end of the main square with my men. Oh, I saw many dead that day as I ran through Wormhoudt in the rain. I passed at least twenty naked bodies, which looked as though they had been slashed with sabre cuts, and four trucks, the engines still running, full of troops ambushed and killed as they tried to leave the town. Only much later did I learn from the mayor of Wormhoudt that after the battle, the SS perpetrated a widespread massacre, and put any Englishman who could still stand to the knife and drowned the wounded in the horse-pond and set four ambulances full of wounded on fire.

Nicholls also discovered that at a gun position next to the café on the road out to Dunkirk, a gun crew from the King's Heath [Birmingham] T.A. Battery, 210 Anti-Tank Regiment, were stripped and shot after they had surrendered. But these random killings in and around Wormhoudt were not the only SS outrages that day. To the east of the town, for example, an officer of the 8th Worcesters had had to watch his men put up against a wall and shot whilst he was lying wounded on the ground; but though the Germans then shot him again to finish him off he survived to tell the tale. These killings paled in scale and barbarity, however, when compared to the fate meted out to the main group of prisoners rounded up by the SS after the Royal Warwickshire's companies had been overrun.

IV

MASSACRE

It is now time to turn to the sequence of events which resulted in the final horrific outcome that occurred on 28 May. These events can only be pieced together from the testimony of surviving eye-witnesses, some British and some German – though the evidence of the latter, not surprisingly, is often evasive and contradictory.

The main nucleus of British prisoners captured on the outskirts of Wormhoudt consisted of the fifty or so men of D Company who had been overrun by the German tank attack on their positions in the meadows on the west bank of the little river known as the Peene Becque. This was the group that Bert Evans joined shortly after he was captured. Before long the order was given for the prisoners to be marched away and they set off across the fields in the direction of Wormhoudt with an armed guard provided by a detail of 2 Platoon of Otto Baum's No 7 Company, under the command of the platoon leader, twenty-eight-year-old Untersturmführer Heinrich.

The prisoners were now herded across a footbridge over the river and then along a track leading to the main road from Cassel. They turned left on to the road and marched forty yards towards Wormhoudt when they were halted again by a wooden-fronted building on the right, about 450 yards south of Wormhoudt church. Here they were searched, and roughly manhandled in the process, and then their identity discs were removed and some of them were stripped to the waist. Evans had his identity disc, pay book, ring and some of his clothing taken from him. From Captain Lynn-Allen the guards removed a hand grenade, a revolver, his ring and the contents of his pockets. Henceforth the prisoners were no longer easily identifiable from their discs, insignia or personal possessions.

It was there that Richard Parry of the Royal Artillery, who had fallen into German hands after his abortive down-river swim, joined the main group after having his pay book and personal belongings removed from him. A small party of D Company men which included Alf Tombs also joined the main group here. They, too, had had their dog tags and possessions removed. As Tombs testified later: 'They stripped everything from us.' At one point during their march here they had been lined up in front of a farm building with a machine-gun trained on them and for a moment had feared the worst. But then they had been ordered off again and continued to hope for the best – until they passed three burnt-out British trucks. 'There were bodies of our lads lying beside each truck,' Tombs wrote later, 'with oil all over their bodies. Some were burnt to charcoal. One of them was still burning.'

It was while the prisoners were on this road that Bert Evans saw something very alarming. Over on the left was a cannery, and Evans saw that the Germans had lined up about fifteen to twenty men against the wall of the building. Evans watched what happened next:

> As they stood there, the guards who were in charge of them opened up with automatic fire. They killed the lot. I shall never forget seeing them fall down, just like rag dolls.
>
> To this day, I can never understand why we were not shot along with them. I can only think that our guards belonged to a different company, or something like that. But what I remember, very clearly, was thinking that something very nasty was afoot.

For what seemed like fifteen minutes the men in this main group were forced to stand with their hands raised while their guards took it in turns to take refreshments from a vacated bar-café across the road, the Estaminet St Hubert. Close infantry combat is thirsty work in summer. There is no means of knowing what kind of drink the SS men consumed in the Estaminet St Hubert; but it is significant that one witness of the heinous events that were to follow was of the opinion that all the guards were either drugged or intoxicated at the time. As for the British prisoners, by now they were in a fairly traumatized condition. After the shock of combat, they were rain-soaked, dirty, bedraggled, dejected, confused, fearful, but perhaps not yet bereft of hope. Additionally, they were deeply shocked by the execution of the fifteen prisoners before their very eyes a few minutes before. Escape was impossible. They had no other option but to go along with their captors' wishes. What these might be they had no way of predicting. But they were grateful when an SS officer emerged from the bar-café and brusquely gave the prisoners permission to put their arms down.

The prisoners were now marched off in a weary column down the road towards the town, where they were halted briefly and made to look at the burning houses, the sight of which seemed to give the German guards much simple pleasure – perhaps because they seemed an appropriate symbol of their triumph and omnipotence. In some of the doorways a few British soldiers were hiding, but they were soon rounded up and added to the group. At Wormhoudt church the column turned left and trudged on down the Ledringhem road which led south-west out of the town.

It seemed that their intended destination was the guard escorts' Company HQ (No 7 Company), but to get there they had to pass Battalion Battle Headquarters, which was located in a field to the right of this road. The escort commander, Heinrichs, decided that he might as well halt the prisoners here, and find out what he was supposed to do with them, rather than march them all the way to Company HQ. Here a second large group, variously estimated at between 30 and 60 prisoners, most of them from A Company of the 2nd Royal Warwicks, but also some men from the Cheshires and Royal Artillery – presumably survivors from Parry's ambushed artillery battery – joined the first group of prisoners.

─────

It was now about 1630 hours in the afternoon and Hauptsturmführer Mohnke had been in command of the 2nd Battalion Leibstandarte for about half an hour or more. It was his instructions which Heinrichs now sought regarding the disposal of the British prisoners. Then a crucial incident took place. A senior Leibstandarte officer emerged from Battalion HQ and to the surprise of at least one of the 2nd Platoon guards, Rottenführer Oskar Senf, was seen to storm over to Heinrichs and rebuke him in extremely angry tones. Richard Parry remembered the senior officer as a 'big noise' who wore a soft peaked cap and seemed to be giving orders concerning the prisoners. 'He was raving blue murder!' Parry later recounted. Senf was later to testify that the senior officer in question was in fact the new Battalion Commander, Wilhelm Mohnke. 'What do you mean by bringing in prisoners,' Mohnke stormed at Heinrichs, 'contrary to orders?' Heinrichs' reply was inaudible, but the instructions Mohnke gave to him were clear. One of the British prisoners who understood a little German exclaimed: 'My God! They're taking no prisoners.'

Heinrichs went away and for half an hour or more the prisoners stood about in loose order along the side of the road. Then Heinrichs returned with eight more SS men, all of them, remarkably, corporals and sergeants. These men were unknown to Senf, who assumed they must have come from another company. In fact, they were members of the Signals Section of No 8 Company, attached to the battalion for special duties, who had been with the original Battalion Commander, Schützeck, when he was wounded in Wormhoudt a little earlier in the afternoon. The new Battalion Commander, Mohnke, then proceeded to give the NCO in charge of the Signals Section escort, Scharführer Walter Drescher, orders to take all the prisoners to a barn a mile or so away across the fields and shoot them.

Heinrichs now gave the order to the 2nd Platoon guards to have the prisoners move off, and when Senf asked him where they were supposed to be taking them, Heinrichs replied that the new men 'knew what to do'. When Senf asked the new men where they were taking the prisoners, he was told that they had orders from Mohnke to shoot them. Senf was to testify subsequently that he and his fellow SS men from the 2nd Platoon felt 'very much incensed' about this and voiced their disagreement with it. But when he remonstrated with Heinrichs, and told him that this was not in his line, and that 'in his heart' he could not agree with it, Heinrichs merely shrugged and told him: 'You've just seen for yourself the way Mohnke shouted at me.' As Heinrichs left the scene to go back to the main body of his platoon, one of the new men from Signals Platoon reassured Senf with the words: 'We'll do it alright'. According to Richard Parry, the officer who had done all the shouting was still there when the prisoners moved off again.

———

And so the descent into purgatory began. A drastic change for the worse had taken place following Mohnke's appearance on the scene – a more positively cogent dimension of brutality. For over a mile the prisoners, some of them wounded, all of them exhausted, were forced to march at double time – in effect, to run – across the rough, uneven ground of the fields. Many found this beyond their failing physical powers and were treated unmercifully for their pains by the SS guards. Those who stumbled or faltered were kicked and beaten. Those who fell to the ground were bayoneted or clubbed about the head with rifle butts. One soldier had fallen to the ground and was attempting to keep up with the rest by crawling along on his hands and knees, but he had not crawled far before he was bayoneted through the chest by an SS guard. For men like Charles Daley, who was weak from the shoulder wound he had suffered when he was shot after giving himself up, and Richard Parry, who was helping a wounded comrade to keep up with the rest, the forced march was almost beyond their powers of endurance, and only the fear of suffering the same fate as the other stragglers kept them going.

63

The prisoners were being taken to the edge of a big field in La Plaine au Bois. Trees lined three sides of the field and in one corner near the trees stood an old wooden-walled, straw-roofed barn, more a cowshed or milkingshed than anything, with two little milkchurns outside, and full of muck and straw and cowpats inside. This barn was about the size of an ordinary domestic garage, open at one end and with a small door at the other. The column of prisoners now numbered in the region of a hundred men and in addition to prisoners from the 2nd Royal Warwicks, the 4th Cheshires, and 242nd Battery 69th Medium Regiment, Royal Artillery, it now included seven men of the 99th Battery, 20th Anti-Tank Regiment, Royal Artillery, who had been caught while heading north on foot in the middle of a column of French refugees and Belgian colonial troops, together with at least six men from D Company of the 8th Battalion The Worcestershire Regiment, who had been stripped to the waist and had their dog tags removed by their SS guards.

This motley column of prisoners was directed towards the barn by the bawling SS guards and then driven into it through the main entrance at the gable end, which was without doors. Prisoners waiting their turn to go into the barn had time to speculate as to why they should be doing so. Some assumed the Germans had decided to use the barn as a temporary POW reception point. A few, diehard optimists, guessed the SS men wished to shelter their prisoners from the rain shower which had begun to fall.

Even those who had understood Mohnke's orders about the disposal of prisoners kept their fears to themselves. There was no panic, no resistance at this point. There did not seem to be much any of them could do about anything. The men filed into the barn as if it were a camp cinema. Apart from the guards, only a solitary spectator, watching the scene from the cover of a hedge at the edge of the field, seems to have had any inkling of what was about to happen. This was Private George Merry, of D Company, who had been wounded in the arm and escaped capture by feigning death. In a state of near collapse, Merry had staggered across the field to the hedge and watched in disbelief as his comrades crowded into the barn. Tears came to his eyes and he began to shiver, fearful that the Germans would find him and force him to join the others.

For some not all was lost, however. When Driver John Borland and his six fellow artillerymen from the 20th Anti-Tank Regiment entered the barn, it was already occupied by about forty men, some sitting and some lying down. As they looked around, the No 1 (NCO in Command) of Borland's gun, Bombardier 'Nobby' Clarke, turned to John Borland and said: 'I don't like the look of this. What do you think, John?' Borland agreed. 'But we can't go out the same way,' he said. 'Let's look around.' Borland was later to recall:

In the far left-hand corner of the barn was a door which was jammed with mud and muck. We forced it open about a foot or so and squeezed through and were away, keeping low for about one hundred yards. We saw no one about.

As far as can be ascertained, Bombardier Clarke, Driver Borland, Gunner Richards, Gunner Vickers, Gunner Salisbury and another gunner whose name is not recorded, got clean away – almost the only men to do so without sustaining any injury of any kind.

———

Gunner Parry was the last to enter the barn. By this time it was already packed to the doorway. Estimates vary as to how many squeezed into that confined space. Bert Evans thought there were about ninety to one hundred. John Lavelle reckoned there were nearly one hundred. Charles Daley put the figure at about ninety. Others put it as high as 120. A lot of men in a tiny space. Richard Parry, stuck by the entrance, decided to elbow his way to the back to join a wounded gunner friend. Bert Evans couldn't get inside at all and had to stand with the crowd in the entrance, next to his Company Commander, Captain Lynn-Allen. Thus roughly a hundred men, many of them wounded, were now crowded into a rude structure measuring only twenty-one feet by ten feet.

Ranged in a semi-circle outside the barn stood twelve SS men. Four of these were from the 2nd Platoon of Otto Baum's No 7 Company – Rottenführers Oskar Senf, Werner Rüger and Max Schallwig, and SS-Mann Dorth. These four stood some fifteen to twenty yards from the left-hand side of the barn. Eight were from the Signals Section of No 8 Company – Scharführers Walter Drescher and Josef Sorowka, and Rottenführers Dutschmann, Friedhof, Günther, Konieczka, Moebius and one other, name unknown. These eight stood fifteen to twenty yards from the barn and covered the actual entrance.

We have descriptions of a few of the guards as they confronted their prisoners in the brief moment of hiatus before the action. There was Walter Drescher, a Berliner in his thirties, a professional gardener in civilian life, six-foot tall, strongly built, with dark blond hair; Werner Rüger from Silesia, a stout six-footer, with fair hair, blue eyes, and a very prominent nose; and slim, thin-faced Max Schallwig, also fair-haired, also six foot, also in his thirties. Few of these guards were in the earliest flush of their manhood. Perhaps it was felt that what these men had to do could only be entrusted to soldiers of experience and maturity, who would keep their nerve and do their duty, however unpleasant. This duty they now proceeded to carry out.

Captain Lynn-Allen, who appears to have been the only officer inside the barn, was not a very big man but he was a fighter.* On the battlefield he had held out with his men to the end and was subsequently recommended for the Military Cross for his personal courage and powers of leadership. Here in the barn he was determined to battle it out with the Germans over the conditions to which they were now being subjected, and he complained vociferously to the nearest guard – a very dark, almost bronzed man in his mid-twenties, rather less than SS regulation height – that there was no room for the wounded to lie down. 'Yellow Englishman,' the guard replied, in fluent English with a strong American accent, 'there'll be plenty of room where you're all going.'

Still unable to grasp the true nature of the situation, Lynn-Allen seems to have thought the guard was referring to the prisoner-of-war camp they would be sent to. 'I am still not satisfied,' he told the guard.

This made the SS man very angry and he reached down, took a stick-grenade out of the top of his boot. Captain Lynn-Allen tried to prevent him from carrying out his obvious intention but to his horror the German went ahead and tossed the grenade into the dense crowd of prisoners inside the barn. A shattering explosion followed and grenade splinters flew like bullets into the press of human bodies. Bert Evans was aware of a shock wave in his ears and a numbness where the grenade had blown the bottom part of his right arm to pieces.

Then Lynn-Allen shouted at him: 'Quick! Run for it!' Seizing the split second when the guards were still taking cover from the blast, the Captain dragged Evans by his good arm out of the barn entrance and together they ducked round the corner and sprinted for their lives along the edge of the field, making for the cover of the trees at the end, the Captain supporting the wounded young Private for a distance of some 200 yards. Evans was surprised that once they were clear of the barn Lynn-Allen did not drop

---

* It is just possible that there was a second officer in the barn – Lieutenant Basil Glasspool of the 4th Cheshires. Glasspool was one of about twelve Cheshires who were killed at Wormhoudt on 28 May and though there is no definite evidence that he died in the barn, one of the survivors of the barn incident – Corporal Gill (2nd Royal Warwicks) – later gave confusing testimony which might perhaps indicate that two junior officers were present, rather than one. Gill stated that before the first grenade was thrown 'a Captain Allen' went forward and was riddled by a burst of fire from a German tommy-gun. 'I had a look at Captain Allen a quarter of an hour later,' Gill said, 'and he appeared to me to be dead.' Alf Tombs has said something similar:

'Captain Allen went outside to protest and was shot dead. I saw his body lying on his face outside. He had been shot in the back.' Since we know that Lynn-Allen was shot by a pistol in a pond 200 yards from the barn, and that the body disappeared under the water and could not have been seen by Corporal Gill, we have to conclude that either the memories of Gill and Tombs are at fault, or there were indeed two officers in the barn, Lieutenant Glasspool being the most likely other one.

him and make off on his own, for he did not really know him; but he was grateful for the officer's courage and self-sacrifice. Two shots rang out behind them but missed their proper target. It is possible that the bullets hit instead one of the SS guards, Werner Rüger, who had inadvertently stepped into the line of fire and been struck in the chest and jaw by two 6.35mm bullets fired from a small German automatic pistol. As a result of Rüger's injuries, two or possibly three of the SS men from No 7 Company may have pulled out of the execution squad at the barn – Oskar Senf, who went off for an ambulance; SS-Mann Dorth, who helped tend and carry the wounded man; and Werner Rüger himself, who required urgent hospitalization.

Meanwhile Lynn-Allen and his fellow Warwick, gasping for breath, reached the trees. There was a little pond there, full of stagnant water. Lynn-Allen waded straight in and pulled Evans after him till they were both up to their chests and partially concealed from view. 'Get down and keep your arm out of the water!' Lynn-Allen told Evans. They crouched down and waited. But not for long. They heard footsteps running, growing louder. The figure of a German soldier loomed above them at the edge of the pond. The soldier had a pistol in his hand – in all probability he was the same man who had hit Rüger with two pistol shots a few moments before – and he raised it, aiming it at the officer.*

'Oh my God!' Captain Lynn-Allen cried out. The German fired two shots, one of which went through the Captain's forehead, killing him instantly. As John Lynn-Allen's body tumbled into the water, the German took fresh aim, this time at Bert Evans, who was standing transfixed beside a tree at the far edge of the pond, not much more than three yards from the German. The German loosed off another two shots, one of which ricocheted off the tree and struck Evans in the neck, so that he fell face-forward into the pond as if dead. The guard, evidently believing he had despatched both men, moved off to where the real killing was now in full swing, leaving the twice-wounded Evans, floundering in the stagnant pool, to make shift as best he could.

For Evans the nightmare was total. He was bleeding profusely from his

---

* According to Untersturmführer Helmut Kramer, the 2nd Leibstandarte's armourer at the time of the Wormhoudt incident, small 6.35mm pistols were not standard service issue but generally the privately-owned property of SS officers. However, a senior platoon leader of non-commissioned rank might also carry such a weapon if he had his company commander's permission to do so. This would indicate that the SS man most likely to have shot Lynn-Allen and Evans – and for that matter Rüger – was the escort commander, Scharführer Walter Drescher, who was the senior NCO present. Subsequently the SS guards claimed – undoubtedly falsely – that it was one of the British prisoners who shot Rüger with a 6.35 pistol and that this was the Germans' justification of the massacre that followed.

shattered arm and the new wound in his neck, and very weak and very frightened. Moreover, as he testified later, 'I'd got practically no clothes on me.' From the barn he could hear automatic gunfire and men screaming. He groped around for the body of his dead Captain, who had saved his life but lost his own by staying with him, but he could not find him, and as he stood and swayed there in the corner of that hateful foreign field, head cocked and mind full of the cries of the dying, the enormity of all the horror and all the suffering overcame him, and he wept. He wept for his dear, dead comrades, whom he was powerless to comfort or save; for the inhumanity of it, the sadness, and the pain.

For what seemed like twenty minutes Bert Evans stood there in the stagnant water. Then he crawled out of the pond, and set off to get away. As he cleared the trees, he was hit again by a stray round coming from the direction of the barn, which just seared the top of his right shoulder. He crawled away down a ditch, taking what cover he could, but he had no idea where he was going, nor did he greatly care, so long as it was as distant as possible from the SS.

Inside the barn the men of Wilhelm Mohnke's 2nd Leibstandarte set about their butchery in a manner so cruelly random and haphazard that it served to prolong the process of killing and the agony of dying. They all seemed very excited, almost manic, and to at least one British prisoner, Corporal Gill, they all appeared drugged or intoxicated. The first grenade had caused great commotion and confusion among the prisoners, for many of them could not understand what had happened, and shouted out their questions, and some even raised a cheer, believing their comrades had struck back at their guards.

In the uproar two voices took command, calling loudly for order, so that the barn fell silent, apart from the groans of the wounded. These were the voices of Company Sergeant-Major Augustus Jennings and Sergeant Stanley Moore, who had obviously attracted the attention of the SS men, for suddenly more grenades were tossed in their direction. The mass of prisoners instinctively receded in a human wave against the walls of the barn where they crouched protectively in a tightly pressed huddle. In an act of selfless bravery the two NCOs threw themselves on the grenades, shielding the others with their bodies. Both Jennings and Moore died instantly in the ensuing explosions.

More grenades were now thrown into the crowd of prisoners, tearing flesh, smashing bone, gouging tissue and organs. Screams filled the barn and the dead and dying covered the floor. Private Kelly, of the Warwicks, had his right leg blown clean off. Alf Tombs fell flat on the floor and felt two men fall on top of him and heard someone call out that the Germans were gassing them. Tombs tried to bury his face in the dirt floor to escape the fumes, then realized it was only the smoke from the grenades. Richard Parry counted at least five explosions, the first of which had wounded him in the right leg and blown him almost clean through the wall of the barn, with only his feet still inside the building. Stuck in this awkward position, unable to move, Parry's view of the interior of the barn was restricted, though he was well placed to observe what happened outside it.

By peering through a crack in the barn wall, Private John Lavelle, who had been struck by a grenade splinter in the foot, was also able to see outside. The Germans had evidently decided that hand grenades were a messy and inefficient way of killing a large number of people, for they now opted for a different method, and began to bawl out fresh orders. Lavelle caught the word '*Raus!*' which a man next to him translated.

'They're demanding five men should go outside,' he said.

At first nobody moved, and the order was shouted again. Alf Tombs heard a voice say, 'Come on, if we've got to go, we've got to go,' and saw a man make his way to the barn entrance, followed by four other volunteers. The men walked slowly and proudly, holding themselves straight, heads high. They were led to a spot twenty yards to the right of the barn entrance, and then halted and made to stand in a line. An SS man armed with a rifle stood opposite each of the five British prisoners, forming a rough-and-ready firing squad. It was immediately obvious to the five men, and to their comrades inside the barn, what the Germans' intentions were. Two of the five asked to be allowed to smoke a last cigarette, thereby gaining a few more minutes of precious life, but the request was refused and the men were ordered to turn round with their backs to the firing squad.

The prisoners inside the barn, who had been muttering their disgust at what was happening, now fell silent, and even the wounded stopped moaning. Some of those who had been watching the scene through the cracks in the wall took their eyes away. In the silence the shots rang out. John Lavelle, peering through a crack, saw the five prisoners slumped on the ground. One of them, he noticed with interest, was not dead, but only wounded.

There was some speculation later as to the identity of the wounded man. According to two men who were in the barn, John Lavelle and Charles Daley, the man's name was Johnson, a soldier in the 2nd Royal Warwicks. It seems that this was subsequently corroborated by a wounded Warwicks officer, Lieutenant Kenneth Keene, who was repatriated from a POW camp in Germany in 1943. Keene had met Johnson in Ghent Military Hospital in Belgium in August 1940 and thus heard his story at first-hand. He was able to confirm that Johnson was indeed shot by a firing squad, was indeed suffering from a wound in the chest and lung, and before the war had been resident at 10 Dulverton Avenue, Coventry.

The guards strode back to the barn and shouted for five more men to come out. Five prisoners elected to face the firing squad. One of them was Private Garside, of the Royal Warwicks, who had been a No 1 on the mortars with Alfred Tombs. This time they were taken to the left-hand side of the barn entrance and again ordered to turn round with their backs to the firing squad. Richard Parry, who was stuck half in and half out of the back wall of the barn, and well placed to observe both executions, saw that this time the prisoners swivelled round on their heels just as the firing squad was about to open fire, defiantly confronting their murderers face to face when they were shot.

For a long time it was never known who these five men were, apart from Private Garside. But recently a former Royal Artilleryman who had been wounded and captured at Wormhoudt, Brian Fahey, has come forward and stated that he was one of the prisoners in the second execution party. As the only member of his unit to end up in the barn, he was apparently unknown to the other occupants inside. According to Fahey, when he was shot the bullet passed completely through his body without hitting any vital organ, and when the Germans turned him over and saw the blood pouring from his nose and mouth, they assumed he was dead and left him alone.

There was uproar inside the barn as the surviving prisoners gave vent to their anger and disgust, hurling defiant abuse at their tormentors. Again the SS men strode back to the entrance and again they demanded five more volunteers. Eventually a stubborn mood of collective resistance gripped the captives. The Germans could do their damnedest, but henceforth it would be without co-operation from the British. There would be no more volunteers. Private Cyril Harbour and another man decided they might as well make a run for it as wait to be executed in cold blood. They crawled out through a hole in the back of the barn, only to be sprayed with automatic fire and left for dead. Harbour, in fact, was still alive, but badly wounded in an arm and a leg.

The Germans now conferred with each other in the barn entrance. Their orders were clear and simple. They had to kill all the prisoners in the shortest possible time. But to liquidate a large group of human beings is not as easy as it sounds – as the Nazis were to discover in similar situations all over Europe in the years to come. To kill all the prisoners in batches of five by formal firing squad would take all evening. As it happened, at this point it began to rain heavily again, another torrential downpour like the one that had fallen at the time of the prisoners' capture earlier in the afternoon, and pinpointing the time as approximately 1700 hours. This made the Germans' mind up for them. Their natural instinct was to take shelter, and they stormed into the barn with the evident intention of finishing off the shooting under cover.

The Germans started shooting the prisoners at once. Men in the entrance were ordered to turn round and then shot in the back. One of them was Charles Daley, who had already been shot in the shoulder after his capture, and was now wounded a second time, once in the left leg and again in the right leg, which was shattered by a grouping of bullets from a machine-pistol, and caused him such shock and blood loss that he lost consciousness. As the Germans advanced further into the barn, trampling on the dead and wounded with their boots as they did so, they opened fire on the prisoners with automatic weapons, spraying the barn from end to end. The dead fell on top of each other. The living tried to hide themselves under the bodies of the dead or retreated to the walls of the barn in a dense pack, so that here the dead were piled up against the walls, while the wounded, propped up in the press of bodies, remained half-standing or slumped in incongrous or grotesque positions.*

Everywhere the nightmare cameos of agony and death were irremovably etched into the memories of those who survived the massacre. Alf Tombs, who had been badly wounded in the shin, heard a man cry out imploringly: 'Shoot me! Shoot me!' A single shot followed and the man fell silent. Nearby a corporal, the bottom half of whose face had been blown away, lay dying in the arms of a comrade, who cried out, 'What a bloody way to die!' Private George Hopper lay on a pile of cow manure beneath a heap of bodies, the staring eyes of a dead soldier only inches from his own. Near to George Hall lay a badly mutilated young soldier who, as his strength ebbed from him, began to recite the Lord's Prayer, each word spoken more slowly than the last, till with the words 'Hallowed be Thy name,' he exhaled deeply, and died. George Hall finished the prayer and others joined in, so that above the bursts of gunfire and moans of the wounded could be heard the murmurs of the dying and about-to-die, 'For Thine is the Kingdom, the Power and the Glory, for ever and ever. . . .' Looking round, George Hall was sickened to see a man whose thigh had been smashed in the shooting writhing on the floor and beating the ground with his fists in his agony.

* According to Private Robert Wildsmith, a stretcher-bearer in the Royal Warwickshire Regiment, who was in the barn, it was at this juncture that SS Rottenführer Werner Rüger was wounded. Wildsmith stated: 'The Germans opened fire on us with tommy-guns, two firing from the front of the barn, two from the side and one from the rear. I heard a scream from outside. Through a crack in the side I saw that the German who had been firing from the back had been wounded. While the Germans went to attend the wounded guard I escaped out the front, crossing the field and into a ditch.' This gives a different explanation for Rüger's mishap from that provided by one of the SS men who was present. It also indicates that Wildsmith may have been the third man to escape from the barn at the time of the massacre.

Many men had died with photos of their families and loved ones in their hands.

The last shot of all was aimed at Richard Parry. Parry had lost consciousness during the last stage of the massacre and when he came to he was aware of a figure standing over him, silhouetted against the sky. He raised his hand to shade his eyes and saw that the figure was that of an SS guard who was aiming a rifle at his head. Parry swore at the German and placing one hand on the ground he raised himself up so that he could look the German square in the face. His mouth must have been open, for when the German fired his rifle the bullet passed between the teeth and emerged at the back of jaw, causing the wounded Gunner to lose consciousness again and fall back on to the ground. Evidently the guard assumed he was dead, as well he might, for no further shot was fired. The SS men waited for a little while till they were sure nobody was left alive in or around the barn – presumably even the wounded stifled their moans and played dead at this point – and then they prepared to leave.

———

All this time George Merry, lurking in a hedge at the border of the field, had been witness to the sights and sounds of this dreadful event in the Plaine au Bois. As far as he could tell, virtually he alone had been spared. But as the Germans began to leave the scene of their crime, Merry was horrified to see that they were coming in his direction, and as they drew near he grew cold and began to shiver uncontrollably. His only hope of survival was to pretend to be dead, and he shut his eyes and tried to control his shivering. 'God help me,' he whispered to himself as he listened to the Germans approaching. Then he felt something cold and metallic prod him, he opened his eyes and saw an SS guard standing over him, holding the muzzle of his rifle against his face. Merry expected the German to pull the trigger there and then, but instead the German shouted an order, motioning for him to put his hands up. But Merry found he could not move his injured arm. Bending down, the German examined the arm, then straightened up and gave Merry a shove with his boot and rolled him over. Then, to Merry's total surprise and relief, he went away. Lying on his stomach, Merry watched the SS men leave the field and disappear in the direction of the Leibstandarte Battalion HQ. For the moment he was safe – and still alive.

V

AFTERMATH

Once it became clear that the SS death squad had finally left the scene of the crime, those survivors who were still miraculously unhurt roused themselves and took stock of their situation. The scene that met their eyes inside the barn was nothing less than a nightmare. Reginald West had been a coal-miner before he joined the Army, and he had seen dead and mutilated bodies before. But no pitface accident matched the horror of that French barn – all those bodies piled high against the walls, all those limbs wrenched and smashed out of all human shape. Alf Tombs, struggling free from beneath the two corpses piled on top of him, realized that his back was soaked in their blood. The sight of the wounded pained him, and was shocked when he saw the corpse of Sergeant Moore, who had smothered the first grenade with his own body, for he had been a personal friend.

There was little the few non-wounded could do for the wounded, for they had no medical supplies and insufficient medical expertise to cope with the kind of wounds their comrades had suffered. They soon perceived that the best and only course open to them was to get out of the barn and try and find expert medical help as soon as possible. Altogether about eight men are known to have been fit enough to do this, leaving (according to several survivors' estimates) about seven or eight men who were too seriously wounded to move. This would make the total of survivors of the massacre in the region of fifteen or sixteen. However, in a statement to the House of Commons on 28 June 1988, the Parliamentary Under-Secretary of State for the Armed Forces, Mr Roger Freeman, said: 'In all, it would appear that there were fourteen survivors of the massacre in the barn.' It is not clear whether this figure excludes the men who died during the forty-eight hours or so following the massacre, who numbered at least three. In any case, a combined total from all sources, including men who came forward after the British Government had closed their investigations into the case, would put the figure higher than this – perhaps as high as twenty.

73

As far as can be ascertained, a complete list of possible survivors would include the following names, in alphabetical and regimental order: Private Bennett, Lance-Corporal Box, Private Cooper, Charles Daley, Private Dutton, Bert Evans, Corporal Gill, George Hall, George Hopper, Private Johnson, Private Kelly, John Lavelle, Alf Tombs, Private Townsend, Reg West and Robert Wildsmith (Royal Warwicks); Private Cyril Harbour and Private Robinson (4th Cheshires); and Gunner Richard Parry. In 1988, following Press publicity and a British Government statement about the case, Brian Fahey (Royal Artillery) made himself known as another Wormhoudt survivor.

Not all these names can be vouched for as being genuine survivors, however. Some of these men were never heard of again and never surfaced at the end of the war; they may have died during their years of captivity in Germany, or simply chosen not to report their experiences to the military authorities when they returned to Britain at the end of the war. In any event, the survival status of some of these men can be neither confirmed nor denied. The number of men who were still alive immediately after the departure of the SS guards from this dreadful place was greater than the final total of survivors. But many of these were so severely wounded that without immediate medical attention their chances of survival were slim. Among those who for one reason or another died in the next day or two were Private Bennett, Lance-Corporal Box, Private Kelly, and probably Private Townsend. If these four are deleted from the list of survivors, we are left with a total of sixteen, of whom five were still alive in 1989.

———

One of the first men to leave the vicinity of the barn would have been Robert Wildsmith, who had managed to break out of the barn and hide in a ditch during the massacre. Another was Bert Evans, who had fled to the nearby pond where Captain Lynn-Allen was shot at the beginning of the massacre. When Evans finally scrambled out of the pond, he aimed for a nearby farm. What happened next he described in his own words:

> I'd just got into the grounds of this farm and I happened to
> see a motor cycle and sidecar and I saw a German officer there
> and a man doing something to the bike – he'd got a puncture or
> something had gone wrong. On seeing me, the German officer
> got hold of me and laid me out on the ground. He ripped the
> sheets off this woman's [clothes] lines, and bound them round
> my arm and stopped it bleeding. He put his German overcoat
> onto me. He rode on the back of the motor bike with me in the

74

sidecar. He was Medical Corps, I think. When we arrived at the German dressing station (fifteen minutes) there was a German Intelligence Officer. He ripped the overcoat off me and carried on [something] alarming to this German officer. But when he ripped the coat off me and saw the state of me he came over and spoke English to me and said he was sorry. He apologized quite nicely and made apologies to the German officer afterwards – me wearing the officer's coat had annoyed him. They put these maggots in my arm, to clean it. All the bone was missing. He said, 'I'm afraid you'll lose your arm. Gas gangrene has set in.' All the inside of my arm was bottle green. The maggots were to clear the blood. From there I was taken into a German Hospital at Boulogne. I was amputated on straight away.

———

One of the first to leave the barn itself was George Hopper. Unfortunately, he was also one of the first men to be recaptured. Keeping low under the cover of the hedgerows, Hopper made his way across the fields till he came to a farmhouse, which after some soul-searching he decided to enter – only to find himself in a room full of startled German soldiers. This time there was no repetition of the brutality meted out by the SS earlier in the day, and Hopper became a conventional, correctly treated, prisoner of war.

Next to leave the barn was a group which included Corporal Gill, Lance-Corporal Box, Alf Tombs and Privates Cooper and Dutton. They fared little better. With the main entrance to the barn clogged with corpses, the group forced their way out through the small door at the back, and crawled off down a water-filled ditch and across a field to a hedge in the corner. To their chagrin, a small squad of German troops appeared in a gap in the hedge at this moment. One of them shouted, '*Halt!*' and the British fugitives were immediately surrounded. Tragically, Lance-Corporal Box decided to make a run for it rather than endure a second bout of captivity in German hands, and he bolted for the hedge in an effort to regain his liberty. As he ran, one of the German soldiers shouldered his rifle and taking careful aim shot the runaway in mid-flight – as he was entitled to do in the case of a prisoner attempting to escape. Lance-Corporal Box had come unscathed through the fighting of the morning and the shooting in the barn, only to perish when there was no need.

The prisoners' new captors seemed a different breed from the thugs they had encountered previously. After Lance-Corporal Box had been shot, the youngest member of the party, Private Dutton, who was only a teenager, broke down and fell to his knees, sobbing: 'Don't shoot me, please don't shoot me, my mother's only got one son now.' Alf Tombs realized that the young lad's brother had also been in the barn, and perished there. This time the Germans were more sympathetic in their attitude. They motioned to the soldier to stand up, which he did, still trembling; and a polite German officer came up and reassured them in perfect English: 'It's all right, boys. The war is over. We will be in London and we will send you to Berlin to work.'

The four prisoners were escorted to the main Ledringhem road and handed over to a Wehrmacht unit. While the Germans tried to find out what they were supposed to do with them, the prisoners were allowed to sit at the side of the road and watch the military might of the Third Reich pass by. Troops in trucks tossed biscuits to them – British biscuits filched from captured British Army rations; while infantrymen foot-slogging up the road to Wormhoudt offered them plundered wine to drink, which the prisoners declined, and drank some themselves as they marched along. Then the little group was taken to a German HQ in a farm not far from the barn. Gill related:

> I was interrogated by an Oberleutnant who spoke perfect English. He told me he had been in London. He endeavoured to get military information, which I refused. He did not appear to know anything about the barn incident, until I told him, and he told me to keep quiet in case any of the other Germans understood English. He prevented a Feldwebel from striking me when I asked for a drink of water.

Corporal Gill's group was taken to a church for the night and next day started a long, three-week march into captivity in Germany.

———

George Hall and Reginald West, separately and individually, also succeeded in making good their escape. When the shooting stopped and the guards went out of the barn, George Hall peeped through a crack in the back wall to check that all was clear at the rear, then pulled out a rotten plank at the bottom of the wall and began to slither through the hole.

'For God's sake, don't go,' cried a voice. 'It's not safe.'

'I've had enough of waiting here to be killed,' Hall replied, wriggling through the aperture.

George Hall crawled away on his hands and knees like a man possessed. He reached the hedge and battered his way through to the other side, oblivious of the deep scratches inflicted on his face and arms. From his

76

temporary sanctuary he could hear the cries of his comrades, and German voices, and an occasional shot.

Reginald West, after a long and difficult cross-country traverse, much of it bent double or on his hands and knees, eventually stumbled upon a small party of Warwicks who had so far evaded capture. One of them was the battalion second-in-command, Major Harborne, who had been seriously wounded in the fighting around Battalion HQ earlier in the afternoon and lay moaning on the ground. With him were three other soldiers, one of them also wounded. Their dilemma was considerable. Fighting was still going on here and there around Wormhoudt and German troops were everywhere. The little group from the Warwicks were reluctant to give themselves up, but at the same time they could not see how to get the wounded men away, or find medical help for them, without breaking cover and running the almost certain risk of capture.

Their problem was solved by the sudden appearance of Regimental Sergeant Major Turner, whom Battalion Headquarters had given up for dead by the time they withdrew from the town. Turner saw that they had no other option but to give themselves up. With all his considerable authority he ordered the party to come out of hiding and arranged for the wounded officer to be carried on a make-shift litter made out of an army greatcoat.

Only West disobeyed the order. Having survived one SS massacre he was little inclined to volunteer for another. And having learnt that Battalion Headquarters had already pulled out of the area he could see no way he could organize help for the wounded men he had left behind in the barn. With the Germans in occupation, it was every man for himself. While the others moved off towards their long captivity in some distant German prisoner-of-war camp, Reginald West stayed defiantly in the bushes, and only when it began to grow cold and dark did he move out in search of a more secure hiding place for the night.

Uncertain exactly where he was going, he trudged across the day's battlefield, where the tanks and trucks had churned the fields into mud, and the bodies of the dead still lay where they had fallen, along with the rifles, steel helmets, ammunition pouches and other jetsam of war. Ahead of him he saw flames flickering from the buildings that were still on fire and heard the sound of gunfire from pockets of resistance where a few British diehards still held out against the victorious enemy.

The dark bulk of a row of houses loomed up against the twilight sky and West headed towards them. Their French occupiers would have abandoned them earlier in the day, he was sure; and he hoped against hope that no Germans had moved into them for the night. Choosing the most damaged and least inviting of the houses, he went in, and stumbled upstairs to the bedroom, where he took off his boots and lay down on the bed. A profound silence had fallen on the killing fields all around. Though he had meant to stay awake and keep watch, he let his eyes close, and fell into a deep, unbroken sleep.

Out in those same hushed and darkening fields George Hall also prepared to rest up for the night – but exposed to the elements in a hedge on the outskirts of the town, where he shivered uncontrollably in the cold. Not a soul was stirring and not a shot was fired.

———

Back at the barn the hapless wounded made shift as best they could. Most were in pain and few of them could move. Outside the barn Cyril Harbour lay helpless and in pain with a badly wounded right arm and nearly severed left leg. Richard Parry, who had been blown through the wall of the barn and was trapped by his legs, was unconscious most of the time. In the barn entrance Charles Daley, who had been wounded in the shoulder, chest and both legs – his right leg had been shattered by a machine-gun burst – was stretched helpless on the ground amid the heaps of corpses.

———

By 1730 hours on 28 May the British HQ had withdrawn to the north and British stragglers were extricating themselves from the area as best they could. Though pockets of British resistance remained, and shooting was to continue for several hours more, to all intents and purposes the town was now under the occupation of Nos 5 and 7 Companies of the 2nd Battalion Leibstandarte, commanded by Hauptsturmführer Wilhelm Mohnke.

By now, too, Sepp Dietrich was back in command of the Regiment. After being pinned down by the British all day he had finally been rescued at about 1700, still under fire, by a special task force whose commander was killed in the action. Dietrich presented a sorry sight from his long hours in the ditch on the Esquelbecq road, as General Heinz Guderian, his Commanding Officer at XIX Corps, to whom he reported, later noted: 'He appeared soon afterwards at my command post, totally covered with mud, and had to suffer not only injury but ridicule as well.' Afterwards, Leibstandarte officers were abjured from ever mentioning the embarrassing plight to which their commander had been subjected at Wormhoudt.

Dietrich's return to the Regiment had been too late in the day to save the British prisoners of war in the barn from their dreadful fate; but it evidently did bring about a change in the 2nd Leibstandarte's treatment of prisoners during the period following the massacre. From about 1700 hours onwards it seems that all British prisoners who fell into German hands in

In an impressive display of Nazi pomp and power, Wilhelm Mohnke marches through the streets of pre-war Berlin at the head of a company of Hitler's chosen – the SS-Leibstandarte

Mohnke (left) and the SS-Leibstandarte march into the Saar in 1935 to carry out Hitler's first act of territorial aggression

Saarbrücken. Einmarſch der S.S. Leibſtandarte Adolf Hitler

The barn at Wormhoudt into which 80-90 British prisoners were herded and then massacred by their Waffen-SS guards

The pool near the barn where Bert Evans and Lt Lynn-Allen were hunted down and shot

Charles Daly before the war. His leg was shattered by a machine-gun burst in the massacre

Alfred Tombs, who miraculously survived the grenade and machine-gun attack in the barn

Four survivors of the massacre attend the unveiling of the memorial to the victims outside Wormhoudt in 1972. From left to right – Bert Evans, John Lavelle, Alf Tombs and Charles Daley

Final resting place of the victims of the Wormhoudt massacre – many of them never identified

In eyeball to eyeball contact at the Leibstandarte barracks in Berlin, Hitler acknowledges the sword dipped in salute by Wilhelm Mohnke (fourth from left), the man destined to defend the Führer to the last

Crossing arms and quaffing beer and schnapps, Kurt Meyer and Wilhelm Mohnke celebrate the Oak Leaves to the Knight's Cross that Hitler had just awarded Meyer in Berlin in 1943

Regimental Commander Wilhelm Mohnke greets Sepp Dietrich during an inspection of the newly-formed 12th SS Hitler Youth Division, Belgium, winter 1943–4

Four top front-line commanders from the SS-Leibstandarte. None emerged from the war unscathed. Left to right: Theodor Wisch (severely wounded in Normandy); Wilhelm Mohnke (ten years captivity in the USSR); Kurt Meyer (sentenced to death by the Canadians, commuted to life); Bernhard Siebken (hanged by the British for war crimes)

SS-Sturmbannführer Gerhard Bremer. One of the first of the Leibstandarte to win the coveted Knight's Cross, Bremer was on the war crimes suspect list at the end of the war but never prosecuted. He now lives on the Costa Brava, Spain

*Canadian troops push warily inland through perilous Mohnke country, Calvados,
Normandy, 8 June 1944*

Wormhoudt were correctly treated in accordance with the rules of the Geneva Convention governing the treatment of prisoners of war.

Many of these prisoners were medical personnel and wounded men, captured at the Royal Warwickshire's First Aid Post located in the cellar of a big house at the end of a driveway by the park at the western end of Wormhoudt. One member of this batch of prisoners was Private Albert Montague, a stretcher bearer from A Company, Royal Warwicks, who had spent three or four hours in the cellar helping the Medical Orderly, Lance-Corporal Lodge, treat the wounded as they were brought in from the fighting. All efforts to evacuate the wounded by ambulance (in reality an army lorry) had failed, as whichever way the ambulance driver went he was fired on by enemy troops. On his final attempt the ambulance was set on fire, and when the MO and his team rushed out of the post to help rescue the wounded they found their way barred by an SS man armed with a pistol who repeated the well-drilled phrase: 'Tommy, the war is over for you.'

In vain the MO explained that this was a First Aid Post and that his duty was to stay with the wounded. The German would not allow it, and all the medical staff, along with the walking wounded (including the Warwicks' Adjutant, Captain Tomes), were marched off at gunpoint, leaving the seriously wounded, who were too ill to move, behind. Albert Montague testified later that they first went into a small wood and then marched along a sandy roadway for about fifteen or twenty minutes till they came to a farmhouse standing on its own in the open. This was the farm known as Le Fort Rose, which the 2nd Leibstandarte had established as their new HQ at about 1800 hours. The prisoners were wheeled left into the farm courtyard, where about twenty-five other prisoners, some of them from other regiments, others in all probability members of Corporal Gill's group of survivors from the barn, were already assembled. On the left-hand side of the courtyard there was a brick wall, in front of which stood two guards, one armed with a machine gun, the other with a rifle.

The new arrivals were lined up in front of the barn, facing the guards, and told to throw their steel helmets and gas masks in a pile on the ground. Then their pockets were emptied and their rings, wrist watches, cigarettes and other possessions were taken from them and dumped on the ground. Ominously, their dog tags were removed from them, suggesting that, initially at least, the SS had the same fate in mind for this last batch of British prisoners as it had had for the previous one. Montague managed to retain his pay book, but his personal snapshots – mostly of his young bride in England – were torn up in front of him. 'Tonight,' the SS storm trooper told Montague, grinding the photos into the dirt with his boot, 'I sleep with your wife.'

The soldier next to Montague turned to him and said: 'I don't like the look of this. What's going to happen?'

'I don't know,' Montague replied. 'But I think they're going to shoot us.'

Years later Montague was to comment: 'As a prisoner of war I got to know the ordinary German Wehrmacht very well. They treated us decently. But the SS were really vicious – true killers.'

For three hours or more the prisoners were compelled to stand in the courtyard with their hands behind their back, and forbidden to talk or smoke. They were dog tired and soaking wet and their uniforms were in shreds. Eventually Captain Crook was allowed to return in the dark to the Warwicks' First Aid Post – escorted by an armed guard of ten men under the same Scharführer Drescher who had commanded the death squad at the barn only a few hours earlier – in order to tend the wounded left behind there, numbering some twenty-five men, and bring them back to the German lines. Somehow Crook then gave his guards the slip and went out to collect a number of British wounded lying in the fields, including Major Harborne. According to Captain Tomes, Crook managed to commandeer a truck, put the wounded on board it, and drive off under the very eyes of the Germans, nearly reaching Dunkirk before he was recaptured.

In the meantime, Wilhelm Mohnke – whose change of heart as far as British prisoners were concerned had undergone a remarkable metamorphosis since the reappearance of Sepp Dietrich – was observed to be stopping trucks on the road and loading the prisoners of war at Le Fort Rose on to them with solicitous concern. Tomes, Montague and the other prisoners fortunate enough to be loaded on to these trucks – those for whom there was no room had to proceed on foot – were then driven along a very dusty track to a schoolhouse a few miles outside Wormhoudt. It was dark by the time they arrived, and the schoolhouse was already packed to the walls with other prisoners, so that it was impossible for any of them to lie down. Here they were to spend the night before their long march into POW captivity in Germany. Though it was to be a depressing and highly uncomfortable night, the prisoners enjoyed one precious advantage not shared by their ill-fated comrades who had been captured earlier in the day – they were still alive.

In Wormhoudt, meanwhile, sporadic fighting had continued into the evening, and just after 1900 the Leibstandarte were surprised by a British tank attack directed from the streets leading into the market-place. Though the British were driven off with the loss of two of their tanks, Mohnke took the precaution of withdrawing his troops from the town into the surrounding fields, in case the British decided to bombard the town during the night. At 2300 the Leibstandarte were again involved in a short, sharp fire-fight, as their adjutant, Fritz Beutler, testified:

> Sometime before midnight, wild shooting broke out near Battalion HQ. Sentries from the covering positions rushed in and reported: 'The British are here!' All available runners and drivers were sent out in the darkness to the danger point and in a few minutes all was quiet again. ... The companies were ordered to muster for the coming night and to draw up, platoon by platoon, on the northerly and north-easterly edge, as though defending a strong point.

Not until 2315 did the fighting in and around Wormhoudt die out completely, the night grow quiet, and the fighting men of both sides snatch the solace of sleep.

———

At dawn the Leibstandarte re-entered Wormhoudt, still burning fiercely, still littered with the corpses of the enemy dead. They reported that the British were in full flight to the north, and rapidly passed through the little town in pursuit of them. After the stocktaking of the previous day's battle, the Leibstandarte calculated that their 1st and 2nd Battalions between them had captured 13 enemy trucks, 2 light tanks, 1 armoured car, 1 prime mover, 2 motorbikes, 27 artillery pieces, 8 anti-tank weapons, innumerable light and heavy infantry weapons and other equipment – and a total of 6 British officers and 430 NCOs and men. It is not clear whether the tally of prisoners of war was confined to those who were fortunate enough to be still alive on the day following the battle, or whether it included those who had perished in SS hands, and whose mutilated and incinerated bodies still lay where they had fallen in the fields, streets, squares, buildings, ponds, streams and public fountains of Wormhoudt.

In the Leibstandarte the talk among the officers and men was all about the massacre of the British prisoners of war the previous day, which had caused something of a sensation. Though they were later to deny it, the fate of these men was universally known throughout the 2nd Battalion and even new arrivals soon got to hear of it. Korvettenkapitän Alfred Rodenbücher, for example, an officer in the Naval Reserve of the Marine Station Commando 'Baltic' who had been posted to the Leibstandarte to obtain combat experience, heard mention of a force of seventy British prisoners who were 'all finished off' soon after he reached the 2nd Battalion late on 28 May, and made a mental note never to tolerate anything of that nature in his command.

As far as can be gathered, the massacre was not something of which the 2nd Leibstandarte felt proud, and there were some who even voiced their opinion that they would not take part in such an incident if anything of the sort ever occurred again. Even the Regimental Commander, Sepp Dietrich, no stranger to violence on his own account, must have been aware that Mohnke had gone too far and could bring trouble down on them from higher authority; after all, the incident was the talk of the mess. When the facts of the massacre were made known to him it seems likely he invoked the SS oath, forbidding all officers and men from mentioning the matter further on pain of the direst penalty – an oath which has held good till today.

———

As the sun rose on a new, warm and unclouded day, George Hall peered out from the shadow of his hedge across the empty, silent fields; while Reginald West, woken by the noisy singing of the birds, stirred on the soft French bed on which he had passed the night, and peering through the bedroom curtains, saw that nothing moved and no one was about. Wormhoudt was empty – a burnt-out ghost town. A mile or so away, in the corpse-filled barn across the fields, the British wounded lay in pain and misery in a twilight world between despair and hope.

During the day Private Kelly, who had his leg almost ripped off by one of the German hand grenades, gave up the unequal battle for survival. Private Johnson, meanwhile, tried to get help from the French farmer at the farm in whose field the barn stood. But the farmer declined to give any assistance, and refused even to provide any water. All the survivors were subsequently to complain that this same farmer came very near to the barn on many occasions, sometimes even carrying milk, but stubbornly refused help or drink. On the second evening he arrived with another farm worker to fetch the milkchurns which had been standing outside the barn when the prisoners had first arrived there. Peering into the barn they were confronted with a vision from hell; and in spite of the pleadings of the wounded they fled from the scene, too shocked and frightened to offer succour or take their milkchurns with them, and clearly reluctant to meddle in matters which might get them into trouble.

Johnson and Bennett took it in turns to watch for help – but they were right off the main road and nobody came. When Johnson and Bennett, making a supreme effort, crawled over to a ditch to fetch water, the demands made on Bennett's waning strength proved too much for him and on the way back he collapsed.

Ironically, Bennett's dying moments proved the others' salvation, for as he lay dying outside the barn he was spotted by two English-speaking

82

members of an Austrian Red Cross unit searching the area for German wounded, who went into the barn and spoke with some of the British wounded. According to Daley, the two Austrians looked shocked at what they saw, as well they might. They departed to fetch an ambulance and were back within an hour – though not in time to save Jack Bennett's life.

The noise of the ambulance grinding up the cart-track to the barn roused Richard Parry, who had been unconscious for the best part of the two days since he was blown up by a grenade and shot through the foot and face by an SS guard. Somehow in that time he had managed to extricate himself from the barn, crawl along a ditch and tumble into a thicket of tall weeds or grass at the back. From where he lay Parry could see a truck with Red Cross markings on it and men being carried out of the barn on stretchers. Then he realized that in all probability the ambulancemen could not see him because of the tall vegetation in which he was lying. He tried to cry out but his mouth was clogged with a blood clot from the gunshot wound in his face, and his leg was too badly injured to allow him to stand. Near to despair, he suddenly had a brilliant idea. If he could raise his arm the Germans might see it and rescue him. Slowly and with considerable difficulty he raised his arm into the air until it soared out of the high grass like a flagpole. Years later he related the final moments of his long agony:

> Fortunately they saw me – and the one thing which stands out is that their handling of me was ever- so gentle. There were six or seven of us taken from the barn wounded but alive, thank God. I remember the great feeling of relief which came over me as I was placed in the ambulance. Inside the vehicle, I fell asleep.
>
> I woke up in a farmhouse and saw what I took to be a French farmer, whose wife was standing by his side. She was trying to feed me with some milk. Afterwards, I remembered a 100-franc note which I had in my pocket. Feeling so grateful, I took it out, and offered it to her. But she wouldn't take it, but when she saw that I was becoming upset at her not accepting my gift, she took it.

Charles Daley also fell asleep in the ambulance and when he came to it was not a farmer's wife he set eyes on but an old German surgeon with a white beard, who made careful notes of everything he told him and treated him with great kindness, as did all the medical staff at the Wehrmacht field dressing station where his wounds were dressed. John Lavelle, who had been wounded in the ankle by grenade fragments, remembered that when the Germans at the dressing station learned what had happened to the British prisoners, one of them said, 'The swines.'

By close of day on Thursday 30 May, as the last remnants of what was left of the 2nd Battalion, The Royal Warwickshire Regiment, were being evacuated in small boats from the sand dunes of the Dunkirk beaches, only two members of the Regiment to have survived the atrocity at Wormhoudt were still at liberty. One was George Hall, who spent the next six days wandering across the French countryside, bloodstained, unkempt and famished, before he was picked up by a German unit and fed soup and beans and lent soap and a razor by a nice German who had relatives in England. After days of privation and hunger, even a prison camp seemed a soft option for this indomitable survivor of some of war's worst horrors.

The other was Reginald West, who miraculously managed to remain at large for five more months. Dressed in French civilian clothes, and sheltered by friendly French farmers and members of the Resistance, West headed for Spain with the aim of reaching British territory at Gibraltar. Travelling mostly on foot, he got as far as Marseilles before he was interned by the Vichy French, and much of the later part of the war he spent in an Italian and then a German prisoner-of-war camp.

———

The Battle of Wormhoudt, one of the blackest days in the German conduct of the war in the West, had been fought and won. The 2nd Leibstandarte SS had moved on to other, newer battlefields in the final German push against the British and the French in Northern France. All that was left to be done by those who replaced them was to clear up the obscene garbage, the Golgotha of fresh young corpses, the mess of blood and limbs, which Mohnke's troops had left behind them. Upon someone – it is not known whom – fell the onerous but honourable task of removing the scores of bodies from the barn and digging the great mass grave in the nearby field into which the British dead were then flung, nameless and unshriven, a few days after the massacre. To various caring medics – British, French and German – was given the responsibility of salvaging the bodies and salving the minds of the handful of men who had survived the savageries of Mohnke's henchmen. Charles Daley lost a leg, Bert Evans an arm. Alf Tombs and John Lavelle suffered constant pain from their injuries. Most remained scarred in body and mind by the experience they had gone through, and other prisoners who met them in hospitals in France weeks later were struck by their shocked condition and their multitude of wounds. Such was the personal price these men had paid in doing their duty for their cause – the British rearguard action, 'to the last man and the last bullet', which had held the BEF escape route open that long and bloody day at Wormhoudt in May 1940.

The exact total of British prisoners of war who were butchered by the 2nd Leibstandarte SS at Wormhoudt will never be known, but a conservative estimate would put the figure at a minimum of a hundred, and in all probability appreciably in excess of this. The generally accepted figure for the number of men killed in the barn is between eighty and ninety. It is impossible to be more precise than this, as many official records were lost during the Dunkirk evacuation, and most of the prisoners who died had had the means of identification removed before they were killed.

VI

ENQUIRY

Time passed, the war progressed, the armies moved on. In 1941 the bodies of the murdered men in the mass grave at Wormhoudt were dug up by local French workmen under German supervision and re-interred. For it seems that when the Nazi authorities finally got to hear of the massacre, their reaction was not to punish the crime but hide the evidence. This they did by dispersing the bodies in a number of smaller graves around the area – one in Wormhoudt, another in Esquelbecq, and another in an unknown place elsewhere. Since most of the dead men had had their identity discs removed before they were killed, it was impossible to say, either then or later, who was buried there. And in England nobody sought to enquire, for nobody had any knowledge of what had happened to the luckless prisoners at Wormhoudt. As Jeff Rooker, MP, told the House of Commons when he raised the matter in Parliament on 25 May 1988, nearly forty-eight years to the day after the massacre:

> They never returned. There were no records. There was no one to tell about it. . . . Many who lost relatives at the end of May 1940, and who received letters from the Ministry of War or the various regiments to say that their loved ones were missing in action and presumed dead, can never be really certain whether they were in that barn at Wormhoudt.

Not until the war was almost half over did the news break at last. In October 1943 an exchange of seriously wounded British and German prisoners of war took place. Among the British prisoners repatriated from Germany were several survivors of the Wormhoudt massacre who were in need of further hospitalization, including Richard Parry, Charles Daley and Bert Evans. The Press were there to greet them. One newspaper printed a photo showing Daley reunited with his Alsatian dog, Bob. Another newspaper sent a lady reporter to talk to Bert Evans. He told her about Wormhoudt. The next morning the paper carried the story of the massacre on its front page. It was the first the British public had heard about it. It was also the first the British Army had heard about it. The War Office reproached Evans for his breach of military protocol. But the unintended leak had a galvanizing effect on the wheels of military justice.

In December the Royal Warwickshire Regiment, to which two of the three survivors belonged, took up the case. Lt-Col. Kendall wrote to the three men: 'On behalf of the Colonel of the Regiment,* I should be very much obliged if you could see your way to putting the facts as you know them on paper and sending them to me, and if there are any particular remarks which you have to make or anything which you remember Captain Lynn-Allen or anyone else said or did, I would be very much obliged if you would let me have them. With best wishes and the congratulations of the Regiment on your own escape from such a terrible fate.' A few months later the survivors were required to swear an affidavit on oath before a solicitor. Then there was a long silence during which they heard nothing.

At the end of the war other survivors returned home. Some were either unknown to the War Office or did not make themselves known; they simply slipped back into the country and kept the memory of the horror of Wormhoudt to themselves. But Robert Gill, John Lavelle and Alfred Tombs were added to the War Office list and required to make statements about their personal experiences at Wormhoudt. Then in April 1947 the survivors received a letter from the Judge Advocate General's Office:

> I shall be grateful if you will come to London on Tuesday 22 April 1947 and, on arrival, proceed to the London District Prisoner of War Cage: 6–7 Kensington Palace Gardens, Bayswater, W8, and report to the Commanding Officer, Lt-Col. A.P. Scotland, OBE.

———

At first sight, Lt-Col. Alexander Paterson Scotland, OBE, presented a considerable paradox. To look at, he was an unprepossessing sort of man in his mid-sixties – a stoutish, bespectacled, silver-haired figure, more like an avuncular retired schoolmaster than the popular notion of someone from

---

* In 1943 this was Brigadier C.T. Tomes, CBE, DSO, MC. In January 1947 he was succeeded by Field Marshal the Viscount Montgomery of Alamein, who had served in the Regiment from 1908 until he relinquished command of the 1st Battalion in 1934.

87

British Intelligence. Scotland was the first to admit that his outward appearance was the least impressive part of him. 'Physically, I looked half as tough as I was,' he was to write. 'My voice was rather flat and colourless, and I had a face that seemed easily forgotten. Indeed, I was, and still am, an unusually ordinary-looking individual.'

The paradox was that behind the dull exterior there lurked one of the ablest and most experienced minds in British Intelligence. In the world of espionage and counter-espionage his very ordinariness was one of his finest assets – 'a defensive camouflage of immeasurable value'. Only a week or two before the Wormhoudt survivors had received their summons to his headquarters, Colonel Scotland's name had been splashed across the front pages of the British Press in a blaze of sensational publicity. 'Britain's Master Spy,' the papers cried; 'Scotland of the Wehrmacht', 'MI5 Colonel on Nazi General Staff'. Scotland was portrayed as a mystery man who had swapped British and Nazi uniforms whenever the occasion required, had been decorated by Hitler, and had flitted intrepidly back and forth between Nazi-occupied Europe and the War Office in Whitehall with briefcases packed with Hitler's military secrets.

The source of all this journalistic hyperbole was an item of evidence Scotland had introduced into the war crimes trial of Field Marshal Kesselring, former supreme commander of German forces in Italy, at the British military court in Venice earlier that year, in February 1947. During the course of the proceedings the chief counsel for the prosecution had turned to Scotland and said: 'Now, Colonel Scotland, I am going to ask you some questions about the German army.'

At this, Kesselring's German lawyer jumped up to protest. 'I object to the question,' he cried. 'The witness was never in the German army, and cannot give evidence about its organization.'

There was a pause before the prosecution counsel spoke.

'Colonel Scotland,' he asked, 'were you ever in the German army?'

Amid gasps from the public gallery, Colonel Scotland replied, somewhat drily: 'Yes.'

'Was information on the organization of the German army your function during the war?'

'Yes,' the Colonel replied again, before sitting down in a courtroom buzzing with speculation and surprise.

Afterwards Colonel Scotland discovered that as a result of this courtroom disclosure Field Marshal Kesselring had formed the impression that the unassuming Scot had commanded a German division in his own forces. 'Dammit,' Kesselring told Scotland in prison, 'I thought I knew all my commanders, but I don't remember *you*.'

It was perfectly true that Scotland had served in the German army – not, as Kesselring and the British Press supposed, in Hitler's Wehrmacht, but in the Kaiser's colonial forces in German South-West Africa in the early years of the century. As a young man, Scotland had left his native Perth-shire to find adventure and seek his fortune in British South Africa, where he soon found work as a company trader, spending days in the saddle among the native Hottentots and Klipkaffirs in the desert bushland of the south. As his most lucrative business was with the German forces fighting the Hottentot Wars across the border, he began to organize ox wagon treks and cattle drives across the desert to the German garrisons – and from supplying the German army with provisions it was but a step to being enrolled in it as provisions officer, complete with rifle and uniform and the Germanized name of Schottland. At the same time, he was reporting everything he learned about the German forces to the head of Britain's Intelligence Service in Cape Town.

This distant but unusual experience in the Kaiser's army enabled 'Scottie' Scotland to speak German without any trace of an accent and gave him an intimate insight into the German way of thinking and behaving. More was required, however. As he was to write later:

> It was not enough, in the perilous field of security work, to court the Germans, speak their language, join in their activities and study their techniques. You had to talk, think and live like a German. You had to become one of them if you wanted to stay alive. You had to know the discipline of the soldier, and how to impose it. You had to understand the nature of the German military machine and the mental processes of the men who directed it.

All this and more Scotland learned in a lifetime of watching Germans and Germany. Arrested as a British spy at the outbreak of the First World War, he spent almost a year in a German gaol in Windhoek before he was released on the intervention of the future Prime Minister of South Africa, General Jan Smuts. Back in Europe he became a German expert at the British GHQ in France, responsible for manpower information on the German army, and undertaking a number of intelligence missions behind the enemy lines in Belgium to verify the facts for himself. With the end of hostilities, Scotland continued to report on German activities, this time in the proverbial hotbeds of German intrigue in Argentina, Brazil, Paraguay and Uruguay. When the Nazis came to power, Scotland switched his attentions to the Fatherland itself, and during one of his fact-finding tours was surprised to receive a confidential visit to his hotel room from Adolf Hitler himself, who had come to sound him out, over coffee and a plate of plain biscuits, about the potential for a revival of German colonial ambitions in South-West Africa and elsewhere. When the time came for him to leave, the Führer paused in the doorway and turning to Scotland remarked: 'You are an ingenious man, Schottland. Now I can understand the reports we have on our files about you.'

By the time Colonel Scotland became head of the wartime Prisoner of War Interrogation Section, which at the end of the war became the War Crimes Interrogation Unit (or WCIU), there were few men in Britain better qualified for the specialized task of winkling the truth out of captured Nazis. Though initially there were interrogation centres in each of the army commands throughout the United Kingdom, the London District Cage (often referred to by its initials, LDC) was the headquarters of Colonel Scotland's organization, an operational unit under direct War Office control, and a part of MI19, the branch of Military Intelligence responsible among other things for obtaining intelligence from enemy prisoners of war. This was where all the big war crimes cases were investigated and all major Nazi suspects were brought for interrogation. The Cage occupied three grand and elegant houses surrounded by barbed wire at the Bayswater Road end of exclusive Kensington Palace Gardens – the so-called 'Millionaires' Row'. The two outer buildings housed the guards and the administrative staff, while the middle one accommodated prisoners under interrogation.

To staff his organization, Colonel Scotland had assembled a small, hand-picked group of German-language intelligence specialists, never numbering more than a dozen or so at any given time. These included the second-in-command, Major Antony Terry, who, as the son of a British diplomat in Berlin, had been educated in pre-war Germany, and was later captured in the daring commando raid at St Nazaire in 1942; Major T.X.H. ('Bunny') Pantcheff, a young, Cambridge-educated linguist; Major William Kieser; Warrant Officer Richard Richter, of Austro-Irish parentage, brought up in Vienna; Warrant Officer Michael Ullman, a German Jewish refugee; and RSM Jerry Stanton, another German Jewish refugee, who had anglicized his name, and died in a plane crash not long after the case was closed.

For two or three years after the war, as Colonel Scotland and his team investigated a wide variety of war crimes cases, the London Cage in 'Millionaires' Row' held at one time or another some of Hitler's most dangerous and despicable thugs. Among the major war crimes investigated were several cases involving the mass murder of unarmed British prisoners of war by their Nazi guards. One such case was that of the 'Great Escape', which involved the murder of fifty RAF officers who were shot for escaping from their POW camp near Sagan in Upper Silesia in 1944. For this crime thirteen Gestapo men, brought to justice by Scotland's team, were hanged in Hamelin Gaol early in 1948, while others were sentenced to terms of imprisonment ranging from life to ten years. With commendable dedi-

90

cation and resolve, contrasting strongly with the lacklustre performance of the British and German investigators into the Wormhoudt massacre, RAF investigators were still working on the 'Great Escape' case into the mid-sixties, and brought the last culprit to trial in 1964.

A similar case involved the massacre of some ninety-seven prisoners of war of all ranks from the 2nd Battalion of the Royal Norfolk Regiment near the village of Le Paradis in Northern France on 27 May 1940. Overwhelmed by a superior force after a stubborn rearguard action against elements of the SS-Totenkopf Division – a unit originally formed to provide guards for concentration camps, of which Dachau was the first – the prisoners from the Norfolks were herded into a field and stood in front of a brick barn. Then they were machine-gunned to death on the orders of the Company Commander of No 3 Company of the Totenkopf's 2nd Infantry Regiment, SS-Hauptsturmführer Fritz Knoechlein, an arrogant, irascible thug with a pathological loathing of the British who had received his training at Dachau. Though SS soldiers were sent in to finish off the wounded with pistol and bayonet, two Norfolk men miraculously survived the massacre to tell the tale and furnish Colonel Scotland and his team with crucial evidence with which to indict Knoechlein.

The Le Paradis massacre shared many things in common with the Wormhoudt massacre, and may indeed have had an indirect, or even a direct link with it – for it took place only the day before, at a place not very far distant, under circumstances that were similar in many respects, and at the instigation of a sister SS unit of the Leibstandarte. As at Wormhoudt, the massacre took place after a hard day's fighting in which the Germans suffered heavy casualties, and roughly the same number of prisoners were murdered. As at Wormhoudt many of the prisoners had had their pay books and even their identity discs removed from them before the killing, so that only half of them could subsequently be identified. In both massacres the fateful orders had been given by an unpopular, evil-tempered Company Commander – one a deputy Battalion Commander, the other in temporary command of his Battalion. As it happened, both men had been born in the same year (1911) and both were later to win the coveted Knight's Cross for bravery in combat. The big difference was that the man who gave the order at Le Paradis fell into the custody of the London District Cage, and was eventually charged, tried and hanged; the man who gave the order at Wormhoudt was not.

During the course of his trial in Hamburg in October 1948 Knoechlein had attempted to justify his crime by claiming that his actions were completely legal under an old German law which provided for the setting up of an emergency standing court, known as a *Standgericht*, on the field of battle. This concept threw the court into foggy confusion for a while, until Colonel Scotland took the stand and explained that even if such a *Standgericht* had

91

been set up at Le Paradis – which was unlikely in the extreme – it could not possibly have been lawful since what would have been in question was not a matter that arose while the battle was in progress, but the fate of men who had laid down their arms after the battle was over. Scotland was well aware that Knoechlein had introduced an obscure ruse in an attempt to save his neck, and that he had been put up to it by another prisoner with whom he had been confined in prison camp – a certain Colonel Baum, who was also under interrogation at the London Cage. It is a matter of regret that the conversations of Knoechlein and Baum were never recorded for the benefit of future historians of SS massacres, for the two men had a lot in common, both having served in units intimately involved with the mass murder of British prisoners during the same twenty-four-hour period in two places in northern France only a few miles apart – the first at Le Paradis, the second at Wormhoudt.*

For Scotland's Colonel Baum was undoubtedly the same Haupt-sturmführer Otto Baum who seven years previously had commanded No 7 Company of the 2nd Battalion of the SS Leibstandarte during the battle for Wormhoudt and had provided some of the men who had escorted the British prisoners to their rendezvous with death at the barn in La Plaine au Bois. Five more years of savage infantry combat stretched before Baum after that dark day in France, during which he had distinguished himself by his outstanding courage and been the recipient of one of Germany's highest awards for valour, the Knight's Cross with Oak Leaves and Swords, roughly the equivalent of the British VC. Yet miraculously he had survived it all, only to be tracked down to some prisoner-of-war camp somewhere in Europe when the Wormhoudt case was opened by Scotland's War Crimes Interrogation Unit in 1945. One of his men was to testify at the LDC that Baum was 'a very quiet and poised personality'. His interrogators found him otherwise. Richard Richter, for one, found him to be 'a very arrogant chap, dedicated to secrecy about all he knew.'

What was amazing was how many more of the dramatis personae of the 2nd Leibstandarte had survived all those years of bloody fighting and now languished in camps in England and Germany. To find them had been a

---

* Mr Tom Field-Fisher, who was the prosecutor in the Knoechlein trial, commented in 1989: 'Knoechlein always denied he was responsible for the shooting or that he was at the spot at the time; the nearest he admitted to being to the incident was several hundred yards. The reference to the "*Standgericht*" was made in the context that if the incident took place at all it was unlawful without such a standing court being convened. It was not without interest that the German army legal equivalent of the Judge Advocate General made enquiries about the shooting but these were aborted on Himmler's direct order. In addition, the officers in Knoechlein's own unit mess refused to talk to him, and a junior officer challenged him to a duel "for the honour of the regiment".'

major achievement on the part of Scotland's team, for at the end of the war the German forces were scattered in their millions in a vast military diaspora that stretched round the world from the wastes of Siberia to the backwoods of Canada and the United States of America. It helped greatly, however, that all members of the SS fell into the automatic arrest category and that meticulous records of such arrestees were kept on an inter-Allied inventory of German prisoners.

By the time the hunt was over, more than fifty voluntary statements had been taken from thirty-eight former SS men who had been in the regiment concerned on 28 May 1940; additionally a number of others were interrogated and reported on. The statements of twenty of these former members of the Leibstandarte were finally submitted to the Judge Advocate General's office in two reports produced by the LDC in 1947. Out of the twenty-four, thirteen of these men had been with No 7 Company at the time of the massacre, including the Company Commander, Otto Baum. By and large it had been an impressive haul. It included no less a figure than Sepp Dietrich, who had been the Commander of the Leibstandarte Regiment; the Adjutant and Assistant Adjutant of the 2nd Battalion, Fritz Beutler and Eric Maas; the Commander of No 7 Company, Otto Baum; and a number of NCOs and men who had been with the Leibstandarte in Wormhoudt at the time of the massacre. A number were only peripheral to the case, however, and though they undoubtedly knew more than they were prepared to admit, they were not directly implicated in the crime. Several potential key witnesses were conspicuous by their absence. Many had been killed in the blood-letting on the Eastern Front, including key witnesses like Untersturmführer Heinrichs, who had been present when Mohnke gave his orders concerning the final disposition of the British prisoners, and several men in the escort, including Dorth and Linkenheil. Others had disappeared and could not be found. One of those was Wilhelm Mohnke, whose fate was not initially known to the investigation team.

One of the witnesses roped in by Scotland had not even been in Wormhoudt at the time of the massacre. This was Korvettenkapitän Alfred Rodenbücher, who did not reach the Battalion Headquarters of the 2nd Leibstandarte until the day after the Wormhoudt battle. Rodenbücher, however, was a witness of peculiar interest and a man who spoke with greater authority than perhaps even his expert interrogators realized. For a start, he was not what he seemed. For in some mysterious way Alfred Rodenbücher enjoyed a dual identity, though it is not clear that the people at the London Cage appreciated this. On the one hand he was a former Gruppenführer (Lieutenant-General) of the Allgemeine-SS, and once one of the most senior men in the SS – number thirty-two in the SS order of seniority at the beginning of 1938. On the other hand he had also held a Reserve Commission in the German navy, in which capacity Himmler had sent him to join the Leibstandarte at Wormhoudt 'for fourteen days front-line service'. This enigmatic figure – 'a dapper little bloke and a proper Nazi' according to one of his interrogators – gave useful evidence at the London Cage, though it appears the investigators never fully understood his real importance.

So far, then, so good. British survivors of the Wormhoudt massacre had made their affidavits. On 6 June 1947 four of the men who had been captured at Wormhoudt – Charles Daley, Albert Evans, Richard Parry and Albert Montague, the first three being survivors of the barn massacre – were taken back to the area by Major Pantcheff and RSM Stanton of the War Crimes Interrogation Unit in order to reconstruct the crime on the spot and hopefully develop additional evidence, including anything the local French populace might care to tell them. Pantcheff recalled the return of the survivors to the scene of the crime:

> None of them broke down or went off in a rage. Except for Montague, who had once been Monty's batman, and who hadn't been in the barn – a very alert little man and very much in his right mind – they were in very poor health. One of them, indeed, wasn't quite *compos mentis*, he was quite disturbed in mind at that particular time and made a very poor witness. The other two barn survivors were quite lucid but obviously unwell, and because of their wounds they couldn't move about very fast.

Among the various points determined, it was proved that when Parry lay down with his feet inside the barn, as he had lain at the time of the massacre, and Montague was positioned on the side where the first batch of five prisoners were shot by the SS firing squad, and Evans on the side where the second batch were shot, he had a perfectly clear view of both spots and therefore of both executions. Pantcheff recalled:

> After he had shown me how he had lain in the wreck of the shed, he pointed and said:
> 'Over there, you see, sir, is the ditch that I crawled through on my way out. And over there was where I was found.'
> 'But Parry,' I said, 'you were in a terrible state, you'd been shot through the leg and shot through the head, and you were in a mess. What possessed you to go crawling anywhere?'
> 'Well, you see, sir,' Parry replied, 'it was about the same time of the year as now, and the corn was just coming up, and as I'm a country boy I just thought I'd like to die in the green.'

The details of the various locations, the movements of the personnel involved, and the bare outline of the facts of the case were thus clear. A terrible crime had undoubtedly been committed at Wormhoudt, as at Le Paradis. There seemed at this stage no reason why sufficient evidence should not be obtained and a trial of the guilty men of Wormhoudt satisfactorily prosecuted in a war crimes court, just as in the Le Paradis case. But it was not to be.

In spite of every effort by the British interrogators, the SS men either would not, or could not, volunteer the facts which were undoubtedly known to many of them. The interrogators could be quite tough when they chose and in any case had little enough reason to treat with totally scrupulous respect the members of an organization whose reputation for gratuitous violence and brutality was legendary throughout Europe. Otto Baum was to complain later that he did not form an affable opinion of Colonel Scotland, Major Terry, Warrant Officer Ullman and their colleagues. They shouted at him, he said, and slapped him and threatened to have him extradited to the Soviet Union. 'Bunny' Pantcheff was very dismissive of this allegation. 'We were never rough but we could be very rude. As for slapping and so forth – a fairy story! But I'm delighted to hear Baum didn't care for the London Cage – it shows we were doing our job.'

On occasion other German prisoners held in the London Cage for interrogation about other cases complained that they had been victims of physical intimidation – Knoechlein, the mass murderer of Le Paradis, even claimed in his trial that he had been tortured 'in a most brutal and gruesome fashion'. Colonel Scotland adamantly denied such charges, which were generally raised as a defence plea – confession extracted by force – in the trial court. 'We were not so foolish as to imagine,' Scotland wrote later, 'that petty violence, or even violence of a stronger character, was likely to produce the results we hoped for in dealing with some of the toughest creatures of the Hitler régime.' Scotland continued:

> As for our methods at the Cage, it was to be expected that the world should be intrigued by the success with which we had persuaded substantial numbers of Nazi criminals not only to confess their role in murder plans, but also to write the detailed story of the events surrounding the crimes and the activities of their own colleagues.
>
> Those documents were our real triumph. But how was it all done? What were the secret methods employed to obtain such confessions?
>
> It was no easy task, but there was no mystery. Consider the situation of our German guests at the London Cage. They were all experts in the arts of extracting information from others, with no scruples as to the technique. When they in turn became

prisoners and were brought to London for questioning, they were eager enough to tell sufficient of their story to demonstrate their individual blamelessness.

Many, however, committed the fatal error of underestimating our intimacy with German habits, personalities and language.

After the preliminary interrogation my practice was to send each man to his room to write his version of events – in his own style. He was permitted contact with no other prisoner while this exercise went on. It was not long before we had at our disposal up to half a dozen histories – dealing in each case with the same crime viewed by different men.

In this manner, discrepancies were noted, lies detected, names and places and times checked, triple checked and checked yet again. Gradually we came to know when we were arriving at the probable truth and, eventually, with the whole truth, or at least enough to establish a case for the court.

Unaccountably, the system broke down when it came to the investigation of the Wormhoudt case. This investigation confined itself to the murder by men of the Leibstandarte regiment of the eighty to ninety British prisoners of war in the barn near Wormhoudt on 28 May 1940 and did not concern itself with any of the other murders committed against unarmed British prisoners at other locations in and around Wormhoudt during the course of 28 May 1940. These other murders included the shooting of about fifteen prisoners on the Cassel road, which was witnessed by Bert Evans; the murder of four men who were burned to death in a vehicle soaked in petrol (an incident referred to by Colonel Scotland, which may be the same incident witnessed by Gunner Baxter); the series of murders in the centre of Wormhoudt, witnessed by Private Oxley of the Cheshires; and the bayoneting and shooting of stragglers and wounded prisoners during the forced march at the double across the fields to the barn from the Leibstandarte Battalion HQ.

In the Wormhoudt case, prisoners seemed well rehearsed and in some cases to have got together to produce an agreed, collaboratory version of events. Several who had escorted prisoner columns at Wormhoudt appeared to have deliberately confused the group of prisoners they had marched to the barn (who were murdered) and the group of prisoners they had later marched to Battalion HQ at Le Fort Rose farm (who were properly treated). Few denied that prisoners had been shot, but a number gave as an explanation of the killings the fact that one or more prisoners had fired a pistol or thrown a grenade – or both – at their guards, wounding one of them, Werner Rüger, and causing the other guards to open fire, either in self-defence or to prevent a mass escape. Read as a whole, the prisoners' statements seemed to impart a thin fog of systematic, calculated and not unskilful misinformation about the true nature of events at Wormhoudt.

The senior SS men were as little help as their minions. The Leibstandarte's regimental commander at the time of the Wormhoudt killings, Sepp Dietrich, who was being held in US Army custody in Dachau, Germany, on other war crimes charges (including the massacre of American prisoners at Malmédy in the Ardennes), cut a sorry figure when he was interrogated by Colonel Scotland during 1946. Hitler's favourite SS commander, a man renowned for his dash and bravado, who had finished the war as an army commander in the field, was but a miserable wreck of a man when Scotland confronted him. A squat, balding figure, rough in manners and crude in speech, he seemed a far cry from the SS ideal of the Aryan superman. When Scotland questioned him about Wormhoudt, all he could say – in wailing tones, repeating himself over and over again – was: 'I spent the day in a ditch. . . . I know nothing of any shootings. . . . I spent the day in a ditch.' Later he made and signed a more coherent statement, which read like the statement of a man who knew more than he was admitting, and certainly did not amount to an outright denial:

> The deed of which the Leibstandarte is accused, i.e. the murder of a number of British prisoners of war, never came to my ears. There was a general order that the prisoners were to be handed over to the Regiment, Division or Corps. At this time, I gave no further orders regarding the prisoners, and above all, not to shoot them. Whether another officer gave such an order, I do not know. Neither do I know whether the murder was done on the orders of an officer, or by some soldiers on their own responsibility. The possibility may, however, have existed that soldiers in an intoxicated state may have done such a deed, without reporting it to their superiors. The fact that I met some soldiers with bottles and packages would strengthen that supposition. If this case had come to my knowledge, I should have brought the culprit before a court martial, if only for the sake of order and discipline. This, however, could not be done, because I knew nothing of the matter. It is clear to me, however, that the commander is responsible for the actions and conduct of his Regiment.

The Regimental Adjutants threw little additional light through the smokescreen. Fritz Beutler, clearly referring to the second group of British prisoners, testified that he had seen about thirty prisoners at the battle HQ and that Mohnke himself had ordered them to be taken to the rear either on foot or in vehicles. He had never heard of prisoners being shot – nor for that matter of prisoners shooting their guards. As for Eric Maas, he confined himself to a pedantic statement about the principles and practice of proper prisoner-processing procedures, a scholarly dissertation which had little to do with the fate of the prisoners who had the misfortune to be taken at Wormhoudt, about whom – with much mincing of words and scratching of memory – he professed to know nothing. Otto Baum conceded that his No 7 Company had indeed taken British prisoners, some of whom had been shot. But this, he claimed, was because they had fired at Rüger and attempted to escape. More than this he could not say, for the commander of the escort had conveniently perished on the Russian Front.

No case filled Colonel Scotland with greater frustration. 'In the end,' he was forced to admit, 'we were beaten largely by the compelling force of the SS oath of secrecy.' The power of the SS oath of loyalty to the person of Adolf Hitler was all-pervading – never more so, in all probability, than in the Führer's own honour guard, the Leibstandarte. When a man swore that oath, he dedicated his whole life to the Führer, putting his personal service to Hitler even before service to his country or to his family. 'I was very conscious that many of the happenings in SS units were sacred and secret,' Scotland wrote, 'never to be disclosed on penalty of death. There was no saving any man who broke his oath, and often as not the penalty would also be paid by his family. The SS had their own courts, ruthless and illegal. And even when the war was over we found prisoners so intimidated by their training in secrecy that it was often impossible to persuade them to disclose what they knew about a particular crime; there were many who would not talk even to save their own skins.' In Scotland's view, when Dietrich heard the story of the murders, he at once invoked the SS oath. 'Every officer present was sworn to silence. They in turn passed on the vow to the men under their command. So powerful was the fear of this oath that those who survived the war, and were captured and interrogated, maintained enough secrecy to baffle our experts and thwart all our hopes for a trial.'

The War Crimes Interrogation Unit at the London District Cage had succeeded in tracking down a number of SS men who must have known the full story of the massacre at Wormhoudt, and had laboured hard and long in a vain effort to bring some of the guilty men to court to answer the charge of murder. They had the evidence related by the British survivors. They had the evidence of the British soldiers' graves at Wormhoudt. But the key German witnesses had been able to dissociate themselves from the crime. Though it was evident to his interrogators that Otto Baum knew a great deal more than he was prepared to admit – 'How could he not have known?' one of them asked incredulously – he was able to satisfy Scotland that he had not been personally responsible for issuing the orders that led to the massacre. None of the other men interrogated so far seemed to have been involved in the killings. In short, Scotland felt unable to pin any German in the London Cage with culpability for the crime. Even though he was in a position to interrogate Senf, and held Sorowka and Konieczka – all three of them SS gunmen who actually had been present at the barn massacre – he was, remarkably enough, unable to crack either them or the case.

There remained, however, one witness who had not appeared in the London Cage. As Scotland wrote: 'One man we were never able to trace. He was said to have been in the eastern zone of Germany at the end of the war – Major-General Moenke [sic]. I am convinced that he was the man who could have assisted us, as the police say, in our enquiries.'

This was, in fact, the conclusion contained in the first of two reports on the Wormhoudt inquiry (reference number WCIU/LDC/1500) submitted early in 1947 by the War Crimes Interrogation Unit to the Judge Advocate General's office in London. In assessing responsibility for the crime, the report was quite unequivocal:

> As in similar investigations, one of our aims was to find out whether there was a general policy in the formation concerned that no prisoners were to be taken. There is no evidence that this was the case. Responsible for the crime of Wormhoudt is the CO of II Bn LSSAH [Leibstandarte], MOHNKE, who gave an order to shoot the prisoners concerned.

Wilhelm Mohnke's name was therefore added to the WCIU's *Consolidated Search List of Persons Wanted in Connection with the Wormhoudt Murders*. Under the heading 'Personal Description' Mohnke was presented as '6'2" tall, powerful build, small face, dark hair, 33–34 years old. Badly wounded in right (?) leg.' Under 'Present Whereabouts' he was entered as: 'Badly wounded in the fighting around Berlin, and taken prisoner by the Russians. The *Tagespiel* (Berlin newspaper) mentioned his "liquidation" in a Russian POW camp, but it is thought that he may still be alive in Russia.'

The WCIU report complained of the handicap caused by the long interval of time that had elapsed since the massacre, and the heavy casualties sustained by the Leibstandarte. 'It has thus only been possible to trace one man directly concerned with the crime, who is in hospital in Germany with advanced tuberculosis. Owing to his state of health it has not been possible to interrogate him adequately or to obtain a written statement from him.' This man was Oskar Senf, who had been a member of the No 7 Company escort that had accompanied the British prisoners to the barn at Wormhoudt. 'Apart from this man,' the report continued, 'it has not been possible so far to trace any individual who has either been concerned with, or was an eye witness of the Wormhoudt massacre. Most of the evidence obtained from Germans is therefore only hearsay, but the names of the men who carried out the massacre have been established and these men should be brought to justice.'

Hearsay evidence, it should be added, was permissible under regulations specially introduced for war crimes trials – the question was the weight which should be given to it.

Apart from Dietrich, Mohnke and Baum, the men on the WCIU wanted list included Willi Dorth, Max Schallwig and Sturmmann Dehos, whose whereabouts were unknown; Werner Rüger, who spoke with a lisp as a result of his accidental shooting at the barn, and had last been seen in February 1945 working as an Orderly Officer in the Reich Chancellery in Berlin; and Oskar Senf, who was in hospital in Germany. All these men were from No 7 Company, however. The WCIU had not yet got round to discovering the sinister part played by the detail from No 8 Company Signals Section – the men delegated to carry out the actual execution at the barn.

After submitting their first report, the investigators continued to work on the Wormhoudt case, and in June 1947 produced a second report (WCIU/LDC/1650). Both these reports form part of the secret British Government File on the Wormhoudt case, which is closed to the public under the Official Secrets Act until 1 January 2021.

On the title page of the second report it was stated that this report superseded the previous report. In fact, it did no such thing. For example, no less than nine depositions by SS prisoners contained in the first report were missing from the second one, *including three which clearly pointed a finger at Mohnke*. If this second report was read as a final report superseding the first, it would have appeared to present only a misleadingly incomplete, incoherent, patchwork case. The second report was really a supplementary report which updated the first one and introduced some important new material. Not only were the investigators able to reconstruct the barn massacre with the help of British survivors, but they were able to obtain further statements from some of those survivors. Even more crucially, they had obtained a full, written statement from one of the SS men, Oskar Senf, who had actually been at the barn.

In late 1946, one of the WCIU investigators, Richard Richter, was sent to Germany to interrogate Senf. He found the SS man alone in an isolation hut of the hospital compound of Eselheide POW camp and was told by the ex-Wehrmacht doctor who was looking after him that he was unfit to undergo interrogation as he was suffering from galloping consumption and his days were numbered. Richter did manage to see Senf but found him weak and bedridden and decided to accept the doctor's advice. 'There was no doubt in my mind that he was a very sick man,' Richter recalled. 'He was not even fit enough to sign a statement.'

But as one of the SS guards who had escorted the British prisoners to the barn, Senf was regarded as such a crucial witness that it was decided to go ahead with his interrogation anyway, and in 1947 RSM Stanton was sent out to question him in a hospital in Germany. The detailed statement that Stanton obtained from Senf could possibly be regarded as what is called in courtroom parlance a 'deathbed confession' – the kind of verbal evidence in which a more than ordinary confidence can be placed. If Senf was indeed dying of TB at this point, then he presumably had no one to fear but his Maker. TB would exact a quicker and more terrible toll than anything the Allied war crimes people could devise for him. Senf could therefore be presumed to have little need to cover-up or lie about his part in the Wormhoudt massacre or that of others and his statement was subsequently described by the investigators as a 'full and reliable eye-witness account'.

Richard Richter still has his doubts, however, and still believes that Senf's reluctance to talk to him on medical grounds may have been 'a put-up job designed to evade his involvement in the murder' and that his 'pretence of remorse was of course whitewash'. Certainly Senf was at pains to give himself a good cover story and distance himself from any involvement in the massacre, even though he had already shopped the others and was on the point of death. Be that as it may, Senf's evidence was crucial, and especially valuable in that it included direct, eye-witness evidence, and was not simply hearsay evidence of the kind previously presented during this enquiry. Moreover, from Senf the investigators may also have learned of the sinister role of the No 8 Company Signals Section and the names of one or two of the execution detail, for two of these – Hans Konieczka and Josef Sorowka – were then tracked down and interrogated by the WCIU. These two provided the names of a few more members of the execution squad: Drescher, Dutschmann, Friedhof, Günther and Moebius. But Konieczka and Sorowka could not be broken down in questioning and lamentably were let off the hook without charges being brought. 'There was no point in going on and on for nothing,' 'Bunny' Pantcheff explained. 'We were a very small team, our time was very limited, there was enormous pressure on us to get on with other things. Obviously if Mohnke had been around and put on trial we would have gone back to those two Signals Section men. But he wasn't, and the Judge Advocate-General would have said very simply: "If you can't find the prime accused, there's no point in going on. Let's keep looking for the one we haven't got, but in the meantime let's get on with the one we have."' Thus two of the suspected trigger-men at the Wormhoudt massacre were allowed to slip away into the obscurity of post-war German society – even though the trigger-men in the Knoechlein case had been put on trial.

The presentation of the second report of Colonel Scotland's War Crimes Interrogation Unit into the Wormhoudt case seems to have marked the end of their involvement in the matter. No effort was made to produce a

101

single reconciliation report combining all the evidence developed in the two reports, and there was little or no effort to produce a final collated analysis of the information which had been obtained. Possibly this was left to the prosecution lawyers of the Judge Advocate General's office in London, on whom fell the responsibility of considering the legal grounds for any war crimes prosecution arising from the WCIU's investigation. As we know, no such prosecution was ever brought against any members of the German armed forces in the Wormhoudt case. In large measure, this was probably because the chief suspect in the case, Wilhelm Mohnke, was not available for interrogation or indictment in the West. Mohnke was at that time, and for some years thereafter, in the custody of the Soviets, who would not co-operate in any Allied move to prosecute him, nor release him to the West. In any case, in April 1948, only a few months after the submission of the WCIU's final report on the Wormhoudt massacre, the British Government took the decision to cease war crimes trials after the coming September. The WCIU was wound up and responsibility for any further German war crimes trials was handed over to the German courts.

The case may have turned out differently if Mohnke had not been incarcerated in Russia. This was the opinion of one WCIU investigator, 'Bunny' Pantcheff, who stated recently: 'I'd have said that there was a prima facie case against Mohnke and that if we'd had him in 1947 we'd have tried him. What the lawyers would have made of it I don't know – they have their own ways of looking at things. We may not have brought a successful prosecution – but we'd have had a try. And whatever the legal outcome, there's no overlooking the moral turpitude of the thing.'

Mohnke's name, which was already on the original Central Registry of War Criminals and Security Suspects (or CROWCASS) in Paris, was added to the United Nations War Crimes Commission list – one of some 25,000 other 'A Class' names with serious charges to answer – and the Wormhoudt massacre was registered as a United Nations war crimes case, No 128/UK/G/28. This was significant, for it meant that a prima facie case had been independently established to the satisfaction of the Judge Advocate General and the responsible authority of the United Nations War Crimes Commission. And that, it seemed, was that.

VII

INDICTMENT

Anyone examining the tragic events that took place at Wormhoudt on 28 May 1940 will first have to satisfy themselves that the massacre that is alleged to have taken place did in fact take place.

This is not mere casuistry. A number of German witnesses interrogated by the WCIU in 1946 and 1947 maintained, not altogether surprisingly, that they had never heard of such an incident. Thus Sepp Dietrich, the commander of the Leibstandarte Regiment, whose men are alleged to have carried out the execution of British prisoners at the Wormhoudt barn, claimed in his testimony: 'The deed of which the Leibstandarte is accused, i.e. the murder of a number of British prisoners of war, never came to my ears.'

Similarly the Adjutant of the 2nd Battalion of the Leibstandarte, Fritz Beutler, who occupied a central position in his unit's attack on Wormhoudt, stated:

> When I was interrogated this afternoon, I was asked if I heard, or got to know anything about, German soldiers being wounded by British prisoners, and whether British prisoners had been shot by Germans. I neither heard nor learnt anything about British prisoners being shot. The British prisoners whom I saw, or about whom I heard, were always moved back to Regimental Battle Headquarters, if only for security reasons.

Likewise, Sepp Dietrich's Assistant Adjutant at Regimental Headquarters, Eric Maas, claimed complete ignorance of any such atrocity:

> I was asked during my oral interrogation whether I knew anything about the shooting of prisoners during the fighting. I must reply to that in the negative. I have occupied myself for three

103

days with the actions that took place at the time, and was able to recall much by studying the maps. If I heard anything then, I would not have forgotten it, even today, after six years, because it concerns an extraordinary way of acting, which in my opinion one cannot forget. If the dead had become known to the Regiment, the Regiment Commander would without doubt – I think I know him well enough to maintain this – have taken very drastic action by means of court martial procedures.

Even as recently as 1988, Otto Baum, who commanded No 7 Company of the 2nd Leibstandarte, which captured many of the British prisoners taken at Wormhoudt on 28 May 1940, maintains that no massacre of enemy prisoners ever took place, or at least that he never heard of it until he was confined and interrogated about it in 1946 in the old Kensington building that housed the London District Cage. Jost W. Schneider, a West German Second World War historian and authority on the SS, wrote to the present authors on 27 October 1988:

> I've met Mr Otto Baum and had the opportunity to talk with him on the 14th and 15th inst. [1988] He openly replied to my 'inquisitory' questions on Wormhoudt, etc. Mr Baum never heard about a massacre. He told me about his LDC experiences, when his interrogators showed him photographs of the ruined shed [barn]. Again, as other veterans confirmed to me, if there had been such a misdeed, news would have soon spread within the regiment, but this wasn't the fact – until he came as POW and internee into LDC. I got an excellent impression of Mr Baum – a good brain, helpful, and frankly making his judgements on all the units he once led in the Second World War: positive as well as negative . . . I consider him as being absolutely trustworthy.

Similarly, three of Baum's former NCOs and men from No 7 Company stated to WCIU interrogators that they had neither seen or heard of any such incident.

As we shall see, even though a number of German witnesses did admit to having heard that British prisoners had indeed been killed after they had surrendered, they went on to claim that these killings were justifiable and lawful, and thus did not amount to a massacre in the sense of involving the crime of murder. We shall return to these claims, which form the basis of the main German alibi in the Wormhoudt case, later. For the moment, it is obviously important from the legal point of view to know that a number of the Germans implicated in the events which we have gone to some pains to

104

describe in the foregoing pages – including the Commander and Assistant Adjutant of the Leibstandarte Regiment, the Commander and Adjutant of the Leibstandarte 2nd Battalion, and the Commander of No 7 Company – have at one time or another denied that the most crucial event, namely the murder of a large number of British prisoners in a barn, actually took place at Wormhoudt at all.

———

The evidence that a massacre had in fact taken place at Wormhoudt was collected with reasonable thoroughness by the War Office and the War Crimes Interrogation Unit over the period 1944–7, and has been supplemented from various sources subsequently. This evidence took several forms.

To begin with, there were the bodies. According to the estimates of the British survivors, between eighty and ninety British prisoners were killed by their German guards in the barn at Wormhoudt, a figure accepted in the final report of the WCIU investigators. According to some of the German evidence, the figure was nearer seventy. The exact figure is unknown, but at any rate it amounted to a substantial number of men. Regarding these bodies, the WCIU report states:

> The bodies of the victims were buried near the Barn in which they had been killed, though it cannot be ascertained by whom. About a year later they were disinterred and taken to the Military Cemetery at Esquelbecq. A French civilian who assisted in the disinterment states that the bodies were unrecognizable and carried no means of identification, and that they were all buried at Esquelbecq as '*Inconnu*' (or unknown).

In fact, according to a statement made by a local Wormhoudt official in the early 1970s, the Germans dispersed the bodies in at least three re-interment sites – one at Esquelbecq, one at Wormhoudt, and another elsewhere – in a deliberate effort to cover-up all traces of a massacre. In a statement to *The Times* of London dated 25 June 1988, a Wormhoudt gravedigger, Monsieur Georges Gautier, recalled that in 1941 he was one of the men ordered by the Germans to inter the dead, and found thirty-six corpses covered lightly with soil and 'buried like animals'. According to the Army Graves Service records of 1952, a total of thirty-five unknown British soldiers were reburied by the Germans in the Esquelbecq Military Cemetery (a British cemetery of the 1914–18 war) in four multiple graves, three containing the bodies of nine soldiers and one containing eight.* In Wormhoudt cemetery today there are thirty-three burials which are classified as 'unknowns'.

If these three sets of figures represent the numbers of unidentifiable dead soldiers reburied by the Germans in three roughly equal batches in three different sites, then the grand total comes to 104 bodies of soldiers who cannot be identified because they carried no means of identification – no dog tags, no pay books, no personal papers – when they were originally buried (or at any rate when they were reinterred). This is not necessarily an accurate total of the British prisoners killed at Wormhoudt, and the figure may even have been larger, bearing in mind the likelihood of battle casualties and the possibility that some British prisoners were killed – not necessarily just at the barn – without having their means of identification removed from them beforehand by their killers, and would therefore be buried in *named* graves.

In a statement on this subject made on behalf of the British Government to the House of Commons in London on 28 June 1988, the Under-Secretary of State for the Armed Forces, Mr Roger Freeman, made the following reference to the numbers involved:

> There can be no doubt that on 28 May 1940 a considerable number of British soldiers were murdered near the small village of Wormhoudt in France. It has never been possible, despite all efforts, to discover the exact figure. That is partly due to the number of men missing from various units as a result of that day's fighting, and partly due to the removal of the means of identification from the men when they were taken prisoner – they subsequently died – and the loss of many official records during the ensuing evacuation. It was not possible for us to make investigations at the spot until the area was again in allied hands in 1944.

It goes without saying, of course, that the significance of so many soldiers being buried without means of identification – meaning the small metal identity disc (or 'dog tag') with the owner's name, number and religious

---

* That was in 1952. Since then some names have been supplied, based on information from Wormhoudt survivors or other sources, but the names that can now be seen on the headstones do not necessarily bear any relationship to the bodies beneath them, as is evident from the words inscribed, 'Buried near this spot'. One of the names supplied was that of Private B.P. Kelly, of the Royal Warwickshire Regiment, who had had a leg half blown off during the grenade attack in the barn. Though Private Kelly was still alive after the massacre, he evidently died of his wounds, and according to the Army Graves Service he was reported to have been initially buried along with a number of other British soldiers '800 metres north of the road to Rubrouck on the field path south of the farmyard and sheds.'

persuasion (for burial service purposes) inscribed on it, which every soldier wore round his neck at all times throughout the war – is very great. On any normal wartime battlefield it would generally have been possible to identify a considerable proportion of soldiers killed in combat with conventional weapons by means of their dog tags. The absence of dog tags from so many of the dead buried in the vicinity of Wormhoudt would indicate that the dog tags had been deliberately removed, either before they were killed (to conceal the crime), or afterwards (to cover-up the scandal), or both. We shall return to this important issue a little later.

———

In addition to the evidence of the bodies, there was the evidence of the people who, in the cold light of the aftermath of the battle, were confronted with the dreadful reality of all that slaughter on their own doorstep, so to speak – the French civilian inhabitants of Wormhoudt. The battle had been fought in and out of the houses and round and about the farms of Wormhoudt, and the front parlours and sheds and farmyards and fields were littered with the bodies of the slain of both sides – and with the bodies of the English dead who had been cruelly and unjustly put to death after they had laid down their arms. The village was traumatized by the experience, and ashamed to have played host against its will to events of such horror and degradation. Worse, Wormhoudt had not covered itself with glory in this crisis. French farmers had been the first to come upon the scene of the massacre in the barn, and the first and last to refuse succour, even milk or water, for the wounded and the dying. In the four years of Nazi occupation that followed, the village turned in on itself. When the British finally returned in the summer of 1944 they found a brooding, unforthcoming populace closely guarding a secret whose existence was as yet barely suspected.* When the investigators from the London Cage arrived

* A Royal Marine Commando officer, George Amos, who was based at the 4th Commando Brigade HQ in Wormhoudt in August 1944, recalled: 'The attitude of the local French was hostile – they seemed to have a lot of women who had been injured and claimed that Spitfires had straffed them in the fields. But there did seem to be a sense of guilt which was very difficult to understand at the time.' When a number of German prisoners were brought to Wormhoudt they were taken to a field in which stood a ruined barn. 'The atmosphere changed,' George Amos wrote, 'and they became unco-operative and surly and huddled in groups. There was a very strange atmosphere about the whole situation. I then ordered them to dig a hole in which to bury their empty food cans but they would not co-operate. Eventually two of them dug a hole, the cans were pushed in and the hole filled. The reaction was immediate, one young German dancing and singing *Happy Days Are Here Again*. I am sure they knew of the massacre and thought we were going to take revenge.'

107

to explore the scene of the crime after the war, they might have expected the full co-operation of their French allies, who had been so close to the events of 1940. But all the investigators found were the huge bare mounds of earth where the unnamed British dead lay buried like cattle, and a populace that was determined to play its cards very close to its chest. In the end, it seems, only the occupants of the Le Fort Rose farm, Monsieur and Madame Decouvalaere-Courtois, agreed to talk to the investigators. Their conversation did not advance the enquiries very far. The husband had been away from the farm on the day in question, and the wife had left when the first German troops arrived at 1300 hours. The couple did not return for two or three days, and when they did come back they found that the Germans – Mohnke's men – had packed wood and straw into the cellar and set light to it in an attempt to burn the house down; and when that failed they had helped themselves liberally to the wine and spirits supply, so that when the couple returned they found their kitchen table buried under rows and rows of empty bottles. Thirty-seven British soldiers had been killed on their farm, they said. But they professed to know nothing about the massacre in the barn across the fields.

But the French knew more than they had let on to the war crimes investigators, and slowly they began to talk – to the trickle of old soldiers from across the Channel who had borne arms in Wormhoudt on that infamous day, and more latterly to a new generation of investigators, anxious to learn the truth and pin the blame after all those blank, silent, unrequited years. Gradually, from the mouths and memories of those French onlookers of 28 May 1940, a wider vision of hell began to take shape – a picture of a paroxysm of violence, a kind of catharsis of bloodlust, during which (if the citizens of Wormhoudt are to be believed) every Englishman who could stand, and even those who could not, was disarmed and stripped and done to death, stabbed, clubbed, shot, and tossed aside by a rampant, wild and vengeful force of SS men who for an hour or two of the late afternoon of that day abandoned all pretence of observing international law and civilized values. This is what the French told later. It names no names. It is not evidence in any specific sense. But, wrested grudgingly from the painful communal memory of this little town, Wormhoudt's horrified overview of a nightmare provides a backdrop which helps make sense of the more closely focused incidents in the trauma of 28 May.

———

A third, more exact, more forthcoming source of information was the men who survived the incident in the barn and returned to Britain to tell their tale, either during the war or after it. These witnesses fall into four main groups.

The first group comprised the four prime movers in the case, so to speak – the men who, on account of the severity of the wounds they had sustained at Wormhoudt, had been repatriated from German prisoner-of-war camps in a prisoner-of-war exchange at the end of 1943. These men were Charles Daley, Albert Evans and John Lavelle of the Royal Warwickshire Regiment, and Richard Parry of the Royal Artillery. At the request of the Treasury Solicitor all four of these survivors made separate, formal, sworn statements before Commissioners of Oaths in 1944 in which they recounted their individual recollections of their capture and of their experience in the barn. These recollections were written down while they were still relatively fresh in the memory, and were as precise and unequivocal as could be expected given the nature of the events they described. Moreover, bearing in mind the possibility of future legal action being brought in this case, it is to be presumed that these legally witnessed affidavits are as valid as depositions of evidence today as they were at the time they were made. This evidence, which has been retold at length in the preceding narrative of this book, clearly shows that a large number of unarmed British prisoners were force-marched at the double across the fields to a small barn, into which they were driven at gunpoint and then subjected to a grenade, rifle and machine-gun attack by their German guards, who left them for dead.

The second group of British witnesses comprised survivors who returned from captivity in Germany at the end of the war and were required not long afterwards to make statements about their experiences when the War Office began to take up the Wormhoudt case. These men were Alfred Tombs, who produced a detailed handwritten statement about his experiences, possibly at the instigation of the Royal Warwickshire Regiment; Corporal Robert Gill of the Royal Warwicks, who made a sworn affidavit about the massacre in the barn before an officer of the Legal Staff at the Judge Advocate General's office in August 1945; and Albert Montague, who at a later date gave a signed statement to the War Crimes Interrogation Unit about his capture at Wormhoudt after the barn massacre had already taken place. Gill's evidence was somewhat hazy and confused about certain details, especially the names of fellow Warwicks in the barn, while Montague was never in the barn at all. Nevertheless, both these men were able to throw additional light on the events of 28 May which in one way or another was useful in the evaluation of the case.

For reasons which are not clear, Alfred Tombs' statement was not appended to the reports of the WCIU, and is not referred to in the investigators' summary of events; and though Tombs was requested to attend an identity parade of German suspects at the London Cage in April 1947, along with three other survivors, he declined to do so on the grounds that all the SS men had looked the same in their helmets – 'all tall and of smart appearance'. (The SS men felt much the same about each other, as one of them – Oskar Senf – testified to the WCIU: 'We all looked alike and were of the same height.')

Colonel Scotland and his team therefore had the statements of six British ex-POWs who had been at Wormhoudt on the fatal day – seven if Tombs is included – and from them obtained the names of a number of other British prisoners who had either definitely survived or very likely survived the massacre in the barn.* For one reason or another, none of these other prisoners were contacted by the WCIU, as far as is known, and most of them vanished into the obscurity of post-war civilian life. One or two, however, surfaced many years later, when interest in the Wormhoudt case was revived and the matter of a legal process was raised with the State Prosecutor's Office in West Germany in the early 1970s. These new witnesses, who comprised a third group, included Reg West, George Hall and George Hopper of the Royal Warwicks, who gave evidence that they had also survived the barn massacre, and Bill Cordrey of the Royal Warwicks, who was taken prisoner at Wormhoudt but correctly treated by his captors. Other Wormhoudt veterans also came forward at this time and claimed that they, too, were survivors of the barn massacre. But in some instances their stories seemed improbable, or difficult to corroborate, and they were therefore not listed among the final tally of survivors, which may have numbered fourteen or fifteen.

Though the British witnesses could relate clearly enough the misfortunes that had befallen them and their less fortunate comrades at Wormhoudt, they were less than clear when it came to identifying the individuals responsible for inflicting those misfortunes on them. After all, seven years had now passed since the tragic events at Wormhoudt. Bert Evans was able to positively identify one of the German suspects paraded at the identity parade at the London Cage in April 1947. None of the other survivors who took part were able to identify any. Corporal Gill was able to give a perfunctory description of the SS man who threw the first hand grenade among the prisoners in the barn – 'about twenty-six years of age, 5′ 7″ in height, very dark, bronze, SS markings on the collar of his tunic'. But clearly it was going to be difficult to track a man down simply on the basis that he had caught the sun during weeks of campaigning in the field.

More importantly, perhaps, Richard Parry was able to testify that on the way to the barn he had seen a German officer who was interviewing a soldier called Daley. In an additional statement, made after he had been

* According to a statement made by Roger Freeman in the House of Commons, a total of eight survivors were interviewed by the WCIU. Only six statements were finally included in the WCIU's reports, however.

taken back to Wormhoudt by LDC officers, Parry enlarged on this description. 'The German officer seemed a "big noise", wore a soft peaked cap (I think it was black), and was giving orders to his subordinates on the road – from his gestures, I should say about ourselves. He was raving blue murder! I cannot say whether this German officer was there when we arrived, but he soon attracted my attention by his shouting. He was still there when we marched off.' Parry stated in his original affidavit: 'I think that I could recognize the German officer [whom we believe to be Mohnke as observed by one of his victims shortly after he had been given command of the 2nd Battalion Leibstandarte], and I am certain that I could recognize the soldier who shot me through the face.' But Parry saw neither at the London Cage and no further clues about the Germans involved came from the British survivors. Nor, surprisingly, did the investigators at the London Cage make any effort to obtain the files and photos of their SS suspects from the Berlin Document Centre, which housed a comprehensive collection of such material.

――――

For information about the Germans the investigators had to turn to the Germans themselves, who constituted the third important source of evidence in the case.

It was a straightforward enough matter to determine from the German Order of Battle which unit had been engaged at Wormhoudt on 28 May 1940 and which officers had commanded what formations during that engagement. Once such 2nd Leibstandarte officers and men as had survived the war had been tracked down, further progress in the investigation depended on chipping away at the wall of sullen silence and obdurate evasion and half-truths which most, though perhaps not all, of the prisoners presented to their interrogators. Few, if any, of the ex-SS Leibstandarte prisoners interrogated by the WCIU were motivated by any great urge to unburden themselves of the truth. The overriding imperative was first to save their own skins and second to save the skins of their erstwhile comrades-in-arms – possibly, as Colonel Scotland suggested, through adherence to the binding secrecy of the SS oath. The processing of the SS personnel hauled before the WCIU interrogators in the Wormhoudt case was therefore a dour and dogged affair and breakthroughs were few and far between. Colonel Scotland might perhaps be excused when he complained: 'I failed to obtain anything of value that might lead to identification of the guilty party. In short, I had no case to present to Court.'

Of course, Scotland was greatly handicapped by not having Wilhelm

Mohnke in his custody. But it is the present authors' opinion that a thoroughly incisive and exhaustive analysis of such evidence as had been developed in the case would have yielded greater grounds for optimism than were perceived by the hard-pressed Colonel Scotland at the time. After all, there was clear evidence which named the trigger-men and showed that Mohnke was responsible for the fatal order. Moreover, like other war crimes officers, Scotland was greatly aided by the regulations governing the procedures of Allied war crimes courts, which differed from normal civil courts in a number of important and controversial respects. Nowhere was this more apparent than in the rules of evidence, for no evidence was excluded, be it hearsay, circumstantial or whatever, if it was thought to have a bearing on the case being tried; and pre-trial interrogation transcripts, statements and properly sworn and witnessed depositions were held to be admissible, even when the witnesses themselves could not give evidence personally in court, having died or disappeared by the time the trial took place. The important thing in war crimes trials was not the *type* of evidence that was produced but the *weight* to be attached to it. This being so, it is surprising that Colonel Scotland felt he had no case to present, for the evidence that could be brought to the Wormhoudt case under Allied military court regulations was substantial.

A statistical analysis of the evidence put forward by the seventeen SS prisoners directly relevant to the case produces the following results:*

In the first place, all four of the officers who had been at Wormhoudt on 28 May 1940 stated that they had never heard of British prisoners of war being killed at Wormhoudt and knew nothing about it. On the other hand, only two of the twelve other ranks gave the same reply, while one gave an ambiguous reply. This suggests that the power of the SS oath was very much less powerful lower down the military hierarchy, and certainly suggests an awareness amongst at least a proportion of the Leibstandarte men that something unusual had happened in connection with the prisoners at Wormhoudt. At the same time, an officer who was not present at Wormhoudt on 28 May 1940, and possibly for that reason, and possibly because he was not a regular member of the Leibstandarte Regiment or even the Waffen-SS – we are talking here of the ambiguous SS-

---

* Statements by a total of twenty German witnesses were included in the WCIU reports on the Wormhoudt case, but three of these statements – by Buchsein, Heinrich and Kramer – had no direct bearing on the actual killings.

Lieutenant-General cum Naval Reserve Lieutenant-Commander Alfred Rodenbücher – testified that he, too, had heard of the killing of a large number of British prisoners at Wormhoudt on 28 May 1940; in fact, it was the talk of the mess.

In the second place, three of the four officers who had been at Wormhoudt on 28 May, also claimed that they had never heard anything about British prisoners wounding a guard and being shot in reprisal either. In other words, with perfect logic they maintained not only that they had heard nothing about any killings, but also that they had heard nothing about any cause or justification for any killings. Alfred Rodenbücher also seemed ignorant of any such incident, and again it could conceivably be construed that, being an outsider to the Regiment who was not even present on the day in question, he was not party to the alibi story either. The one exception among the officers was Otto Baum, the Commander of No 7 Company, who claimed that some such incident involving British prisoners attacking a guard had been reported to him. Nine out of the ten men from his company who were interrogated gave much the same story, as did one of the two men from the Signals Section of No 8 Company who had actually been present at the barn killings. Moreover, all but one of the SS men who related the story of the wounding of a guard by British prisoners mentioned the name of Werner Rüger as a victim, while seven mentioned a small-arms shot as the means of attack and only two mentioned a grenade.

In other words, some six or seven years after the Wormhoudt incident the SS alibi remained remarkably watertight, broadly conforming to the line that an SS guard called Werner Rüger was shot by a British prisoner (or prisoners) and that the wounding of the guard was the reason for the killing of a number of prisoners at that time. The one exception to the otherwise universal solidarity among the other ranks was Oskar Senf, who gave a completely different version of the shooting of the SS guard – a version which, if true, completely exploded the SS alibi.

Finally, five of the seventeen SS prisoners who gave statements relevant to the matter named Wilhelm Mohnke in connection with the disposal of British prisoners of war. (Four of the five named him on the basis of hearsay evidence, while one, giving direct evidence as an eye-witness, specifically named him as ordering the execution of prisoners.) The name of this eye-witness was again Oskar Senf.

What this statistical review of the German evidence shows is that a substantial number of the German witnesses at the London District Cage had at least *heard* that British prisoners of war had been killed at Wormhoudt – not from the British but from their own comrades in the Leibstandarte; and though many of them put forward an alibi to excuse the killing, this alibi did not entirely hold water, as at least one of their old comrades was to reveal. Moreover, an appreciable number of the German witnesses indicated a clear and unanimous opinion as to who might be responsible for the deaths of the prisoners.

———

International law governing the treatment of prisoners of war at the outbreak of the Second World War was laid down in the Prisoner of War Convention signed in Geneva in 1929, of which Germany was a signatory. Article 23 (c) of the Geneva Convention was quite unambiguous: 'It is particularly forbidden to kill or wound an enemy who, having laid down his arms, or no longer having means of defence, has surrendered at discretion.' Article 23 (d) was equally forthright: 'It is forbidden to declare that no quarter will be given.' These laws were as well known to the Germans as they were to the other belligerent nations of Europe in the Second World War. In fact, the German army went so far as to print in every German soldier's paybook a list of the so-called 'German Soldier's Ten Commandments' governing his conduct in war. 'While fighting for victory the German soldier will observe the rules of chivalrous warfare,' the brave warriors of the Führer were exhorted. 'No enemy who has surrendered will be killed. . . . POW's will not be ill-treated or insulted. . . . Offences against the above-mentioned matters of duty will be punished. . . . Reprisals are only permissible on order of Higher Command.'

The actual procedure for handling prisoners in a battlefield situation was equally well known to the responsible officers in the Leibstandarte Regiment. Sepp Dietrich put it in a nutshell at regimental level: 'There was a general order that prisoners were to be handed over to the regiment, division or corps.' Eric Maas, as Assistant Adjutant to the Regiment, was well acquainted with the nitty-gritty of the business. He gave his interrogators at the LDC an admirably precise outline of the process at Battalion level:

> Before the start of a fairly big operation, every unit received orders and directives about the treatment of POWs. These orders were given by higher authority and agreed with the regulations of the Geneva Convention. Beyond this, special orders contained directives and orders about the transport of POWs from the fighting and danger zone. I know these orders because of my capacity as Assistant Adjutant to the Regiment.
>
> I would like to add a few words about the sending back of POWs. Every section leader whose section had to accompany POWs had to have a certificate showing the number of prisoners, [with] officers and men divided into separate groups.

114

When the prisoners were delivered at an assembly point or at a camp, the actual transfer of the prisoners was receipted on this certificate. This certificate was to be given back to the respective Company: it had to be kept in the Company files.

The movement was on foot if the distance was small. Usually, however, empty convoy space was used. . . . Prisoners who seemed important were sent to the division for interrogation, and the rest were sent back to the rear.

Hermann Hasewinkel, a section leader at No 7 Company HQ, gave a practical outline of the procedure for shipment of prisoners at company level. The commander of the prisoner escort was required to report to the company commander or company HQ section leader and then take the prisoners on to Battalion HQ. If for some reason the escort could not do this, the company commander would have to summon a special escort – consisting of men from the reserve platoon or reserve section – to take the prisoners down the line from Company HQ to Battalion HQ. In the 2nd Leibstandarte on 28 May this reserve section was the Signals Section of No 8 Company. These seem to have been the only people Hasewinkel could find at Battalion HQ when he was sent there to report casualties and request ambulances at the height of the battle – round about the time the Battalion Commander was wounded in the front line and Wilhelm Mohnke took over command.

So much for the theory and practice laid down for the safe-conduct of prisoners in battle. At Wormhoudt on 28 May 1940 the reality as conceived by the 2nd Battalion of the Leibstandarte Adolf Hitler was radically different. For a start, prisoners were not just killed – they were not taken either. At various times and various points around the battlefield it is apparent that various SS units decided to give no quarter. Gunner Arthur Baxter of the 53rd Anti-Tank Regiment witnessed the cold-blooded machine-gunning of a British officer and his driver as they tried to surrender, and almost immediately afterwards the murder of another British soldier who had refused to part with his watch. Lance-Corporal Oxley, of the Cheshire Regiment, was one of a small party of soldiers who were gunned down after they had put their hands up to surrender in Wormhoudt square, and later he saw a wounded British sergeant brought out of a house and shot, and a party of soldiers killed by a grenade at the entrance to an air raid shelter as they attempted to surrender. The company commander of A Company of the 2nd Royal Warwicks, Captain Padfield, was shot down after he had been surrounded, and Private Charles Daley was shot through the shoulder while he had his hands up in surrender by a German soldier who called him an 'English pig'. Private Alf Tombs watched an SS man shoot one of his wounded Warwickshire comrades, Private Gould, through

115

the head as he lay helpless on the ground. Private Bert Evans saw fifteen British soldiers, possibly Cheshires, stood against a wall and shot with automatic weapons. An officer of the Worcesters saw his own men suffer a similar fate to the east of the town.

These are instances of no quarter being given for which there is eye-witness evidence – all of them in violation of Article 23 (d) of the Geneva Convention. They do not include instances where the only evidence consists of the bodies of soldiers seen *after* they had been killed – the naked bodies seen by Gunner Nicholls and Lance-Corporal Oxley on the driveway to the First Aid Post in Wormhoudt village, their backs lacerated by what looked like sabre cuts; the charred bodies covered in oil beside the burnt-out trucks which Alfred Tombs saw; the bodies of the British soldiers with their heads bashed in which a French farmer's daughter saw.

As for those British soldiers who successfully surrendered to their German foe, their fate in many cases was no less dire. What emerges is a whole series of aberrations, of sinister deviations from the norm, which totally invalidate any claim that the processing of the first main batch of British prisoners, numbering some one hundred men and assembled between 1600 and 1700 hours in the afternoon, was ever envisaged by their captors as a routine shipment of prisoners back down the line 'to the Regiment' or 'to the rear'. Consider, for example, the ascending scale of indignities to which the prisoners were subjected, contrary to the inter-national rules of warfare:

Firstly, some of them had the jackets of their battledress removed and were stripped to the waist. Others had their paybooks taken from them and their dog tags removed from round their necks. As Bert Evans testified: 'We were searched and stripped of everything (identity discs and the lot) . . . I'd practically no clothes on me.'* This was confirmed by Richard Parry: 'My steel helmet, paybook and personal belongings were taken from me.' Many prisoners, in all probability the majority, were thus deprived of just about every clue to their identify – name, number, rank, regiment, religious denomination. This would not normally much bother the prisoners themselves, since most of them were perfectly well aware of their own identity. But for the Germans engaged in a genuine prisoner shipment it would prove a considerable handicap for all sorts of practical and administrative reasons. That most prisoners were deprived of their identi-fication is strong evidence, therefore, that no such genuine prisoner shipment was ever intended, and that the identity of these unfortunates was meant to remain unknown for ever after.

---

* The thoroughness of these searches makes it improbable any British prisoner could have retained a firearm and thus invalidates one of the main props of the German alibi.

Secondly, far from being taken to the Regimental HQ in the rear, which is where they were *supposed* to have been taken, and where some German detainees told the LDC that they *were* taken, the prisoners were led off into the back of beyond to a place that by reason of its location and the accommodation it provided could never be mistaken, even in the wildest fantasy, for a prisoner-of-war assembly point. At this time on 28 May the Regimental HQ was somewhere between Bollezeele and La Cloche, about fifteen miles to the east of Wormhoudt, on the other side of Esquelbecq, about three or four hours away on foot. This is not where the prisoners were taken. A prisoner-of-war assembly point might reasonably be expected to be sited near a command post and adequate road communications to the rear, and to be able to provide at least rudimentary living space in which the prisoners could find shelter and be fed. The tiny, ramshackle barn in La Plaine au Bois to which the prisoners were herded fulfilled none of these basic requirements. The barn was the size of an ordinary domestic garage and the only way one hundred or more men could be accommodated in it was by standing cheek by jowl, wounded included, like rush-hour commuters in a packed underground train. This wretched shack was not near Regimental HQ, nor even on the way to it. It was not near a road, nor indeed anywhere in particular. It could only be reached across the fields and down a farm track that on 28 May was so soft and muddy that a German ambulance could not get down it to fetch one of the Germans' own wounded. This was no place to bring prisoners who were meant to be shipped on to prisoner-of-war camps in Germany. But it was a good place to despatch them to Valhalla with the fewest possible people looking on.

Thirdly, the prisoners were treated with exceptional violence and brutality, as though their lives were already forfeit. They were marched at the double across the fields for nearly a mile and a half, and harassed, beaten and even bayoneted if they could not keep up; and when they got to the barn they were herded into it in the most squalid and sordid possible way, until they were squeezed in it 'like sardines' (as one British survivor described it). Was *this* the routine procedure for handling enemy prisoners so methodically outlined by the Assistant Adjutant of the Leibstandarte Regiment, Eric Maas?

So far what we have seen is a highly abnormal prisoner handling process. Now we come to the crucial action – the killing of the prisoners. This has been described in detail in the preceding pages from the evidence of a number of British witnesses and from one German witness in particular, Oskar Senf. Senf apart, most of the German detainees interrogated by the WCIU reacted to the allegation of murder in various ways. Some sought to evade the charge by pleading ignorance, or denying that it had happened, or weaving a web of disinformation by deliberately confusing the first group of prisoners, who were killed, with the second group, who were spared.

Against those who in one way or another sought to deny that any British prisoners had been killed should be considered the following statements made to the War Crimes Interrogation Unit by various members of the 2nd Leibstandarte:

Hermann Hasewinkel (a thirty-one-year-old married ex-hairdresser from Altmark who had ended the war as an SS Captain): 'I heard a large part of the prisoners lost their lives.'

Karl Krause (a thirty-one-year-old ex-farmer and former Nazi Party member from Dresden in East Germany, a Sergeant Major when the war ended): 'I learnt that prisoners were shot.'

Karl Kummert (a thirty-three-year-old former SS First Lieutenant from Hamburg: a CSM in charge of the baggage train at Wormhoudt): 'One of the platoon leaders told me that British prisoners had been shot. The adjutant told me . . . that the commander told him the prisoners were to be shot.'

Hans Neidereck (a typically blond, blue-eyed, athletic-looking ex-SS Sergeant Major from the Black Forest, with a wife in Berlin): 'It was said that Rüger . . . had been wounded . . . while taking back British prisoners, but that he was nevertheless present at the shooting of forty to fifty prisoners. Reference was made to a barn near Wormhoudt.'

Alfred Rodenbücher (forty-five years old by the time he was locked up in the London District Cage – once one of the top-ranking men of the Allgemeine-SS, who had somehow blotted his copybook): 'There was talk about a force of seventy men. It was said these men were all finished off. The depressing thing was the supposition that prisoners were shot.'

Franz Rofallski (a twenty-nine-year-old East Prussian with a young child; shot through the head at Wormhoudt and subsequently invalided out of the rough and tumble of the Waffen-SS into the gentler pastures of the frontier police): 'I heard that all the fifty prisoners were said to have been shot.'

Josef Sorowka (a member of the execution squad; a corporal at Wormhoudt and only one rank higher by the war's end, five years later): 'I remember hearing that British prisoners had been shot.'

Bruno Wachowiak (a former unemployed labourer of Polish descent from Berlin who ended the war a Leibstandarte Staff-Sergeant, aged thirty-three): 'Rumours went around our company to the effect that British prisoners had been liquidated . . . No prisoners were to be taken in the battle for Wormhoudt.'

Hugo Waetzman (a thirty-one-year-old former SS First Lieutenant from Saarbrücken with only one leg): 'The rumour went round our company that some British prisoners had been shot.'

Admittedly, the statements quoted so far only purvey hearsay as to the actual killings, which were not witnessed by most of the men that made them.

However, they do represent first-hand evidence as to the subject of conversation and speculation – the background state of mind – within the 2nd Leibstandarte following the massacre; and since this comes from more than a single source it could be argued that it collectively amounts to circumstantial evidence as to an awareness and a widespread assumption within the 2nd Leibstandarte that something unusual and untoward had occurred in connection with the British prisoners.

With the exception of Josef Sorowka, none of the German witnesses quoted above – who all acknowledged that prisoners had been shot – had played any part in the killings, and therefore had no need to fear any British retribution as a result of anything they said to their interrogators. Even freer to speak his mind in this respect was Alfred Rodenbücher. Rodenbücher was a mature person of very senior rank. He was not a proper member of the Leibstandarte, he was not present in Wormhoudt at the time of the massacre, and, bearing in mind that he had been sent into the front-line from a top-ranking desk job in Berlin on the express orders of Himmler, he may conceivably not have felt constrained by any vestigial ties of loyalty to the SS or Nazi cause. There is no reason to doubt Rodenbücher when he said that on the evening of the massacre and on the evening after that the talk of the SS officers at the Leibstandarte Regimental Battle HQ was the shooting of the British prisoners. Other detainees at the London District Cage would confirm that men were still talking about it in the Leibstandarte Barracks in Berlin as late as 1942. Even in 1945 the subject was a considerable preoccupation, not to say source of anxiety, with several of the men of the Leibstandarte. Thus Carl Kummert related to his interrogators in the LDC how his old comrade Waetzman had looked him up after he had been interrogated by US Army Counter Intelligence at Darmstadt:

> When I asked him whether he suspected anything, he answered: 'I can only suppose that they found a guard duty book in Metz . . . where I had to guard some prisoners; but that does not matter because I behaved according to instructions . . . I can only suppose it has something to do with the filth about Rüger. But they cannot do anything to me; I had nothing to do with the matter.'

The 'filth about Rüger' lies at the heart of the German alibi – the pillar of the Leibstandarte defence. As we have seen, eleven of the seventeen men whose statements were filed in the LDC reports on the case mentioned that British prisoners had attacked their guards, and all but one of these eleven mentioned the name of Werner Rüger as the SS victim. One of the clearest versions of the Rüger alibi was provided by Max Reimelt:

119

A member of Seven Company related the following incident after the battle.

During the battle approximately four to five men were detailed to guard large numbers of English POWs. The number of POWs was given to him as sixty to seventy men. Amongst the guards there was a Rottenführer Werner Rüger from Seven Company. Rüger was admitted to hospital severely wounded by several shots, amongst others a jawbone injury. I was told that this injury was caused by shots which came from the English POW ranks.

In the eyes of most of the SS men the incident provided adequate and reassuring justification of the killing of the British prisoners of war. As Hermann Hasewinkel testified at the LDC: 'The incident was undoubtedly extraordinary. But since the attack came from the prisoners it was not felt that an injustice had occurred. The matter was probably regarded as an incident for which the escort could not be blamed.'

Franz Rofallski related a similarly vivid account of the incident which had been told to him by a comrade from No 7 Company in 1941:

About eight men of No 7 Company were ordered to bring some fifty prisoners back to the Battalion Battle HQ. Four of these eight men were the following members of II P1: Werner Rüger, Alfons Linkenheil, Oskar Senf, Willi Dorth. All four were SS Rottenführers at the time. When these prisoners and their escort were about one hundred metres from the company, suddenly shots were fired. I do not know whether they were pistol or rifle shots. Thereupon confusion resulted amongst the prisoners and it was about half an hour before the column was reassembled. The onward transporting of prisoners was then resumed . . . Rüger is said to have been wounded then and taken to the dressing station by Senf.

Later Rofallski heard that all the prisoners were shot by order of the Battalion Commander.

Rüger later told his own version of the story to Bruno Wachowiak in Berlin – by which time Rüger boasted a major facial scar and spoke with a pronounced lisp on account of the wound he had sustained under such mysterious circumstances in Wormhoudt:

I was present when the captured British soldiers were to be taken to the rear. We had the prisoners drawn up in three rows and told them to lay down their arms. When that was done we

120

marched off. When we were near the Battalion Battle HQ some shots were suddenly fired from among the prisoners and they hit me. I was wounded in the face and the back and then all the guards opened fire on the prisoners. Even hand grenades were thrown among the prisoners. There was great confusion, but in spite of that three prisoners escaped.

The Rüger alibi cannot be dismissed out of hand. Though most of the British prisoners of war had laid down their arms when they surrendered, and though most of them had been searched after they had done so, it might conceivably have been possible for a prisoner to have retained a pistol or a grenade, and, having retained it, used it. Captain Lynn-Allen still had his revolver on him when he was searched a little while after he had surrendered. And Fritz Beutler, the Adjutant of the 2nd Battalion Leibstandarte, made a great play about another British officer who, according to him, had hung on to his revolver all the way to the German Battle HQ and then refused to part with it. Beutler described the ensuing conversation in his testimony – though we must bear in mind that this is the uncorroborated testimony of a potential German suspect in the case:

'You still have a revolver on your belt,' Beutler told the officer. 'Give it to me.'

'I am an English officer,' the prisoner replied, somewhat annoyed, in German, 'and I may keep my arms during captivity!'

Beutler is clearly referring to an incident at the Fort Rose Farm, to which the final batch of prisoners were safely conducted late on the 28 May, *after* the massacre of their comrades an hour or so earlier. An English officer making this sort of response to his SS captors earlier in the afternoon would have been given short shrift. But on this occasion Beutler simply shrugged and said:

'In the rear it will be taken off you in any case.' And he left it at that.

In the testimony provided by the British survivors, the nearest evidence we find to anything resembling the Rüger incident came from Bert Evans, who described how, as the group of prisoners from D Company were being marched across the fields to the Cassel road, a British soldier hurled a grenade at a German tank. This made the SS guards very angry, and shortly afterwards another group of British prisoners, numbering about fifteen men, were stood up against a wall and shot – possibly as a reprisal. But the incident witnessed by Evans had nothing to do with the alleged attack on Werner Rüger. The soldier who threw the grenade was not a prisoner of war, not a member of the group of which Evans was part, but a fighting soldier who was still at large and still carrying on the fight. And his

121

grenade attack was not aimed at the guards of the prisoner escort, one of whom would have been Rüger, but at an active enemy combatant – namely, a German tank, of all things. Possibly the Germans subsequently wove the story of the grenade attack on the tank and the shooting of the fifteen British prisoners and the injury genuinely sustained by Rüger a little later into a single elaborate fantasy to exonerate the atrocity that took place at the barn. But the massacre at the barn cannot be so easily excused, any more than the gratuitous slaughter of the fifteen unarmed men on the Cassel road.

***

In several German testimonies the names of Rüger and Senf are linked. Most agree that it was Senf who took his wounded comrade to the dressing station after he had been shot, an action which is confirmed by Senf himself. Senf's own testimony, it goes without saying, is crucial to this case. At the time he gave it to RSM Stanton in his ward in the isolation hospital of an internment camp in Germany in 1947, Oskar Senf was about thirty-three years old, a slim, fair-haired six-footer who was reaching the end of his days. After Wormhoudt and the campaign in France, where he had served as an infantryman in No 7 Company of the 2nd Leibstandarte, Senf had gone on to Russia with the Battalion, and had served as a Technical NCO there until he had been invalided out after sustaining a damaged lung which turned into encysted TB. By the time Colonel Scotland's interrogators had caught up with him, Senf was in the grip of galloping consumption, a terminal condition from which in the 1940s there was no prospect of remission or recovery.

As we have stated earlier, the testimony which Senf eventually gave to RSM Stanton was tantamount to a deathbed confession. Not only does this fit the context in which Senf found himself, but it is almost the only explanation why Senf should have thought fit to depart so diametrically from the account of events previously given to the WCIU by a number of his former comrades-in-arms. While the other accounts provided an alibi for the whole unit, Senf's provided an alibi for himself alone. With only a few months to live, it would seem that Senf had none of the inhibitions of his old comrades about naming names and describing a sequence of events which corresponded much more closely to that outlined by the British survivors of the Wormhoudt massacre. The present authors share the view of the War Crimes Interrogation Unit that in his statement Senf provided a full and reliable eye-witness account to which a considerable measure of credence should be given.

The salient part of Senf's statement has already been included in our narrative of the events immediately preceding the massacre. How Senf and half a dozen or so of Heinrich's 2 Platoon of No 7 Company had taken about forty British prisoners during their attack on the south side of Wormhoudt. How they had marched them to Battalion Battle HQ, where Heinrich was fiercely reprimanded by Mohnke for having brought in prisoners 'contrary to orders'. How Heinrich went away and came back after a while with a special squad of SS men from the Signals Section of No 8 Company, who told Senf that they had received orders from Mohnke to shoot the prisoners. How they all ran across the fields to the barn. How two of the prisoners – we know them to have been Evans and Lynn-Allen – escaped and were shot at by one of the No 8 Company men. How Rüger was wounded in the shooting and how Senf carried him to an ambulance and was thus able to leave the scene of the massacre.

Certain aspects of Senf's testimony need to be highlighted. In the first place, he effectively destroys the SS alibi that the prisoners were shot because they opened fire on their guards, wounding Rüger. Senf is unequivocal in stating that the prisoners died as a result of orders given by Wilhelm Mohnke that they were to be shot. This order was not given as a reprisal for something the prisoners had done, but simply because Mohnke, for reasons best known to himself, wanted them out of the way as quickly as possible. This is how Senf described the incident in his own words:

> We took the prisoners to the Battalion Battle Headquarters ... because on the way to Company Battle Headquarters we had in any case to pass Battalion Battle Headquarters.... Just a little way in front of the Battalion Battle HQ, Hauptsturmführer Mohnke, Company Commander of Five Company, who had just taken over the command of the Battalion, came up to us and reprimanded SS-Untersturmführer Heinrich *in our presence* because he had, contrary to orders, brought in prisoners. His words were '. . . What do you mean by bringing in prisoners, contrary to orders. . . .'

This was almost certainly the same moment which one of the British survivors, Richard Parry, described in an affidavit – the moment when a German officer who looked like a Prussian and seemed a 'big noise' was 'raving blue murder' and giving orders to his subordinates about the prisoners. More recently Parry was to say that one of the prisoners standing near him, who could speak a little German, exclaimed at this point: 'My God! They're taking no prisoners.'

After half an hour or so Heinrichs returned with the men from Eight Company – the execution squad. Senf continued:

123

That was late in the afternoon, around six o'clock. It was raining and misty. Heinrichs ordered us to bring back the prisoners with the other men. When I asked, Where? he said that the men – that is the other ten men, who were all Rottenführer or Sturmmänner – 'Knew what to do'. I then asked the men where we were going, and was told that they had orders from Mohnke to shoot the prisoners. . . . The men who had joined us told us that they would do it alright. I told Heinrichs before he left us that this was not in my line and that I could not agree with it in my heart. Heinrichs replied that we had just heard ourselves how Mohnke had shouted at him.

Once in the barn, Senf went on, the prisoners 'must have got an inkling of what was going to happen to them.' Fortunately, he himself had to go off and tend to the wounded Rüger. Senf continued:

I was glad that I could escape the horrible deed which was to follow then . . . I now had a reason for going to the Company and reporting Rüger's wounding. I reported to the Company Commander, Baum, that some prisoners were going to be shot on the orders of the Commanding Officer, Mohnke.
   In my heart, I disapproved of this horrible deed from the beginning. . . . My other comrades [from No 7 Company] also thought as I did. Had we thought differently it would have been easier to carry out this crime there and then.

To sum up, according to Senf's testimony the killing of the British prisoners was a cold-blooded and pre-meditated crime which was quite clearly *not* a result of the wounding of Rüger or the escape of British prisoners but on the contrary had been set in motion some time *before* the wounding of Rüger on the orders of the Commanding Officer. Though Senf echoes other SS witnesses in supposing that Rüger had been shot 'apparently by a British soldier who must still have had a pistol on him' – a most unlikely contingency – in his version of events the wounding of Rüger is plainly a *consequence* of the Leibstandarte's intent to kill their prisoners, not a *cause* of it, irrespective of from where the two shots that wounded him came.
   In other words, the wounding of Rüger is irrelevant to the case, for the British prisoners were going to be killed whatever happened to him. That being so, the German alibi falls to the ground and we are left with a situation in which a large proportion of the SS men who made statements to the LDC acknowledged that 'many' or 'all' or 'up to fifty' or 'a force of seventy' British prisoners had been killed at Wormhoudt – but without any

viable or acceptable explanation in mitigation. Given this scenario, it is no longer important who shot Rüger.

Though Senf still appears to have believed that a British prisoner must have taken a pot at his comrade from No 7 Company – presumably, and improbably, from among the tight press of men packed like sardines inside the walls of the barn – his testimony on this score tends to invalidate his own conclusion. According to him, the prisoners had been searched immediately after capture. 'We made a cursory search of the prisoners,' he told his interrogator. 'Some had previously thrown their weapons away. Weapons belonging to the rest were thrown by us into a heap.' Senf also confirmed that Rüger was shot by a 6.35mm calibre pistol. 'As we were equipped with 8mm rifles,' he went on, 'I could only assume that the shot was fired from a British revolver.' But Senf was unaware that almost immediately after Rüger had been shot with a pistol, Captain Lynn-Allen and Bert Evans were also shot with a pistol – a pistol fired by one of the German guards. So no matter how much the British prisoners might like to have hit back at Rüger and his friends, it is most unlikely they ever had the opportunity of doing so – especially as at least one hand grenade had exploded amongst them by the time Rüger was hit. In any case, we have the evidence of one British survivor, Private Robert Wildsmith, of the Royal Warwicks, who confirmed that a German guard was indeed wounded at the barn. Wildsmith's evidence differs somewhat from Senf's, however – according to him, Rüger was wounded by his own SS comrades while he was himself shooting at the prisoners through a gap at the back of the barn. If this is correct, Rüger was not wounded until the massacre was very nearly complete; in which case his pal, Senf, would have been present throughout the entire period of the atrocity, and very probably taken part in it himself.

A few more points need to be made about Senf's testimony. Firstly, even if Senf's sentiments of contrition are genuine and sincere – he twice speaks of 'this horrible deed' and of his disapproval of it – and even if he never pulled the trigger of his gun at the barn, and there is no evidence that he and his comrades of No 7 Platoon did not, it is most unlikely he was not a witness of part or all of the atrocity, in spite of his statement that following Rüger's wounding he did not know any details of what happened to the prisoners. The killing had already started – with the tossing of the first hand grenade into the press of prisoners – when Evans and Lynn-Allen made their break for freedom. If this was when Rüger was shot, the killing would have gone on while Senf tended the wounded man. By the time he had gone to fetch an ambulance and come back with it – a fairly lengthy business because the field track was too wet for the vehicle to drive all the way to the barn – the massacre would have been completed. At least ten bodies would have been plain to see on either side of the barn – the bodies of the two batches of prisoners shot by firing squad. The groans of the wounded would have been clear to hear. The most cursory inspection round the outside of the barn would have revealed Richard Parry lying unconscious with his feet stuck through the wall of the barn and a bloody gunshot wound in his face. And a peep inside the open end of the barn would have revealed the entire horror in all its ghastliness. Senf may not have taken part in the crime but as one of the escort from No 7 Company he was undoubtedly a partial witness to it. This perhaps gives an even greater authority to his testimony, for Senf was the only one of the SS men who had been present at the barn to make a relatively accurate and coherent statement to the WCIU.

Secondly, though Senf went to some pains to promote his own innocence and humanity, he did not shrink from naming others. On the verge of death, the life-long binding force of the SS oath did not have quite the same compulsion as it did for his healthier comrades. The first casualty was his Company Commander, Otto Baum. In spite of ten interrogations at the LDC, some of them quite tough ones, Baum stoutly maintained, as he maintains today, that he never heard of any British prisoners being shot at Wormhoudt. Not so, says Senf. After taking Rüger from the barn to the first-aid post in the ambulance, Senf states:

> I now had a reason for going to the Company and reporting Rüger's wounding. I reported to the Company Commander, Baum, that some prisoners were going to be shot on the orders of the Commanding Officer, Mohnke, and that Rüger had been wounded during the shooting . . . Baum at this time was still at the old Company Battle Headquarters. He accepted this report without asking further questions. Whether he knew of Mohnke's order to have the prisoners shot was not discernible in his behaviour. As, however, SS-Untersturmführer Heinrichs had already previously returned to the Company, I must assume that Heinrichs had told Baum of Mohnke's order.

If this is so, then Otto Baum was not ignorant of the massacre of British prisoners of war at Wormhoudt, as he has always claimed to be. On the other hand, he was clearly not involved in it either. The standard procedure for the disposal of prisoners was shipment from Platoon to Company to Battalion to Regiment. But at Wormhoudt the Company was by-passed and the Regiment was never reached. When Heinrichs set off with the prisoners captured by his Platoon, he was aiming initially for his Company. But to reach No 7 Company Battle Headquarters, where his Company Commander, Otto Baum, was stationed at the crucial period, Heinrichs had to pass Battalion Battle Headquarters, and it was here that Mohnke fatefully intervened in the prisoners' progress. Thus the prisoners never reached Baum's Company HQ and he had no say in their final disposition.

126

By the time he heard about their fate, it would have been too late for him to have done anything about it – not that there was anything much he could have done anyway to countermand or defy the order of a superior officer in the Waffen-SS.

So if Baum was not responsible for the massacre, who was? Not Untersturmführer Heinrichs, the original commander of the prisoner escort, for he left the prisoners at Battalion Battle HQ to return to his Company and had no more to do with them. In any case he is not here to answer further questions, for he perished later on the Russian Front, along with other members of the escort from his Platoon, Dorth and Linkenheil. 'I buried him myself,' Senf told his interrogator. The commander of the execution squad at the barn was Scharführer Drescher, who would have been the man who actually gave the order to open fire. But an NCO like Drescher (who is also thought to have perished on the Russian Front) would ever have presumed to have taken a larger number of enemy prisoners of war to a lonely spot and liquidated them on his own initiative. He was only carrying out orders. But whose?

––––––

We have already seen a considerable amount of testimony from German detainees – some of it eye-witness evidence, some of it hearsay, but much of it so consistent and so persistent that it amounts to all intents and purposes to circumstantial evidence – to the effect that it was Hauptsturmführer Wilhelm Mohnke, the new Commanding Officer of the 2nd Battalion of the SS-Leibstandarte Adolf Hitler Regiment, who gave the order for the prisoners to be shot. But did this order originate with Mohnke or was he, too, obeying orders, and if so – whose?

Apart from Mohnke, there were only three other officers who could have issued such an order. One was the Regimental Commander, SS-Obergruppenführer Sepp Dietrich. It has to be said that there is no evidence of any kind that any such order was given by Dietrich. There is no evidence in his testimony to the War Crimes Interrogation Unit in 1946. There is no evidence in the written orders he issued to his Regiment on the eve of the attack on Wormhoudt. There is no evidence – not even a whisper or a rumour – that he gave any oral orders that prisoners were not to be taken at Wormhoudt. And it is unlikely that he came up with such an order after the attack had started, for as we know he was forced to spend most of the day pinned down in a roadside ditch by withering British fire, and had no opportunity to issue any further orders of any kind until he was rescued late in the afternoon – by which time the prisoners were already dead. It is also worth noting that another of the Leibstandarte battalions under

Dietrich's command, the 1st Battalion, which was also in the thick of the action on 28 May, was in no way involved in any wrongdoings against prisoners, though many were taken.

'There was a general order that prisoners were to be handed over to regiment, division or corps,' Dietrich told his interrogators. 'At this time I gave no further orders regarding the prisoners, and above all not to shoot any of them [sic]. Whether another officer gave such an order, I do not know . . . It is clear to me, however, that the Commander is responsible for the actions and conduct of his regiment.' Doubtless it could be construed that as the captain of the ship Dietrich could be indicted for the ship's misdoings, whether he knew about them or not, or exercised any influence over them or not. But for present purposes the matter is academic, for Dietrich has been dead for many years, and since he does not appear to have issued any original order for prisoners to be shot, we are still left with the question – who did?

A second alternative is Sturmbannführer Wilhelm Trabandt, who took over command of the Leibstandarte Regiment when Dietrich went missing. But Trabant's name does not feature in any testimony, not even in the faintest whisper of SS gossip or innuendo. A more serious contender – and the only other alternative to Mohnke as the officer responsible for the prisoner order – is the original commander of the 2nd Leibstandarte Battalion, Sturmbannführer Ernst Schützeck. Schützeck was in command of the 2nd Leibstandarte from the start of the attack early on the morning of 28 May 1940 until approximately 1600 hours in the afternoon, when he was severely wounded in the head and removed from the scene for urgent medical attention, to be replaced by Mohnke. Schützeck was therefore on the field of battle for ten hours or more – time enough to issue an order to the battalion for prisoners to be shot, which he was presumably in a position to do, in view of the indisposition of his Regimental Commander, Sepp Dietrich, for most of that time.

As we have seen, some of the SS men interrogated by the WCIU were in no doubt that such an order had been issued. Thus Wachowiak mentioned the existence of 'an order of the Battalion Commander to the effect that no prisoners were to be taken in the battle for Wormhoudt'; while Rofallski says that 'fifty prisoners were said to have been shot by order of the Battalion Commander.' However, there seems to have been some genuine uncertainty as to which Battalion Commander was meant. As Kummert remarked: 'The then Adjutant, Obersturmführer Beutler, told me that the Commander – I can no longer recall whether it was Sturmbannführer Schützeck or already Hauptsturmführer Mohnke – had told him in answer to his question as to what was to be done with the prisoners, that they were to be shot.'

Even Mohnke himself is unable to clarify the matter. When he angrily

128

rebuked the commander of the prisoner escort, Heinrichs, at Battalion Battle HQ, the words he used were: 'What do you mean by bringing in prisoners, contrary to orders?' It is not plain from this whether he meant standing orders, or at any rate orders already known to be in existence – and therefore promulgated in the Battalion by the then Battalion Commander, Schützeck – or orders which had been recently issued to cope with a newly arisen situation, namely the large number of prisoners that had been taken in the decisive stage of the battle – orders that would have emanated from himself, Wilhelm Mohnke, the new commander of the 2nd Leibstandarte. Oskar Senf, who overheard Mohnke's remark, told his interrogators at LDC: 'I myself knew nothing about such an order, which I suppose must have been issued by the previous Battalion Commander, Schützeck. Nor do I know if Heinrichs was acquainted with such an order.'

There are a number of reasons why it is unlikely that it was Schützeck who originated the order for the shooting of prisoners. In the first place, if it was he who issued the order, he did not do a very good job of disseminating it. Untersturmführer Heinrichs, for example, whose platoon captured many of the prisoners, does not seem to have heard of such an order, because instead of shooting prisoners he spent a lot of time marching them around the place, trying to find out what to do with them. From this it could also be deduced that his Company Commander, Otto Baum, was likewise ignorant of such an order, otherwise he would presumably have acquainted his platoon commanders, including Heinrichs, with its contents. If an order had been given by Schützeck at the outset of the attack that no prisoners were to be taken in the battle for Wormhoudt, it would be reasonable to expect the order to have been carried out. As it happened, the course of the battle was such that the question of prisoners did not arise to any significant extent until late in the day, the first sizeable batches of British prisoners being taken round about the time Schützeck was wounded and Mohnke took over the Battalion.

However, it could be argued that the few prisoners captured earlier in the conflict were indeed given short shrift, as Gunner Arthur Baxter's story of his encounter with an SS platoon on the south-west perimeter of Wormhoudt vividly demonstrates. Baxter and his comrades of the Worcestershire Yeomanry, it will be recalled, were stripped to the waist and had their dog tags torn from their necks by their captors. They were then beaten and knocked to the ground. Two British trucks then roared up and were stopped. The occupants of the first truck were gunned down in the act of surrender and the truck set on fire and the bodies incinerated. One of the soldiers in the second truck was shot and robbed and the rest were hauled out and stripped and made to join the other prisoners. Baxter was convinced that they were going to be executed, and made a break for it and escaped. His comrades, however, were killed and now lie buried in Wormhoudt Cemetery.

129

But there is a significant difference between the killings which Arthur Baxter saw with his own eyes and the massacre which was perpetrated at the barn. The killings which Baxter saw were carried out on the spot and were soon over; they could thus be loosely described as battlefield killings carried out in hot blood – a no less reprehensible but slightly more comprehensible category of slaughter in the ghastly codex of prisoner-of-war murder. By contrast, the barn massacre was not a spontaneous act of violence triggered off in the volatile heat of combat emotion, but a cold, calculated, systematic brand of mass murder, in which a considerable lapse of time and a lot of to-ing and fro-ing took place between the prisoners' capture and their slaughter. The fact remains that the great mass of killings of unarmed prisoners took place *after* Mohnke had assumed command of the battalion, not before – and in the relatively narrow band of time, moreover, between the disappearance of Schützeck and the reappearance of Dietrich, when control of the Leibstandarte's actions in Wormhoudt was in his hands alone.

One other thing needs to be said here. Ernst Schützeck miraculously survived his wounds and lived to fight another day. After the Allied landings in Normandy he was back in combat on the Western Front again and he died in combat there in November 1944. At no time before or after Wormhoudt was there any suggestion that this officer conducted himself in battle other than within the rules of warfare laid down by the Geneva Convention. The same could not be said of Wilhelm Mohnke. As will become apparent during the course of this book, Wormhoudt was not the only prisoner-of-war massacre with which Mohnke's name was to be associated. Not only in the campaign in northern France in 1940, but in Normandy in the summer of 1944 and in the Ardennes in the winter of the same year, Allied prisoners were shot in large numbers (and small) whenever this particular SS officer appeared on the scene. The massacre of an unarmed and defenceless enemy was as much this man's trade mark – his 'fingerprint' – as the individual style of wiring in a delayed-action explosive is a particular terrorist bomber's.

Hugo Waetzman, a Leibstandarte man who was at Wormhoudt on 28 May but took no part in the massacre (and is alive and well in Germany today), told his interrogator from the London District Cage that a rumour had gone round his company that 'on the order of 2nd Battalion Commander Mohnke some British soldiers had been shot as a reprisal.' On the grounds of all available evidence, including eye-witness testimony and circumstantial evidence, together with a consideration of such factors as opportunity, method and even motive, there is every ground for believing that this is in fact the case and that it was indeed Wilhelm Mohnke who gave the order for the liquidation of the British prisoners at Wormhoudt. Even if it could be proved beyond all reasonable doubt that it was Schützeck who had given the original order after all, Mohnke is not exonerated, for as the new Battalion Commander the power to countermand such an order – which would clearly have been a criminal order in flagrant violation of Article 23 (c) of the Geneva Convention – lay within his discretion. If such an order had been given by Schützeck, then it was clearly Mohnke who opted to enforce it – and in the most cynical and cold-bloodedly brutal way possible. At the time of day on 28 May 1940 when this ghastly atrocity was perpetrated, the only man in the 2nd Battalion of the Leibstandarte Adolf Hitler who was empowered to send the British prisoners to their fate in the barn was Mohnke; and the only man empowered to detail the Signals Section of No 8 Company to implement that fate and carry out the executions was Mohnke, for the Signals Section was attached to Battalion Headquarters for special duties that day, and ultimately answerable to the Battalion Commander alone – and the Battalion Commander at that time was Mohnke.

Whether Mohnke simply reaffirmed Schützeck's original order or issued a new order of his own amounts to the same thing – the order to shoot the prisoners came from the mind and mouth of Hauptsturmführer Wilhelm Mohnke and no one else. So with hindsight it could perhaps be said that when the Royal Warwicks in their own defence fired that fateful anti-tank missile at Schützeck's car in Wormhoudt square, *they shot the wrong man!* Had Schützeck not been wounded, Mohnke would not have become CO, and many British soldiers might have been maintained in security and health under the laws of the Geneva Convention until the end of the war – not killed like cattle in squalor and in anguish in a run-down milking shed.

———

We have seen that a major war crime – the murder of between eighty and ninety British prisoners of war – was committed by German troops of the 2nd Battalion of the SS-Leibstandarte Adolf Hitler at Wormhoudt on 28 May 1940. We have seen that the crime was not committed in the heat of battle or in self-defence or to prevent a mass escape, but as a consequence of a direct and criminal order to shoot the prisoners. We have seen that beyond all reasonable doubt that order was given by Hauptsturmführer Wilhelm Mohnke, the Commanding Officer of the Battalion at the time. We must now consider one final question: why was that order given?

One convenient explanation has to be dismissed out of hand at the outset. In a recent account of the Dunkirk campaign, it was claimed that during the British counter-attack at Arras on 21 May 1940 some 400 German prisoners of war from the SS Totenkopf Division were slaughtered by the Durham Light Infantry to whom they had surrendered.* It was further claimed that it was to avenge this alleged atrocity by British troops (and the alleged use of outlawed dum-dum bullets by the Norfolks, a completely spurious charge) that British prisoners of war from the Norfolks were in turn murdered by soldiers of the SS Totenkopf at Le Paradis a week later, and by soldiers of the Totenkopf's sister regiment, the SS-Leibstandarte, at Wormhoudt on the day after that. This claim was unfounded. In 1981 an investigation was carried out which resulted in statements being made by the officers and men of the Durham Light Infantry who either had control of the Totenkopf prisoners or came directly in contact with them. These statements showed that the Germans had been escorted back to 151 Infantry Brigade rear headquarters and from there to the headquarters of the 50th Northumbrian Division and thence to Dunkirk. Official casualty figures also show that only two Totenkopf personnel were found to be missing after the battle. Furthermore, no reference was ever made to the alleged massacre by the German propaganda machine, for whom the incident would have made spectacular copy, at any time during the war; nor was it used as a defence plea when Fritz Knoechlein was tried for the Le Paradis massacre.

It is possible that the Totenkopf do have a bearing on the Wormhoudt case, however, and that some connection may exist between the massacre of British prisoners by the SS at Le Paradis on 27 May and the almost copycat massacre of British prisoners by the SS at Wormhoudt on 28 May. This is what Colonel Scotland felt, too.

> 'There was good reason for assuming,' he wrote, 'that the SS Totenkopf murders of the Royal Norfolk prisoners at Paradis on the previous day had been the subject of chit-chat which went over the air from the Totenkopf signals branch to the signals of the Leibstandarte, their sister unit, at Wormhoudt. There was little doubt in my mind not only that Mohnke knew what had happened at Paradis, but was himself not averse to the elimination of prisoners.'

Against this, it has to be said that the Totenkopf and the Leibstandarte were in different Corps and different chains of command and that communication between them would not be an everyday matter in the normal course of events.

The massacre at Le Paradis was not the reason for the Wormhoudt

---

* This claim was made by Nicholas Harman in his book *Dunkirk – The Necessary Myth* (1980).

killings, however – it merely established a precedent, sowed the germ of an idea. The real underlying cause of the Wormhoudt massacre, as of the parallel one at Le Paradis, was undoubtedly the anger felt by the men who took part in the attack at the casualties inflicted on so many of their comrades by a stubborn, brave and professional enemy. Until this point the German campaign in Flanders and northern France had been a relatively painless pursuit of an apparently compliant and toothless enemy for the SS units involved. Indeed, though many of the Leibstandarte troops had taken part in the fighting in Poland the previous September, several Leibstandarte men interrogated at the London Cage admitted that the battle for Wormhoudt was their first real baptism of fire. After days and weeks of chasing the demoralized Dutch and French and low-profile British, the severity of the fire-fight encountered at Wormhoudt would have come as a sharp shock, just as it had at Le Paradis.

The truth of the matter is probably that the men of the Waffen-SS were bad losers. They had been trained to believe that they were invincible, and when they encountered good troops who inflicted heavy casualties on them they did not like it and turned nasty. Both the Royal Warwicks and the Royal Norfolks were ordinary, decent, straight-up-and-down, county yeomen infantry regiments. They were not particularly fashionable or glamorous regiments, but they were imbued with a strong tradition and a staunch *esprit de corps*. Moreover, the Germans encountered the *regular* battalions of these regiments, which were composed of long-term volunteers who boasted the high standards of weapon-training and marksmanship of the old British regular army.

By contrast, though the Leibstandarte was an élite unit, it had only been in existence for half a dozen years and its long-service volunteers were probably diluted by a number of called-up Allgemeine-SS men; while the Totenkopf had not existed at all until the outbeak of the war and certainly included a large number of conscripts. This is not to say that they did not fight with skill and courage. But from the German point of view the victory at Wormhoudt had been bought at a high price. The battle had presented the Leibstandarte with the sternest test in their history to date, and cost them the heaviest toll of casualties in their experience so far. The 2nd Battalion had lost their Battalion Commander, and as far as they could tell they had lost their Regimental Commander as well. Many of their comrades had been killed and wounded, especially those who had run into the murderous fire of the Cheshires' machine-guns. French civilians in Esquelbecq reported that they had heard one wounded German soldier declare that 'everyone talked of revenge'. It would seem, then, that the Germans reacted badly to their unexpected reverses and that anger and the desire for vengeance were the prevailing emotions of many of the Leibstandarte soldiers.

This could well account for the roughness and even downright brutality displayed by a number of individual SS soldiers while rounding up surrendered British troops. But on its own it would not account for the well master-minded, well orchestrated, systematic and wholesale butchery that eventually took place. It would not account for the licence to kill that turned a respectable German feat of arms into a day of calumny that would for ever sully the reputation – such as it was – of the Leibstandarte Adolf Hitler. The battle anger of the Leibstandarte was an explosive mixture – but without a detonator, a trigger, it could not go off on its own accord. That trigger was Wilhelm Mohnke. It required *his* uniquely volatile, nitro-glycerine brand of temper, *his* innate urge to violence, *his* inherently brutal nature – notorious even by the less-than-tender standards of the Waffen-SS – to unleash the slaughter. To understand why that should be it would be necessary to understand the arrangement of the molecules that made up the chemistry of Mohnke's mind. For it is in that mind that the massacre at Wormhoudt had its dark origins. But that is an unchartered territory into which even the present authors are loath to venture.

———

After Jeff Rooker, MP for Perry Barr, Birmingham, first raised the Wormhoudt affair in the House of Commons in April 1988, Mohnke told a West German newspaperman: 'I had nothing to do with the massacre. I wouldn't be able to do such a thing. I was only a soldier doing my job. I couldn't kill unarmed people.' In the *Washington Times* he was reported as having, in characteristic fashion, 'exploded in indignation' when asked by a Hamburg reporter whether he had been involved in the killing of British troops. 'I've never concealed a thing,' Mohnke said, 'unlike Waldheim. I was in Dunkirk. It's true. But what kind of beasts must they have been to slaughter prisoners of war with bayonets and so on? This is an appalling crime.'

With that statement the British Government was in complete agreement. But the implementation of justice was now in West German hands. Many years had passed since the British war crimes investigators had first grappled with the Wormhoudt case in the early post-war period. Many of the dramatis personae had disappeared or died. But one man who was not on the scene in those days had reappeared and was available to answer questions now. That man was Wilhelm Mohnke. 'The obvious conclusion,' a former member of the War Crimes Interrogation Unit, Richard Richter, wrote to Jeff Rooker recently, 'is that there is more than sufficient evidence to bring Mohnke to trial in the very near future.' And the successful prosecuting counsel at the Le Paradis trial, Tom Field-Fisher,

QC, told *The Times* in June 1988: 'If there are still survivors, there is no conceivable reason why the man should not be prosecuted.'

The British Government seemed of like mind. 'The Wormhoudt massacre was a sordid, brutal and dishonourable event in a bloody war,' Mr Roger Freeman, the Under-Secretary of State for the Armed Forces, told the House of Commons on 28 June 1988, 'and the British Government will do their part to facilitate justice.'

PART IV

—

Between East and West

1940–1944

After the successful conclusion of the Blitzkrieg in the West in June 1940, the Leibstandarte was ordered to Metz for refitting and further training. Hitler was well satisfied with the battle prowess of the regiment that bore his name, and to mark his appreciation of its feats of arms he awarded the Knight's Cross to its commander, Sepp Dietrich, and ordered the regiment to be enlarged to brigade strength, declaring: 'What my fate is, oh my men of the Leibstandarte, I do not know. But one thing I *do* know is that you will be at the forefront of every endeavour. It will be an honour for you, who bear my name, to lead every German attack.'

For a short while Mohnke and his comrades of the LAH were caught up in preparations for Hitler's seaborne invasion of England, and spent days cocooned in life-jackets, poring over maps of the Home Counties and assaulting the vine-clad banks of the Moselle in small boats by way of practice in amphibious landings. But this half-hearted scheme was soon shelved, and in March 1941 the Leibstandarte was turned about and sent off in the opposite direction, eastward to the Balkans, where Hitler envisaged a more feasible invasion of an altogether less daunting chunk of the continent of Europe – Yugoslavia and Greece.

Leaving Metz in twenty-eight transport trains, the LAH and all their guns and trucks and martial paraphernalia were shunted across the breadth of Europe, across Southern Germany, Czechoslovakia and Romania, to the staging post in Bulgaria from which they would be let loose on the craggy mass of the Balkan peninsula to the south. Sturmbannführer Wilhelm Mohnke was commanding the 2nd Battalion of the LAH at the start of this campaign, just as he had done at Wormhoudt, and a member of his command vividly recalled Mohnke's march to the Bulgarian capital that fatal springtime – a stepping stone on the road to Greece and the Aegean isles:

It was a warm spring evening in March 1941 as the march

139

column of the 2nd Battalion LAH finally snaked out of the tortuous Balkan mountain road onto the big overland road from Burgas to Sofia.

The first elements of the Regiment's march column had already reached Sofia and had halted in order to close ranks with the rest of the unit for its scheduled march through the Bulgarian capital. We stood by the vehicles, stamping our feet, beating the dust from our driving coats, and smoking cigarettes. Then a motorcycle messenger stopped at the jeep of our commander, Sturmbannführer Mohnke, and handed him an order from the Regiment. No march into Sofia was now planned. In order to preserve the semblance of neutrality, Czar Boris wanted no German troops to appear in the capital. The Regiment was to march through the southern and western suburbs and find billets north of Sofia.

The column drove on. It was already twilight as we drove into the city. The streets were filled with people in a festive mood, and they waved enthusiastically at us. It occurred to us that all the boys and girls were wearing matching blue clothes (school uniforms, we later learned). Cigarettes, flowers and chocolates were handed to us from all sides. Again and again we heard chants from the crowd: 'Give our greetings to Soviet Russia and the White Sea.'*

The 'White Sea' meant the Aegean, the thousand-year-old dream of a great Bulgarian empire. We were to reach its shores in the coming campaign. It was night when we reached our billeting area, the village of Mramor. A typical Bulgarian town with individual farm buildings, clay-covered houses with wooden porches, and thick fences around the yards. Quarters were prepared for the Commander, Sturmbannführer Mohnke, in the priest's house. The battalion staff headquarters were set up in the school house.

In the impending attack across the Yugoslav border, Mohnke was to lead a battle group – Kampfgruppe Mohnke – consisting of his 2nd Battalion reinforced as an advance guard with the addition of a number of other fire units. The 'Enemy Information Sheet' attached to the Leibstandarte's Attack Orders issued on the eve of the invasion of 5 April 1941 laid special stress on danger from the air:

---

* The Bulgarians were traditional allies and blood-brothers of the Russians. Since the Russian–German Pact was still in force at the time of the LAH's march through Bulgaria, the Germans were automatically greeted as friends of friends.

The Yugoslavian air force is of considerable strength. It hardly seems possible that it can be destroyed in the first few days. They are flying German, Yugoslavian and Russian models. Low-level attacks can be expected in the mountainous terrain with so many valleys.

On the morning of 6 April the German forces began to roll over the Yugoslav frontier. The main body of the LAH did not move at once, however, but stayed in position, waiting for the order to move out in the direction of Kratova later in the day. But in accordance with orders received from Sepp Dietrich, Mohnke's Kampfgruppe did move forward to reconnoitre the forward area, and it was at this point that Mohnke himself was forced to part company from his Regiment, and very nearly from this world, as the result of a Yugoslav air strike which hit the LAH before it had even crossed the frontier. Mohnke was dreadfully wounded in the foot in this attack and lay in intense pain, bleeding profusely, his shattered foot a hopeless, mangled mess. When Mohnke eventually was brought to the medical aid post, the army doctors decided the only course was to amputate the leg, but Mohnke, who was still conscious, had other ideas. Drawing his pistol, he gasped his last order of the Balkan war: '*Das Bein bleibt dran*. That leg stays where it is.' So the medics, powerless to resist either the order or the pistol, had to content themselves with sawing off the foot alone.

For Mohnke at the age of thirty the fighting war seemed over. While his comrades in the Leibstandarte marched away to dusty death in ever more distant battlefields at the furthest fringes of the European continent, first in Greece, then in Russia, the amputee SS major was shipped back as a stretcher case to Germany, where long months of painful hospitalization and rehabilitation lay before him. It was probably as a result of the heavy morphine doses which were administered to him by German army doctors in order to ease the extreme pain caused by his wound that Mohnke gradually became a morphine addict, a condition of narcotic dependency which was to last for the best part of the rest of the war.

Men of a frailer constitution and less determined resolve might have called it a day at this point and turned their back on active service in a combat unit. But Mohnke was made of sterner stuff. Whatever else it might do, the Waffen-SS looked after its own people well. The Führer, too, showed solicitous concern for those who, like Mohnke, had served him personally. So in spite of his physical handicap, Mohnke was kept on in the Leibstandarte 'Adolf Hitler'. He recovered his health and grew adept in getting about on an artificial foot. In February 1942 he returned to full-time duty as CO of the LAH Panzer Abteilung (Tank Unit), and on 20 March 1942 was transferred to the command of the LAH Ersatz

(Replacement) Battalion, a training unit based at the Lichterfelde Barracks in Berlin.

But it was a long way from the fighting front and from the slaughter in which his old Leibstandarte was now engaged as it drove deeper and deeper into the vast and endless spaces of the Russian steppes. For the best part of two years, as his comrades fought and died in the purgatory of the Eastern Front, Wilhelm Mohnke had to cool his heels (one of flesh and blood, one of wood) in the backwater of a home posting. And month after month the British and American bomber raids on the cities of Germany grew more frequent and more devastating, and the news from the Eastern Front more ominous and grave. Mohnke was in Berlin when the announcement of the shattering defeat of the German armies at Stalingrad plunged the German nation into mourning and turned the whole tide of the war. It was in Berlin, too, that intimations of the nature of the fighting in the East reached him by word of mouth from comrades who returned from that vast hell for convalescence or home leave.

It did not make pretty hearing. So intense was the enmity and hatred between the Nazi SS and Bolshevik Red Army, so ferocious the fighting, so primeval and dehumanized the moral conduct of both sides, that every rule of war was abandoned and every human life there held for nought. Mohnke learned that it had become the German practice to shoot their wounded rather than allow them to fall into Russian hands, and to shoot most if not all the Russian prisoners who fell into German hands. From the earliest days of the conflict the killing of prisoners of war was so widespread as to be the norm on both sides. An LAH company commander wrote in August 1941: 'I have never seen such disgusting scenes, whole groups of men from all units have been murdered by the Soviets upon their surrender . . . It will not last for long.' In April 1942 the LAH Division shot every Russian prisoner taken over a three-day period, a total of some 4,000 men, in retaliation for the torture and murder of six LAH men by the Russians. At the Nuremberg Trials the Russians were to allege that the Leibstandarte and Totenkopf Divisions between them had been 'responsible for the extermination of more than 20,000 peaceful citizens of Kharkov and for the shooting and burning alive of prisoners of war.' A propaganda pamphlet issued to SS combat troops in Russia sought to persuade them that they were locked in a life-and-death struggle between two races. Portraying the enemy Slav as a sub-human gorilla, the Nazi propagandist wrote: 'This creature is actuated by a ghastly chaos of savage, unrestrained passions – limitless destructiveness, primitive lust and shameless vulgarity.' The irony of this diatribe evidently escaped the propagandist, for the creature he had so vividly described now bore more than a passing resemblance to the evolved SS warrior of his own side on the Eastern Front.

As the Germans began their long, slow, weary fighting withdrawal from

142

Stalingrad and the high-tide line of the eastern advance, the Anglo-Americans began their build-up for the long-awaited invasion of France, the Second Front that would liberate Europe for ever from Nazi tyranny. It was in this atmosphere of invasion fever that Wilhelm Mohnke was returned to active combat command. Promoted to the rank of SS-Obersturmbannführer, Mohnke was posted on 15 September 1943 to a newly created SS division of fanatical teenagers called the 12th SS Panzer Grenadier Division 'Hitler Jugend', a sister division of Mohnke's own Leibstandarte. Thus it was that the brutal lessons of the fighting in the East, the ultimate in *Härte*, were imparted to the young bloods who were to confront the Allied invaders on the beaches of Normandy in the coming year.

PART V

—

The Murder Division
NORMANDY JUNE 1944

Where there was evidence of more than one war crime by the members of a unit, while under the command of a single commander, the Court might receive such evidence as prima-facie evidence of the responsibility of the commander for such crimes.

Lt-Col. Bruce Macdonald, OBE, QC

In war it becomes very easy to kill someone. It takes hard discipline to overcome that urge.

Wilhelm Mohnke (1988)

INVASION

Strange reports had been coming through from all over the Normandy coast during the early hours of 6 June 1944. The reports were incomplete, contradictory, confused, even nonsensical – but they all contributed to a growing impression at various German headquarters in the immediate locality and in the rear that something was, as they say, 'up'. But what? Enemy parachutists reported to have landed amid the tangle of fields and hedgerows in the *bocage* farmland behind the coastal defences turned out to be straw dummies with firecrackers attached to their legs. From somewhere out in the dark, tumultuous English Channel ships' engines could be heard, but nothing could be seen, and precious little registered on the German radar, much of which had been put out of action by Allied bombers only days before. In the black, squally, cloud-wracked sky there was the constant growling of aircraft droning unopposed this way and that, but the why and the wherefore of it all quite escaped the German defences, who could only perceive that the Allies were exceptionally busy that night, but were unable to fathom the cause.

All through the spring and early summer the German forces in the West had stood bracing themselves against the expected Allied invasion of Europe – the Second Front that would bring about the liberation of Europe from Nazi rule. But the Channel weather for the last week had been so foul, and the German forecast for June 6 so gloomy, that one thing German Intelligence and the High Command felt they could be sure of – there would be no invasion of France that weekend. So confident did they feel about this that many senior commanders had left their posts to attend more pressing or diverting appointments elsewhere. Even Field Marshal Rommel had gone away, partly to visit his family in Bavaria, but mainly to try and persuade Hitler to part with a few more reinforcements for the West. So the odd happenings up and down the Calvados coast of Normandy were put down to enemy fun and games – pinpricks, intelligence probes, diversionary feints. After all, everyone knew that once the invasion came it would come by the shortest route – across the Channel from Dover to Calais.

But the strange reports persisted, and grew more frequent, and more widespread, and more ominous. A second drop of parachutists turned out not to be dummies but the real thing firing real weapons behind the German lines. At first light news came that ships' guns had opened up in a prolonged barrage against the German coastal defences and that enemy aircraft had flown up and down the beaches laying a pin-point carpet of bombs on to the German bunkers and gun emplacements and their shattered inhabitants. The German field telephones grew ever more clamorous and urgent. Enemy troops were coming ashore. The German coastal crust was being overrun. Something was happening – and it looked like an invasion. But was it?

Convinced that the Normandy assault was only a diversion, the German High Command hesitated to release the Panzer strategic reserves that could decide the issue on the beaches. Among these reserves was a new, youthful, élite formation called the 12th SS Panzer Division (Hitler Jugend), which at that moment was held on its leashes in a state of alert at Evreux, just west of the Seine. This Hitler Jugend Division boasted 20,500 zealous but non-battle-hardened troops, 177 tanks, 52 artillery pieces and 1,600 machine-guns. It was a formidable fighting force and it was raring to go. Already the order had been given for the Division to move forward with the aim of counter-attacking the invasion forces early the following morning. Meanwhile, a company of its Reconnaissance Battalion was ordered to probe forward immediately towards the beaches with the task of finding out what was really happening and report back.

Daylight found the armoured cars and motor bikes of the reconnaissance company in Caen, a town already aroused by the sounds of battle, and choked with a throng of German troops and vehicles and a milling confusion of bewildered French civilians. In Bayeux the confusion was even more intense, and there was more than a whiff of panic in the air, for British and American fighter-bombers were up and about in force, swooping on all targets of opportunity, making all movement on the ground a slow and hazardous nightmare.

Drawn by the distant roar of artillery fire, the armoured cars now headed directly towards the sea, picking their way gingerly forward under such cover as could be offered by the stone walls and hedgerows along the road. Then, breasting a gentle slope halfway between Bayeux and the Channel coast, they were suddenly confronted with an unbelievable view – a glimpse of a cross-section of history, no less. Before their incredulous eyes they saw the sea crowded with hundreds upon hundreds of enemy warships stretching beyond the horizon, and great battleships pumping their salvoes at

149

unseen targets on the land, and landing craft packed with infantry swarming to shore and unloading wave upon wave of troops. The soldiers wore British-style steel helmets, the reconnaissance company of the Hitler Youth Division noted, and they were advancing inland with amphibious tanks in support. Whatever the intelligence chiefs and High Command might think, the reconnaissance men atop their little hill had no doubt what it was they were looking at.

The reconnaissance commander radioed an urgent message to headquarters:

> Hundreds of enemy ships sighted, protected by barrage balloons. British infantry and heavy equipment coming ashore virtually unopposed. A dozen heavy tanks counted. Coastal defences either out of action or overrun. Enemy infantry in battalion strength moving south towards Bayeux. The city itself, and the road leading into it, under naval bombardment.

What these astonished young SS men were witnessing was one part of the total Allied invasion front – a small section of the 6,483 ships that made up the greatest armada the world had ever seen, a few formations of the mighty Allied Expeditionary Force that would land 150,000 men on the soil of France before the day was done. As it happened, the men they had watched jump from the landing craft and advance into the dunes were members of the Second British army, made up of the 50th Northumbrian, 3rd British and 3rd Canadian Divisions. Though they did not know it then, the Hitler Jugend men were watching the arrival of their nemesis upon the field of battle. For it was against the 3rd Canadian Division, now heading inland in the direction of Bayeux and Caen, that the Hitler Jugend Division would itself be locked in fierce, protracted and implacable combat in and around the little Normandy towns and tight and compact countryside in the days of conflict to come. And it would be in the brutal crucible of this savage combat that crimes would be committed against the Canadian invaders that would darken for ever the reputation of the 12th SS Panzers and their commanders. These crimes were inevitable – inherent in the very mind and nature of this latest creation of the Waffen-SS.

In the period of military and national crisis that followed the cataclysmic defeat of the German forces at Stalingrad, the idea was born of raising a new, super-élite division of the Waffen-SS that would harness the youthful enthusiasm and ideological fanaticism of the Hitler Youth movement and

150

go some way towards replacing the vast loss of men now buried deep in the wastes of Russia. The new formation was seen as a 'Guard of the Führer' on a par with the Leibstandarte 'Adolf Hitler' – a Panzer Grenadier (armoured infantry) division consisting of some 20,000 of the fittest, keenest and most deeply indoctrinated young Nazis of the Hitler Youth that could be found among the seventeen-year-olds of the class of 1926 anywhere in the Third Reich. It was hoped that all would be volunteers, young zealots who would dedicate their lives to the defence of Führer and Fatherland. By this stage of the war, however, the dreadful reality of the military struggle was evident even to the Hitler Youth, and in practice many recruits had to be bullied and bribed to join the new division, or simply drafted. This in no way diminished the superlative quality of the human material of which this teenage formation was composed, however. Though Allied propagandists mocked the new division as the 'Baby Division', with a baby's bottle as its symbol, Hitler himself knew better. 'The Hitler Youth Division will fight fanatically,' Hitler promised Himmler in the summer of 1943. 'The enemy will be struck with wonder.' A year later, in Normandy and the Ardennes, the boy warriors who bore his name were to prove their Führer right time and again.

In July 1943 the new formation officially came into being as the 12th SS Panzer Grenadier Division (Hitler Jugend) and intensive training began at the German training centre at Beverloo in Belgium to turn the division's boy recruits into front-line tigers. To build up their strength and fill out their immature frames they were fed special rations and put through an intensive course of physical training. But tobacco, alcohol and girl friends were forbidden and the trainees were given sweets instead. Their method of training eschewed old-fashioned drill and bull and concentrated on battlefield familiarization instead, with an emphasis on close combat and night fighting using live ammunition and explosives. There was an insistence, too, on ideological indoctrination designed to transform the Hitler Youth into a fanatic SS warrior. Gradually the boy soldiers of the Hitler Jugend Division were honed into an organization of immense élan and fighting ability.

Though it was always possible to fill the ranks of the Hitler Jugend Division by simply drafting recruits into it, there were never enough experienced officers and NCOs, due in part to the heavy losses sustained at the front and in part to the rapid expansion of the Waffen-SS overall. The transfer of some 700 officers and men from the Leibstandarte helped make up the shortfall in some measure; it also infused the new division with a distinctively élitist Leibstandarte character, so that the Hitler Jugend Division became not so much a sister formation of the Leibstandarte as a clone of it. Many of the senior offices were old Leibstandarte hands – some of them veterans of the battle at Wormhoudt three years before.

The commander of the 1st SS Panzer Corps of which the new division was part was none other than Sepp Dietrich, the Regimental Commander at Wormhoudt, now an SS-Obergruppenführer. The Commanding Officer of the 12th SS Panzer Grenadiers (Hitler Jugend) was SS-Brigadeführer* Fritz Witt, a large, genial, able soldier of thirty-five, who always led from the front and was held in great esteem by his men and fellow-officers alike. Like Dietrich, Mohnke and several other senior commanders in the division, Witt was one of the original founding members of the Leibstandarte, and for his bravery in the 1940 campaign in Northern France he had won one of Germany's most coveted military awards, the Knight's Cross, supplemented in March 1943 by the Oak Leaves to the Knight's Cross for his leadership as a battalion and regimental commander in the Balkan and Russian campaigns.

The Commanders of the three major elements of his division – the two infantry regiments and the tank regiment – were likewise old Leibstandarte hands. The Commander of the 25th Panzer Grenadier Regiment was the dynamic and charismatic SS-Standartenführer Kurt Meyer, an early recruit to the pre-war Leibstandarte and a legendary war hero among Waffen-SS veterans. Nicknamed 'Panzer Meyer', this thirty-three-year-old Nazi ideologue, who had been a company commander of the 3rd Battalion of the Leibstandarte at the time of the battle of Wormhoudt, was a model of the ruthless and aggressive Waffen-SS officer – brave, belligerent and calculatedly reckless, a natural warrior and leader of men, a skilled and flexible tactician with a flare for the unorthodox. Meyer's dashing exploits in the Balkans and the USSR earned him the Knight's Cross and the Oak Leaves to the Knight's Cross, and later in the fighting in the West he was destined to win the Swords to the Knight's Cross and promotion to the rank of SS-Brigadeführer and Major-General of the Waffen-SS – making him at thirty-three the youngest general in the German armed forces.

The other infantry regiment in the Hitler Jugend Division, the 26th Panzer Grenadiers, was commanded by SS-Obersturmbannführer Wilhelm Mohnke, the controversial SS officer at the centre of the Wormhoudt massacre. The intervening years had done little to mellow Mohnke's dour but turbulent personality, but they had severely scarred him physically. The serious wound he had sustained at the beginning of the Greek campaign had left him not only with a wooden foot and a limp but – so it was said – an addiction to morphine acquired while undergoing medical treatment for this same wound. His drug addiction may not have been the cause of his notorious explosive temper, but it may well have

* The ranks given here are the ranks held at the time of the Normandy invasion in June 1944.

exacerbated it, especially when under battlefield conditions there was difficulty in obtaining the drug to gratify the addiction. Nevertheless, Wilhelm Mohnke was still judged by his superiors to be one of the steadiest senior commanders – one hundred per cent loyal ideologically, staunch and determined in battle, an ideal obdurate iron man of the Waffen-SS. Serving under him as a Battalion Commander in the 26th Panzer Grenadiers was another founding member of the Leibstandarte, thirty-three-year-old Bernhard Siebken, who was destined to pay a heavy price for his Regimental Commander's idiosyncrasies.

SS-Obersturmbannführer Max Wünsche was the third member of the triumvirate of Regimental Commanders serving under Fritz Witt in the Hitler Jugend Division. Twenty-nine years old, handsome, dashing, blue-eyed and blond, the Commander of the division's Tank Regiment was a Nazi propagandist's dream model of a Nordic Nazi knight. A member of the Leibstandarte since 1934, Wünsche had spent the greater part of the battle for Wormhoudt trapped in a ditch with Sepp Dietrich, and later fought with skill and courage as a tank commander in the Balkan and Russian campaigns, in recognition of which he had been awarded the Knight's Cross in February 1943.

Max Wünsche was looked upon as one of the idealists in the Waffen-SS, against whose name no suggestion of war crimes ever seems to have been raised. By contrast, SS-Sturmbannführer Gerhard Bremer, the pugnacious twenty-six-year-old Commander of the new division's Reconnaissance Battalion, was regarded as one of the brawlers. Bremer, too, had been with the Leibstandarte at the time of the Wormhoudt battle, serving as Adjutant to the 3rd Battalion, the same battalion in which Kurt Meyer was then a Company Commander. Like Meyer, Bremer had a reputation as a 'Draufgänger' – a reckless, fearless dare-devil – and was a veteran of all the Leibstandarte's campaigns in east and west and one of the regiment's earliest recipients of the Knight's Cross in 1941. In the battle for Normandy this hard-driving and ruthless soldier was to prove a formidable – and controversial – opponent.

Former Leibstandarte officers such as these, hardened by years of combat in one of the most outstanding fighting units of the German armed forces, gave the 12th SS Panzer Division an inimitable character. This character stemmed not only from the wealth of modern combat experience gained in the East by the Leibstandarte officers and NCOs, but the peculiar nature of that experience. For the war on the Russian Front was no ordinary war. It was the collision of behemoths, a fight to the death on a scale without precedent, fought with a savagery that makes the blood run cold. These two huge gladiatorial armies, tearing each other apart in the vast arena of the Russian steppes, were the ultimate violent expression of two revolutionary and diametrically opposing totalitarian states, both of them police states, death camp societies, controlled by a single, supreme, monolithic, transcendentally wicked despot. In such a conflict between two such armies it would be naïve indeed to have expected a gentlemanly and honourable adherence to the rules and practice of warfare as defined by the Geneva Convention. The Russian Front was no place for gentlemen and there was little room for honour. Both sides took prisoners, millions of prisoners, and treated them barbarically. More importantly, both sides regularly, persistently, and without compunction killed their prisoners, either by offering them no quarter or by massacring them after they had surrendered.

This was an aspect of warfare with which the Leibstandarte had grown familiar in Russia, and which it practised from time to time as a matter of expediency. The philosophy behind this cruel and cynical violation of the codes of warfare and civilized charity was extremely simple and underpinned by an iron logic: we can expect no quarter from them, therefore they can expect no quarter from us – and vice versa. Examples were rife – many of them in connection with the exploits of Kurt Meyer and his unconventional methods of fighting in Russia. A favourite tactical trick of his, it was said, was to take his reconnaissance unit through the Red Army lines and allow himself to be encircled – at the same time keeping an escape route open whenever possible. He would then wipe out a whole village, slaughtering all the men, women and children that could be found in it, on the grounds that it was impossible to bring them back to the German lines as prisoners.

Meyer's philosophy of ruthless, remorseless war, honed and hardened during his time with the Leibstandarte in the Russian crucible, was imported into the new Hitler Jugend Division when he was transferred to it as a Regimental Commander. Even while the Division was still in training at Beverloo, Belgium, Meyer had taken the opportunity to remind an assembly of troops: 'My Regiment takes no prisoners.' A member of the reconnaissance company attached to Meyer's regimental HQ was to testify at the end of the war that on the eve of the Hitler Jugend Division's move to Normandy in April 1944 his company was given secret orders, the relevant part of which read as follows:

> The attitude at front: SS troops shall take no prisoners. Prisoners are to be executed after having been interrogated. SS soldiers should not surrender but commit suicide if no other choice is left. The officers have stated that the British do not take prisoners as far as the SS are concerned.*

* From evidence given to the SHAEF Court of Inquiry at Chartres, France, by a soldier of the 15th Reconnaissance Company, 25 SS Panzer Grenadier Regiment HQ, and used in evidence at the trial of Kurt Meyer. Neither this soldier nor some of the other SS men giving evidence for the prosecution at Meyer's trial were allowed to be named by the Court. See Macdonald: *The Trial of Kurt Meyer*, pp. 92–4.

Another SS soldier from the same company confirmed his comrade's testimony and added that shortly before the Allied invasion of France Kurt Meyer had told his company at their HQ in Le Sap, Normandy: 'My Regiment takes no prisoners.' An SS man from the reconnaissance company by the name of Jan Jesionek also remembered this speech by Meyer and recalled that Meyer had exhorted them to take reprisals on English prisoners in retaliation for the bombing of their German homeland, which they took to mean that prisoners were to be shot. Shortly afterwards the Company Commander had told his men: 'May the others do what they please – our Company takes no prisoners.' This sentiment, according to a soldier from the 1st Battalion of Meyer's 25th Regiment, was echoed by his Company Commander as they were moving up to the Front on D-Day.

Though Meyer was to deny that he had ever given orders – and certainly never secret orders – for prisoners to be executed, there was evidence that his entire Regiment, indeed the whole Division, was riddled with a dark, secretive understanding on the subject. Not all the officers in the Hitler Jugend Division, it should be said, subscribed to such an understanding. Some had been posted to the Division from the rather more conventional Wehrmacht, and even from the Luftwaffe; the murder of prisoners was not in their blood to the extent that it was in the blood of some of their SS colleagues; and certainly when the occasion arose the Hitler Jugend Division did take prisoners in considerable numbers in a perfectly correct manner. But there was a cadre of SS commanders who for one reason or another – be it personal, tactical, or ideological – saw enemy prisoners as objects of hate and retribution and the murder of them as a powerful weapon of terror and force. Such commanders included Meyer himself, and Mohnke, Bremer, Milius and Müller. It was thanks to the likes of these men that the 12th SS Panzer Division (Hitler Jugend) lost its sobriquet as the 'Baby Division' and became known even amongst the other units of the German forces in France as the 'Murder Division.'

———

During the course of D-Day the Hitler Jugend Division received its marching orders from the Seventh Army:

'To 12 SS Panzer Division: Division to move forward immediately . . . Assignment: To throw the enemy into the sea and destroy him.'

And so this great caravan of men and tanks, guns and troop carriers that made up the 12th SS Panzers lurched off down the narrow Normandy lanes to make an appointment with the resolute men of the 3rd Canadian Division – and with destiny. Kurt Meyer's 25th Panzer Grenadier Regiment was the first to take up its position on 7 June, defending the south-west perimeter of Caen, ready (as he put it) to 'throw the little fishes back into the sea'. Wilhelm Mohnke's 26th Panzer Grenadier Regiment, hindered by Allied air attacks, did not reach its battlefield position until the following day, 8 June. Here, in the course of the next few hotly fought days, both Meyer and Mohnke were to put into practice the message they had long preached concerning enemy prisoners of war.

———

First into the thick of it was an SS combat group commanded by Obersturmbannführer Karl-Heinz Milius. This group was composed of the 3rd Battalion of Meyer's Regiment, supported by the 'Prinz' Battalion of the 12th SS Panzer Regiment, after its commander, Sturmbannführer Karl-Heinz Prinz. Milius's combat group was the first element of the 'Murder Division' to make contact with the Canadian invasion forces, and during this initial battle on 7 June savage fighting took place in and around the villages of Authie and Buron, during which a number of Canadians were taken prisoner. The Milius combat group wasted no time in practising what they preached. Many of them had never been in combat before, none of them had been in action on the invasion front for more than a few hours, before they were slaughtering Canadians as heedlessly and systematically as some of them had once done on the Russian Front. At least twenty-seven and more likely thirty-three prisoners were murdered in a whole string of incidents, many of them squalid and vicious beyond measure.

The fate of the Canadians who fell, individually and collectively, into the hands of their teenage captors make grim reading. One seriously wounded prisoner, lying unarmed and helpless on the ground, was bayoneted repeatedly by a number of SS men, one of whom was an officer. Another prisoner,* while being searched and disarmed, was found to have a grenade on his person which he had not yet had the opportunity to discard. He was thereupon shot, but not killed outright, and as he lay in extremis where he had fallen he was kicked by the guards and after fifteen minutes of torment finally despatched by shots fired into his head. In another incident, a wounded soldier was caught in the position where he was hiding, and as he tried to get to his feet a Hitler Jugend trooper placed his boot on his neck and trampled his face into the ground. The trooper then drew his knife and stabbed the wounded Canadian eight times in the body.

Any excuse, or none, was enough for the men of the Milius combat group to murder prisoners indiscriminately wherever they found them. Thus a

* Private J. Metcalf of the North Nova Scotia Regiment.

prisoner* standing in line with other prisoners, unarmed and with his hands above his head, was shot in the stomach for turning his head and took two days to die of his wounds. Again, a prisoner wounded by a shell which killed his two comrades was having his wounds dressed by a French civilian when a German officer and a stormtrooper came up to the prostrate Canadian; whereupon the officer, obviously enjoying what he was doing, drew his pistol and shot the prisoner twice through the head, killing him. Time and again, groups of prisoners were machine-gunned without warning by their guards. Six were killed in this way as they were being marched along to the rear in a group of nine prisoners with their arms in the air.

In one incident the guards seemed to go completely out of control, behaving in such a wild, frenzied and completely undisciplined way that one of the surviving Canadian prisoners, Major J.D. Learment, DSO, who had commanded the vanguard of the 9th Brigade, was of the opinion they had been taking drugs.†

Eight prisoners sitting under guard at the side of a street in Authie were told to remove their helmets and were then sprayed with automatic fire until not a single prisoner was left alive. The guards then dragged the bodies out into the street and left them to be run over by passing vehicles. French civilians tried to pull the bodies back on to the pavement but the Germans pulled them back into the road again and ordered them to be left where they were. Some bodies were so badly mutilated by the passing traffic that they were unrecognizable. Two were crushed to pulp when a tank was deliberately driven over them from head to foot. The Hitler Jugend lads found it amusing to put an old tin hat on one of the corpses and an empty cigarette packet in the mouth of another. The bodies remained in this desecrated and nauseating condition for six days before the SS gave the local French civilians permission to bury them. By then there were thirty-nine bodies to be buried around the village, four of them too mutilated for identification as to name or unit.‡

On occasion, however, things went a bit too far for the Hitler Jugend top brass. When an army lorry was deliberately driven into a column of captured Canadian POWs at high speed near 12 SS Division Headquarters in Caen, killing two prisoners outright and severely injuring a third, the Germans went to some pains to cover up the incident, even to the extent of putting on newsreel film the solemn funeral they had laid on for the victims.

---

* Corporal J.A. Taylor of the North Nova Scotia Highlanders.
† Interestingly, this is what one of the survivors of the Wormhoudt barn massacre thought about the Leibstandarte stormtroopers who carried out that atrocity.
‡ The thirty-five who *could* be identified were made up of twenty-six North Nova Scotia Highlanders, three Sherbrooke Fusiliers and two Camerons of Ottawa.

So the random but widespread killings went on through that long, bitter day of D plus 1. No prisoner was sacrosanct, even when it was obvious he had played no part in the fighting on the ground. Near Argentan, on the road to Caen, three American airmen who had been forced to bale out were taken to the back of a barn and shot by German troops in camouflage uniforms, thought to be from the 12th SS Panzers. That evening a Canadian padre, Captain W.L. Brown of Windsor, Ontario, attached to the Sherbrooke Fusiliers, inadvertently fell into SS hands when his jeep strayed into the German lines near Cussy. Wearing a clerical collar and a Red Cross armband and with his hands above his head in a token of surrender, this courageous man of God then walked towards the German positions, where he was given the usual Hitler Jugend reception and stabbed to death with a single knife or bayonet thrust through the chest.

The murder and mayhem perpetrated by Kurt Meyer's 25th Panzer Grenadiers on their first day in action was not confined to the troops locked in combat along the hotly disputed front out in the Normandy *bocage*. Even to the rear, at Kurt Meyer's Regimental HQ in the medieval Abbaye Ardenne, near Caen, the killing of prisoners continued – sometimes at the behest of the Regimental Commander himself. Eleven Canadian POWs were murdered in the grounds of Meyer's HQ during the course of 7 June, and another seven the following day. A seventeen-year-old SS despatch rider of Polish origin by the name of Jan Jesionek witnessed the killing of the seven prisoners on 8 June. Jesionek, waiting for his motor bike to be repaired, saw the prisoners being marched into the Abbaye grounds and bustled into a stable under the watchful eye of an escort of two soldiers from the 25th Regiment, and it was he who led one of the guards into the old chapel of the Abbaye to report the arrival of the prisoners to the Regimental Commander, Kurt Meyer. Meyer was perceptibly angered by the arrival of the prisoners. 'Why do you bring prisoners to the rear?' he asked the guard. 'They only eat up our rations.' Meyer turned to another officer standing nearby and spoke with him briefly in tones too low for Jesionek to catch. Then he announced in a voice loud enough for all to hear: 'In future no more prisoners are to be taken!'

The officer and the guard then left the chapel and made their way towards the stable where the prisoners were being kept. Jesionek followed them as far as the stable courtyard. He had intended to take a wash at the water pump there, but he was directed instead to the concrete pool near an archway leading to a garden, and from there he had a perfect view of the prisoners, who were being interrogated one at a time in English by the officer at the stable entrance. Later Jesionek related:

One of the prisoners had tears in his eyes, and the officer laughed at him in a sneering manner. The officer seemed to be enjoying himself and frequently burst out laughing as he spoke to the prisoners. He took their papers from them and returned to the chapel.

The guard who had spoken to Meyer took up a position at the archway leading to the garden. Each of the seven prisoners was then called by name and in turn had to walk from the stable entrance to where the guard was at the archway. They were then directed up some steps and into the garden. Here each made a left turn, and as he did so an Unterscharführer, who had previously gone into the garden and was awaiting the prisoners, shot him in the back of the head.

As each of the prisoners came out of the stable, he shook hands with the others before walking into the garden. They all seemed to know what was about to happen, and the sound of the shots and occasionally a scream could be clearly heard.

After the shooting, Jesionek went over to the pump by the archway and saw the Unterscharführer reloading his pistol and the bodies of the seven Canadians lying in a large pool of blood in the garden. Nearly nine months were to pass before the murders at the Abbaye Ardenne were revealed during a routine interrogation of Jan Jesionek at a POW camp in Chartres, France, during the last fortnight of the war. A Canadian investigation discovered that a total of twenty Canadian prisoners of war had been murdered in the Abbaye Ardenne and buried in its grounds.* Eleven had been killed in small groups at the Abbaye on 7 June, seven on 8 June and two on 17 June. The bodies were identified by the discs which were still on them and a pathologist confirmed that all of the prisoners had died as a result of head wounds sustained either by a single shot in the base of the skull, or multiple bullet wounds, or blows from a blunt instrument such as a rifle butt or, more probably, the two bloodstained clubs found later in the Abbaye park.

––––––

It was not just the hot-headed stormtroopers of the infantry battalions who indulged in this orgy of brutality against their luckless captives. The

* These included Lieutenant F. Williams and Lance-Corporal Pollard of the Stormont, Dundas and Glengarry Highlanders; Lieutenant Windsor and Troopers G.V. Gill, T. Henry, K.J. Bolt, of the Royal Canadian Armoured Corps; Private C. Doucett, North Nova Scotias; Privates C.R. McNaughton and J.A. Moss; Private H.L. McKiel.

violence was so widespread and so infectious as to seem like the symptoms of an epidemic, and tank men, recce men and engineers took part in the violence as the fit took them or the opportunity arose. Thus two Canadian riflemen from the Regina Rifles, captured by the crew of a disabled German tank while on outpost duty near Norrey-en-Bessin, were made to run a distance of 500 yards to the south, where they were interrogated by a German SS Panzer officer. Dissatisfied with their answers, the Panzer officer suddenly pulled out a machine-pistol and opened up on the two men, killing one of the prisoners outright with three bullets in the stomach and one in the head, and wounding the other in the thigh. Feigning death, the wounded prisoner survived and eventually returned to his own unit, where he reported the incident. Later it was established that the 1st and 3rd Companies of the 12 SS Panzer Regiment, commanded by Hauptsturmführer Anton Berlin and Hauptsturmführer Rudolf von Ribbentrop, the twenty-three-year-old son of Hitler's Foreign Minister, carried out the attack, though neither of these officers was ever brought in for interrogation after the war.*

———

Similarly, the Reconnaissance Battalion of the 12 SS Panzer Division under the command of Sturmbannführer Gerhard Bremer, a veteran SS warrior of the Nazi campaigns in Poland, northern France and Russia, was involved in at least two criminal violations against prisoners of war on the Normandy invasion front.

At about midday on 8 June the HQ of Bremer's formidable outfit rolled up to the Château d'Audrieu and set up their battalion command post in the shade of a huge spreading sycamore tree in the grounds behind the château. Shortly after its arrival at the château the Reconnaissance Battalion began to shoot Canadian prisoners of war in batches after they had failed to impart required information during interrogation. The first batch consisted of three Canadian soldiers who were seen to emerge from the command post under an escort commanded by an NCO. The escort was directed into the woods by an officer, believed to have been Obersturmführer Hansman, and the prisoners were then promptly shot by their guards. The bodies were left unburied and were found by British troops who moved into the area a few days later.

---

* The two Canadian prisoners were Riflemen L.W. Lee and E.N. Gilbank. Gilbank was the one who died.

Not long after this incident, a second batch of three Canadian prisoners* were marched into the woods. One of the riflemen was a stretcher bearer and wearing a Red Cross armband which entitled him to special treatment as a non-combatant. This fact did not engage the sympathy of the SS guards, however, and the only special treatment they gave him was their own inimitable brand. The stretcher bearer and his two comrades were shot, just as the first batch of prisoners had been.

A little later in the afternoon, at about 4.30 p.m., a group of thirteen more Canadian prisoners, all of them members of 9 Platoon, A Company, the Royal Winnipeg Rifles, were also marched out of the command post to a spot about a hundred yards distant and shot in the presence of officers and NCOs of Gerhard Bremer's Reconnaissance Battalion.

Seven other Canadian soldiers were also murdered at the Château d'Audrieu during the course of that afternoon. Though no eye-witnesses ever came forward to describe the manner of their killing, their bodies were found without weapons and equipment, and subsequent investigations indicated that they too had been shot by heavy small-arms fire while prisoners of war. In any case, since no Canadian troops were ever in action in the vicinity of the Château, it would have been impossible for these men to have met their deaths in combat there.

Three of these four murder incidents were later verified by a Court of Inquiry specially convened by SHAEF (Supreme Headquarters Allied Expeditionary Forces) to investigate the murders of Allied prisoners during the battle of Normandy. A total of twenty-six Canadian soldiers were killed at the Château d'Audrieu during the afternoon of 8 June 1944, of whom nineteen were officially verified. It was originally thought that at the time of the murders the Commander of the Reconnaissance Battalion, Gerhard Bremer, was away from his unit, having received some minor shell wounds that required treatment at the rear, and that his second-in-command, twenty-five-year-old Hauptsturmführer Baron Gerd von Reitzenstein, was the officer responsible for ordering the executions as reprisals – though the actual firing parties were commanded by an Oberscharführer who rejoiced in the name of Stun. It was subsequently determined, however, that though Bremer was indeed wounded, it was not until *after* the murders had been carried out, and a French witness was later to testify that the German Commander present at the time of the murders wore a Knight's Cross around his neck – which could only have been Bremer.

Gerhard Bremer's Reconnaissance Battalion was again involved in a murderous incident when a US Army Air Force pilot who had crash-landed

---

* Riflemen D.S. Gold, J.D. McIntosh and W. Thomas of the Royal Winnipeg Rifles.

near Rugles was handed over to a detachment commanded by Unter-sturmführer Kirchner. It was Kirchner who gave permission to one of the detachment's senior NCOs, Unterscharführer Hugo Wolf, to take the downed pilot to the château at St Sulpice, where other troops of the Reconnaissance Battalion were located. Here Wolf showed his American prisoner the bodies of two German officers who had been killed in an Allied air attack that day. Wolf then drew his gun and cold-bloodedly shot the prisoner dead.

————

During this period another of the Hitler Jugend Division's specialist units, the Engineering Battalion, was also involved in a major act of violence against unarmed prisoners of war. This incident took place at the village of Mouen, which was then the Engineering Battalion's Rear HQ. A group of seven Canadian prisoners – six from the Queen's Own Rifles and one from the 1st Hussars – were brought to Müller's HQ in the village one evening, having been captured following an abortive Canadian attack on the village of Le Mesnil-Patry. The prisoners were in such an exhausted state when they reached Mouen it is possible that they had spent time in hiding. After their arrival at Rear HQ the Canadians were interrogated by an officer, and four hours later, when it must have been getting very dark, they were taken out to the edge of the village and executed by a firing party of fourteen SS men under the command of a senior NCO. Though the name of the officer who interrogated the prisoners could never be determined, it was known that the 12th SS Engineering Battalion was commanded at the time by Sturmbannführer Müller, who is said to have directed his company com-manders to give no quarter.

THE MOHNKE MURDERS

On the morning of 8 June, while holding a position on the north side of the Caen-Bayeux railway line near the village of Putot-en-Bessin, the Royal Winnipeg Rifles, together with elements of the Cameron Highlanders of Ottawa and the 3rd Canadian Anti-Tank Regiment RCA, came under attack from the 2nd Battalion of the 26th Panzer Grenadier Regiment, commanded by a veteran Waffen-SS officer, thirty-four-year-old Sturmbannführer Bernhard Siebken. During the course of this action twenty-five to thirty Canadian soldiers were taken prisoner, including two officers and a number of wounded stretcher cases. These prisoners were marched back along a trail till they came to an orchard where a large number of German vehicles were parked. Here the wounded were given first-aid and another party of Canadian prisoners, numbering about fifteen, joined them, making a total of some forty prisoners of all ranks. The prisoner party was then marched off again along trails and across country until they reached the house of a certain George Moulin in the village of Le Mesnil-Patry, which was being used as the 2nd Battalion's Headquarters. Here they were kept in a barn for several hours, apparently without being interrogated.

In the evening the prisoners were led out of the barn and marshalled in the courtyard in front of George Moulin's house, where they were looked over by a group of officers from the Headquarters. The prisoners were then marched off along a track leading south towards the Caen to Fontenay-le-Pesnel road under an escort, composed of the same guards who had escorted them to Le Mesnil-Patry commanded by a sergeant. As they marched along they encountered a German officer in a camouflaged vehicle, halted along the track. The sergeant halted the prisoners and spoke to the officer. He appeared to be asking for instructions and the officer appeared to be very annoyed and pointed in a southerly direction along the trail they were on. Some of the prisoners formed the impression that the officer wanted them to be killed.

163

The column of prisoners set off again and marched along until they were within sight of the Caen to Fontenay road, where they could see a large column of German vehicles, including tanks and half-tracks, passing through. When they were within about 150 metres of the road they were directed into a field where they were told to sit down with the wounded in the centre. Two of their escort remained close to them and kept crowding the prisoners up into a tighter and tighter bunch. In a short while a half-track vehicle turned into the field and a squad of eight or nine German soldiers, including two officers, jumped down from it brandishing Schmeisser machine-pistols. After a brief conference, the prisoners' guards went to the half-track and took out some extra Schmeissers which had been thoughtfully provided for them, plus a haversack containing magazines. Then all the German soldiers advanced in a line towards the seated prisoners, and at a signal they opened fire on the prisoners.

Thirty-five prisoners were killed. Five, their suspicions aroused before the shooting started, ran for their lives when the Germans opened up, and went to ground in the next field, which contained a crop of tall standing wheat. Four others made a break for it but were gunned down before they could effect an escape. A shallow mass grave was dug for the thirty-one Canadians who were in the main group of prisoners and a bulldozer shovelled the bodies unceremoniously into it. The other four were buried nearby. The five survivors were eventually rounded up by a different German unit, and after spending the rest of the war in a German prisoner-of-war camp, were eventually repatriated and reported the massacre to the authorities.

The evidence of the five survivors of the massacre on the Fontenay-le-Pesnel road* was corroborated by two other Canadians who had witnessed the incident from a distance. These two, a lieutenant and a rifleman,† had been prisoners themselves at the time, but broke free from their guards and escaped once the shooting in the field began.

The murder of the thirty-five Canadian prisoners had many of the hallmarks of the bigger and more notorious massacre at Malmédy in the Ardennes at the end of the year, when an even larger group of American prisoners were similarly mowed down by machine-gun fire in an open field by SS troops of the 1st SS Panzer Division. But unlike the Malmédy massacre, the Germans responsible for the massacre on the Fontenay-Le-Pesnel road were never identified or apprehended by the Allies after the war. Why the Canadian authorities failed to follow up this Canadian

* The five survivors were Gunner W.F. Clark of the Anti-Tanks and Corporal H.C. McLean, Riflemen A. Desjarlais, G.J. Ferris and J. MacDougall of the Royal Winnipegs.
† These two witnesses were Lt D.A. James and Rifleman W.R. LeBarr.

'Malmédy' – the worst crime ever inflicted against their armed forces at any time in their history – remains unknown to the present day.

———

On the day immediately following the massacre of the Canadians at Fontenay-Le-Pesnel – for convenience of reference we shall refer to it henceforth as the Canadian Massacre – another brutal set of murders was perpetrated by men of Wilhelm Mohnke's regiment, again (in our view) at his behest. Again for convenience of reference we shall call this second set of murders the First Aid Post killings. These killings were unknown to the Allies for several weeks after they had been committed, and it was not until the beginning of July, when a Field Regiment of the Royal Artillery, moving up towards Caen, set up gun positions on the south-western outskirts of the village of Le Mesnil-Patry, that clues to the crime were discovered. In the grounds of a farmhouse belonging to a Madame Saint-Martin, the British gunners came across the partly buried bodies of six Canadian soldiers in two separate shallow graves – one a large L-shaped mound and the other an adjoining fire trench, partially filled in. As the position was militarily too exposed to permit exhumation and proper burial, the bodies were hastily covered with earth and a report sent through to rear échelon.

At the end of the month, when the fighting front had moved on, the bodies were disinterred by members of the No 3 Canadian Graves Concentration Unit. An examination of the wounds indicated that these were not battlefield casualties, however, and the bodies were immediately reburied and a guard placed on the graves. On 30 August a pathologist of the Royal Canadian Medical Corps exhumed the six bodies already reported, together with a newly-discovered seventh body found in a separate grave, and carried out an autopsy on each. All but one were found to have received fatal bullet wounds in the head, and several appeared to have suffered non-fatal wounds in other parts of the body before receiving the shots to the head that killed them. The wounds of the seventh body appeared to be that of a normal battlefield casualty – probably a member of a tank crew who had died of burns received when his tank was hit.

It was established that the three bodies in one of the mass graves were those of Canadian infantrymen who had last been seen in action near Putot-en-Bessin on 7–8 June – Private H.S. Angel of the Cameron Highlanders of Ottawa and Riflemen F.W. Holness and E.C. Baskerville. The three bodies in the other mass grave were identified as those of two Canadian tankmen and an infantryman who had been in action on 11 June during an attack on the German positions at Le Mesnil-Patry – Trooper A. Bowes and Trooper G.H. Scriven of the 6th Canadian Armoured Regiment (1st Hussars) and CSM J. Forbes of the Queen's Own Rifles of Canada. The seventh body, which was not the subject of a war crimes investigation, was identified as that of Trooper K.O. Peddlar of the 1st Hussars.

Allied investigations soon established that there had been no fighting nearer than 500 to 600 yards of the place where the bodies were found and that between 8 and 16 June the Headquarters of the 2nd Battalion of the 26th SS Panzer Grenadier Regiment was located in the village of Le Mesnil-Patry, with the First Aid Post of this Battalion installed in a farmhouse less than 100 metres from where the graves were discovered. The inference was clear – the Canadians had been brought to the First Aid Post as prisoners to have their wounds treated, and one had died of his wounds and the rest had been murdered. French villagers who had witnessed the First Aid Post killings soon confirmed that the first three bodies were those of Allied soldiers who had been shot on the morning of 9 June, while the rest were those of men who had been shot two days later, on 11 June. The CO of the 2nd Battalion was Sturmbannführer Bernhard Siebken, whose men were known to have murdered a number of other enemy prisoners in this sector of the front during the days following the invasion. But as the United Nations War Crimes Commission charge sheet duly recorded: 'The Regimental Commander, Standartenführer MOHNKE,* was present in the village of Le Mesnil-Patry on 11 June 1944; he led the German counter-attack on that day from the village.' In fact, Standartenführer Mohnke was in that village at an even earlier date. As we shall see, he was very probably at the village in the early hours of that fateful morning of 9 June as well.

———

On the same day as the second set of First Aid Post killings three Canadian soldiers of the 6th Canadian Armoured Regiment (1st Hussars)† were taken prisoner by German soldiers of either the 2nd Battalion of the 26th SS Panzer Grenadier Regiment or No 3 Company of the 12th SS Engineering Battalion near the village of Les Saullets, a stone's throw from the First Aid Post in the neighbouring village of Le Mesnil-Patry, with which it formed an almost contiguous little rural suburb. The prisoners were interrogated by an officer and then marched towards the rear – in other

---

* Capital letters for names were standard in Allied investigative reports.
† The three Canadians were Sergeant E.S. Payne and Troopers H.L. Preston and R.C. McClean. Trooper Preston was the one who died.

166

words towards Mohnke's Regimental HQ – under escort. They had not gone far, however, when the guards opened fire, killing one of the prisoners, wounding another, and missing the third. The two who survived the shooting feigned death and eventually managed to escape independently and make their way to their own lines.

In a separate incident near Les Saullets on the same day, four members of a tank crew from the 6th Armoured Regiment fell into the hands of No 7 Company of the 2nd Battalion, 26th SS Panzer Grenadier Regiment, in the course of an unsuccessful attack on the village. The SS Company Commander, Oberleutnant August Henne, who had joined the Hitler Jugend Division from the Wehrmacht and still kept his Wehrmacht rank, later claimed that he sent the four Canadian prisoners* back to battalion headquarters, which was only a short distance away in Le Mesnil-Patry, under the guard of a stormtrooper by the name of Mischke. Whatever happened, and whoever was responsible, it was clear that the Canadians never reached their destination. Their bodies were later found in a common grave not far from the route between Company and Battalion HQ in circumstances that showed quite clearly they were shot while prisoners of war.

On the same day as the two sets of shootings at Les Saullets – the same day, moreover, as the second set of First Aid Post killings just down the road from Les Saullets – yet another outrage was perpetrated against Canadian prisoners of war by Mohnke's regiment, this time indisputably on his direct orders, and in his presence. For convenience sake we shall call this crime, the fourth in a series of four committed by Mohnke's 26th Panzer Grenadiers, the Stangenberg Case, after the SS man who was later to give eye-witness testimony about it.

At about 1600 hours on 11 June three Canadian soldiers† who had been captured by German troops while laying mines, were brought to the Headquarters of the 26th SS Panzer Grenadier Regiment, which at that time was located in an orchard at Forme du Bosq, near the village of Haut du Bosq. Here, after being handed over to a sergeant and an SS stormtrooper of the Feldgendarmerie (military field police) attached to the

---

* The four Canadians were Captain H.L. Smuck, Private A.H. Charron, Troopers A.M. McLair and A.B. Hancock.
† Rifleman A.R. Owens of the Royal Winnipeg Rifles and Sappers J. Ionel and G.A. Benner of the Royal Canadian Engineers.

Regimental HQ, they were taken to the entrance of the Regimental Headquarters, which was accommodated at that time in an army vehicle, where they waited a few minutes. The Regimental Commander, Obersturmbannführer Wilhelm Mohnke, then appeared and proceeded to interrogate the three Canadians through an interpreter in the presence of his Adjutant, Hauptsturmführer Kaiser. The interrogation lasted for fifteen to twenty minutes, during which time Mohnke, who must have struck the prisoners as a terrifying figure, shouted and gesticulated and appeared (as always when confronted with enemy prisoners of war) to be very angry. At the end of the interrogation, the prisoners were searched and stripped of all their personal possessions, including their identity discs, which were tossed into some nearby bushes.

The two members of the Feldgendarmerie now marched the three prisoners away from Mohnke's Regimental Headquarters across a meadow in the direction of the Allied lines. After they had gone about 275 yards, they stopped at the edge of a bomb crater, one of many with which the surrounding area was pockmarked following an Allied air raid a few hours earlier.

At no time did the prisoners make any effort to escape and as soon as they were abreast of the crater the SS sergeant opened fire on them from behind and at very close range with his machine-pistol. He fired in a continuous long burst of about twenty to twenty-five rounds and the prisoners fell to the ground and lay motionless at the edge of the crater. As they lay there one or both of the Feldgendarmes fired single shots into the bodies. They then doubled back to Regimental Headquarters, where Mohnke and all the other officers had been standing watching the prisoners being marched away and then so brutally and criminally shot to death – none of them, it has to be said, making any effort to intervene or interrupt the three murders, least of all the Commanding Officer, Wilhelm Mohnke, who as the senior officer present was the *only* person who could have given the order to carry out the murders and was therefore perfectly aware that what he was witnessing *was* indeed murder in the first degree – murder for which he and he alone was prima facie responsible.

As it happened, these events were witnessed by a young eighteen-year-old Polish motor mechanic and SS Obergrenadier by the name of Withold Stangenberg, who had been drafted into the Waffen-SS against his wishes in the previous year and was at Mohnke's headquarters on 11 June as a member of the Motorcycle Platoon, Headquarters Company, 26th SS Panzer Grenadiers. Four of his comrades also saw the interrogation, search and execution of the prisoners. After they had returned to their slit trenches following the shooting – it was dangerous to remain standing about in the open for too long, because of the incessant risk of Allied air attacks – the men of Stangenberg's section talked about what they had seen. Most of

168

them agreed it was a bad thing that prisoners were shot 'because if one of our own comrades were taken prisoner he would be shot too.' But one of them felt it was right to shoot prisoners, and the section commander told them that anyway the English shot all the prisoners *they* took.

And there, but for a quirk of fate, the matter might have ended, one of the myriad catastrophes of war, hidden away and obliterated from memory in the chaos of the military débâcle that was to follow. That evening Mohnke's headquarters pulled out. But on 28 June Withold Stangenberg's position was overrun by British troops and he was captured and shipped back to a prisoner-of-war camp in England. There, on 10 July 1944, he told the army authorities of the incident he had witnessed at Wilhelm Mohnke's Regimental Headquarters at the Haut du Bosq less than a month previously. His story was later corroborated in a statement made by another German prisoner of war, Heinz Schmidt, who also described the two members of the Feldgendarmerie who did the actual shooting. All this information, in all its shocking detail, landed like a parcel of bloody parts on the desk of a SHAEF Court of Inquiry sitting in London. As a matter of urgency an investigation into the crime was started at once.

INVESTIGATION

Not long after the invasion of Normandy reports began to filter through to Canadian and British headquarters that a considerable number of Allied soldiers, most of them Canadians, were suspected of having been murdered in cold blood after surrendering to fanatical SS troops in the area north-west of Caen held by 12th SS Panzer Division (Hitler Jugend). These reports came from Canadian prisoners who had contrived to escape the fate of their less fortunate comrades and managed to return to their own lines; and from French civilians who had been eye-witnesses to some of the incidents. Their reports were confirmed when the Allies advanced into territory that had been held by the 12th SS Panzers and discovered the bodies of Canadian soldiers, some buried, some unburied, and all of them bearing signs of having met their deaths not on the battlefield but in executions carried out while they were prisoners of war.

News of the murder of Canadian prisoners of war created something of a sensation in Allied headquarters and gave rise to a storm of outrage in Canada. The Hague and Geneva Conventions had formulated clear-cut laws prohibiting the killing of unarmed prisoners of war. The killings in Normandy were a flagrant violation of the laws and customs of war that had been understood and accepted by the civilized nations of the world for many years. They had to be stopped; and they had to be punished. The Canadian Government made a formal protest which was conveyed to the Nazi Government via Red Cross channels in neutral Switzerland. Leaflets were dropped by aeroplane on German troops in Normandy containing an Order of the Day issued by General Crerar, Commander of the First Canadian Army, in which he promised retribution for those responsible for these crimes – a promise which he only partly kept.

At 21st Army Group General Montgomery set up a Court of Inquiry to determine the facts of the matter.* Shortly afterwards General Eisenhower did the same. The first investigations looked into the killings at the Château d'Audrieu, near Pavie, where twenty-six Canadians had been executed by the Reconnaissance Battalion of the Hitler Jugend Division on 8 June; and at Mouen, where seven Canadian prisoners had been shot in similar circumstances by the Engineering Battalion of the same Division. As more incidents of this nature were reported it began to appear that the killings were not isolated acts but part of an overall policy on the part of elements of the Hitler Jugend Division.

It was therefore decided that the first two courts should become a standing SHAEF Court of Inquiry, under the direction of Major-General R.W. Barker, US Army, head of G1 Division at SHAEF. The Standing Court was assigned the task of investigating at once, on the ground, all reports of violations of the laws and usages of war, determining the facts, taking testimony on oath, identifying where possible the units and personnel responsible, and building up a corpus of evidence to be used in such war crimes trials as might subsequently arise. A staff of Intelligence and Provost officers were made available for this new organization, and a back-up staff of interpreters, shorthand writers, pathologists and other experts. A fleet of vehicles were on hand to whisk the investigation teams to any spot where a war crime might be newly discovered.

At the end of August 1944 this new standing SHAEF Court of Inquiry assembled in the field to open its first session in Caen, Normandy. Present were the President of the Court, Colonel Paul Tombaugh, US Army, and two Members – the British representative, Lt-Col. J.H. Boraston, CB, OBE, a barrister by profession, and during the Great War the Military Secretary to Field Marshal Earl Haig; and the Canadian representative, Lt-Col. Bruce J.S. Macdonald, OBE, QC, likewise a barrister by profession, and Battalion Commander of the Essex Scottish Regiment during the early fighting in Normandy. First on the agenda were the atrocities committed by Kurt Meyer's 25th Panzer Grenadiers at Authie and Wilhelm Mohnke's 26 Panzer Grenadiers at Le Mesnil-Patry (the First Aid Post killings) and Les Saullets. Among the recommendations recorded by the court on that occasion was the following:

That Obersturmbannführer MOHNKE be apprehended
when possible and held until final effort is completed to obtain

---

* It was something of an irony that, unknown to him, Montgomery should initiate an investigation which would look into the activities of Wilhelm Mohnke, the very officer who had been responsible for the outrage against the Royal Warwickshire Regiment at Wormhoudt in 1940 – the regiment of which Montgomery himself had been Battalion Commander before the war and was to be Colonel-in-Chief after it.

all further evidence, and, if such action then be justified, he be tried on a charge of murder.

As the number of cases multiplied more members were added, including the American writer and explorer, Lt-Col. Charles S. Cutting, and the London barrister and actor, Lt-Col. Leo Genn, who had recently distinguished himself in Laurence Olivier's film version of *Henry V* and was soon to transfer to the International Military Tribunal at Nuremberg as one of the British prosecution team in the trial of the major German war criminals.

The SHAEF Court of Inquiry continued to sit at periodic intervals, and during two-day-long sessions at the London District Prisoner of War Cage in Kensington Palace Gardens, London, on 26 and 27 March 1945, it questioned at length former Brigadeführer (Major General) Kurt Meyer to determine the part he played in the atrocities committed by the men under his command.

In due course, the court presented its findings, classified as Secret, and entitled *SUPPLEMENTARY REPORT of the SUPREME HEADQUARTERS ALLIED EXPEDITIONARY FORCE COURT OF INQUIRY re SHOOTING OF ALLIED PRISONERS OF WAR by 12 SS Panzer Division (Hitler-Jugend) NORMANDY, FRANCE, 7–21 June 1944.*

Bearing in mind that at this stage the investigations into these war crimes were not yet completed and that much work still had to be done before sufficient evidence could be assembled to justify initiating any trials of those responsible, the crucial sections of the Findings of the Court read as follows:

1. That seven cases of violations of the laws and usages of warfare and the terms of the Geneva Conventions, 1929, by members of the German Armed Forces have been established.

That these cases occurred between the 7 and 17 June 1944 in Normandy, France.

That the victims of such violations were all unarmed Allied prisoners of war in uniform, many of whom had been previously wounded, and none of whom had resisted, endeavoured to escape or otherwise committed any act to justify their captors in killing them.

That the cases represented 20 separate incidents and 64 prisoner of war victims, 62 Canadian, 1 British and 1 American, of whom only 2 of the 64 survived, all others being killed.

That the perpetrators were members of the 12 SS Panzer Division (Hitler-Jugend) and of the following units:

12 SS Reconnaissance Battalion
12 SS Engineering (Pionier) Battalion
'Prinz' Battalion of 12 SS Panzer Regiment
III Battalion 25 Panzer Grenadier Regiment
II Battalion 26 Panzer Grenadier Regiment

2. That there is no sufficient evidence upon which responsibility for the said atrocities can be placed upon the Commander of any formation higher than the Division under examination.

3. That there is at present no sufficient evidence directly implicating personally the two respective Divisional Commanders, FRITZ WITT and KURT MEYER.

4. There is no corroborated evidence directly implicating personally the two Regimental Commanders, KARL HEINZ MILIUS and WILHELM MOHNKE.

There is no evidence directly implicating personally any of the battalion commanders, officers and non-commissioned officers of the Division by name.

5. That there is, however, circumstantial evidence directly implicating personally the following officers:

Sturmbannführer GERHARD BREMER, Hauptsturmführer VON REITZENSTEIN and Obersturmführers SCHENK and KIRCHNER, and the following non-commissioned officers: Stabscharführer HAGETORN (said to have been killed), Unterscharführer HUGO WOLF.

6. That enlisted men/other ranks of No 15 Company 25 Panzer Grenadier Regiment were given secret orders by Stabscharführer HAGETORN at a formal parade of the Company to the effect that 'SS troops shall take no prisoners; prisoners are to be executed after having been interrogated', and were also told that the officers had stated that the British did not take prisoners, so far as SS soldiers were concerned.

That an Obersturmführer of the III Battalion 26 SS Panzer Grenadier Regiment told his men that the British did not take prisoners and that they were not to take prisoners either.

That the men of the 12 SS Engineering (Pionier) and Reconnaissance Battalions were likewise told by their officers and non-commissioned officers that the British did not take prisoners.

That no orders had been issued by the Divisional Headquarters respecting observance of the terms of the Geneva Convention until after the protest made by the Canadian Government through the International Red Cross in July 1944; although it was said by KURT MEYER under interrogation that provision was always made in Divisional Orders for the selection of points for the collection and evacuation of prisoners of war.

That in five of the total number of twenty established incidents of separate atrocities, shootings were carried out in an organized way by firing squads under command of non-commissioned officers (Audrieu 3, St Sulpice 1, Mouen 1), while in two more cases officers or non-commissioned officers personally committed the reported atrocities (Authie).

The Court of Inquiry then came to its conclusions, which are highly relevant to the line of investigation pursued in this present book, and immensely damaging to the subject of it, Wilhelm Mohnke. The italics are the authors' own:

That, by reason of the foregoing and the general prevalence of such cases throughout the Division, in which officers and non-commissioned officers participated, the conclusion is irresistible that it was understood throughout the Division, if not actually ordered, that *a policy of denying quarter or executing prisoners after interrogation was impliedly if not openly approved by the Regimental and Divisional Commanders or at least would be treated by them with acquiescence.*

That, if such a policy was not so approved, or acquiesced in by the said Commanders, then *a lack of discipline and proper supervision prevailed throughout the Division in this particular matter, for which the respective Battalion, Regimental and Divisional Commanders are responsible.*

8. That, if the uncorroborated sworn statements of Allied soldiers and German prisoners not so far examined by the Court are accepted as true, then *the following officers are personally implicated as actual perpetrators of atrocities:*
Standartenführer WILHELM MOHNKE
Obersturmbannführer KARL HEINZ MILIUS
Sturmbannführer SIEGFRIED MÜLLER
the total number of incidents and victims then being increased respectively to totals of 31 and 107 (103 Canadians, 3 British and 1 American).

That, if the evidence referred to above ... is eventually established, then one or other of two conclusions follows: either such conditions and conduct in the Division existed with the knowledge and approval of the Divisional Commanders WITT and MEYER, or the said Divisional Commanders failed in their duty to see that the provisions of the Geneva Conventions, 1929, were observed by all ranks under their command; in either of which cases they are responsible for the results of a condition of affairs in their Division which they in the one case sanctioned and encouraged and in the other criminally failed to prevent.

A few months later these findings of the SHAEF Court of Inquiry with regard to the activities of Mohnke, Meyer, Milius, Müller, Bremer and von Reitzenstein, who had all survived the war, were submitted as evidence at the trial of the Major War Criminals – Goering, Hess, Keitel, Jodl, Doenitz, Speer and other top-ranking Nazis of the Third Reich – on charges of war crimes and crimes against humanity, which opened before the International Military Tribunal at Nuremberg on 14 November 1945. The SHAEF findings were logged as Document 2997-PS (Exhibit USA-472), and were sandwiched in the published records of the Trial between a document on SS massacres of Jews in Poland and a document on the duties of the Chief of the Reich Chancellery up to the end of the war.

Not included in the section of the SHAEF report submitted as evidence at the Nuremberg Trials were the Court of Inquiry's General Recommendations to the effect, firstly, that Kurt Meyer, Wilhelm Mohnke, Gerhard Bremer, Karl Heinz Milius and Siegfried Müller should be brought to trial on charges of denying quarter to prisoners of war and failing to protect them when captured, and of failing to prevent violations against prisoners of war by the men under their command; and secondly, that Gerhard Bremer, Siegfried Müller, Gerd von Reitzenstein, Obersturmführers Kirchner and Schenk, Stabscharführer Hagetorn, and Hugo Wolf and Leopold Stun should be charged with murder, either as the direct perpetrators of the crime or as accessories before or after the fact.

With the end of the war, meanwhile, the SHAEF Court was disbanded and a Canadian unit – the No 1 Canadian War Crimes Investigation Unit – was formed to continue the work in the Canadian sphere of interest. Commanded by Lt-Col. Bruce Macdonald, this unit consisted of two detachments – the North West Europe (NWE) Detachment, based at Bad Sulzuflen, and the UK Detachment, based in London. Macdonald's new unit soon determined that the number of Canadian prisoners murdered in Normandy in the space of ten days by the 12 SS Panzers was in fact 134, which was a greater total than the initial SHAEF findings had arrived at. According to Macdonald, there were indications that many more than 134 Canadians had been murdered, but certain proof of this was lacking.

Among the various cases investigated by the Canadian War Crimes

Investigation Unit was the Stangenberg case – the shooting of three prisoners at the Haut du Bosq in Normandy on 14 June 1944, a crime which had been witnessed by the young Polish storm trooper, Withold Stangenberg. After reporting the incident to the army authorities in England after his capture, Stangenberg spent the rest of the war as a POW in the United States but on 28 June 1945 he was duly shipped over to appear before the war crimes investigators at Colonel Scotland's London Cage in Kensington Palace Gardens to tell them all he knew.* The Pole faithfully recounted what he had seen on 14 June 1944 and during the course of the interrogation a few more interesting details emerged. The transcript of the relevant section of the interrogation reads as follows:

Q: Did you ever see any other incident of this kind?

A: No, I never saw anything of this kind except once when they brought in a civvy to the Feldgendarmerie. He was asked what sort of man he was. He said he was a Pole, and [they said] 'We will take care of him.' I believe he was shot, but I don't know.

Q: Where did this incident about the Pole happen?

A: That was in the same place as before.

Q: Would you recognize the Regimental Commander [Mohnke] if you saw him? Would you describe him to us?

A: I believe that he had a wooden leg, quite tall, powerfully built, not much hair, if any. I believe both hair and eyes were black. Anywhere from 175 to 180 centimetres high, full oval face.

Q: How old do you think he was?

A: I believe over forty years old.

Q: You say he had a wooden leg. What makes you think so?

A: Because he always walked with a limp and everybody said he had a wooden leg.

Q: Now you said that Oberscharführer Kaiser [also present at the shooting] was Company Commander. Can you describe him?

A: He was a little smaller, about 170 centimetres, also powerfully built, narrow face, black hair and eyes, I believe in his late thirties. I believe his face was scarred.

---

* The Investigation Team was composed of Lt-Col. J.W. Walker (Investigator Cross-Examiner), Major C.B. Campbell (Investigator Examiner), Captain I.T. Burr (Interpreter) and Sergeant W.S. McDonald (Court Reporter).

Q: When your training was going on did the Regimental Commander ever talk to all the troops?

A: Yes, when we first came to Berlin and were in civilian clothes, he spoke to us then.

Q: Did he speak to all of the troops after that?

A: Yes, he also spoke to us in Belgium twice. I remember now he also spoke to us in France shortly before the invasion.

Q: What did he tell you then?

A: The same as he always did – everybody has to be a good fighter and to always think and talk of the Führer.

Q: Were any secret orders [about prisoners of war] ever given to you about the time of the invasion or shortly afterwards?

A: No, I personally received no orders.

Q: Did you hear any orders of any kind given to anyone about the prisoners?

A: No, no order was given that I know of.

Q: Do you know who gave the order for the prisoners to be shot?

A: I don't know, but I suppose from the Regimental Commander.

Q: What makes you think that?

A: Because when orders come they can only come from above – from the officers.

A few weeks later Stangenberg was taken to Normandy and on 19 July identified the location of the Headquarters of the 26th SS Panzer Grenadiers and the scene of the shooting. A search for the bodies and personal effects of the three Canadians was then organized by Canadian Graves Concentration Unit and a few days later the identity disc of Sapper Ionel was discovered in the bushes in the exact spot where the Regimental Headquarters had been located at the time of the shooting. By now the shell crater where the prisoners had been shot was full of water to a depth of about eight feet and a working party in the vicinity was requisitioned to help locate the bodies. The bodies were found to be covered by a layer of mud and it was necessary to pump the water out to recover them. When the bodies were finally exposed it was clear that they had had no proper burial and had nothing about them that could help identify them. All three wore Canadian battle dress uniforms with 3rd Canadian Infantry Division patches on them. One had the letters 'RCE' (Royal Canadian Engineers) embroidered on his uniform, the others wore the shoulder titles of the Royal Winnipeg Rifles. The Identification Section of the 2nd Canadian Graves Concentration Unit examined the bodies and an autopsy on all of them was carried out by a pathologist of the Canadian Army Medical

177

Corps. Due to the advanced stage of decomposition, it was impossible to determine the exact cause of death, but two of the bodies displayed many fractured bones and a skull fractured in many places, injuries consistent with multiple bullet wounds. With the aid of the identity discs and dental charts the corpses were finally identified as those of the three Canadian soldiers who had been cut off from their unit the day after D-Day and murdered on Wilhelm Mohnke's orders a week later at Haut du Bosq.*

In due course the Canadian War Crimes Investigation Unit filed its reports on the atrocities committed by the 25th and 26th SS Panzer Grenadier Regiments and their Commanders Kurt Meyer and Wilhelm Mohnke, with the United Nations Commission in London. The Commission was headed by a famous law lord, Lord Wright, and included a former Lord Chancellor, Lord Finlay, and a number of eminent representatives of the United Nations among its ranks. *The United Nations Commission found that a prima facie case had been established against both Meyer and Mohnke and recommended that they should be sent for trial before a military tribunal on war crimes charges.* Meyer was already a prisoner in Allied hands, but Mohnke could not be found, so his name was filed on the wanted list at the Central Registry of War Criminals and Security Suspects (CROWCASS) in Paris.

On 16 November 1945 Colonel Macdonald wrote to the War Crimes Advisory Committee at the Department of External Affairs in Ottawa, Canada, from Canadian Military Headquarters in London:

1. I beg to advise you that two charges against Standartenführer Wilhelm MOHNKE, Commander 26th SS Panzer Grenadier Regiment, 12 SS Panzer Division (HJ), were submitted by this Office to the United Nations War Crimes Commission on 5th November 1945.
2. The charges arise out of the conduct of MOHNKE and of troops under his command during the fighting in Normandy, between 7–17 June 1944.
3. On 8 November 1945, the Commission considered the charges as filed and, being satisfied that a prima facie case had been established, decided to place the name of MOHNKE on

---

* The murdered soldiers now rest in peace in the Canadian war cemetery at Bresseville-sur-Laize.

the list of accused persons under Secretariat Registration Number 1752/C/G/2.

4. A 'Wanted' Report, covering MOHNKE, has been filed with CROWCASS but to date no information has been received by this office as to his present whereabouts. Unconfirmed reports suggest that when last seen, this man was fighting in the area of the Chancellery in Berlin, immediately prior to the capture of the city.

Some time later, in his personal account of the trial of Kurt Meyer, Colonel Macdonald enlarged on the subject of Mohnke and his part in crimes against the Canadians in Normandy:

We tried to find out from the Russians whether he was in their hands. Our intransigent Allies, however, had either mislaid the file, our previous correspondence, or had not heard from Moscow. So eventually an officer was despatched to their Berlin HQ with orders to sit there until he got some kind of an answer. After several days they threatened to throw him out if he came back again, so we had to give up our efforts at that time to bring one of the really vicious SS commanders to justice. Later it was reported by Major-General Walter Schrieber, Surgeon-General of the German Army, that he had seen Mohnke in a Russian prisoner-of-war camp at Strausberg, where he himself had been a prisoner.

Mohnke was one German commander for whom even his fellow officers had nothing good to say. In their estimation he was quite capable of performing the deeds alleged against him. It was suggested that he was addicted to dope, was a man of violent emotions, and was regarded by them as quite brutal. [It is remarkable how consistently these character traits are attributed to Mohnke by officers and men who served with him at various times throughout the war.] With such leadership it is not to be wondered at that officers of the 26th Regiment appeared to derive so much pleasure out of witnessing the murder of helpless prisoners, and that so many were shot by members of his Regiment . . . in Mohnke's case while he himself actually watched.

———

Meanwhile, the case against Mohnke's opposite number in the 12th SS Panzer Division, Kurt Meyer, had been proceeding apace. The Canadian investigations had had the advantage of having had Meyer in custody since his capture by American troops near Liège on 7 September 1944, only a few weeks after the atrocities committed by his Regiment in Normandy had been discovered. Colonel Macdonald's team were able to build up an adequate body of evidence implicating Meyer in the murder of Canadian prisoners of war, and on 10 December 1945 brought him to trial before a Canadian Military Court in Aurich, Germany, arraigned with much the same set of charges as Wilhelm Mohnke would have faced had he been made available to the Allies in the West. The trial was the first of its kind to be tried by a Canadian Military Court. Colonel Macdonald served as prosecutor during the trial, which fully occupied his time until two days after Christmas.

Meyer was charged with committing a number of war crimes – the unlawful killing of prisoners of war – either as a principal in the killings or as an accessory before or after the fact. There were two charge sheets. The first listed five charges, including the killing of 23 Canadian prisoners of war at Authie and Buron and 11 prisoners of war at Abbaye Ardenne by troops under his command, the killing of 7 other prisoners at Abbaye Ardenne either by troops under his command or (as an alternative charge) on his direct orders, and inciting and counselling his troops to deny quarter. Meyer was thus accused of being directly responsible for one set of murders, and indirectly responsible for all the others in his role as commander. A second charge sheet, which was concerned with Meyer's responsibility for the killing of seven Canadian prisoners at Mouen, was not finally proceeded with, on the grounds that by the time of the Mouen murders he had become the Divisional Commander and his responsibility was therefore appreciably more remote.

During the course of his four-week trial, Kurt Meyer impressed the Court with his polite, restrained and poised behaviour. His accusers even came to admire his soldierly virtues and respect the courage and dignity he displayed throughout the trial. About the murders described to the Court during the trial, Meyer had this comment to make:

> I have here during these proceedings been given an insight into things which, in the aggregate, were unknown to me up to now. I wish to state to the Court here that these deeds were not committed by the young soldier. I am convinced of it, that in the Division there were elements who, due to the year-long battles, due to five years of war, had in a certain respect become brutalized.

Meyer was here referring to the Leibstandarte component of the Hitler Jugend Division, who had brought to the Western Front the dirty tricks they had long employed on the Eastern Front. Ignorant though he may have been of the crimes committed 'in the aggregate', the evidence was stacked against him. It was clearly established that Canadian prisoners had indeed been murdered by troops under his command, and therefore, whether he had given those troops a direct order to murder the prisoners or not, he was responsible as the commander. This was the first time in a war crimes trial in Europe that an attempt had been made to establish the vicarious responsibility of a senior commander for crimes committed by the troops under his command (a responsibility which, conveniently for the Allies, was decreed to be only applicable to German commanders, not to Allied ones). This could be called the chain of command principle. It was explained in greater detail by Colonel Macdonald:

If murders repeatedly took place in the presence of NCOs and officers, one would be entitled to suspect that they took place with the knowledge and tacit approval of the commanding officer, if not on his direct orders. At least he should be called on to explain how, if he was making any effort whatever to perform his duties, this could have happened without his knowledge and consent. So, to put the responsibility on the highest possible level, rather than on the 'trigger man' acting on orders or according to the known policy of his superiors, it was provided that (a) where the war crime was the result of concerted action upon the part of a unit or body of troops, each member would be presumed as sharing in the responsibility for that crime and all could be jointly tried for it [this was the basis of the trial brought by the Americans against the perpetrators of the Malmédy massacre of December 1944]; (b) where there was evidence of more than one war crime by the members of the unit while under the command of a single commander, the Court might receive such evidence as prima facie evidence of the responsibility of the commander for such crimes [this was the basis of some of the war crimes charges listed against Wilhelm Mohnke by a SHAEF Court of Inquiry and the United Nations War Crimes Commission involving the murder of prisoners of war in the Canadian Massacre, the First Aid Post killings and the Les Saullets murders]; (c) where a war crime had been committed and at such time or immediately prior thereto an officer or non-commissioned officer was present, this might be received as prima facie evidence of the responsibility of such officer or NCO and of his commander [this was the basis of one particular war crime charge listed

181

against Wilhelm Mohnke involving the murders of prisoners of war, viz. the Stangenberg case].

These principles not only affected the outcome of Kurt Meyer's trial; they also had a major bearing on the assessment of Wilhelm Mohnke's culpability in the crimes of which he was suspected in Normandy. Interestingly, the name of Mohnke cropped up once during the course of the trial. This was when General Hans Eberbach was giving evidence as to character. General Eberbach was from the Wehrmacht, not the SS, and in July and August 1944, as Commander of Panzer Group West, he had been Meyer's senior commanding general. Describing the types of officers to be found in the Hitler Jugend Division, General Eberbach said that, apart from forty officers who had been drafted into the Division from the Wehrmacht, the SS element could be divided into two categories – 'the young people who joined the SS from sheer idealism, and the brawlers and bad mercenaries.' In his view and that of his predecessor, General Geyr von Schweppenburg, and of the Wehrmacht in general, the two Hitler Jugend Divisional Commanders, Fritz Witt and Kurt Meyer, were among the idealists, along with Panzer Commander Max Wünsche. By contrast, Wilhelm Mohnke and Gerhard Bremer were regarded as 'bullies and brawlers'.

On 27 December 1945 the Court assembled to pronounce sentence. Kurt Meyer was found not guilty of responsibility for the murders of twenty-three Canadian prisoners in Authie and Buron and not guilty of ordering the execution of a group of seven prisoners at the Abbaye Ardenne. But the Court found Meyer guilty of inciting his troops to deny quarter and held him responsible, as commander, for the murder of a total of eighteen prisoners killed at the Abbaye Ardenne on 7 and 8 June 1944. 'The sentence of this Court,' the President pronounced, addressing the convicted SS commander, 'is that you suffer death by being shot.'

On 13 January 1946, to the intense outrage of the Canadian public at home, the Commander-in-Chief of the Canadian Occupation Force in Germany, Major-General Chris Vokes, commuted Meyer's sentence to life imprisonment. 'When I studied the evidence against Meyer,' he was to write later, explaining his decision, 'I found it to be a mass of circumstantial evidence. There was certainly the inference to be drawn that he had given the order to have Canadian soldiers executed. But nowhere in the evidence could I find the order to be proved. Not to my satisfaction. There was hearsay evidence. There was nothing direct. So I ordered the execution stayed.' But the General seems to have had a deeper, more personal gut feeling about the case, for he was to admit later that the fact that his own troops had killed German prisoners of war in Italy and North

West Europe may have had some influence in his decision to acquit Meyer.*

———

At the end of the Meyer trial, Macdonald returned to London to continue his investigations into the Normandy atrocity cases still outstanding. These cases proved much more difficult to develop than the Meyer case. Lack of evidence caused a number of them to be dropped altogether. Some suspects, like Prinz and Hagetorn, were dead. For reasons which were never officially made clear, no action was taken against Karl-Heinz Milius, Siegfried Müller or Gerhard Bremer, though the latter was securely locked up in the custody of the French (and remained so until 1948). The number one suspect now under investigation was Wilhelm Mohnke, as the 'Index of War Crimes now under Investigation by 1 Canadian War Crimes Investigation Unit' confirmed. This listed six cases of crimes committed against Canadian prisoners of war in which Mohnke was suspected of having been implicated:

> 8 June. Fontenay le Pesnel [the 'Canadian Malmédy' massacre]. 39 victims. 35 dead. Mohnke indirectly responsible.
> 8 June. Putot-en-Bessin. 6 or more victims. All dead. Mohnke indirectly responsible.
> 9 June. Bretteville l'Orgueilleuse. 2 victims. 1 dead. Mohnke indirectly responsible.
> 11 June. Les Saullets. 3 victims. 1 dead. Mohnke indirectly responsible.
> 7–11 June. Le Mesnil-Patry [the First Aid Post killings]. 6 victims. All dead. Mohnke indirectly responsible (with Müller).
> 11 June. Haut du Bosq [the Stangenberg case]. 3 victims. All dead. Mohnke directly and indirectly responsible (with Kaiser).

---

* Kurt Meyer served more than five years of his sentence in a penitentiary for common criminals in New Brunswick, Canada, and was then transferred to a British solitary confinement prison for convicted war criminals at Werl, near Dortmund, Germany, where he joined other notable imprisoned German military leaders such as Field Marshal Kesselring. Released in 1954 after exactly ten years' captivity, he got a job in a brewery and was active on behalf of a Waffen SS veterans' organization. In 1961 he died prematurely of a heart attack at the age of fifty-one, worn out by a life of privation. 5,000 old comrades attended his funeral, the largest his home town had ever seen, and the West German Chancellor, Konrad Adenauer, sent his sympathies. The war criminal had become a war hero.

Though the Putot-en-Bessin and Bretteville cases were subsequently removed from the list, the other four remained permanently logged against Mohnke's name. Colonel Macdonald was later to write:

> Confirmation of Mohnke's complicity was obtained when on 16 March, 1946, Bernhard Siebken, the commander of the 2nd Battalion of the 26th Regiment, was interrogated. Siebken stated that at some time during the first three days of fighting, Mohnke had called him on the field telephone and had said: 'Do not send so many prisoners back.' He interpreted this to mean that his commander intended that no quarter should be given or that prisoners should be shot after capture.

The preparation of the case against Mohnke received a setback, however, when the investigators inadvertently lost their star witness, Withold Stangenberg, along with the leading prosecution witness in the Kurt Meyer trial, Jan Jesionek. In February 1946 Colonel Macdonald complained to the Judge Advocate General's office in London that when he requested Major Antony Terry of the London District Cage to have these prisoners brought in for interview, he was 'much upset' to find that they had been sent to Germany for eventual repatriation to their native Poland. Not long afterwards it was found that a third prisoner, a Rottenführer Pastorek, who had given evidence in the Meyer case, had been 'lost or mislaid by the Americans in the process of transfer from one camp to another and they have been unable to find him.' Someone had boobed. Stangenberg's evidence was even more crucial against Mohnke that Jesoniek's had been against Meyer.

'The Canadian Government,' railed Macdonald, 'is at present considering the advisability of requesting Russia to turn over Mohnke to us for trial, if he should still be in their hands and alive. Consequently, the loss of this main witness will be not only embarrassing, but probably fatal to any chance of obtaining a conviction against Mohnke . . . I certainly would not like to see either of these being turned loose in Germany where they might, if the facts became known, become victims of underground Nazi punishment. On the other hand, if they are sent to Poland, they leave our control and become subject to the Russians. That, for all practical purposes, means they are lost for use at any war crimes trials. I hope that none of the other 12th SS Division prisoners who were similarly brought here have also been returned to Germany. I would greatly appreciate it if you could get an urgent message through to whatever camp in Germany might still be holding Stangenberg, if he has not yet been released, requesting them to hold him until a final decision has been made as to the prosecution of Brigadeführer Mohnke.'

But Stangenberg had slipped away, a molecule in the maelstrom of displaced humanity swarming across Central Europe. In due course he returned to his native Poland, now under Communist rule, and there he stayed and there, five years ago, he died. Neither the British nor the Canadian authorities ever made any effort to locate him, and it was left to the present authors to do so more than forty years later. The potential damage inflicted by the ineptitude of losing a key witness was limited, however, by the modification of the Rules of Procedure for Field General Courts Martial to enable certain types of evidence not normally admissible in Canadian courts to be introduced into war crimes trials. Provision was made that where witnesses were dead by the time the trial began, or were unable to attend the trial, the statements they had made under oath during the earlier investigation, together with the records of their interrogation, were admissible as evidence. Unless this provision has been abolished in the intervening years, such evidence should presumably still be eligible for submission if a trial were to be held today. At any event, as late as May 1946 the Canadians were still bullish enough about the Stangenberg case for them to report to the Judge Advocate General: 'This is a case which should certainly be proceeded with if Mohnke is made available.'

———

By early summer 1946, however, with Mohnke still unavailable for questioning, virtually the only senior commander from the 12 SS Panzer Division against whom Colonel Macdonald had any real prospect of bringing charges that would stand up in court was the former commanding officer of the 2nd Battalion of Mohnke's 26th Regiment, Obersturmbannführer Bernhard Siebken, who had been apprehended in May 1945 after his return from war service with the Leibstandarte in Hungary and was now confined in a prisoner camp in Fischbeck, near Hamelin, Germany. By then, however, moves were afoot for the disbandment of the Canadian War Crimes Investigation Unit and for further investigations and trials to be transferred to the UK military authorities. Thus the investigation and subsequent trial of Bernhard Siebken and of his orderly officer, Dietrich Schnabel, became a British affair, as would Wilhelm Mohnke's have been, if he could have been physically brought to court. There was every prospect that Siebken and Schnabel were likely to face a severer hearing from a British Military Court than their predecessor in the dock, Kurt Meyer, had received from a Canadian one.

———

It took the British more than two more years of investigations before they were able to develop a strong enough case to bring Siebken and Schnabel to trial for the First Aid Post killings at Le Mesnil-Patry. Even then, the case in the end was confined to the first set of murders – the three wounded Canadians who were shot at the SS First Aid Post on the morning of 9 June 1944 – and not the second set, involving three (or possibly four) prisoners shot at the same place two days later. There was evidently considerable confusion about the second set of killings. It was evident that several Canadian soldiers had been captured and shot following a Canadian attack on the German positions at Le Mesnil-Patry on 11 June 1944. Three bodies had been found and it was clear they had been shot in the head. A fourth body may have died of wounds sustained in combat. But accounts as to exactly what happened, and why, and even when, were contradictory. This was Colonel Macdonald's version:

> Two French civilians, M. [sic] St. Martin and M. Poisson, described an execution which they witnessed about 9.30 on the morning of 9 June [sic] in the vicinity of the place where these bodies were later found. They referred, however, to having seen five (not four) Canadian prisoners being executed by a firing party of five acting under the orders of an officer. They said that there were many German troops watching, including about ten officers. The latter stood behind the firing squad and manifested every evidence of pleasure in this deed apparently being performed for their instruction and entertainment. The officer in charge, as before, finished off the victims individually with his own pistol.

Allowing for a discrepancy in the date and time, which appears to have been muddled up with the date and time of the execution of the first three prisoners in the First Aid Post killings at Le Mesnil-Patry on the morning of 9 June, the scene described above could be an approximate description of the fate of the Canadians killed at the same place at a later date. But subsequent evidence only confuses the matter on this point. According to Michael Wimplinger, the driver at the First Aid Post, he was told by the medical orderly, Oberscharführer Ischner, that on 11 June four Canadian soldiers had come to the First Aid Post to search the rooms there and he and a number of other German soldiers had shot them in close-quarter combat. Wimplinger himself had seen the corpses in the yard. Madame Saint-Martin also saw the four corpses stretched out at the entrance to her yard, two on each side, and noticed that one of them had been wounded in the temple. The corpses were left like that for three or four days, she said, and when she complained to the mayor about it he said there was nothing he could do as it was an affair of the occupation troops.

186

Finally, the second set of murders were left on the record book and further active inquiries abandoned. Who were the officers who assembled to gawp at the death by firing squad of three hapless prisoners of war at a First Aid Post set up by the 2nd Battalion of Mohnke's 26th SS Regiment? We can only speculate.

The four men accused of the first set of murders in the First Aid Post killings at Le Mesnil-Patry were the Battalion Commander, Bernhard Siebken, now thirty-eight; his orderly officer, Dietrich Schnabel, twenty-eight; and the two medical orderlies from the First Aid Post, Heinrich Albers and Fritz Bundschuh. The first was suspected of having given the order to shoot the prisoners, the other three of having pulled the trigger. The two officers, Siebken and Schnabel, were the big game the British were after, and there is little doubt that the two orderlies who had participated in the murders were offered their scalp, if not their liberty, in return for the eye-witness evidence that might help convict their erstwhile superior officers. As the date set for the trial of the four SS men drew near, they were invited to make such statements on the case as they thought fit. On 18 June 1948, at Hanau, Dietrich Schnabel made a deposition on oath before Captain H. Schweiger, of the Field Investigation Section, War Crimes Group (NWE), in which he stated:

> During my duty with the battalion till 9 June only once in my opinion did I see prisoners of war. That was a group of forty–fifty men, I believe they were Canadians. I saw this group in Mesnil-Patry before the forward HQ of the battalion. It must have been on the afternoon of the 8th, I think, before MOHNKE's visit. Nobody had interrogated these prisoners and they were taken back to the Regimental HQ on the same day. I cannot remember having seen any other prisoners. I also cannot remember if I saw any prisoners when I visited the dressing station.
>
> I never attended official instructions about the treatment of prisoners of war, even before the invasion. Also I cannot remember during the invasion that SIEBKEN had ever given me instructions regarding prisoners of war.
>
> I remember that there was some talk about prisoners of war in the night from the 8th to the 9th, when MOHNKE visited our forward battalion HQ. It was in connection with the forty or fifty prisoners of war whom we had sent to the Regimental HQ that

187

MOHNKE said: 'Where shall I put all those prisoners of war you sent back?' He very much abused the enemy. I cannot remember the exact words any more, *but the way he expressed himself made it clear*. He further complained that German prisoners had been shot by the enemy *and said words to the effect that we should do the same*. One could not take this as an order and I did not think of it as an order. I do not know how SIEBKEN took it, but we all swore. A few hours after MOHNKE had driven off again, SIEBKEN repeated these remarks in the same manner. *One could already take this as an order*.

I cannot remember the details of the incidents on these days. I cannot remember if at the dressing station at Le Mesnil-Patry I ordered the shooting of prisoners of war . . . I would like to add that I was completely tired out and overstrained during the days from the 7th to the 9th [of June] and I was only nourished by a drug which contains cocaine, and therefore my nerves were completely overstrained.

Like Napoleon at the Battle of Waterloo, Schnabel was also suffering from piles, and later in the day on 9 June had to take leave of absence to seek proper medical attention.

––––––

On 21 July 1948 Dietrich Schnabel volunteered a second statement regarding the First Aid Post killings and this was taken down at the police prison in Hanau before the same Captain Schweiger of the War Crimes Group (NWE). This latest deposition markedly reinforced his earlier statement of three days previously. Schnabel told the war crimes investigator:

I have been cautioned that I am suspected of having committed a war crime. I have been cautioned that I am not compelled to make a statement, only if I do so by my free will . . . It is my free will to make the following statement under oath and I do this without being under pressure or compulsion or threatening and not based on promise or reward. I believe in God and I declare that I consider a solemn declaration in the name of God as a binding oath. . . .

It was MOHNKE who gave the order to shoot the prisoners of war. In the night from the 8th to the 9th MOHNKE was at the Battalion HQ in the farm at Le Mesnil-Patry. Mohnke said that

188

the Allies were shooting down German prisoners, and he started raging as we had sent a fairly large number of prisoners to his HQ. Present were myself, SIEBKEN, and either Andersen or Luetschwager. MOHNKE said 'What shall I do with them? I don't even know where to put them,' and added, '*it is an order that no further prisoners are to be taken.*' It was not clear if he was himself the originator of this order, or if he meant that this order came from higher authority. At this time I assumed the order came from higher authority.

SIEBKEN passed this order on to us, and did this as the occasion arose. I do not wish at present to make a statement in which way SIEBKEN passed on these orders and what happened later, but I wish to refer to this first with my solicitor.

Though the Court was not to take this line, we would venture the opinion that this statement, if true, not only damns Siebken, but damns Mohnke equally – and not simply on account of the First Aid Post killings but the Canadian Massacre too. Both statements implicate Mohnke, but the second elaborates on the theme. We shall return to this point later.

———

On 26 July 1948 one of the gunmen who had carried out the actual killing, Heinrich Albers – who had acquired an English fiancée during his time as a POW in England – made a deposition on oath at the War Criminal Interrogation Centre in Minden. His statement was very damaging to Siebken. What he said was:

I make the following statement under the condition that it will be kept confidential and that it is not published in the presence of those concerned (Bernhard SIEBKEN) and also that it is not produced to his legal advisor. The reason for my above restraint is that I am in fear of being exposed to personal danger and severe persecution by the followers and leaders of the SS.

SIEBKEN spoke to me several times in Fischbeck and also in Brunswick about the case of the Regimental Aid Post, Le Mesnil-Patry. He asked me what I said in my statement and then said that I should hold firm and keep to the statement which I made. He added that Dr Schütt was an arsehole and that Bundschuh may possibly be dead and therefore that I would well be able to put it on Bundschuh. Before I left Brunswick to be

189

transferred to Minden he said to me: 'Keep firm and stick to your statement. Tell SCHNABEL if he comes to Minden to *put the blame on MOHNKE.*' SIEBKEN also said that SCH-NABEL had to be protected, especially as he had been an adjutant to the *Werwolf* [the Nazi resistance].*

During the trial the Prosecutor was to make much of Albers' deposition. In his view, for Siebken it was deadly. The Judge Advocate General, in a review of the evidence after the trial, was to concur. No doubt they were right. But simply because Albers' statement would appear to condemn Siebken, and for that matter perhaps Schnabel too, does not mean that it automatically exonerates the person on whom the blame was supposed to be put – Wilhelm Mohnke. It is one thing to pass a brief message down the prison grapevine – 'put the blame on Mohnke' – but it is another to convey a full and detailed, blow by blow, minute by minute *account* of Mohnke's involvement in its totality by this means, and doubly so if Siebken's and Schnabel's accounts were meant to coincide and corroborate each other, as they would have to do, and as, by and large, they did do. In the event, both Siebken and Schnabel were to provide a detailed description of Mohnke's alleged intervention in the fate of the three Canadian prisoners, and this description tallied at many points, and was corroborated by a number of witnesses. We have to ask, how could two prisoners, segregated in separate prisons some substantial distance apart, have cobbled together a complex narrative packed with minutiae – unless it had to do with events that were already familiar to them both, and for that reason, therefore, true? At the trial they were to give an account of Mohnke's involvement and the chain of events which led up to the shooting of the prisoners which, though dismissed by the Court, seems to us all too authentic, all too feasible. In any case, the apparently damaging phrase, 'put the blame on Mohnke', is an inherently ambiguous one, capable of more interpretations than the one seized upon by the Court. Siebken here might just as well have meant, put the blame on Mohnke *as well* – in other words, make sure you remind everybody that it was Mohnke that gave the order.

---

* Under cross-examination Albers was asked by counsel why he had been viewed with suspicion by Siebken and the other occupants of his POW camp. Was it because he had – incredible though it may seem – an English fiancée? To which Albers replied: 'Not just because of that.' The drift of counsel's questioning was clearly to suggest that if Albers, an acknowledged SS gunman, wished to save his neck and see his English fiancée again, he might be required to come to some kind of arrangement with his interrogators – in effect, perhaps, to turn Crown Witness.

On 12 August 1948 Bernhard Siebken, then interned at the suspected war criminals prison at Minden, made a sworn deposition at Bad Oeynhausen before two British officers of the War Crimes Group (NWE) detailed by the C-in-C British Army of the Rhine to interrogate him. His statement was taken down in English, a fact to which he raised no objection, since he was conversant with the English language. It was a curious statement – at face value the work of a man of either confused idiocy or saint-like devotion to honour and truth. In any event, it would seem that Siebken was naïvely unaware of the implications of what he was saying, and that the SS code of loyalty and honour still bound him in some sort of protective allegiance to his former regimental commander, Wilhelm Mohnke, even at the expense of his own defence. Siebken stated:

> I have never at any time received directions or orders from MOHNKE to shoot prisoners of war nor any directions or orders which I could interpret as meaning I should shoot prisoners.
>
> I have been told of the case of the shooting of three Canadian prisoners of war at the battalion first-aid post on the morning of 9 June 1944. I deny all knowledge of such an incident and the first time I heard of the shooting of prisoners of war by members of my battalion was in Fischbeck in June 1947 when Albers told me that two prisoners had been shot on 9 June 1944 on the orders of SCHNABEL. . . .
>
> During a telephone conversation with MOHNKE on 9 or 10 June 1944 he told me that I must not send back prisoners so often. I interpreted this order that I should not send back prisoners individually or in small numbers but wait until I had collected a large number and then send them back. This order I passed on, I think to Andersen, my adjutant . . . I did not welcome the order of MOHNKE to assemble a large number of prisoners at my headquarters in order to avoid sending them back in ones and twos because a large number of prisoners near my headquarters constituted a danger of its being observed from the air. Since I gave no orders for the shooting of prisoners of war within my battalion I can only assume that such an order must have been given by MOHNKE to members of my battalion without my knowledge or that members of my battalion carried out such shootings on their own initiative and without reference to me. I have no knowledge of MOHNKE having issued such an

order over my head nor have I any knowledge of any of the members of my battalion having issued such an order without reference to me. It would have been highly irregular for MOHNKE to have issued orders to my subordinates to shoot prisoners of war without my being at some time informed of it.

This marks a considerable departure from the statement Siebken had made to the Canadian investigators on the same subject two years earlier. On that occasion he had recalled Mohnke's telephone call somewhat differently. Then, he had interpreted Mohnke's complaint, 'Do not send so many prisoners back', to mean that his Regimental Commander intended that no quarter should be given and any prisoners that were taken should be shot. Why, by August 1948, had he changed his tune on Mohnke so radically? Why had he departed so far from the position Heinrich Albers had attributed to him in the secret deposition he had made only a few days previously – 'Tell Schnabel to put the blame on Mohnke'?

It is difficult now to enter the mind of a man like Siebken. He was an early recruit to the Nazi Party and, like Mohnke, a founder-member of the Leibstandarte 'Adolf Hitler', the prototype of the Waffen-SS. He was thus a dyed-in-the-wool acolyte of Hitler's Reich. He was also a good SS soldier and by the end of the war he had been decorated with the Knight's Cross for bravery in the field and won promotion to the rank of Obersturmbannführer and the command of a Regiment. Such a man would have felt himself rigorously bound by the strict and enduring code of honour and loyalty enjoined on all members of the Waffen-SS, especially the officers. It was the staunch adherence to this code, the SS oath, which Colonel Scotland had blamed for his failure to crack the Wormhoudt case. It may well have been this same SS oath which governed Siebken's dramatic changes of stance towards his former Commanding Officer, Wilhelm Mohnke. In the early spring of 1946 Siebken in all probability believed, as others believed, that Mohnke had perished in defence of his Führer in the ruins of the Reich Chancellery in Berlin. That death, had it been true, may have released him from the awesome bonds of the SS oath, and from any fear of retribution for having broken it. But by the summer of 1948 he may well have discovered that Mohnke had not perished in Berlin but was still alive. With that knowledge, perhaps, the chill fear of retribution may have gripped his soul – the same fear that prompted even a lowly ex-orderly like Albers to tell his war crimes investigator, 'I am in fear of being exposed to danger and severe persecution by the followers and leaders of the SS'. Such a fear, we should add, might also have affected the nature of Albers' testimony; for by testifying against Siebken, who was locked up in British hands, helpless and probably doomed, Albers would be in a position to say, if the worse came to the worse and the need ever arose, that he had supported Mohnke.

192

Whatever the reason, Siebken's deposition of 12 August 1948 had two effects. Firstly, it helped torpedo his defence in the trial, even though, now that he was fighting for his life, he was to renege on his earlier deposition once he took the witness-stand. Secondly, it helped confuse the exact picture of Mohnke's role in the First Aid Post killings at Le Mesnil-Patry. We shall return to this topic later. Now to the trial.

TRIAL

There have been only two trials involving personnel of the 12th SS Panzer Division (Hitler Jugend) charged with war crimes in Normandy in June 1944. The first was the trial of Kurt Meyer in December 1945, which took place in a blaze of publicity and still looms large in the history books about the period. The second was the trial of Bernhard Siebken and Dietrich Schnabel nearly three years later, which normally attracts only a footnote at best. Yet as far as this present work is concerned the Siebken trial is of the greatest significance, for it was a trial in which the name, character and alleged behaviour of Wilhelm Mohnke were inextricably entangled; a trial, in fact, in which Mohnke in some degree was himself on trial in absentia – accused of complicity in the crime in question, not by the British military, but by his own former SS comrades-in-arms. There is not the slightest doubt that if Mohnke had not been in solitary confinement in a Soviet prison in Russia in 1948, he would have shared the dock with the other two accused in a British military court in Germany – and received the same sentence and shared the same fate. That is why we propose to examine the statements actually made at that trial in the closest detail now.

The preliminary hearing to this trial took place on 28 August 1948 at the Military Court in Hamburg. There, Bernhard Siebken, Dietrich Schnabel, Heinrich Albers and Fritz Bundschuh – 'all German Nationals in the charge of the Hamburg Garrison Unit' – were jointly charged with 'committing a war crime, at Le Mesnil-Patry, France, on or about 9 June 1944, in violation of the laws and usages of war, in that they were concerned in the killing of three unknown members of the Canadian Army, prisoners of war'. The war crime in question was, of course, the First Aid Post killing. Why the Canadian victims should have been described as 'unknown' is a mystery, unless it was to spare their next-of-kin unnecessary pain and grief.

On 21 October the trial proper began when the four accused were brought before the Military Court convened at the Curio-Haus in

Hamburg by the Commander of the Hamburg District. The Court was composed of a typical cross-section of the officer class of the British military establishment, the victorious conquering army which now occupied the British Zone of Germany like some outpost of the Indian Raj.* The Germans called it *Siegergericht* – one law for the victors, another for the vanquished. A young German woman with an impeccable non-Nazi background, Doctor of Jurisprudence Frau Anna Marie Oehlert, a lawyer at the Hanseatic Provincial Court in Hamburg, acted as Siebken's defence counsel. She was confronted with an extremely difficult task in a decidedly alien arena which put her at a distinct disadvantage.

For a start, Anna Oehlert's client was a former officer of the Waffen-SS, a branch of the German armed services which was viewed by the world at large as a criminal organization composed entirely of monsters and yahoos, and indicted as such as Nuremberg. Moreover, this young woman had to exercise her legal expertise in a very unfamiliar and esoteric Court – not just a British Court but a British Military Court, convened in Hamburg, the very heart and capital of British Germany, by a conquering army intent on punishing crimes committed against that very same conquering army by people from the nation to which she herself belonged. And to make matters worse, the review judge at the Judge Advocate-General's department, to whom at the end of the day the trial records and the Court's judgement would be sent for approval, was hardly likely to prove wildly sympathetic to the kind of crime of which Anna Oehlert's client was accused. For this judge was none other than the renowned scourge of Nazi criminals, Lord Russell of Liverpool, whose best-selling book, *The Scourge of the Swastika – A Short History of Nazi War Crimes*, written years later, would graphically catalogue Nazi horrors of the very kind that were committed by the Hitler Jugend in Normandy.

By and large, therefore, Dr Oehlert had to contend not only with the possibility of prejudice against her client, the former SS Colonel, Bernhard Siebken, but also all the disadvantages of unfamiliar legal procedure and military law and all the pitfalls and veiled obscurities of a foreign language rich in ambiguities. These were towering obstacles. The question of

---

* The President of the Court was Lt-Col. H.R. Bentley, OBE, from the Cheshire Regiment (of Wormhoudt fame), and the members were Major C.E. Hind (RHG), Captain K.T.W. Baker (Royal Scots Greys), Captain R.H. Gayer-Watson (Royal Artillery) and Captain P.N.M. Rolles (Royal Artillery). The Judge Advocate – a professional lawyer at an otherwise all-army affair – was Mr O. Bertram, a barrister-at-law. Mr Tom Field-Fisher, QC, who prosecuted at a number of war crimes trials in Hamburg, comments: 'Oliver Bertram was a senior and distinguished junior counsel, i.e. not a QC but still a man of stature. I knew him well, as I did Col. Bentley, who might best be described as a nice old buffer of a professional soldier!'

language alone, in our view, was crucial; for it was on an ambiguity of English expression that Siebken's fate in great measure was to turn.

The trial was a long one and lasted nearly three weeks. A mass of evidence was produced and many witnesses called to the witness-stand. Chief among them was Bernhard Siebken, the most senior and the most controversial of the four accused. It was never called into question that the shooting had indeed taken place. On the witness-stand Siebken himself, contradicting his earlier claim that he had not heard of the killings till 1947, had admitted: 'The killing of the prisoners did take place. It was quite illegal in my opinion.' The crucial question, therefore, was *why* it had happened. Again on the witness-stand, Siebken changed his tune from the deposition he had made a few months previously. Then he had defended his former Regimental Commander staunchly and claimed he had never received an order from Mohnke to shoot prisoners. Now he was quite categorical: the prisoners were shot because Wilhelm Mohnke ordered his orderly officer, Dietrich Schnabel, to shoot them on pain of death.

As for Schnabel, he chose not to give evidence in court in his own defence. Instead he chose to send a former SS soldier by the name of Willi Poehne onto the witness-stand to give evidence on his behalf. Poehne was to relate a very complicated and not entirely credible story about the Regimental Commander, Wilhelm Mohnke, descending on the First Aid Post like the wrath of God on the rear pillion of an army motor bike. As in Siebken's case there was a considerable discrepancy between Schnabel's pre-trial deposition, when he claimed that it was Siebken who had ordered him to shoot the prisoners, and the statement made on his behalf in court to the effect that Mohnke had drawn a pistol and warned him: 'If you do not shoot these prisoners, I will shoot you.' The differences between the pre-trial depositions and the defence put up in court by both the accused must have weighed heavily against them in the final judgement – excessively so in the authors' view.

The story of the brutal events at the First Aid Post was recounted by several eye-witnesses, including one SS man, twenty-two-year-old Michael Wimplinger, the Medical Officer's driver, who had not taken part in the murders, though he had been privy to them. In the early hours of the morning of 9 June 1944, Wimplinger told the Court, he had left the bandaging room, which was located in the kitchen of the farmhouse, and taken a stroll outside (probably to answer a call of nature). He had not ventured very far from the house, however, when he saw a figure lying in the long grass about fifty metres from the door. The figure was lying face down, stretched out on the ground with arms crossed. At first Wimplinger thought he was one of the German wounded who had dragged himself to the First Aid Post. But he had a look at him for a moment in the light of his pocket torch and noticed he was wearing a khaki uniform, which meant that

196

he was an enemy soldier, either British or Canadian. Wimplinger immediately called Albers, who was in the bandaging room, and when Albers came they set the soldier on his feet and searched him for arms. The soldier was unarmed, so they helped him back to the house, then took a pistol and went out to search the area. In the immediate vicinity of the farm they found a second soldier in khaki uniform, who had a minor head wound, then a third, who might have had a foot or leg injury. Both of them were unarmed and neither offered resistance or attempted to escape.*

Wimplinger continued:

> We brought the prisoners to Major Schütt, the MO. Dr Schütt talked to the prisoners in English. He told us that the prisoners were Canadians, and that one was from Ottawa and had four children. A bed of straw and a blanket was prepared for them and the prisoners laid down in the bandaging room. After we had talked about the prisoners for some time, and to them through Dr Schütt, the prisoners went to sleep.
>
> The prisoners got up between 8 a.m. and 9 a.m. and washed themselves at the well in the yard. While they were washing, Albers went to the Battalion to report about them on Dr Schütt's orders. After about half or three-quarters of an hour I came from the yard into the bandaging room, where the prisoners were. I saw that the Orderly Officer, Schnabel, was in the room, as well as Albers, Ischner and Dr Schütt. Bundschuh had arrived some time before, while the prisoners were still asleep, and he was in the bandaging room as well. An elderly woman, who used to live in the farm, was also in the kitchen.

The 'elderly woman' referred to by young Wimplinger was in fact the forty-nine-year-old owner of the house and farm at Le Mesnil-Patry, a Madame Germaine Saint-Martin, who had been turned out of her home when it was requisitioned as an SS lazarette on the previous day. Major Schütt had given Madame Saint-Martin permission to visit the farm from time to time to look after her cows and it was for this reason that she had arrived at the house at about 9 a.m. on the morning of the 9th. When Major Schütt saw her he asked her if he could have some milk to give to the

---

* Lt-Col. Macdonald, in charge of the investigation into the crime, gives a different account of how the prisoners got to the First Aid Post in Le Mesnil-Patry. According to his version, the men were last seen in action near Putot-en-Bessin, about a mile and a half to the north, on the previous day and brought directly to the First Aid Post, presumably by men of Siebken's Battalion. It is hard to explain the discrepancy between the two accounts.

197

wounded, so she went away to milk her cows and returned a little while afterwards. She recounted later:

> I brought the milk to the doorstep of the kitchen and looked inside. There were several wounded Germans and three British wounded prisoners of war in the kitchen. Two were lying on the floor on straw and the third was sitting in an easy chair. One of the prisoners lying down was wounded in a foot and wearing one of my clogs. The third one was wearing one of my slippers. I saw that the prisoners were smoking cigarettes, but I do not know who gave them to them to smoke. An SS soldier took the milk which I had brought and gave it to the British prisoners. I was waiting for the container, and during this time the SS officer near the door, whom I had not seen before, said something in German. I did not understand what he said but I suppose that it was an order given to the British prisoners.

The SS officer to whom Madame Saint-Martin was referring was in fact Dietrich Schnabel, who had just arrived at the farmhouse in his Volkswagen staff car. Though the French woman could not understand what Schnabel had said, it was only too plain to Wimplinger, who was standing only two or three metres away from him. When he entered the bandaging room he heard Schnabel say to Dr Schütt: 'The prisoners must be shot. Because of lack of transport we can't transport them to the rear, and as the Battalion has already suffered heavy losses, we can't spare any men from the front line to escort the prisoners back.' Wimplinger's recollection on this point was confirmed by Bundschuh, who recalled that Schnabel told Dr Schütt: 'An order has been issued to shoot the prisoners.' Dr Schütt answered that this couldn't be done, as they were defenceless prisoners, and as prisoners were not to be shot. Schnabel then explained that this order couldn't be countermanded, as it came from the commander.

It is necessary to pause at this important juncture to consider a number of crucial factors which were to have a weighty, not to say fatal, bearing on the defendants' case. For everything was now to hinge on the meaning of those simple words, 'the commander' – meaning the officer who issued the original order to shoot the prisoners. Once one knew who 'the commander' was who gave that order, one would have discovered the identity of the person really responsible for the crime. As we shall see, a little further on in his deposition, Wimplinger was to give a name to 'the commander'. What he said was: 'Dr Schütt told me that the order to shoot the prisoners, delivered by Schnabel, was issued by Siebken. I remember for certain that he mentioned the name Siebken and did not use the expression "commander".'

198

Not surprisingly, this statement formed a major part of the prosecution attack and was to have a disastrous consequence for Siebken, for if true it pointed conclusively to the fact that it was Siebken who had ordered the killings. But was it true? Wimplinger's testimony at this point amounts to no more than hearsay – albeit admissible in a military court. Furthermore, he was unable to say, when cross-examined in the witness-stand, whether Dr Schütt really knew that the shooting order had come from Siebken or whether he only supposed so by virtue of some rumour or other. Other witnesses who had been in the First Aid Post were even vaguer. Thus Albers was to testify in the witness-stand: 'I have said that Schnabel gave the order and I did not know, nor do I know today, whether Siebken gave the order [to him].'

So we have a situation were the only person to testify that by 'commander' Schnabel meant Siebken was Wimplinger, who was retailing hearsay evidence. Though hearsay evidence was admissible in war crimes trials, the test was what weight it should carry, and here *the main thrust of the prosecution was based on this hearsay*. As we shall see, when Schnabel realized the significance of the construction that the British Military Court had put on this ambiguous word, he made a desperate, belated attempt to clarify it. By 'commander', he declared on oath, he 'naturally meant the Regimental Commander', Mohnke, not the Battalion Commander, Siebken.

To continue with Wimplinger's narrative. Schnabel now turned to the rest of the people in the First Aid Post and said: 'I herewith give you the official order to shoot the prisoners.' To Albers, Ischner and Bundschuh he then declared: 'Those who took them prisoner should bump them off.' The outraged Dr Schütt muttered that it was horrible to shoot defenceless prisoners. But there was little he could do about it. Wimplinger continued:

> After that Albers gave the prisoners a signal and called to them: 'Come on! Come on!' Albers went out of the door and the prisoners followed with their hands raised. Behind the prisoners went Bundschuh. Albers and Bundschuh were carrying a machine pistol. Oberscharführer Ischner, armed with a pistol, followed about four paces behind the others. Four paces behind him, Schnabel left the room. Through the open door I saw that one of the prisoners was walking ahead, with the other two following him. I seem to remember that one of them was supporting the other one. Albers walked slightly to the side of the two prisoners, and Bundschuh behind. Ischner followed at a distance of about three to four metres, and Schnabel walked about three to four metres behind Ischner. I watched this group until they drew level with the barn and then returned into the house.

In this account Wimplinger has obviously forgotten that one other person accompanied the little procession out of the house – Madame Saint-Martin. After Schnabel had given his order he had turned to the French lady and made her understand that she had to follow. When she did not obey immediately, he spoke to her more sharply, in French. '*Venir, venir, Madame* [sic].' he told her. 'Come along, Madame.' Madame Saint-Martin later described what happened next:

> We walked across the yard and then we went out through a small gate at the end of this yard at the left and then we went along the garden which is on the right and then we arrived at the end of the garden. The three prisoners marched in front, hands raised. The prisoner wounded in the leg marched in pain – but anyhow, he marched. The SS soldiers followed at a distance of approximately three metres, holding their weapons at the trail. The SS officer followed the SS soldiers at a very short distance and myself immediately behind. I saw that the SS officer had a revolver in his hand, pointed at the prisoners.
>
> At the end of the garden the prisoners stopped and turned their backs to the SS soldiers. The three prisoners were not armed, they did not make any movement of revolt and did not attempt to escape. There was a small trench at the end of the garden which had been there for some time. The officer gave an order which I did not understand; but I was afraid because I saw that the Germans were going to shoot the three prisoners. The SS officer who gave the order to fire was not too tall and fairly big, approximately 168 cm high, age approximately thirty years, and he had brown hair and very big dark brown eyes.

Eighteen-year-old medical orderly Fritz Guenther Bundschuh, who only that morning had been sent to the advanced dressing station in the farmhouse at Le Mesnil-Patry because of the large number of wounded, now found that he was required to help take lives rather than help save them. He was to state subsequently:

> Albers and I were standing about five to six metres behind the prisoners of war. Ischner was standing behind us either to right or left and Schnabel remained standing behind us on the right-hand side. Schnabel gave the order to fire. I fired about ten to twelve rounds from my sub-machine-gun, spraying all three of the prisoners. I noticed that Albers fired about the same amount of shots from his sub-machine-gun in the same manner.

200

Madame Saint-Martin continued:

> I saw that all three SS soldiers had fired. The three soldiers were hit as they fell down together. After this, the SS officer in his turn fired his revolver at each of the prisoners who had fallen down. I no longer remember if he fired at the head or the body of the three prisoners. The corpses were left on the spot. The SS officer said to me: '*Madame, partir* [sic]. Go away, Madame.' I ran away to my neighbours. I do not know why I was ordered to attend the execution. I thought they were going to shoot me with them.

Back in the kitchen of the farmhouse, Michael Wimplinger had heard several rather muffled bursts of gunfire. He continued:

> A few minutes later, through the open door, I saw Albers, Bundschuh and Ischner returning. In the presence of myself, the doctor and the [German] wounded, Albers told me that he had bumped the prisoners off. I remember Dr Schütt made the remark that if, following a counter-attack, the enemy should find the corpses and discover the German bandages on the prisoners, an unpleasant affair could result and we might all get bumped off for it.

It was then, according to Wimplinger, that Dr Schütt told him the order to shoot the prisoners had been issued by Siebken.

The bodies remained where they had fallen for several days, then on the MO's orders Bundschuh and Albers returned to the execution site and buried the Canadians' bodies in a very shallow grave beside a hedge nearby – so shallow in fact that one of Wimplinger's fellow drivers complained to Wimplinger the following day that he had found one of the Canadians' boots sticking out of the ground. How Wimplinger felt about all this, if anything, was never clear. But later he was to claim that a rumour circulated 'amongst the comrades' to the effect that there existed an order that all prisoners were to be shot, possibly as a reprisal for a large number of SS men who were rumoured to have been found shot in a corn field.* So perhaps, like most of his SS comrades, this otherwise innocent ambulance driver felt the killing of Canadian prisoners of war was justifiable.

---

* No record of this incident has ever been found.

201

It was the prosecution case that Schnabel had been responsible for the execution of the prisoners on the order of his Commanding Officer, Siebken. The depositions of both accused, the prosecution maintained, amounted to as much. In reply, the main thrust of the defence was clear and unequivocal. The three Canadians had been shot as an act of reprisal against the murder of German prisoners of war in Allied hands on the same sector of the front during the days of bitter fighting following the D-Day invasion.

An impressive phalanx of defence witnesses were summoned before the Court to give evidence to this effect, some of them former senior officers of considerable standing in the wartime German army. Before any court at any other time in history the testimony they gave would have been sensational and extremely damaging. Here, however, in a Military Court convened by the victorious British Army amid the ruins of Germany's shattered second city, the charges made by the humiliated representatives of a defeated and dishonoured army did not carry the weight they might have done under other circumstances.

Colonel Meyer-Detring, who had been the intelligence chief on the staff of the German C-in-C on the Western Front, Field Marshal von Rundstedt, stated in the witness-stand that at the very beginning of the Allied landings he twice received documents through channels proving that the Canadian army did not intend to take any prisoners. 'I specially remember the notes in the pocket-book of an officer killed in action,' Colonel Meyer-Detring told the Court, '– I cannot now say with certainty whether he was Canadian or British – containing an extract from some order concerning the invasion. In these notes I found the sentence: "No prisoners are to be taken".'

On the same question the next witness, Hubert Meyer, who had been chief operations officer on the divisional staff of the 12th SS Panzer Division, stated that on 7 June 1944 a notebook was found on a Canadian captain containing notes on the pre-invasion briefing. 'Apart from tactical instructions,' Hubert Meyer told the court, 'these notes also contained rules on the actual fighting. These rules stated: "Prisoners are not to be taken".' Meyer affirmed that he had personally seen this notebook and had handed it over to the Commander of the Seventh Army, Colonel-General Dollmann, to be forwarded to higher authority. He had also seen the minutes of the interrogation of other prisoners, officers and other ranks, made during their interrogation by the divisional staff. 'They confirmed the fact that they had received orders from their commanding officers not to take any prisoners,' Meyer stated. 'One of them stated they were not to take prisoners whenever these would be in their way. These violations of the rules of war mainly took place during the initial period.'

The next witness was Lt-Col. von Zastrow, who had been the intelligence chief on the staff of General Leo Geyr von Schweppenburg, the Commander of Panzer Group West. During the first days after the Allied landings von Zastrow's unit had been located in the Caen area, where several violations of the Hague and Geneva Conventions by Allied troops came to his notice. Von Zastrow described an incident in which a number of captured German soldiers, having been taken prisoner and disarmed, had been shot down by Canadian troops. Von Zastrow also described his interrogation of a Canadian captain who had been taken prisoner in the Somme region later in the campaign in France. As the captain had belonged to the same unit which had been found in possession of the incriminating orders immediately after the landings, and had been guilty of corresponding violations of the rules of war, he was charged with these offences under International Law. To the question whether he had any knowledge of the shooting of German prisoners of war, this Captain had replied that he had heard that violations had taken place, but later on strict orders had been given threatening severe punishment for such actions.

A more serious instance of Allied violation of the rules governing the treatment of prisoners of war was cited by the defence counsel. A new witness – Count Clary-Aldrigen, formerly Regimental Adjutant in the 130th Armoured Artillery, Panzer-Lehr Division – was brought into the witness-stand. This witness told the Court that on the morning of 8 June 1944 he was taken prisoner by an armoured car patrol of the Inns of Court Regiment, along with his Regimental Commander, Colonel Luxenburger, one of the Battalion Commanders, Major Hubert Zeissler, and six other ranks. When the German officers refused to allow themselves to be used as a human shield for the British armoured cars during their drive back to the Allied side through the German lines, Colonel Luxenburger, though seriously disabled (he had lost an arm in the Great War), was beaten unconscious by two British officers, and then, bleeding all over, tied to one of the armoured cars. As the armoured cars moved off they opened fire on Count Clary, Major Zeissler and the other German soldiers, killing them all, according to the witness, except Count Clary, who was shielded by the dead body of one of his comrades lying on top of him.* While driving through the German lines from the rear, the armoured cars came under fire and the vehicle carrying Colonel Luxenburger was hit by a German

* This version of events would appear to be challenged in a recent German history of the Panzer-Lehr Division, which concludes that though Colonel Luxenburger was indeed struck down his comrades managed to escape. This would seem to be confirmed by the fact that at least Major Zeissler survived his unpleasant encounter with the Inns of Court armoured cars, for three months later he was mentioned in despatches. See *Die Geschichte der Panzer-Lehr-Division im Westen 1944–1945* by Helmut Ritgen (Stuttgart, 1979).

anti-tank gun. The Colonel was wounded and died shortly afterwards. Count Clary, meanwhile, regained consciousness and crawled in a severely wounded condition in the direction of the village of Le Mesnil-Patry, where he was found by members of the 2nd Battalion, 26th SS Panzer Grenadiers, brought to the command post and given first aid by the battalion clerk, Sturmmann Klöden.

Klöden confirmed to the Court: 'I administered first aid to him. I had previously been told that a seriously wounded officer of the German army was going to be brought to us who had been involved in a special incident.' Questioned as to whether Count Clary had told him about the incident on that occasion, Klöden replied: 'Yes, in my own presence and in the presence of Andersen [Siebken's adjutant, later killed in action] he told about a shooting incident from which he had escaped.' Questioned whether Count Clary's report was submitted to higher levels, Klöden replied: 'Yes, it was a special incident, which had taken place in the sector of our battalion. It had to be entered in the War Diary and was transmitted by phone to the regiment.'

It was defence counsel's contention that such an incident, occurring in the sector held by Siebken's battalion only a few hours before the three Canadian prisoners were shot, was a matter of considerable significance – a clear-cut case of reprisal, which in the defence counsel's view, based on an extremely technical legal argument citing various interpretations of International Law and Practice, exonerated the accused from the charge of committing a war crime.

The defence then turned to the crucial matter of *who* gave the original order to shoot the three Canadian prisoners. The defence's position on this was best encapsulated in a petition delivered on 20 November 1948 following the judgement. This read:

> It is an indisputable fact that the three Canadians were shot on the order of a commanding officer. The Prosecutor maintains that this order was given by Siebken. I have maintained that this order came from no other person but Mohnke, who was in command of the regiment, and that Siebken not only refused to obey this order but did everything to prevent the order being carried out.

That was the defence stance in a nutshell. Examined in greater detail in the petition referred to above, it would appear to develop a highly persuasive line of argument. The relevant section of this argument runs as follows:

> In the witness-stand Siebken declared that, in view of the violation of the rules of International Law on the part of the

Allies, Mohnke had requested him not to take any more prisoners and to order such prisoners as were already in his hands to be shot. Mohnke, it seemed, was 'very excited' about the occurrence reported by Count Clary, who was at this time having his wound treated at Siebken's First Aid Post in Le Mesnil-Patry, and according to evidence given by Company Commander Henne, Mohnke argued his point 'in a very rude tone'.

At the time, Siebken expressed the view that all such an action would achieve would be a redoubling of violence by the other side. There, for the moment, the matter rested. Mohnke departed and Siebken transferred his command post from the village church to a nearby farmhouse.

Soon after midnight of 8–9 June 1944, while Siebken was deeply preoccupied with preparations for a fresh battalion attack on the coming morning, Mohnke reappeared. Unfortunately, his visit coincided with that of the Battalion's Medical Officer, Dr Schütt, who reported that he had three wounded Canadian soldiers at his First Aid Post – the first Canadian prisoners to be taken since the Count Clary incident. According to Siebken, Mohnke ordered the prisoners to be shot immediately. Siebken refused – 'categorically'. Mohnke's reaction was very violent. He remonstrated with Siebken and reproached him angrily. The enemy were not taking prisoners, he argued, so why should we? Still Siebken turned a deaf ear – or so he claimed on the witness-stand. Mohnke then pulled rank. As Siebken's Regimental Commander, he said, he was now giving Siebken a superior order. But Siebken was still unpersuaded.

By this time Mohnke seems to have been beside himself – 'beyond all measures excited', as Siebken's counsel put it in her awkward Germanic English. Roaring at Siebken, *'We'll see about it!'* Mohnke turned on Siebken's orderly officer, Schnabel, whom he had called into the room, and ordered him point blank to shoot the three prisoners. When Schnabel attempted to adopt his Battalion Commander's attitude towards this order, 'he was crushed down by Mohnke'. Mohnke repeated his personal, direct, official order to shoot the prisoners one more time, and then departed.

According to the defence counsel, Siebken had told his Commanding Officer, Mohnke, without mincing words, that he would neither accept nor hand on such orders, let alone give such orders personally.

The witness Klöden, who at that time was Siebken's clerk, after stating that Mohnke had ordered Siebken not to take any prisoners, said: 'Siebken rejected any such measures.' This statement has been confirmed by the witness on being re-examined as follows: 'It was a clear refusal to obey orders.'

Questioned whether he remembered the exact words used by Siebken in refusing to obey the order, Klöden said: 'The gist of his reply was, "I am not going to do any such thing. I shall send back the prisoners in the proper fashion and I refuse to treat them in an unfair manner."'

The witness Steinmann, who was in charge of the telephone exchange of that sector, made the following statement concerning an earlier telephone conversation between Siebken and the Regimental Headquarters: 'When informed that the 26th Regiment did not wish to have prisoners, Herr Siebken replied that he was going to send back the prisoners all the same.' Questioned as to who was at the Regimental HQ's end of the line, the witness, who did not overhear the conversation from the beginning, said: 'I am not quite sure who it was, *but judging by the manner and tone in which the conversation was carried on it must have been Mohnke.*'

On the witness-stand Siebken then described how, immediately after the argument with Mohnke, he tried to get in touch with the Divisional Commander over the phone. On the face of it, this was an extraordinary thing to do, for he was breaking strict military protocol by leap-frogging the chain of command, going over the head of the Regimental Commander in order to complain about him to his Divisional Commander. 'That this call was put through was confirmed by the witness Klöden,' defence counsel reminded the Court. 'According to the statement made by Siebken, he failed to reach the Divisional Commander and he therefore asked the Divisional Chief of Staff [Hubert Meyer] whether an order had been issued by the Division to the effect that prisoners should be shot. The "IA" officer replied in the negative and asked Siebken for further information, whereupon the latter explained that Mohnke had maintained that such an order had been issued. At the same time Siebken asked to be put through to the Divisional Commander immediately on his return.'

The witness Hubert Meyer stated as follows:

On the night of 8–9 June Siebken rang me to ask whether the Division had issued an order to shoot all prisoners. I said no and added that it would be desirable to take as many prisoners as possible as they were the only source of information for us. I asked him what was the reason for such a curious question. He replied that Mohnke had said something to this effect. He then asked me to put him through to our Divisional Commander at once.

Hubert Meyer went on to say that following Siebken's telephone call he at once tried to get in touch with Regimental Commander Mohnke. These are Meyer's words:

206

Max Wünsche (with head wound and Knight's Cross) drives despondently off after watching his tanks being knocked out in the Normandy fighting. In the sidecar (with spectacles and wounded arm in a sling) is Rudolf von Ribbentrop, son of Hitler's Foreign Minister

Mohnke (centre) at the operations briefing with fellow officers of the SS-Hitler Youth Division, Normandy, June 1944

Wilhelm Mohnke glares at the photographer as elements of his 1st SS Panzer Division gets stuck in a traffic jam – a frequent occurrence on the narrow Ardennes roads during the Battle of the Bulge

A Peiper look-alike stops to take his bearings near Malmédy. Long thought to be Jochen Peiper himself, the cigar-chewing SS warrior is in all probability Unterscharführer Ochsner, of Peiper's recce battalion

The real Jochen Peiper, complete with death's head badge, Knight's Cross and charmer's smile. Sentenced to death at the Malmédy massacre trial in 1946, Peiper was reprieved but eventually murdered in a fire-bomb attack on his home in France in 1976

Typical handiwork of the Peiper combat group. Unarmed American GIs mowed down in a field after surrender during the advance of Mohnke's spearheads in the Malmédy area

Belgian civilians – men, women and children – murdered by men of Mohnke's SS division in the Ardennes onslaught

Desperate and closely guarded Waffen-SS man surrenders to grim-faced Americans, during the Ardennes offensive, December 1944

Nemesis for the Malmédy killers. Lt Lary, a survivor of the massacre, points out the man who fired the first shot, SS-Sturmmann Georg Fleps, at the mass trial before the American Military Tribunal in the former concentration camp at Dachau, Germany

Hitler's Reich Chancellery under new management, Berlin, July 1945. It was from the cellars below that Mohnke led the first escape bid through the besieged capital. By the time this photo was taken, he was already in the Lubyanka Prison, Moscow

(opposite) Knight's Cross holder Wilhelm Mohnke as SS Oberführer and Divisional Commander during the Battle of the Bulge

General Patton was one of American's most dashing commanders of the war. But was he responsible for an allied war crime at Biscari?

Jeff Rooker, Member of Parliament for Perry Bar, Birmingham, brandishes the secret investigative file after raising the Wormhoudt case in the House of Commons in 1988

As Mohnke was absent I talked to his Adjutant. I asked him what was going on with regard to this order that all prisoners should be shot. He did not know anything about it. I again pointed out that it would be desirable to take as many prisoners as possible and that they should be treated in accordance with the provisions of the Geneva Convention. I then ordered the 'IC' Officer to draw up an order about the taking and treatment of prisoners, which was to be distributed down to company level. The tenor of the order was to be in keeping with what I had told Siebken and Mohnke's Adjutant. When the Divisional Commander returned in the morning I reported to him about Siebken's telephone call. The Commander signed the draft order, which was at once distributed. He said to me he was going to ring up Siebken.*

Forty years after the trial, Hubert Meyer did not hesitate to confirm that these telephone calls took place exactly as he had described them to the Court in 1948. If, therefore, Siebken really did phone Divisional HQ, as we believe, and complain about Mohnke's prisoner order, then we have to ask one fundamental question which seems to have gone unasked during the trial. If Siebken was the commanding officer who issued the order to shoot the prisoners, why on earth should he have by-passed the proper chain of command and rung his Divisional Commander to talk to him about it? Would that have been the behaviour one might reasonably expect from a man with a guilty secret? We think not. The corollary that follows, therefore, must be that Siebken did *not* issue the order.

Meanwhile, Siebken had other, no less pressing matters on his mind, for with a battalion attack due to start at 10 a.m. the next morning he had to work out his plans and form up his troops. Dr Oehlert continued:

Following the telephone conversation, he went into the fighting line after making it clear that his order stayed, according to which prisoners should be sent back speedily and in the

* If the Divisional Commander's draft order really was distributed it does not seem to have had much impact, certainly not in the sector held by the 26th Panzer Grenadiers. Two days later, for example, there was a spate of prisoner murders, including a second set of killings at the First Aid Post in Le Mesnil-Patry, two sets of shootings just down the road at Les Saullets, and three executions at Mohnke's Regimental HQ (the Stangenberg case). If Witt *did* issue an order to stop shooting prisoners and this was disregarded, then Mohnke would appear to be to blame for the further series of murders carried out in his sector. But if Witt did not issue the order, then both Witt and Mohnke would have to be implicated in the killings, since Witt was now apprised of what was going on.

proper fashion. This statement which was made by Siebken in the witness-stand was confirmed by the witness Klöden. Moreover the witness Henne, who was at that time in charge of a company under Siebken, has confirmed that on the night of 8–9 June 1944 Siebken was in the fighting line.

Siebken has further stated that he returned to Battalion Headquarters about 10 a.m. on the morning of 9 June. On his arrival his Adjutant, Andersen, reported to him that Mohnke had rung up during the night to ask why Schnabel had not yet reported the shooting of the three Canadians, which he, Mohnke, had ordered. When Andersen replied that this order had not been carried out, Mohnke had made a terrible row. Some time after that – when Siebken was still absent – Mohnke arrived at the Battalion Headquarters, raging because Schnabel had not executed his order, to ask where he could find Schnabel. Since the latter was absent, Mohnke left again.

A short while after Andersen had made his report, Schnabel turned up at his headquarters and stated that Mohnke had compelled him to carry out the order given by him. According to the statement made by Siebken, he [Siebken] violently rebuked Schnabel and ordered that the incident should at once be put on record in the War Diary. The facts were also put before the Divisional Commander in a verbal report.

This statement which my client made under oath was also confirmed by the witness Klöden, who not only testified to Siebken's absence, the telephone call, Mohnke's visit in Siebken's absence between 8 a.m. and 9 a.m. in the morning, but also to what happened after Siebken had returned. This is what he said:

'Andersen reported to Siebken on all orders, etc., that had been received in the meantime, mentioning also that Mohnke had made a row because Schnabel had not carried out the order given to him. After about fifteen to twenty minutes Schnabel came back. He looked extremely depressed when he reported to his Battalion CO, Siebken, that the Regimental CO, Mohnke, had compelled him to carry out the order which had been given to him. Siebken then ordered Andersen to put the incident on record in the War Diary.'

Siebken further stated that he rang up the Divisional Commander on 9 June to inform him about the facts.

On the afternoon of 9 June 1944 the Commander of the 12th SS Panzer Division, Fritz Witt, spoke on the telephone with Siebken, who informed

208

him about the episode with Mohnke. Normally Witt was a calm, even reserved kind of person, who refrained from openly criticizing senior officers in front of officers of lower rank. On this occasion, however, he reacted to Siebken's complaint with uncharacteristic frankness and denounced Mohnke's behaviour in extremely harsh terms. He was especially critical of Mohnke giving direct orders to Siebken's Orderly Officer, Schnabel, and according to the evidence of Witt's Adjutant, Rothemund, he complained: 'Mohnke gives orders without consulting the Battalion Commander, Siebken.'

It was at that point, Rothemund testified, that Witt became convinced that Mohnke was unfit to be a Regimental Commander and arranged for him to be posted away from the Division. As Dr Oehlert reminded the Court:

> The witness Rothemund, Adjutant of the Divisional Commander, stated in the witness-stand that as he was in charge of the officers' list he was informed by the Divisional Commander on about 12 June 1944 that he, the Commander, intended to have Mohnke posted away. One of the reasons for this decision had been the complaint lodged by Siebken against Mohnke. The witness confirmed that soon after receiving Siebken's verbal report the Divisional Commander personally went to see Siebken at his headquarters. Soon after that the Divisional Commander was killed in action.

Mohnke was not posted away from the Division, partly because of Witt's death – he was caught in the open by an air-burst from a massive 16-inch shell when a British battleship opened up its guns on his headquarters on 14 June – and partly because the Division was suffering such heavy losses among its officers at the time that it could ill afford to lose an experienced tactical commander by posting him away from the front. Siebken's counsel concluded:

> Summing up I wish to say that in my opinion the following unequivocal and unassailable facts have been established by the evidence:
> 1. No other person but Mohnke is responsible for the order to shoot the three Canadians.
> 2. Siebken bluntly refused to obey this order.
> 3. Immediately on Siebken's refusal, Mohnke, in his capacity as CO of the Regiment, gave direct orders to Schnabel for the shooting order to be carried out.
> 4. Siebken prevented the order being carried out right away.

5. Disregarding proper channels and severe disciplinary regulations, Siebken, without Mohnke's knowledge or consent, lodged a complaint with the Divisional Commander. This had the effect that the Divisional Commander at once issued another principal order prohibiting any incorrect treatment, let alone the shooting, of prisoners of war.

6. Siebken informed his staff about the decision made by the Divisional Commander and explicitly stated that prisoners would continue to be treated in a fair manner.

7. Subsequently, Siebken went to the fighting line to discharge his duties at Battalion Commander and was absent from his headquarters until about 10 a.m. on the following morning.

8. The order given by Mohnke had not been carried out by 8 a.m.

9. About 9 a.m. Mohnke personally compelled Schnabel to carry out the shooting without the knowledge and against the clear intentions of Siebken, who was absent, as well as in contradiction to the orders given by the Divisional Commander.

10. Immediately on learning what had happened Siebken made a verbal report to the Divisional Commander and lodged a complaint against Mohnke. Following this complaint the Divisional Commander tried to have Mohnke posted away to another unit.

At no time, defence counsel averred, did Siebken ever issue an order for the shooting of prisoners, and there were plenty of witnesses to confirm it. Indeed, the Battalion Clerk, Klöden, whose job was to count and record prisoners of war passing through the battalion, confirmed that during the first few days of the invasion the battalion correctly took more than 400 prisoners, while one of the Company Commanders, Polanski, was actually with Siebken when Siebken ordered a large batch of prisoners taken by one of the companies to be sent back to the regimental POW assembly point. Not only did Siebken have nothing to do with the shooting of prisoners, his defence maintained, but he saw to it that prisoners were properly sent to the rear. 'Siebken was in no way responsible for the shooting of the three Canadians,' counsel stated, 'and did everything, nay, more than he could ever have been expected to do, to bar any possibility of the order being carried out.'

The prosecuting counsel was naturally very contemptuous of the defence case, as all good prosecutors normally are. As far as Albers and Bundschuh were concerned, he contended in his closing address, they should both be convicted of the crime, since they had unquestionably fired the actual shots which had killed the three Canadians – though he conceded that the Court might feel they were young men who acted in fear of death and were conditioned to unquestioning obedience of orders.

But as for Schnabel, the officer in charge of the firing party, there were no mitigating circumstances. There was plenty of eye-witness evidence that he had commanded the firing squad that had shot the three Canadian prisoners and had personally blown their brains out by way of a *coup de grâce*. He knew very well that what he had done was a criminal act and that it was an insufficient defence to claim that he had only been carrying out orders. Where was the evidence in his first deposition, the Prosecutor asked, to indicate that Mohnke had physically coerced him into carrying out the shooting order? His entire defence was not born till later, the moment Siebken stepped on to the witness-stand and for the first time declared: 'Schnabel came and reported to me that he had been compelled by Mohnke by force of arms to shoot these prisoners.' But Schnabel himself did not choose to go on to the witness-stand to give evidence. Instead he put the defence witness Willi Poehne there to give evidence on his own behalf.

Now that gentleman, sir, was a remarkable witness,' scoffed the Prosecutor. 'He placed his company geographically in the wrong spot. It was necessary that he should do so in order to get himself to the spot where he could help Schnabel. Moreover, he forgot that he had himself made a deposition on oath and he gave, sir, a most remarkable series of incidents that happened at a moment when he had already stated on oath that he was lying in a field waiting for instructions to connect the field telephone. But this was not the end of his absurdities, because at the end of this hair-raising story he left Schnabel proceeding down a road in a motor car, then passed by Mohnke on the rear seat of a motor cycle. It is clear from every eye-witness at the First Aid Post that Mohnke never reached it. Not a single eye-witness saw Mohnke, not a single eye-witness saw his motor cycle.

That raises two points. The first is that . . . Willi Poehne is one of the most imaginative liars that it has been my or your privilege ever to see in the witness-box. And the second, of course, is that – even if you by any remote possibility *did* think that Mohnke exercised some force upon Schnabel – it is quite clear that that force had ceased at some time before Schnabel reached the First Aid Post. And, of course, the defence put up by Schnabel could only be a defence if it continued right up to the very moment of the crime. Schnabel cannot excuse any act of his own as being committed under fear of death from Mohnke if Mohnke was not even there. It must be, I think, beyond argument that Mohnke was not at the First Aid Post.

This, we feel, is putting a very narrow time-scale on the notion of 'fear of death' and taking a rather unrealistic view of life in the Waffen-SS. The Prosecutor here has underestimated the power of superior orders (or force) in the SS. Mohnke had no need to be present for his force to be exercised, and that force could indeed continue right up the moment of execution whether Mohnke was there or not, for Mohnke was quite empowered to punish his subordinates in any way he chose at any time he chose. But in any case, the Prosecutor concedes that the Court *might* think that Mohnke did exercise some force upon Schnabel – as well he might have, in our view.

'I think I need waste no more time with the case of Schnabel,' the Prosecutor concluded. 'I invite you with every confidence to say that he is guilty of every crime with which he is charged.'

The Prosecutor then turned to the case of Siebken. The conduct of the defence, he protested, caused him the 'greatest grievance' – not on account of the evidence but the 'irresponsible manner in which his defence has been conducted'. The Prosecutor had in mind the defence counsel's accusation that at the time of the invasion the Canadians (and perhaps the British too) had received orders not to take German prisoners – and acted on these orders. Naturally, such a charge would not have gone down terribly well in a court composed of serving officers of the British army, even if it had been well-founded. But in the Prosecutor's contention, it was not well-founded.

It is shown by a very senior German officer that if this order ever existed at all, it was a divisional order. It seems to have been broadcast to the rank and file of the Hitler Jugend Division under the name of the Eisenhower Order . . . a propaganda invention on the eve of battle to make young men fight more desperately than they [otherwise] would. But, of course, the matter does not end there, because we were told that the existence of that order and of those brutalities were reported up to the highest quarter. And yet the German High Command and government, which was never reluctant to cry out if it felt it was being badly dealt by, never made any complaint to anybody at all. And when the Canadian government complained to the German government about the brutal murder of many soldiers by the Hitler Jugend Division in the area of Le Mesnil-Patry, the German government merely denied the fact of any such murders having been committed. Can you possibly doubt for one

212

moment that – had this order existed, had these alleged Canadian atrocities been committed – the German government would not have set them out in full?*

This was a valid point. But the Prosecutor was on less sure ground when it came to specifics. Defence counsel's reference, in her closing speech in the morning, to the incident in which Colonel Luxenburger was mortally wounded and Count Clary seriously wounded in an encounter with a British armoured car patrol of the Inns of Court Regiment, allegedly while prisoners of war, caught the prosecution counsel by surprise, and he could only blether and bluster in outraged riposte.

Graf Clary's story reminds you of a cinema more than a Law Court,' he protested. 'If true, it showed him up as an officer incautious to the point of lunacy. . . . In her speech this morning Frau Dr Oehlert said that she understood the unit concerned in that incident to be the Inns of Court Regiment. Had she had the confidence to mention that fact at an earlier stage of the proceedings, I might perhaps have been able to call evidence to show where the Inns of Court Regiment was at that time. But, of course, you will overlook all reference to that unit because there is no evidence to that unit at all.

Had the Prosecutor had time to check the War Diary of the unit concerned he would have found that it was exactly where Dr Oehlert had said it was at the time in question. On the morning of 8 June 1944 two armoured scout troops – No 2 and 6a – of 'C' Squadron of the Inns of Court Regiment slipped unnoticed round the left flank of the Panzer-Lehr Division and near the village of Cristot ran into a group of Germans on the staff of the 130th Panzer Artillery Regiment of the Panzer-Lehr. According to the Regiment's War Diary: 'Nos 2 and 6a captured 3 German officers, including a Colonel and 3 [other ranks]. On way back with these they were ambushed and lost all vehicles. Lt [T.L.] Yodaiken, Lt [R.] Wigram killed,

* Yet General Vokes, C-in-C of the Canadian Army Occupation Force in Germany, gave as his reason for commuting the death sentence passed on Kurt Meyer for responsibility in the shooting of Canadian prisoners of war, the fact that his own troops had killed German prisoners of war in north-west Europe and Italy. Moreover, when Dr Craig W.H. Luther, then at the University of California in Santa Barbara, was researching his study of the 12th SS Panzer Division (*Blood and Honour*, 1987), a questionnaire sent to veterans of the 3rd Canadian Division indicated that German prisoners were sometimes shot in Normandy, especially if they were in the Waffen-SS.

213

2 ORs missing, 4 ORs led by Cpl Fowler made way back on foot by compass.' The prisoners did not return with them. According to the official historian of the Hitler Jugend Division, three Canadian prisoners of war in the vicinity of the Command Post of the 2nd Battalion, 26th SS Panzer Grenadiers, were shot by order as a reprisal.

You, sir, have held that reprisals are no justification for a war crime,' the Prosecutor reminded the Court. 'Reprisals are illegal. The doctrine . . . may have arisen from a German proverb, which certain German writers of International Law sought to uphold between the years 1900 and 1914, that necessity in law overrules the manner of warfare. To attempt to return to that doctrine now would in my opinion be to attempt to return to barbarism.

However, it was not on a doctrine of law that Siebken should be judged, the Prosecutor continued, but on the basis of evidence. Two points of evidence were damning for Siebken, he maintained. The first was Schnabel's deposition, in which he stated that Siebken 'passed on an order to us as the occasion arose'. That, the Prosecutor submitted, was 'deadly'.

At this juncture we have to ask why the Prosecutor was so confident on this point and why no one challenged him about it. The deadliness of this statement depends on a particular interpretation of an extremely ambiguous utterance. What exactly does the sentence mean? It is a very vague and general sentence and we cannot see why it should necessarily and conclusively mean what the Prosecutor implies it means. If it does indeed refer to the shooting of prisoners, no matter how obliquely, we would further ask – what exactly is meant by the phrase 'passed on an order'? When a commander is the original source of an order, he is said in normal parlance to 'issue' or 'give' that order. On the other hand, if a commander 'passes on' an order, this suggests that he is not the original source of the order but merely relaying it as an intermediary between the original source and the ultimate recipient – that he is acting, in other words, as part of a chain of command. In his affidavit of 9 November 1948, Schnabel argues more or less this point:

As I have said in my two statements of 18 June 1948 and 20 July 1948, it was Mohnke who gave me the order for shooting the three Canadian prisoners. I received the order from Mohnke at the conference which took place on the night of 8–9 June 1944. In the morning of 9 June, threatening to use force of arms, he compelled me to have the shooting carried out. In both

214

statements I said the order was *transmitted* [authors' italics] to us by Siebken . . . What I wanted to say was merely that Siebken was present at the conference and that he knew about the shooting.

If, then, the allegedly deadly phrase 'pass on an order' means what we think it means and what Schnabel seems to suggest it means, it follows that the order in question originated higher up the chain of command than Battalion level; and since it has never been suggested that the Division was responsible for any order to shoot prisoners, that only leaves the Regiment – specifically, Wilhelm Mohnke's 26th Panzer Grenadiers. This may not exonerate Siebken, but it certainly does not exonerate Mohnke. That the outcome of a trial could turn on the ambiguity of the English language serves to illustrate, perhaps, the difficulty under which the German defence counsel were labouring in this trial.

The Prosecutor now came to an even more 'deadly' admission on Schnabel's part. The only reason given for shooting the prisoners, the Prosecutor declared, was 'because we could not afford any more prisoners in the battalion'. Those were the words which all the witnesses who had been at the First Aid Post in Le Mesnil-Patry independently stated that Schnabel had used to set in motion the execution of the prisoners. 'They were the most deadly words that were spoken in this crime,' the Prosecutor argued. 'In the light of those words, where are the reprisals? Where is Mohnke? Where is the regimental order? Where is the report to the division? Those words establish the case for the Prosecution, which is that this order originated at battalion level with Siebken . . . I would really say, sir, that you would be perfectly safe in convicting Siebken of being the prime mover in this very unpleasant crime without considering any other evidence at all.'

In fairness to Schnabel, we ought at this point to introduce his post-trial rebuttal dated 8 January 1949 giving his reasons for having said what he said to the SS orderlies at the First Aid Post. 'I could not admit to the men,' he said, 'that the Regimental Commander was forcing me by force of arms. 1. Because it did not concern them. 2. Because I believed that I would thereby lose my authority in front of all the men. 3. To avoid breeding ill blood in the fighting forces resulting from such matters.' In any case, in the light of all the rest of the evidence in this case, what he had actually said at the First Aid Post was not true anyway. And if it were not true, then it was hardly a sound reason for convicting Siebken. But why was the Prosecutor so confident that the words were so deadly for Siebken? Was this not a case of over-optimistic pleading by the Prosecutor? In the context of all that we know, it could just as well have been Mohnke who was most hurt by these words, if anyone was rightly hurt at all.

The Prosecutor then proceeded to address his concluding remarks to the Court. These remarks are interesting, not only for the influence they had in deciding Siebken's fate, but for their implications à propos of Wilhelm Mohnke.

> Now, sir, I want to remind you of this – that I asked Siebken questions why, if these acts were ordered by Mohnke, he had never said anything about it before; and his answer was that he was concerned, jealously concerned, for the honour of the 12th SS Panzer Division. *That might be a good reason for his not having said that Mohnke ordered the killing.* But, of course, it is absolutely meaningless as a reason for not right at the beginning describing the atrocities which the other side had committed. I would ask the Court to consider very carefully why, if there is one word of truth in the whole of this fantastic defence, it was not raised earlier.
>
> I can perhaps sum up very briefly what I have said to you and the conclusions to which I have urged you to come. First, that there were never any illegal acts by the other side that would even serve to mitigate the gravity of this crime; that these were not reprisals at all, because these acts were done secretly and the essence of reprisals is that they are done openly; that reprisals in any event form no defence; that the three wounded Canadian POWs were shot for no other reason than that the 2nd Battalion, the 12th SS Panzer Division, could not be bothered with them; that Schnabel superintended the killing on direct orders from Siebken.
>
> It is not disputed that Albers, Bundschuh and Schnabel were there and did the deed. All of them heard rumours that Siebken gave the order and all of them said that the reason was because the battalion could not afford to take prisoners. And having attracted attention again to that last sentence, which I do regard as important, I think there is nothing further I can say to assist the Court.

———

The Prosecutor sat down. He had done his bit. What he could not contend he had not mentioned. Indeed, it is as much what he did *not* say as what he did say in his closing address that makes the outcome of the trial all the more surprising to us today. A total of eight witnesses had been brought before the Court to corroborate Siebken's version of events at various points along its length. These witnesses had corroborated Siebken's claim that Mohnke had indeed come to Siebken's command post on the night of 8–9 June 1944, that he had lost his temper, that he ordered the Canadian prisoners to be shot, that Siebken had resisted the order, that Siebken had

216

then telephoned the Division and lodged a complaint against Mohnke, that he was then in the front line until after the shootings had taken place, and that when he heard the news he spoke about it to the Divisional Commander, who then made plans to have Mohnke transferred out of the Division. Not a single witness was produced by the Prosecution to refute Siebken's story. Instead, the Prosecutor sought to destroy the witnesses by contending that all of them were liars. But, conveniently, they were only liars up to a point. Whenever any of them said anything that was inadvertently useful to the Prosecution case, this was held up as a glittering trophy, a rare, solitary, diamond-hard trophy, a rare, solitary, diamond-hard specimen of absolute truth. It is, of course, the Prosecutor's job to secure a conviction if he can. But under the peculiar circumstances of a trial of members of a defeated German army by a British Military Court in Occupied Germany, we are bound to ask, having studied the trial records, whether in this instance the securing of a conviction was synonymous with the dispensing of justice.

———

The officers of the Court deliberated. Then the President, Lt-Col. H.R. Bentley, OBE, solemnly pronounced the verdict. Albers and Bundschuh were acquitted. Though they had clearly been the trigger men in the First Aid Post killings, the Court felt that as simple soldiers carrying out compelling orders they could not be held truly culpable of the crime. In the Court's view the same could not be said of Siebken and Schnabel. The Court clearly believed that the former had issued the order to kill the prisoners and the latter had carried it out. Both the accused were thus pronounced to be guilty of the crimes with which they had been charged and were sentenced to suffer death by hanging. The Court then dispersed into the gathering gloom of the bleak Hamburg November dusk, while the two condemned men were returned under guard to their penitentiary cells and the cheerless contemplation of the impending gibbet.

———

On 9 November 1948, while in prison in Hamburg awaiting execution, Schnabel submitted an affidavit to the legal authorities in which he endeavoured to exonerate not only himself but his fellow-condemned, Bernhard Siebken, from culpability for the First Aid Post killings. Schnabel again affirmed that it was Mohnke who was at the back of the entire wretched business. It was Mohnke, he reiterated, who had given him the order to shoot the three Canadian prisoners, and it was Mohnke, threatening to use force of arms, who compelled him to have the shooting carried out. Though he had earlier stated that the order had been transmitted by Siebken, this statement was not made on his own initiative. 'It was the outcome of an interrogation which lasted for hours,' he said. 'What I wanted to say was merely that Siebken was present at the conference referred to [with Mohnke] and that he knew about the shooting. At the time I was interrogated it was not clear what Siebken's responsibility in the matter was. I therefore did not attach any great importance to the words I had used.'

One might perhaps ask why, at this eleventh hour, Schnabel should go to the trouble of trying to save Siebken by yet again laying the blame on Mohnke, unless what he was saying happened to be true. Whatever the facts of the matter, however, his affidavit fell on deaf ears.

———

Following the judgement, Siebken's Hamburg-based attorney, Doctor of Jurisprudence A. Oehlert, submitted a petition on her client's behalf in which she sharply rebuked the finding of the British Military Court. Dr Oehlert does not appear to have been enchanted by her contact with British military justice and did not mince her words about it.

> 'I submit that both the findings and the sentence are in direct contradiction to the evidence brought forward during the trial,' railed Siebken's attorney. 'The summing up of the Judge Advocate did not constitute a truthful summary of the evidence. Very important depositions both as to the principles and the facts of the case, which without any doubt would have influenced the findings as well as the sentence in favour of the accused, were not even mentioned in the summing-up, and certainly not weighed. I submit that this constituted an unequivocal case of Misdirection of Court. I explicitly lodge this protest on procedural and material grounds.'

Moreover, continued Dr Oehlert, the English translations of German witnesses' statements at times deviated from their original meaning. She had been able to clarify discrepancies of this kind when she spotted them during the course of the court proceedings, by virtue of the fact that a German shorthand writer trained in recording parliamentary debates had taken down the complete text of statements by German witnesses. But different meanings and interpretations were patently contained in the trial notes of the Judge Advocate and the Prosecutor, and in his concluding address the Prosecutor made use of a number of misquotations.

218

That said, Dr Oehlert maintained that the Military Court had not given due and proper consideration to three major arguments in the defence case. In the first place, the Court had dismissed the reprisal argument as a permissible exonerating factor in the case. 'I submit, however, that this decision cannot be upheld from a legal point of view. . . . There is no doubt that the Geneva Convention upholds the principle that no reprisals must be taken against prisoners of war. I submit, however, that the Court was not entitled to rely on this principle in a case where reprisals were caused by a *violation* of the Geneva Convention.'

So far Dr Oehlert had concerned herself with technicalities of law which were open to interpretation, and about which it would be presumptuous for the present authors to comment. The next prop of her petition was an altogether more cogent argument, however, and one which was highly relevant to the subject of this book. This dealt with the question of Wilhelm Mohnke's culpability in the affair, as outlined earlier in this section. Unlike the questions of reprisal and *tu quoque*, which were more a matter for legal theorizing, the issue of Mohnke was a matter of hard evidence, and Dr Oehlert contended that this had been largely ignored by the Court. She continued:

> I have already pointed out that this evidence for the defence . . . was not at all mentioned by the Judge Advocate when he gave his summing-up.
>
> The evidence has, I submit, proved conclusively that Siebken was not in any way responsible for the shooting of the three Canadians and that, moreover, he did everything, nay, more than he could have been expected to do, to bar any possibility of the order being carried out.
>
> In case the Court should fail to accept this proof to its full extent, I submit that the evidence for the prosecution is subject to such material doubt that the alternative would have to be my client's acquittal for want of sufficient evidence.
>
> The total disregard for the whole evidence in favour of my client as regards the question of fact is tantamount not only to a violation of the rules of law but also to the principles of fair reasoning . . . I am therefore deeply convinced that the judgement disputed is a misjudgement which contradicts the maxims of law as well as the principles governing the administration of justice.

On 27 November 1948 the Deputy Judge Advocate General, Brigadier Lord Russell of Liverpool, forwarded his final review of the Le Mesnil-

Patry case to the Commander-in-Chief of the British Army of the Rhine. He wrote:

The main facts of this case were never in issue and the following was clearly proved.

The 2nd Battalion of the 26th Regiment of the 12 SS Panzer Division (Hitler Jugend), commanded by the accused SIEBKEN, was in Normandy on the morning of the Allied invasion of 6 June 1944. Two days later the Battalion Advance Headquarters was at Le Mesnil-Patry and the first aid post was set up in a farm house on the borders of that hamlet. The first aid post was under the command of Dr Schütt, who had under his command Staff-Sergeant Ischner, the accused Albers, and at least two drivers, one of whom was the prosecution witness Wimplinger. On 9 June Bundschuh joined for temporary duty as a medical orderly.

During this time three wounded Canadian prisoners of war were looked after by the medical officer at the first aid post. During the morning of 9 June the accused Schnabel arrived at the first aid post and said that the prisoners were to be shot as the Battalion was short of transport and wounded prisoners could not be taken to the rear. The medical officer protested that the shooting could not take place in his dressing room and they were therefore taken out into the courtyard of the farm and shot.

There was no dispute at the trial that the fatal shots were fired by Albers and Bundschuh; nor was there any legal dispute that such a shooting, quite apart from its inhumanity, was illegal and contrary to the law and usage of war. Indeed this view was agreed to by the accused SIEBKEN, who, when questioned by the court, said: 'The killing of the prisoners did take place. It was quite illegal in my opinion.'

There was a rather discreditable attempt made by the advocates for SIEBKEN and SCHNABEL to argue that the shooting of these Canadian prisoners was justifiable under international law as a reprisal for unlawful methods of warfare which had been adopted by the Allies' invading armies. There was little evidence to support this argument but, in any event, Dr Oehlert and Dr Graevius must have known that by the provisions of the Convention of 1929 reprisals against prisoners of war are forbidden.

There was also evidence that SIEBKEN had ordered prisoners to be shot and that it was upon the executive command of SCHNABEL, Siebken's orderly officer, that the shots were fired.

220

SIEBKEN'S defence was that although he had received orders from MOHNKE, the Regimental Commander, that all the prisoners were to be killed, he had not carried out this order in respect of the Canadian prisoners but that MOHNKE himself had directly ordered SCHNABEL to shoot the prisoners.

This was not what SIEBKEN had said in his deposition, made only two and a half months before the trial, wherein he stated: 'I have never received directions or orders from MOHNKE to shoot prisoners of war, nor any directions or orders which I could interpret as meaning I should shoot prisoners. . . . I have no knowledge of MOHNKE issuing such an order over my head, nor have I any knowledge of any of the members of my battalion having issued such an order without reference to me.'

That was the statement which Siebken made after caution on 12 August 1948 and signed, stating that he had no objection to his statement being taken down in English, 'being conversant with the English language', and having read it through, found it to be correct and wishing to make no additions or deletions.

And yet on 26 October 1948, when giving evidence at the trial in his own defence, he stated that shortly after he had refused to carry out MOHNKE'S order to shoot the three Canadian prisoners, the accused SCHNABEL 'came and reported to me that MOHNKE, using force of arms, had forced him to have the execution carried out.'

Which was true: the statement or the evidence? A clue to the right answer may, perhaps, be found in the significant testimony of Albers given originally in his statement of 26 July 1948 and repeated in his evidence at the trial. 'I had a conversation with Siebken at the interment camp. SIEBKEN told me if I went to Minden [the location of a small prison camp used by the War Crimes Group (NWE) for interrogation of war criminals] and happened to see Schnabel I was to tell him to put the blame on MOHNKE.'

At the time of the conversation, according to the evidence of SIEBKEN himself, he knew that MOHNKE was safely in Russia and had been seen near Moscow as recently as June 1948.

It is therefore not surprising that the court did not believe the evidence of the accused SIEBKEN.

SCHNABEL did not himself give evidence; instead he called a witness named Poehne, who gave evidence that he saw

221

MOHNKE place a pistol to Schnabel's chest and say: 'If you do not shoot these prisoners, I will shoot you.' In his first deposition he had made no mention of the fact that MOHNKE had ordered him to shoot the prisoners.

In that deposition SCHNABEL had been content to say 'SIEBKEN passed on this order to us and did this as occasion arose. I do not wish at present to make a statement in which way SIEBKEN passed on these orders and what happened later'. It was only later, probably when he realized the full implication of the allegations against his former Commanding Officer, SIEBKEN, that he made any mention of the fact that it was MOHNKE who directly ordered the Canadians to be shot. Small wonder that Schnabel elected not to give evidence in his defence but to put forward a defence of duress through the mouth of one of his witnesses, Poehne. Schnabel had made too many inconsistent statements before trial; cross-examination would have discredited him. Much better to put his defence through Poehne and leave SIEBKEN to fend for himself.

It is not, however, surprising that the court placed more reliance on SCHNABEL'S first two depositions than on his subsequent statements.

SCHNABEL'S counsel pleaded superior orders. The fact that a rule of warfare has been violated in pursuance of an order of an individual belligerent commander does not deprive the act in question of its character as a war crime; neither does it, in principle, confer upon the perpetrator immunity from punishment by the injured belligerent. Undoubtedly a court confronted with the plea of superior orders adduced in justification of a war crime is bound to take into consideration the fact that obedience to military orders, not obviously unlawful, is the duty of every member of the armed forces, and that the latter cannot, in conditions of war discipline, be expected to weigh scrupulously the legal merits of the order received. The question, however, is governed by the major principle that members of the armed forces are bound to obey lawful orders only and cannot therefore escape liability if, in obedience to a command, they commit acts which both violate unchallenged rules of warfare and outrage the general sentiment of humanity.

Upon consideration of the above principles the Court thought fit to acquit the accused, ALBERS and BUNDSCHUH. They were but private soldiers and may not have had the mental capacity to appreciate that they were doing an unlawful act. The accused SCHNABEL was in a different category. He must have known that the order was unlawful, as did his Commanding Officer, and had little reason to suppose that had he disobeyed it the consequence for him would have been serious. Only if the court believed the evidence of Poehne was an acquittal of SCHNABEL, in my opinion, proper.

In my opinion there is ample evidence to support these convictions.

Both the convicted accused have petitioned against finding and sentence. In my opinion these petitions disclose no adequate grounds for interfering with either and should be dismissed. If you agree, you should dismiss the petitions and endorse them accordingly.

In my view the proceedings are in order for confirmation.

If you do not commute the death sentences the proceedings have to be forwarded to the Commander-in-Chief, British Zone of Germany, for his concurrence therein.

———

On 30 December 1948, nearly two months after Bernhard Siebken had been sentenced to death by the British Military Court in Hamburg, and a week after this judgement had been confirmed by the Judge Advocate General in London, Siebken's attorney, Dr Oehlert, addressed a special plea for clemency to the Commander-in-Chief of the British Zone of Occupation in Germany, General Sir Brian Robertson, in Berlin. In stilted but perfectly lucid English, Dr Oehlert expressed regret that the procedures of British Military Courts did not allow for an appeal against the sentence or for the fall-back of a re-trial, especially in view of the fact that she had already petitioned the Judge Advocate General on the grounds of 'misdirection of the court'. Since she had no alternative but to accept the judgement of a Military Court, Dr Oehlert could only reiterate the main points of her original defence of her client. The shooting of the three Canadians at Le Mesnil-Patry, she claimed, was a reprisal for the shooting of German prisoners who had fallen into Allied hands on the same sector of the front. Siebken had resisted to the utmost the order to shoot the prisoners. 'This ought to have been taken into consideration in deciding upon the extent of the punishment,' Dr Oehlert protested, 'and as it has not been done, this makes him worthy of recommendation to mercy.' Furthermore, the psychological background to the case ought to be considered. The deed in question had been committed at a time when both sides on the invasion front were locked in a desperate battle for every inch of soil and the German forces had not slept a wink for three days and two consecutive nights. 'It is not

223

advisable,' the lady attorney pleaded, 'to judge . . . an individual in such moments by the same scale which in peacetime or three years after the cessation of hostilities may seem a matter of course. Therefore if any penalty seems warranted it ought not to be the highest that is possible – the death penalty.'

Dr Oehlert made one last plea for compassion. 'May I say in conclusion,' she wrote to the mighty British Commander-in-Chief from her office amid the rubble of bomb-gutted Hamburg, 'that my mandator [Siebken] has been described by all witnesses – not only former members of the Waffen-SS but also high German officers of the army – as a decent, honest, quiet and reclusive soldier. Up till now my mandator has led a life completely free from objection. He has an old mother of seventy years, a young wife and a child, all of whom hope and pray that this awful sentence may not be executed. Therefore, Sir, I beg of you to alter this sentence of death against Bernhard Siebken by an act of grace.'

But Dr Oehlert was barking up the wrong tree. By continuing to plead that the shooting of the three Canadians was 'a case of genuine war reprisals' endorsed by 'commentators of authority in the international law of warfare and Law of Nations' she was tackling the Allies head-on on an issue in which they would not and could not be moved. The subject of Allied war crimes against the enemy was a closed book. Any evidence in this sensitive area was instantly and totally suppressed, either destroyed or buried deep. No references could be made to it, no charges brought. In effect, the official line was that the Allies committed no war crimes; this was the prerogative of their enemies alone. So Dr Oehlert's plea fell again on deaf ears, as it had done in the court room in the Curio-Haus the month before. As she herself conceded in her letter to the C-in-C: 'The Military Tribunal declined to admit the existence of reprisals in precluding guilt, a decision against which no appeal is admitted.' Thus her defence on this point remained inadmissible.

———

By this time the accused had radically departed from the line taken by the Hamburg attorney. Faced with the awful and absolute reality of the noose, they threw aside the futile legal casuistry pursued by Dr Oehlert and got to the heart of the matter as they saw it – the fatal complicity of their erstwhile superior officer, Wilhelm Mohnke.

On 3 January 1949 a Petition for Clemency from 'Military Government Prisoner Bernhard Siebken (War Criminal)' was forwarded to the Commander-in-Chief of the British Army of the Rhine. Translated into extremely clumsy English (which the authors have tried to improve for the sake of readability and sense), this was Siebken's last bid to escape the gallows, and it pinned the blame for the First Aid Post killings at Le Mesnil-Patry all those years ago squarely on the absent Wilhelm Mohnke:

In the first days of the invasion of Normandy I repeatedly received from my Regimental Commander, W. MOHNKE, the order to take no prisoners, because of what had happened on the opposing side [meaning alleged killing of German prisoners by Allied troops]. But I never obeyed this order and explicitly refused to do so. So on the night of 8–9 June there was a very fateful conflict between MOHNKE and myself at my combat headquarters at Le Mesnil-Patry when the latter required me to have three Canadian prisoners of war, who were in my dressing station, shot. Moreover, MOHNKE required that I should forward a general order to this effect to my companies.

I refused to do both these things. This has been proved, firstly, by the fact that the prisoners were not shot as a result of this special order but only nine to ten hours later as a result of MOHNKE directly forcing my orderly officer, SCHNABEL, to obey this order; and, secondly, by the fact that my Company Commanders never received an order of this kind from me. MOHNKE tried to persuade me as to the necessity of this order as a preventive measure. However, I refused to adopt this viewpoint.

Furthermore, I spoke to my Division about this matter and reported it to my Divisional Commander.

The action itself [i.e. the killing of the prisoners] was carried out in my absence, so that it was impossible for me to intervene.

All this was verified by my witnesses under oath before the Court. And I myself declared the same under oath before the Court.

My reputation as a soldier was anything but that of a reckless dare-devil.

In this place I can only assert again that I always fought as a decent and honourable soldier and did my duty for my country.

I ask you, soldier and officer in this gigantic World War, to reconsider my case once more, for I never acted other than as I had learnt to act as a soldier: to fight and die honourably. And this point of view connects all soldiers of the world with one another.

Yours respectfully
Bernhard Siebken

At the time of the trial of the First Aid Post case some misgivings were expressed – not simply by interested Germans – as to the way the trial was conducted by the British Military Court and the justice of the findings. As far as Schnabel's fate was concerned there never seemed much doubt that he would face the big drop – the Court found him a shifty sort of character and it was never in doubt that he had personally fired a bullet into the skull of each of the three wounded and unarmed prisoners of war for whose murder he was put on trial. But the sentence of death handed down to Siebken was a different matter. His attorney had pleaded Misdirection of Court but was brushed aside. The alleged atrocity committed against German prisoners the day before the shooting of the Canadians was dismissed as immaterial and no attempt was made by the British authorities to investigate the truth or otherwise of the allegation. It was Germans not Englishmen who were on trial.

The former First Orderly Officer of the Divisional HQ staff of the 12 SS Panzer Division, Bernhard Georg Meitzel, had attended the trial in the Curio-Haus in Hamburg and impressed many of those present with his handsome appearance, exquisite manners and excellent English. Clearly a first-class staff officer and a man of sound judgement, Meitzel was aghast at what he saw as a glaring example of *Siegergericht* (or *vis victis*) – a distortion of justice to suit the winning side. On 27 October 1948, while the trial was still in progress, he turned to a British military historian, Colonel Liddell Hart, in a desperate attempt to help both the accused. Liddell Hart, who believed that the German concept of *Blitzkrieg* was his own invention and that the German Panzer generals were his devoted disciples, had grown quite chummy with the defeated German top brass when he was researching his bestselling book, *The Other Side of the Hill*, during the immediate post-war years, and at the time was leading a campaign to stop the British putting Germany's great military commanders, von Brauchitsch, von Manstein and von Rundstedt, on trial.* Meitzel evidently hoped that such a man might be willing to cast a sympathetic eye on this latest German predicament, and as it turned out he was not far wrong. On 9 November Liddell Hart wrote back from his home at Wolverton Park, Buckinghamshire:

> I entirely agree with what you say about both the injustice and the harmful effect of these one-sided trials. As you may know, I have been doing my best to stop them by public protest – in

* For the latest re-appraisal of Liddell Hart's claims see *Liddell Hart and the Weight of History* by John J. Mearsheimer (Brassey's Defence Publishers, 1989).

which many leading people here have joined. I am still active in the matter, and the public support for it is growing all the time.

Liddell Hart cited the case of an Allied war crime witnessed by a friend of his near an airfield in Sicily. A lorry-load of German prisoners were mown down by a heavy machine-gun fired by two American soldiers, who later shot a batch of about sixty Italian prisoners in the same way. What Liddell Hart did not mention was that the culprits were in fact tried for these crimes – though, since the chain of command principle did not apply on the Allied side, no charge was ever brought against the top-level commander of the soldiers involved, General Patton. However, Liddell Hart was too remote from the First Aid Post case to be able to save Siebken and Schnabel from the gallows.

———

On 8 January 1949, as the day of execution drew near, Schnabel made one last effort to obtain a stay of execution of his former Commanding Officer and SS comrade-in-arms. This took the form of a Declaration in lieu of oath, in which Schnabel attempted to make the belated point that when previously he had said the order to shoot the prisoners had come from the Commander, he 'naturally meant the Regimental Commander', Mohnke, not the Battalion Commander, Siebken.

On 19 January 1949, the day before Siebken's execution, Brigadier Lord Russell of Liverpool forwarded his final recommendation on Schnabel's submission to the GOC British army of the Rhine:

> In my opinion SCHNABEL's new statement in no way exculpates SIEBKEN, whose conviction rests on other evidence.
>
> I do not see how any credence can be given to a statement made at this late hour that by the use of the word 'Commander' he meant the Regimental Commander, MOHNKE, and not the Battalion Commander, SIEBKEN.
>
> In my opinion this statement discloses no adequate grounds for interfering with the finding or sentence and should be dismissed.

Schnabel had done what he could for the sake of old loyalty and honour. Nothing could save Siebken now – and his own hopes were long gone.

———

227

In the prison in the Pied Piper town of Hameln on the morning of 20 January 1949 a highly experienced hangman by the name of Albert Pierrepoint arrived from England to carry out an unpleasant but necessary duty. Pierrepoint was no stranger to Hameln, for as the only licensed hangman in the British Zone of Germany he had sped many war criminals to their deaths in the execution block of this same prison in the last three years, and his numerous 'scalps' included such notorious brutes as Josef Kramer, the so-called Beast of Belsen, and the young Belsen girl guard, Irma Grese. Pierrepoint was an experienced professional and seldom allowed human emotions to interfere in the exercise of his unusual skill. It made little difference, therefore, that on that fateful winter morning the two men who stood before him looked less like monsters than a couple of German gentlemen in the prime of life who happened to have fallen on hard times. With a deftness born of long practice Pierrepoint looped the noose over the heads of Bernhard Siebken and Dietrich Schnabel and with a firm, hard pull depressed the trapdoor lever beside the gallows. And thus, more than three years after the end of the war and more than four years after the shootings at the First Aid Post in the little Normandy village of Le Mesnil-Patry, the lives of these two former SS officers of the Hitler Jugend Division were abruptly extinguished. They had been found guilty of murder after a long process of law – perhaps rightly so. But there were some who felt that another SS commander deserved to have stood on the gallows alongside them that grim January morning in North Germany. That man was Wilhelm Mohnke.

INDICTMENT

The execution of Siebken and Schnabel by a British hangman in a British military gaol in the British Zone of Germany was among the last judicial executions carried out by the Allied Occupation authorities in the western zones of Germany. By 1949 Europe was already turning away from the settling of old scores arising from the war and setting its face towards the very different realities of the new post-war world – above all the dangers posed by the escalation of the Cold War with the Soviet Union. Inconceivable as it may have been in 1945, by 1949 Western Germany was already seen as a future ally of the West, and plans for the creation of the new autonomous German Federal Republic for later that year were well in hand. Under such circumstances, the hanging of two former German army officers, one of them distinguished by one of the highest awards for gallantry, by the army of their former enemy, struck a false note, not only in Germany, but in more thoughtful circles in Britain as well. In any case, the British had already begun to abandon their interest in German war criminals, and were soon to hand the whole business lock, stock and barrel over to the Germans themselves. The files were bundled up and tidied away. The war crimes investigators began to hunt about for alternative employment. Wilhelm Mohnke, rotting in a cell in Lubyanka prison, in distant Moscow, was given up and forgotten.

Should Siebken and Schnabel have died? It is doubtful if any jury in the world would have felt inclined to acquit Schnabel of complicity in murder, since he was a responsible officer who should have known what he was doing – and it is an indisputable fact that what he was doing was blowing his victims' brains out.

But Siebken was a different case. After his conviction his defence lawyer had protested that there had been a misdirection of court. We would go further and say that there was a miscarriage of justice.

When we began this study of Nazi war crimes, we never dreamed that we would find ourselves in the position of pleading the cause of an ardent Nazi and long-serving professional SS soldier like Bernhard Siebken. Readers of this book will doubtless understand that our reasons for doing so are not to defend Nazism but to report what we see as objectively as possible in the interests of justice. Nor does it serve our particular interests to vindicate Siebken in order to destroy Mohnke, since Siebken's guilt or innocence makes no difference to Mohnke's own culpability. But we could not sit on the sideline and see someone hanged, no matter how vile the cause he represented, as a result of a miscarriage of justice.

This is not to say that Siebken was necessarily an entirely exemplary character, an irreproachable lilywhite SS commander who had no blood on his hands. After all Siebken was a founder member of the Leibstandarte Adolf Hitler. He was a veteran of the no-quarter-given, no-questions-asked style of carnage practised by both sides on the Russian Front. As it happened, a number of the murders of Canadian prisoners in Normandy were committed by men of his battalion. But Siebken was not tried for any of those things. He was tried for having given the order that led to the First Aid Post killings at Le Mesnil-Patry on 9 June 1944. And it is our contention, on the basis of our examination of the trial records, that the judgement passed on him by the British Military Court in Hamburg and endorsed by the Deputy Judge Advocate General, Brigadier Lord Russell of Liverpool, was unsafe and contrary to the principle of fair and natural justice. We believe that the charge that he had given the order to kill was not proven – on the contrary, there was evidence that the order had been given by his superior officer, the Regimental Commander, Mohnke. We further believe that at the very most Siebken was culpable on the basis of the chain of command principle, and that at the very least the death sentence should have been commuted, as Kurt Meyer's had been. It is our view that if Siebken was tried again today before a properly constituted British court he would not be convicted on the same evidence.

In our account of the trial we have indicated at various points the weaknesses of the prosecution case against Siebken. Two main features are particularly remarkable. In the first place, no less than eight witnesses were brought by the defence to corroborate Siebken's account of the events of 8–9 June; none were brought by the prosecution to disprove his account. In the second place, while all the defence witnesses, including the defendants themselves, were generically lumped together as liars by the prosecution, this did not deter the prosecution from making use of any statements made by them that could be seen to help the prosecution case. These statements often turned out to be extremely vague and ambiguous and hinged on such words and phrases as 'commander' and 'passed on an order' which were capable of more than one interpretation. And yet it was on such ambiguous strands of terminology that Siebken was found guilty of the crime of murder and in due course hanged. In the final analysis, as we have said, this would appear to have been a miscarriage of justice. In which case, of course, the Court would in effect have done what they had condemned Bernhard Siebken for doing.

At Siebken's trial the Court chose to reject the idea of any involvement in the First Aid Post killings on the part of Siebken's Regimental Commander, Wilhelm Mohnke. Why? The reason given by the Prosecutor and repeated by the Deputy Judge Advocate General, Lord Russell of Liverpool, was that in his pre-trial deposition Siebken – not wanting to stain the honour of his Division – had stated that he had never received any order from Mohnke to shoot prisoners of war. Therefore, it was argued, his attempt to pin the blame on Mohnke during the trial was unconvincing. No reference was made at the trial to Siebken's earlier testimony, given during interrogation in March 1946 and later quoted in a book by the chief Canadian investigator, Colonel Macdonald, to the effect that when Mohnke had called Siebken on the field telephone during the early fighting in Normandy and told him, 'Do not send so many prisoners back', Siebken had taken this to mean that prisoners were to be shot. It is, of course, unlikely that the Prosecutor would have found it in his interest to refer to this earlier testimony. It is equally unlikely that the defence counsel, Dr Oehlert, would have been shown it, otherwise she would undoubtedly have belaboured the point for all it was worth. Yet it is, in our view, a telling piece of evidence, and helps to reinforce our view that the sequence of events leading up to the killings at the First Aid Post in Le Mesnil-Patry, as outlined by the defence, was very likely correct – and was, moreover, part of a broader picture of murder carried out on a much larger scale than was ever conceived of at the Siebken trial.

This is our reconstruction of the most probable course of events at and near Bernhard Siebken's command post at Le Mesnil-Patry between 8–9 June 1944.

On the afternoon of 8 June a group of forty Canadian prisoners were brought to Siebken's headquarters in Le Mesnil-Patry. This was the correct procedure, for the Canadians had been captured by one or other of the companies in Siebken's battalion, and the proper course was for prisoners to be taken progressively to the rear – from Company to Battalion, then to Regiment and then to Division. That evening the forty prisoners set off on the next stage of their journey to the rear, this time to the headquarters of the 26th Panzer Grenadiers – Mohnke's regiment. This was confirmed by Siebken's orderly officer, Schnabel, who was responsible for sending the prisoners off. At some point while all this was going on, Siebken received a telephone call from Mohnke, who said (according to Siebken's March 1946 testimony): 'Do not send so many prisoners back.' We would argue that Mohnke here was referring to the shipment of forty prisoners, which was almost certainly the largest shipment his regiment had been required to handle since it had gone into action a few hours earlier. As we have seen, Siebken in his 1946 statement said he believed Mohnke meant that prisoners should not be taken, or, if taken, should be shot.

Whatever Mohnke may have meant, the prisoners never reached their destination. On a track leading to Regimental HQ they were intercepted by an officer waiting for them in a camouflaged vehicle, who ordered the sergeant in charge of the prisoner escort to take the prisoners to a particular field further down the track towards Regimental HQ. There a squad of German soldiers in a half-track personnel carrier joined the escort from Siebken's 2nd Battalion, and thirty-five of the forty prisoners were machine-gunned to death where they sat in the field.

There is no doubt whatsoever that this massacre, the Canadians' 'Malmédy', did take place. Almost unknown, and certainly long forgotten, we have described this major war crime in analytical detail for the first time in these pages. Though the sequence of events is clear, the question remains: who gave the order?

The Allied investigators never succeeded in identifying, still less apprehending, those responsible for this atrocity. Our contention is that, given the circumstances as described, there was only one person empowered to issue such an order – and that person was Wilhelm Mohnke. It could not, in our view, have been Siebken himself. Otherwise why should he have bothered to send the prisoners and their escort off on the long hike to Regimental HQ, instead of killing the prisoners on the spot? Why, if Siebken *had* given an order for the shooting of the prisoners, should Mohnke have telephoned to say, 'Do not send so many prisoners back'? And why should Schnabel have raised the subject of the forty prisoners as part of his defence at his trial – citing them as an example of his exemplary conduct with regard to prisoners of war – if he knew that they had been shot, and on Siebken's orders at that?

If the prisoners were massacred somewhere between Battalion HQ and Regimental HQ, and it was not the Battalion Commander who gave the order, there is logically only one other candidate for this infamy. If the Battalion had ordered the prisoners to be sent off to the rear in a perfectly correct manner, as Schnabel claimed, then only one person had the authority to countermand that order and that was Siebken's superior officer, his Regimental Commander, Mohnke. There was no way that the sergeant in charge of the prisoner escort would have allowed anyone to interfere with the orders given to him by his own Commanding Officer unless that person quite clearly pulled rank over all concerned. Nor could that person have come from outside the 26th Panzer Grenadier Regiment area of operations, which was almost inviolate.

232

This is not necessarily to say that the officer in the camouflaged vehicle, who gave the order for the prisoners to be taken to the field where they met their deaths, was Mohnke himself. There is not enough evidence on that. It could have been an officer delegated by Mohnke. Equally, it *could* have been Mohnke. The interference in the fate of a column of prisoners looks almost like a re-run of Mohnke's interception of the prisoner column at Wormhoudt. The display of anger on the officer's part, as witnessed by some of the Canadian survivors, was very characteristic of Mohnke. 'The officer appeared to be very annoyed,' the investigators were told. 'Some of the prisoners formed the impression that the officer wanted them to be got rid of.' This almost pathological obsession with enemy prisoners was also very characteristic of Mohnke. It could be argued, too, that an order of such a kind, initiating a major transgression and a massacre on such a scale, could only be issued personally by the person who conceived it.

Be that as it may, the massacre was a systematic and cold-blooded outrage which required careful organizing – the half-track and its death squad, the extra Schmeisser machine-guns for the original prisoner escort, none of these smacked of an impromptu, heat-of-the-moment killing on the part of some malevolent subordinate at Regimental HQ. Our firm contention, therefore, is that only one person could have ordered the Canadian massacre near Fontenay-le-Pesnil and that was Wilhelm Mohnke. Interestingly, this crime constitutes one of the charges laid against Mohnke's name by the United Nations War Crimes Commission. Neither the charge nor the name have ever been struck off the UN charge sheet, and at no time has Wilhelm Mohnke ever been called to account for it.

When Siebken himself was asked about the Fontenay incident by the Canadian war crimes investigators after the war, he ventured to suggest that the crime might perhaps have been committed by some unit of the Panzer-Lehr, which he contended had been operating in the area at about that time. This is extremely unlikely, however. Panzer-Lehr was a high-quality Wehrmacht unit with an otherwise clean record of conduct in Normandy and no suggestion had ever been made that this Division ever indulged in the barbarism of the sort that disgraced elements of the SS 'Murder Division'. If that is the case, and if Siebken knew it to be the case, we have to assume that either Siebken was again attempting to protect his former Regimental Commander, Mohnke, or that he had never previously heard of the massacre of the thirty-five prisoners. The latter possibility seems unlikely, especially as some of the executioners had been members of the escort drawn from Siebken's own battalion, and word would surely have got out. On the other hand, Schnabel, his orderly officer, seems to have been under the impression that the forty prisoners he sent to the rear on the evening of 8 June actually got to the rear. The truth of the matter is obviously difficult to arrive at. But let us consider what happened next.

233

According to evidence given in the trial, late that same night, after the forty prisoners had been sent from Siebken's Battalion Headquarters to the rear and been murdered en route, Mohnke stormed up to Siebken's command post and exchanged angry words with him on the subject of prisoners of war. According to the evidence of the accused, Mohnke ranted and raged in his usual inimitable fashion and ordered that all prisoners henceforth should be shot. No mention was made in this evidence of the forty prisoners, who by this time were already dead, though it would be reasonable to assume that it was they who had stoked up Mohnke's wrath. At about this point, the Battalion Medical Officer, Dr Schütt, arrived to report the appearance of three more Canadian prisoners, the ones his orderly, Wimplinger, had just discovered outside the First Aid Post down the road. The unfortunate coincidence of Mohnke being present at that moment may well have sealed the prisoners' fate. Whether Siebken protested as vehemently against the notion of shooting them as he claimed, and whether Mohnke, in his rage, actually did draw his pistol on Schnabel and say, 'If you don't shoot the prisoners, I'll shoot you,' it is common sense to suppose that a Regimental Commander who had ordered the execution of forty prisoners only a few hours previously would be unlikely to suddenly change his tune and spare three more who had inadvertently dropped into his lap – especially if the whole business of prisoners was the subject of an ongoing dispute with his Battalion Commander at that very juncture.

The defendants' version of the subsequent chain of events leading to the shooting of the three prisoners on the morning of 9 June has already been laid out in detail in earlier pages. It rings true to us, but the Military Court in Hamburg rejected it. But would they have rejected it if Mohnke had been available and could have been put on trial himself? We very much doubt it. We believe that the Siebken trial was a case of two birds in the hand being worth one in the bush, so to speak. In other words, since Mohnke is beyond our reach, let us nail the two we have in our grasp. The Canadian and British war crimes investigators had toiled long and hard to solve the Normandy massacres and so far had brought only one suspect to trial – Kurt Meyer. To round off the whole investigation programme, to notch up some kind of investigative achievement, to satisfy Canadian public opinion, to exact a measure of justice for the crimes undoubtedly committed by the Hitler Jugend Division, it was important to bring an overwhelming case against Siebken and Schnabel. But to nail Siebken and Schnabel it was necessary to disregard any evidence about the involvement of Mohnke; this did not matter, since Mohnke was not available to stand trial anyway. But if Mohnke *had* been available to stand trial, the reverse would very likely have been the case, and the evidence of Siebken and Schnabel would in all probability have been looked at in a completely different light and admitted with the greatest alacrity. This would not have saved Siebken's and Schnabel's lives – but nor would it have saved Mohnke's.

As it is, though Siebken and Schnabel swung for the First Aid Post murders, the name of Mohnke still stands on the United Nations charge sheet in connection with this crime – as it does for the shootings at Les Saullets and the murders at the Haut du Bosq (the Stangenberg case). About the Haut du Bosq killings there is no dispute – it is a prima facie case and eye-witness evidence proved conclusively that Wilhelm Mohnke had ordered the shooting of three Canadian prisoners outside his Regimental Headquarters and stood and watched as the executions were carried out – having first lost his temper and then removed the prisoners' identity discs, just as he had done at Wormhoudt four years before. This crime, too, is listed against Mohnke's name on the United Nations list.

Not for nothing was the 12th SS Panzer Division (Hitler Jugend) known in the German Army as the 'Murder Division'. More than 130 prisoners, nearly all of them Canadian, all of them unarmed and some of them wounded, were cruelly and deliberately done to death after surrender by this formidable and fanatical unit. As we know, the Hitler Jugend was composed of two main infantry elements – the 25th Panzer Grenadier Regiment under the command of Kurt Meyer, and the 26th SS Panzer Grenadier Regiment under Wilhelm Mohnke – together with Max Wünsche's 12 SS Panzer Regiment and two smaller, mobile specialist units, one being Gerhard Bremer's Reconnaissance Battalion, the other Siegfried Müller's Engineering Battalion. Atrocities occurred within the operational areas of both these infantry Regiments (and of both these specialist Battalions).

It is our contention, and that of the Allied war crimes investigating units who looked into these atrocities, that both Regiments and both Regimental Commanders were equally culpable. Kurt Meyer was tried for his part in the murders and sentenced to death (later commuted to life imprisonment). Wilhelm Mohnke was not. And yet Mohnke was culpable on two grounds. In the first place, he was incontestably shown to have been *directly* responsible for the shootings perpetrated in the Stangenberg case. In the second place, on the basis of the chain of command principle he was undoubtedly *indirectly* responsible for the other killings in the operational area of the regiment which he commanded; and in our submission he was very likely *directly* responsible for having given the orders in two of them – the Canadian Massacre and the First Aid Post killings. It was Mohnke's former Regimental Commander at Wormhoudt, Sepp Dietrich, who told his interrogators after the war: 'The Commander is responsible for the actions and conduct of his Regiment.' In the area of the Regiment of the 26th Panzer Grenadiers in June 1944 that commander was Wilhelm

Mohnke. It is our inescapable conclusion, therefore, that in locking up Hitler's last general in the gloomy confines of Lubyanka Prison the Soviet authorities unwittingly saved Mohnke's life and that as a consequence two lesser scapegoats died in his place.

Some of the former SS suspects named in this chapter are alive, well and living comfortably in their Fatherland or abroad. As for Wilhelm Mohnke, when recently he was approached at his Hamburg home by reporters of *The Citizen*, a Toronto newspaper, and asked for his views on reports about the Normandy atrocities, he made this curiously ambivalent, if not contradictory, statement: 'A lot of prisoners of war were captured in Normandy. Honestly, I will look at you and tell you that none, repeat none, were shot on my order. Do you understand? In war it becomes very easy to kill someone. Human life becomes worthless. It takes discipline, hard discipline, to overcome that urge and fight to a goal.' And he added: 'I am a man of discipline. The SS was disciplined. War is not some woman's job, you know.'

236

PART VI

—

Malmédy

THE ARDENNES DECEMBER 1944

My men were the products of total war. The only thing they knew was to handle weapons for the Dream of the Reich. They were young people with a hot heart and the desire to win or die according to the word: right or wrong – my country!

Jochen Peiper on the Leibstandarte
(at his trial, Dachau, 1946)

OFFENSIVE

By the autumn of 1944 it was clear that the war was going very badly for Germany. In the West the Allied armies had broken out of Normandy and advanced swiftly across France towards the German frontier. In the East the Russians continued their irresistible advance towards the eastern provinces of the Third Reich. In the south the Allies, battling their way hand-over-hand up the rugged spine of Italy, drew slowly nearer to Germany's mountain borders. In the air the Anglo-American bomber fleets ravaged German cities and industries by day and night. All was not yet lost, however. Though the Allies hoped for an end of hostilities by Christmas, Hitler still dreamed of contriving a dramatic change in the course of the war. By October he had evolved a plan to which he gave the code-name 'Watch on the Rhine'. To the Allies this plan was to become better known as the Battle of the Bulge.

It was Hitler's firm contention that the war would be won or lost in the West. In spite of the catastrophic losses in the summer battles in France, and the destruction of so many of the German army's best and bravest divisions – the Hitler Jugend Division among them – Hitler still believed that Germany could win a decisive victory in the West. His plan was bold, brilliant – and desperate. A major offensive – a new *Blitzkrieg* – would be launched through the Ardennes highlands in Belgium, the historic gateway used by German troops to invade the West in 1870, 1914 and 1940, with the object of splitting the British and American forces in France and the Low Countries, seizing the Allies' major supply port at Antwerp, and hopefully driving the British back to the sea and out of the war in a second Dunkirk. With the British knocked out of the war, Hitler argued, it might be possible to reach a separate peace with the Americans in the West, then concentrate all Germany's resources towards throwing back the Russian tide in the East.

To achieve this ambitious victory, Hitler ordered the assembly of four whole armies – two Panzer armies in the centre and two infantry armies covering the flanks – under the command of Field Marshal von Rundstedt as Commander-in-Chief West. A key part was to be played by a brand new Panzer army – the Sixth – under the command of Hitler's old comrade and favourite general, Sepp Dietrich. Dietrich's Sixth Panzer Army, with the support of Manteuffel's Fifth Panzer Army, would be the iron fist which would punch its way through the lightly held American positions in the Ardennes and race west to jump the River Meuse and take the port of Antwerp, eighty miles away on the North Sea coast. To have any hope of success, total secrecy, speed and surprise would be required. This meant that the offensive – Germany's last chance to gain a favourable outcome of the war – could only be undertaken at a time when bad weather restricted the Allies' overwhelming superiority in the air. Meteorological records indicated that late November, when the Ardennes heights were normally blanketed by low cloud and fog, was the most favourable time. But in the event the launch of the Ardennes offensive was delayed until 16 December.

Though von Rundstedt's forces on paper were mighty in men and equipment, many of the troops were young, inexperienced and inadequately trained. To fill the thirty-seven new divisions which made up the Sixth Panzer Army, for example, troops had to be withdrawn from low-key sectors in Finland and the Balkans, or scoured from the navy, the air force, industry and the ranks of the under-age and over-age. Great stress, therefore, was laid on the correct psychological conditioning of the troops who were to do the fighting, and to this end a hate campaign was organized against the Anglo-Americans. German soldiers were reminded once again of the air raids that had laid waste their towns and homes, and of the rapine and pillage that had allegedly been endured by those parts of Germany which had already fallen into American hands. Above all, Hitler insisted that for the offensive to succeed the German fighting men had to be imbued with a fanatical ruthlessness.

Four days before the start of the offensive, Hitler held a conference of senior commanders down to divisional level at his military headquarters, code-named Adlerhorst (Eagle's Eyrie), near Bad Nauheim. For two hours he rambled and ranted extempore. Only towards the end did he turn to the matter in hand – the attack through the Ardennes. The Americans were later to claim that in this speech Hitler had exhorted his commanders to fight a brutal and ruthless battle in which all human scruples were to be discarded. This claim cannot be supported from the fragment of the speech transcript that has survived. But both Sepp Dietrich and Wilhelm Mohnke attended Hitler's conference, and there seems little doubt that sentiments of this sort were passed down the chain of command within the Sixth Panzer Army by one or both of these loyal veteran commanders.

The orders spoke of 'a wave of terror and fright' preceding the German troops, of resistance being broken by terror, and prisoners of war being shot 'where local conditions should so require it'.*

At a meeting of his unit commanders two days after Hitler's Bad Nauheim conference, Sepp Dietrich, having made no mention of prisoners of war in his orders, was asked: 'And the prisoners? Where shall we put them?' At which Dietrich retorted: 'Prisoners? You know what to do with them.' A Wehrmacht colonel who was present at this meeting commented after the war:

> Addressed to the generals and senior officers of the Waffen-SS and in the atmosphere of the time, a phrase of this nature could mean only one thing: get rid of the prisoners. Sepp Dietrich ... was the man who was really responsible for the Malmédy massacre and for the way in which the 1st SS Panzer Division, the Leibstandarte Adolf Hitler, shot down civilians throughout their advance. The least that can be said is that the commanders were letting their men run riot.

The Commander of the Leibstandarte Division to which this Wehrmacht colonel refers was Wilhelm Mohnke, now promoted to the rank of Ober-führer, or Brigadier. Mohnke had survived the near annihilation of the 12 SS Panzer Division (Hitler Jugend) in the battle for Normandy, during which the Hitler Jugend had lost forty per cent of its men and most of its weapons and armour, and had been awarded the coveted Knight's Cross for his valour at the Normandy front and promoted to take command of the Leibstandarte when the Division's previous commander, SS-Brigadeführer Theodor Wisch, was severely wounded in Normandy during the division's desperate flight from the carnage in the Falaise pocket in August. Until October 1944 Mohnke was preoccupied with rebuilding the decimated ranks of the Leibstandarte and indoctrinating a new generation of recruits with the old élitist *esprit de corps* and ideological fervour. Largely rebuilt by December, but desperately short on training and experience, Mohnke's division was destined to be the leading strike force of the German offensive – for it was inconceivable to Hitler that this last great operation in defence of the Reich should not be carried out by his own bodyguard formation.

---

* Compare these orders with the orders for Operation Black, the German operation against the Yugoslav partisans in the summer of 1943, in which the shooting of enemy prisoners by the German military reached its peak. The orders stipulated 'The troops must move against the hostile populace without consideration and with brutal severity, and must deny the enemy any possibility of existence.'

242

Two days before the start of the offensive, Mohnke summoned a conference of his regimental commanders in a forester's house in the wooded Eifel hills to give them their detailed orders for the impending offensive. His division, he told the assembled officers, had been given a most vital role in the offensive. With the 12th SS Panzer Division it was to lead the attack of the Sixth SS Panzer Army against the American positions on the other side of the border in the Belgian Ardennes. One of the spearheads of the 1st SS Panzer Division's assault would be a powerful armoured battle group, to be known as Kampfgruppe Peiper, after its commander, SS-Obersturmbannführer Jochen Peiper, the handsome and dashing twenty-nine-year-old Leibstandarte war veteran who currently commanded the division's 1st SS Panzer Regiment.

Peiper was a carefully considered choice for the job of commanding such a key operation. Recklessly daring, ruthless and able, Peiper had already had experience of leading similar battle groups on the Russian Front. A middle-class Berliner and early convert to Nazi ideology – though never a member of the Party – Peiper was commissioned in the SS-Leibstandarte in 1936 and in 1938 joined the personal staff of Heinrich Himmler, with whom he once watched an experimental gassing of living human beings. Assigned to Hitler's military headquarters during the Polish campaign, Peiper was back with the Leibstandarte during operations in the Low Countries and France in 1940. Afterwards, in Russia, he distinguished himself as a brave, cool and skilful commander, winning the Knight's Cross in a crucial engagement during the German recapture of the city of Kharkov.

But there was, of course, a negative side to Peiper's spectacular exploits. Thus in a night attack on a village in the Zhitomir sector of the Russian Front in December 1943, his battle group not only totally destroyed the village but annihilated all its occupants, and in the following two days killed no less than 2,500 Russian troops while taking no more than three prisoners. It is little surprise, therefore, that this impetuous, battle-hardened and fanatical young Nazi war hero should adopt similar extreme measures when called upon to spearhead Germany's last throw in the West – particularly after receiving his orders from Wilhelm Mohnke.

Delayed by traffic jams on the narrow, congested road, Peiper arrived late at the conference and had to be briefed separately by Mohnke and his chief of staff, SS-Obersturmbannführer Dietrich Ziemssen. The vanguard of his battle group, which was to be about 5,000 men strong, was to consist of about 70 Mark IV and Mark V Panther tanks and a battalion of 20 King Tigers, together with a battalion of motorized infantry with armoured self-propelled guns commanded by Hauptsturmführer Josef Diefenthal. At the head of Peiper's heavyweight column, though not under his direct command, a special commando unit of the 150th Panzer Brigade (raised and commanded by the legendary SS commando leader, Otto Skorzeny), consisting of English-speaking German soldiers and American tanks, trucks and jeeps, would spread panic and confusion in and behind the American lines – or so it was intended.

Kampfgruppe Peiper's objective was the great bridge spanning the canyon-like banks of the River Meuse at Huy. The Meuse was the major natural barrier in the path of the Sixth Panzer Army and it was felt that Peiper would have achieved his mission if just one of the many tanks in his battle group reached the river and secured the bridge for the main body of the forces following behind. To reach the bridge Kampfgruppe Peiper was assigned a route which ran for the most part over the nearly mountainous Ardennes along narrow minor roads. Starting at the village of Losheim just inside the German border, the route ascended the Ardennes hills to Honsfeld, then carried on to Ligneuville on the River Amblève, and thence followed a very steep, twisting track over hilly, forested country through Wanne to the village of Trois Ponts on the River Salm. Here Peiper could join a first-class road, the *Route Nationale* N-23, which hopefully would take him speedily to his objective at Huy on the Meuse.

Peiper did not conceal the fact that he did not care for the plan outlined to him by Mohnke. The outcome of the mission depended on Peiper reaching the Meuse in the fastest possible time, in spite of the winter conditions and the fact that most of the route lay over precipitous, thickly wooded country and along narrow, winding dirt tracks which in his opinion were more suited for bicycles than tanks. Peiper estimated that on such roads in such terrain his battle group would be strung out in a column fifteen miles long, with virtually no room to manoeuvre if it came under fire. This route had been chosen because it contained the fewest bridges for the Americans to blow to bar his advance. But how was he to know if any of those bridges could bear the weight of his tanks, some of which weighed up to seventy tons apiece? And where was the petrol coming from? No fuel reserves could be provided for his tank force, so the only way he could keep going was to capture American fuel dumps along the way.

The whole mission was desperate and fraught, but Mohnke made it clear to Peiper that the success of the entire offensive depended on him. It was an operation of extreme daring, Mohnke told Peiper, but the Führer expected his Leibstandarte to fight 'fanatically', and to accept self-sacrifice to achieve the impossible. Speed, surprise and ruthlessness were paramount. Nothing could be allowed to slow down or stop the rapid advance to the Meuse. Therefore enemy prisoners were not the concern of the armoured spearhead, but should be left to the infantry following up behind. Any resistance by the Belgian Maquis should be crushed 'ruthlessly'.

Mohnke told Peiper that Hitler had ordered the battle to be fought 'with special brutality and without humane inhibitions'. Mohnke concluded his

244

conference by recalling the speech Hitler had made to his generals at Bad Nauheim two days earlier:

> The battle will decide whether Germany is to live or to die. Your soldiers must fight hard and ruthlessly. There must be no pity. The battle must be fought with brutality and all resistance must be broken in a wave of terror. The enemy must be beaten, now or never. Thus will live our Germany! *Forward to and over the Meuse!*

Otto Skorzeny, who was also present, had heard this sort of thing before. To him, Hitler's impassioned exhortation as relayed by Mohnke was just the 'usual rhetoric'. It might work wonders with the young and impressionable rank-and-file who would have to do the fighting, but to the battle-hardened commanders it was, in his view, so much hot air. 'Old hares as we were,' Skorzeny recalled, 'we only half-listened to Mohnke, who had steadily grown red in the face with the effort.'

Peiper left Mohnke's headquarters to return to his own. He was to testify subsequently:

> I did not read the material given to me at the Division Command Post, because I was in a hurry, and was also in a bad mood, because I disagreed with the entire preparation for the undertaking, which looked highly defective to me.
>
> I returned on the same day to my Command Post, which was located in a forester's house in the Blankenheim woods. First, I ordered my adjutant to call a commander's meeting for the same day at about 1600 hours. This left me about two hours, which I used to study the material handed to me at the division. The very first impression of the terrain which I got, with the aid of maps, reassured my opinion that it was a desperate undertaking. I can remember that in this material, among other things, was an order of the Sixth SS Panzer Army, with the contents that, considering the desperate situation of the German people, a wave of terror and fright should precede our troops. Also, this order pointed out that the German soldier should, in this offensive, recall the innumerable German victims of the bombing terror. Furthermore, it was stated that the enemy resistance had to be broken by terror. Also, I am nearly certain that, in this order, it was expressly stated that prisoners of war must be shot where the local conditions should so require it. This order was incorporated into the regimental order . . . I did not mention that prisoners of war should be shot because local conditions of

245

combat should require it, because those present were all experienced officers to whom this was obvious.

It is possible, although I don't know for sure, that the paragraph of the regimental orders, which dealt with the prisoners of war, and was taken from the army order without receiving any additions, was not sent to the battalions in writing, but for reasons of security was only looked at in the Regiment, and remained there to avoid this order falling into enemy hands.

The above army order, about which I have just talked, was signed by SS Oberstgruppenführer and Generaloberst Sepp Dietrich. I know, however, that the order to use brutality was not given by Sepp Dietrich out of his own initiative, but that he only acted along the lines which the Führer had expressly laid down.

On the morning of 15 December 1944 I was at the Command Post of the 1st SS Panzer Corps, where the Commanding General, SS-Gruppenführer Priess, used the words as they were in the army order, in which he talked about the manner in which to treat the enemy and fight him. Anyhow, out of all his words emerged that we had to fight with brutality and that this was expressly desired by the Führer.*

Before dawn on 16 December 1944 Peiper moved his battle group up to Losheim for the start of his historic but desperate enterprise – part of a simultaneous surprise German onslaught along the entire Ardennes front. It was an inauspicious beginning. The plan was for the 12th Volksgrenadier Division to punch a hole through the American lines on the other side of the border through which Kampfgruppe Peiper could launch itself on its drive to the Meuse. But a bridge blown during the German retreat months before could not be repaired because the Volksgrenadiers' horse-drawn artillery had clogged up the roads and the army engineers could not get through. All morning Peiper sat and fumed. For a while he tried directing the traffic personally, but when that failed to clear the jams he gave the order for his column to start rolling anyway and to run down anything that lay in its way. Kampfgruppe Peiper was en route.

Late that night the column reached Lanzareth, a small place then occupied by a parachute regiment commanded by a staff colonel from the Air Ministry in Berlin. Though the regiment was in the front-line it had put

---

* Peiper subsequently retracted this statement at his trial, claiming that it was made 'under duress'.

out no sentries or guides and most of its men had gone to sleep for the night as if they were on a peacetime exercise. Peiper was furious. He strode over to the Café Palm, the parachute regiment's HQ, to have it out with the CO. Inside the café Germans were asleep everywhere, and in a corner a group of ashen-faced American prisoners, captured by the German paras during the fighting earlier in the day, sat huddled together awaiting events. One of them was Lieutenant Lyle Bouck. He was to write later:

> About midnight, a group of officers came into the room. They were busy and excited about the situation. A map kept falling off the table near the far side of the room. One of the officers stuck the map against the wall with two bayonets. A few of the officers left the room and then returned, mad about something. One of the German soldiers was wounded badly in the arm. He was in shock and shouted: '*Panzerfaust, Panzerfaust, Panzerfaust!*' One of the officers made this soldier go upstairs with the other wounded. He seemed to feel this wounded soldier might grab a weapon and kill the wounded Americans.

A violent argument broke out between Peiper and the para commander. It was only ended when Peiper forced the para colonel to agree to launch a dawn attack to clear the surrounding woods of any lurking American troops. Till then the men could grab what sleep they could. But Peiper would not sleep. He would not sleep for many endless days and nights. For the offensive had now begun.

MASSACRE

In the raw chill and damp of the dark hour before dawn, with the air thick with swirling fog and the road muddy after days of rain, Peiper's armoured column squealed and rattled towards the small country village of Honsfeld, the first major checkpoint on its route west, with paratroopers walking beside each tank to guide it with white handkerchiefs through the darkness. The German tanks were not the only vehicles on the road that morning, however, for long columns of American vehicles were retreating in the same direction that Peiper was advancing, and Peiper had to halt his battle group to allow one American column to pass, then move into the gap between that column and the one following up behind, thus merging into the enemy force.

Honsfeld was a rest area for the 394th Regiment of the 99th US Infantry Division. At the southern end of the village a US Army Lieutenant by the name of Robert Reppa was trying to snatch some sleep in a chair when his ears detected a change in the sound of the traffic passing outside. Opening the door, he was shocked to find an enormous German Panther tank outside, and German paratroopers swarming everywhere, rounding up the American troops in the streets outside. While many Americans were captured in Honsfeld, some managed to break away, and others, holed up inside the houses, put up a spirited defence. For some, however, there was to be a different fate, for it was in Honsfeld that the first of a whole series of mass murders by Kampfgruppe Peiper began.

As the attack developed into fierce house-to-house fighting down the village street, a house containing eighteen enlisted men and four officers was surrounded, and the Germans brought an 88mm gun to bear on the house and began to blast it away piecemeal. At this point the Americans hung a white sheet out of the window and the firing ceased on both sides. A group of twelve Americans then walked out of the house carrying a large white flag, but before they had taken more than a step or two outside they

248

were gunned down in cold blood. The remaining six Americans, having seen what had happened to their comrades, stayed inside the house. They were later brought out by a German soldier and marched away to join a large group of about 200 American prisoners. This group was then marched away to the rear, but as they went down the road the crew of a German tank fired into the column, killing two of the prisoners – one of them, an anti-tank gunner by the name of 'Johnnie' Stegle, shot between the eyes with an American .45 automatic. That same morning, on the outskirts of Honsfeld, two separate groups of Americans – one of fifteen to twenty men, the other of seven men – were shot to death by the Germans after they had surrendered.

After the war the Americans were to claim that SS troops had killed some twenty-five American POWs at Honsfeld in six separate incidents. But it was only a beginning. Wherever Kampfgruppe Peiper went the killings continued.

———

Peiper now decided to divert from his assigned route in order to refuel his tanks from an American petrol dump at Büllingen, a few miles to the north of Honsfeld. Fifty American GIs captured at Büllingen were ordered to fill the tanks with 50,000 gallons of captured fuel; then, their usefulness at an end, they were shot. This was not the only atrocity the Americans claim was committed by Peiper's SS troopers at Büllingen that morning. In one incident, for example, an armoured personnel carrier of the 3rd SS Panzer Company overtook six to eight unarmed American prisoners of war walking along the road towards the rear. At the sight of the prisoners the commander of the carrier, Sergeant Sepp Witkwoski, gave a brief, peremptory order: 'Ready – bump 'em off!' All the crew of the carrier let fly with everything they had – machine-guns, machine-pistols and rifles – and the Americans fell to the ground. This was but the start of a widespread wave of random killings in the vicinity of Büllingen. Out towards Büllingen airfield another half track of the 3rd Panzer Company fired into two separate groups of between five and eight American prisoners, while just outside the town another squad from the same Company dragged seven or eight Americans out of a cellar, and after searching them lined them up against the house and shot them. Shortly afterwards another group of fifteen to twenty Americans were shot outside the same house.

These outrages – the shooting of Americans who had either been taken prisoner and were being marched to the rear or were coming out of the houses to offer their surrender – were repeated by several other German units, including the 10th SS Panzer Company, the 1st Panzer Company

249

and the 9th SS Panzer Pioneer Company – all elements of Peiper's battle group. So universal was the killing of prisoners that an NCO of the 9th SS Panzer Pioneer Company reported to his company commander that *no* prisoners of war were taken at Büllingen and that any Americans found in the houses were 'bumped off'. Nor were the killings confined to Americans. When two SS men named Rieder and Haas, both from the 9th SS Panzer Pioneer Company, entered one of the houses in Büllingen they found a Belgian woman inside; and when she assured the SS men that there were no Americans in the house, Haas turned to his comrade and told him: 'Rieder, bump this woman off.' Rieder then raised his rifle and shot the woman through the forehead.

Altogether between sixty-two and ninety unarmed American prisoners were alleged by the Americans to have been murdered at Büllingen in a total of twelve separate incidents.

Leaving Büllingen after a short but deadly stay, Kampfgruppe Peiper headed west, then divided forces in an attempt to encircle a large American force to the east of Ligneuville. Peiper himself took the assigned southern route to Ligneuville and a smaller group commanded by Sturmbannführer Poetschke, with Hauptsturmführer Diefenthal commanding a battalion of SS Panzer Grenadiers, took a northern route via Thirimont and Baugnez. It was at Baugnez that Poetschke's column was destined to make catastrophic contact with an American column in a bloodletting to which the name 'Malmédy massacre' will for ever be attached. This is what happened.

At 11.45 a.m. on 17 December a small American convoy consisting of thirty vehicles and about 140 men of Battery B of the 285th Field Artillery Observation Battalion of the 7th US Armored Division reached the town of Malmédy while *en route* toward St Vith in the south. At the command post of the 291st Engineering Battalion, the only American unit defending Malmédy against the German advance, the column came to a halt. Lieutenant Virgil T. Lary, who was in the leading jeep, was advised by the Battalion Commander, Colonel David E. Pergrin, to change course and proceed via Stavelot as German tanks had been reported at Büllingen. However, the captain in the jeep with Lary decided to ignore this advice. His job was to keep the column in its proper slot in the divisional convoy, so tanks or no tanks he ordered the driver to continue on the planned route in the direction of Ligneuville.

Shortly afterwards the column reached the crossroads at the scattered hamlet of Baugnez, where no less than five roads converged, including the road from Thirimont along which the heavy tanks of the northern wing of

Kampfgruppe Peiper was at that moment making its way. Outside the café of Madame Adèle Bodarwé, which was situated on the western corner of the crossroads, an MP by the name of Private Homer Ford was standing on duty. As the artillery observation column came up, Ford directed it on to the right road, behind an army bulldozer making its own lone way towards Ligneuville. Private Ford then turned to go back into the café. But he had taken only a few steps when he heard the noise of sudden gunfire and turned back to see the American column under fire from a German armoured column proceeding in the opposite direction on a secondary road almost parallel with the road to Ligneuville. The lead truck of the American column had had its front wheels shot off and several vehicles caught fire and began burning. Across the intervening fields German troops had jumped off their armoured vehicles and were running towards the American positions, firing their rifles and machine-pistols as they ran. Further down the road the US army bulldozer had accelerated away as if it was driven by rocket propulsion.

Pandemonium broke out in Battery B. Some of the Americans jumped out of their vehicles and tried to gain the sanctuary of the surrounding woods. Others ran back to the crossroads and hid with Private Ford, the MP, in an outbuilding behind the café. Others, including Lieutenant Lary, made an effort to hold off the advancing Germans from the cover of a ditch that ran alongside the road. But it was a forlorn resistance. The German tanks had by now reached the crossroads and turned down the Ligneuville road, smashing their way past the American vehicles, which they simply pushed off the road and then machine-gunned, setting them on fire, if they were not on fire already. Lieutenant Lary had meanwhile been crawling along the ditch in an effort to reach a roadside house from which to conduct a more effective defence, but when he got to the house he found fifteen to twenty GIs with their hands already up in surrender. Lary tried to persuade them to make a fight of it but a corporal in the group would have none of it. 'Look up the road, Lary,' he told the Lieutenant. Lary looked and saw an entire column of armoured vehicles bearing down on them. Clearly, the lightly armed Americans were in no position to fight it out against such overwhelming odds, so Lary ducked back across the road to consult the captain in charge of B Battery, who was still crouching in the ditch.

'Captain, are you hit?' Lary asked the motionless figure of the senior officer.

There was no reply, so Lary asked again: 'Captain, are you hit?'

'No,' came the captain's voice from the ditch. 'Go away or they'll come back and kill me.'

'Captain, come out of the ditch,' Lary reassured him. 'Those people have gone.'

Reluctantly the captain struggled out of the ditch and joined the group waiting outside the house with raised hands. As the lead tank growled up an SS man on board motioned them to move up to the crossroads.

Jochen Peiper had not been on the spot when the shooting started, but had allowed his armoured column to go on without him while he paused to interrogate an American prisoner further back down the road. When he heard the noise of cannon and machine-gun fire he drove up to rejoin the column and found that a number of his tanks and armoured personnel carriers had targetted a column of American trucks at a range of about 500 yards. Seeing that the Americans presented no danger, Peiper had ordered his men to stop firing at about the time Lieutenant Lary's group offered their surrender, then pressed on, leaving his subordinates to do the mopping-up. According to Lary's later account, as Peiper passed the prisoners Lary heard him call out to them in English from his perch on top of a Panther tank: 'It's a long way to Tipperary, boys!'

Hauptsturmführer Josef Diefenthal, CO of the 3rd Battalion of the 2nd SS Panzer Grenadier Regiment, now arrived on the scene in his half-track. He ordered the prisoners to be searched and after their cigarettes and valuables were taken from them they were lined up in eight rows in a field next to the café at the crossroads. The MP Private Ford and the men who had tried to hide themselves at the back of the café were rounded up and made to join their comrades in the field. So also was a group of ten Americans from the US 32nd Armored Regiment, which included Sergeant Henry Roy Zach, who had been captured by Peiper's column earlier in the morning and had reached the Baugnez crossroads clinging to the hulls of the German tanks. About twenty other American soldiers, meanwhile, had succeeded in evading capture and hidden themselves as best they could in the vicinity. Warren Schmidt, for example, had crawled into a small stream, where he lay, half frozen to death, camouflaged from view with weeds and mud.

Since the overriding need was to keep moving at all costs, Hauptsturmführer Diefenthal then ordered the leading German column to resume its advance, and left Sturmbannführer Poetschke, commanding the 1st Panzer Battalion, to take care of the prisoners. These now numbered about 120 men, including Medical Corps personnel wearing Red Cross armbands and Red Cross signs painted on their helmets. Poetschke's Panzer Column now rumbled up and for a while the prisoners had to stand and watch as the Germans struggled to manoeuvre their 70-ton Tiger tanks round the sharp bend on to the Ligneuville road. Then Lieutenant Lary saw a self-propelled gun stop and try and depress its enormous 88mm cannon in the prisoners' direction. But the gun was blocking the road and an officer ordered it to move on. Its place was taken by two armoured vehicles which were pulled out of the column and manoeuvred so that they could cover the prisoners with their machine-guns. Poetschke then ordered the commander of one of the tanks, Sergeant Hans Siptrott, to open fire on the prisoners. Siptrott turned to his assistant gunner, Private George Fleps, a young Rumanian *Volksdeutscher* (ethnic German) who already had his pistol drawn, and told him to fire. Hand on hip as he had been taught in training, Fleps three times brought the pointed pistol slowly down to line-of-sight level, then took careful and deliberate aim at Lieutenant Lary's driver, who was standing in the front rank of prisoners, and pulled the trigger, twice.

Lary's driver was hit in the chest and fell to the ground with blood pouring from his wound. The other Americans stared in horrified disbelief, then began to cry out and shout out loud, so that one of the officers, fearful that some of them might make a break for it and give the Germans a perfect excuse to open up on them, yelled a sharp command: 'Stand fast!' But the words were barely out of his mouth when the machine-guns of both tanks began firing, traversing the ranks of Americans and mowing them down where they stood. Many Americans were killed outright. Others were wounded and lay screaming on the ground. A few tried to flee but were cut down before they had run a few paces. One medic, Corporal Indelicate, was shot and killed while he was still bandaging a wounded comrade. Lary was hit twice and fell, feigning death as the bullets thudded into flesh and mud all around him. Homer Ford, Henry Zach, and an ambulance man by the name of Samuel Dobyns and a number of others all did the same. For several minutes, which seemed like a whole quarter of an hour to the men still clinging to life in the meadow grass, the shooting continued unabated – all observed in total disbelief by a Belgian eye-witness, Henri Le Joly, standing in the doorway of the café.

Sergeant Siptrott's tank was the first to stop firing and move off, but the other tank continued to pump a long burst of machine-gun fire into the fallen bodies. Then it, too, rumbled away, duty done.

This was not the end of it, however. As more trucks and tanks rolled past, they too opened up on the bodies, raking them with further bursts of machine-gun and rifle fire. Finally, men of a German SS engineering unit went into the field and walked among the bodies, killing any that still showed signs of life. Lary lay still, hardly daring to draw breath, listening to the single shots and the sound of boots moving nearer. Out of the corner of an eye he could see one of the Germans kicking the bodies for signs of life; any that flinched were summarily shot. Other Germans joined in the fun, kicking and shooting, kicking and shooting, laughing insanely as they went. The whole field echoed with their laughter ; to Lary it sounded 'maniacal'.

The ambulanceman, Samuel Dobyns, who ironically had been commended for rescuing German wounded in the Normandy campaign, saw no point in waiting to be butchered and staggered to his feet and began to run. But a machine-gun opened up on him and four bullets entered his body and another eight tore his uniform to ribbons. He fell and three SS men came up to him; but they turned back again when they decided that he was as good as dead. A few of the prisoners managed to get as far as the road in a vain effort to reach the sanctuary of the farmers' houses; the villagers watched in horror as the German tanks rolled over their bodies as they lay in the roadway. A few of the Americans in the field were bludgeoned to death. At some point, either then or later, a few of the prisoners were bayoneted in the eyes or had their eyeballs gouged out – while still alive, according to the later American autopsy. Finally the Germans left the field and moved on. A small detachment was left to guard the crossroads and a strange silence descended on the massacre site.

By a miracle, twenty or so Americans had survived the unremitting gunfire aimed at them. Most, including Lieutenant Lary and Private Ford, had been wounded, some of them more than once. Incredibly, one of them, Private James Massara, had not been hit all. It was Massara who led this shattered band of survivors as they got uncertainly to their feet from amongst the heaps of bloody corpses of their former comrades and lurched and hobbled away in a desperate attempt to seek the shelter of the distant woods. The German rearguard at the crossroads, astonished to see living figures rise (as it seemed) from the dead, once more let fly with their machine-guns, and some of the Americans, hearing the shooting, ducked for the cover of the café. But the café was a snare and a delusion, for in the most diabolical trick of a diabolical engagement the Germans now set the café on fire, and as the Americans stumbled out to escape the flames, the Germans coolly shot them dead.

Not all had died, however. Shortly after 2.30 p.m., some thirty minutes after the first shot had been fired at the prisoners, four soldiers burst out of the woods near the road block on the Malmédy road, and half-running, half-stumbling, made for a small American patrol which had driven out of Malmédy to check what all the shooting was about. One of these Americans was the CO of the unit defending Malmédy, Colonel Pergrin, and it was to Pergrin that the four survivors, almost incoherent with the shock and trauma of their ordeal, gave the first news of what had happened to them and their comrades – 'screaming incoherently', as Pergrin put it, 'something about a massacre.' Pergrin was aghast. He drove the four men back to Malmédy where two *Time* magazine reporters found them 'half-frozen, dazed, weeping with anger.' By 4.30 p.m. Pergrin's preliminary report had burst on First Army HQ; by 6 p.m. the *Time* reporters had filed their scoop and the army had decided to give the story maximum publicity so that every unit in the command would be fully aware that a large number of American prisoners had been brutally put to death by German forces advancing west through the Ardennes. Shortly afterwards the news was beamed to Germany and the German forces in the West by the Allies' black propaganda radio station, *Soldatensender Calais* (Forces Broadcasting Station Calais). Subsequently the American government delivered an official protest to the German government via Switzerland. The German government passed it on to the German High Command, which in turn passed it back down the line to Sepp Dietrich at the Sixth Panzer Army, who passed it on to Hermann Priess at 1st SS Panzer Corps. Priess was to testify later:

> Army ordered an investigation and demanded a report as to whether prisoners of war had been shot in the area of Malmédy ... The first thing I did when this order from Army came through was to ask my Chief of Staff, 'Do you know anything about this?' I received the answer, 'No.' I then called the Division Commander [Mohnke] by telephone. He also reported to me that he knew nothing. I then ordered him by telephone that this investigation ordered by Army would be put into action very energetically and as soon as possible ... But the Division Commander, Oberführer Mohnke, reported to Army that his division had not shot any prisoners of war. One or two days after that I again talked with Oberführer Mohnke. He orally reported his written report to Army to me. Apart from this, Corps did not make any further inquiries about this matter.

———

Meanwhile, more survivors straggled out of the woods and reached US army road blocks. By midnight seventeen had reached Pergrin's unit, two of the last being Lieutenant Lary, who had passed out at a farmhouse on the way, and Warren Schmidt, exhausted after his prolonged immersion in an icy stream. By then heavy snow had fallen and covered the bodies at the crossroads in a thick white mantle that hid all evidence of the crime from view.

In all, some forty-three Americans are reputed to have survived the encounter with the northern wing of Jochen Peiper's battlegroup at the Baugnez crossroads on Sunday, 17 December 1944.

According to official estimates, eighty-six Americans died – not all, it has to be said, as prisoners in the massacre, since a few had died in the preliminary skirmish before the American surrender.

The effect of the massacre on the morale of the American army in general and First Army in particular was very different from what had been intended by Hitler when he ordered the German offensive to be waged ruthlessly and without pity. For instead of the cowed and abject foe the Germans had hoped for, they found an enemy steeled by a grim resolve to avenge the murdered men of Malmédy. Moreover, this vengeance was sometimes to be paid out in kind. On 21 December, for example, the men of the 328th Infantry Regiment were given the order: 'No SS troops or paratroopers will be taken but will be shot on sight'. And in the savage fighting for Chegnogne, twenty-one surrendered German soldiers were shot by men of the 11th US Armored Division, while the inmates of a German first aid post which had been set on fire were gunned down as they emerged carrying a Red Cross flag as a flag of surrender.

The Malmédy massacre was the worst summary atrocity ever carried out against American troops in the western hemisphere. But it was only a beginning, for an even greater number of American soldiers were to die in a series of similar outrages as Kampfgruppe Peiper pursued its ruthless advance westward towards the Meuse.

After leaving the scene of the massacre at the Baugnez crossroads, the SS column resumed its advance towards Ligneuville, where the Divisional Commander, Wilhelm Mohnke, soon set up his command post in the Hotel du Moulin. Near the town another large group of dead American prisoners of war were seen lying near the road. They had no weapons and were grouped too closely together to have been killed in combat. At about 4 p.m. that afternoon a further eight American prisoners were shot by SS men of the 9th SS Panzer Engineer Company, who had been responsible for the earlier killings at Büllingen. On the road leading out of Ligneuville to Stavelot a further fifteen POWs were reportedly shot at a farmhouse by the crew of a German troop carrier. Thus, according to subsequent American investigative reports, a further seventy-three American prisoners had been murdered in the vicinity of Ligneuville in the immediate aftermath of the Malmédy massacre.

On the morning of 18 December, the day after the Malmédy massacre, Kampfgruppe Peiper reached Stavelot. Here it was the turn of the Belgian populace to learn the meaning of war waged 'without humane considerations'. Peiper and his men were later to claim that in Stavelot they had been fired on by members of the Belgian Maquis and had simply reacted in accordance with their orders to crush civilian resistance. There is no evidence that the Resistance did in fact launch an attack on Peiper's heavily armed battle group at this juncture and it is unlikely that many of the victims of SS retaliation, who included the very young and the very old, could have been members of any resistance group. Indeed, many of the shooting incidents indicate a totally wanton and gratuitous taking of life – random fun killings carried out on the spurious grounds of military necessity.

The litany of murders makes stark reading. On the road leading to the hospital one of the crew of a parked tank opened fire with his machine-pistol on a group of civilians walking past only a few yards away. The group included a couple with an eighteen-month-old baby, and another couple with two young children. Two of the adults were killed and two severely wounded in the gunfire. None had committed any hostile acts towards the Germans. That evening two more Belgians were murdered in their house on the outskirts of Stavelot; and on the road out to La Gleize German tanks fired into a group of fifteen to twenty women, killing and wounding between six and eight of them. Two more Belgian civilians were shot by Peiper's men under a railway bridge near the town.

The next day units of Kampfgruppe Peiper rounded up twenty-one Belgian civilians, took them to a shed measuring only eight by twelve feet, then set up a machine-gun and proceeded to empty two belts of ammunition into the tightly pressed throng as they stood huddled together in the shed. Several troopers then went into the shed to finish off anyone still left alive. They then piled straw on top of the bodies and set it on fire. Miraculously eight of the occupants managed to escape and two of these later gave evidence against Peiper's men. That night the Germans found a group of twenty-nine Belgian civilians who had sought refuge in the cellar of a house on the road to Trois Ponts at a time of heavy street fighting. The Germans threw two hand grenades into the cellar, which failed to kill anyone, then ordered the occupants to come out. Claiming they had been fired on from the cellar, the Germans shot the people as they came out. Twenty-six of the group were believed to have been killed in this way – two men, eight women and thirteen children and young girls.

Thus a total of ninety-three Belgian civilians were believed to have been killed by Peiper's SS troops during their brief occupation of the town. None of these civilians had at any time taken up arms against the German troops.

———

At the town of Trois Ponts Peiper's battle group encountered its first serious set back. American engineers blew the key bridges leading to the N-23 highway, forcing Peiper to divert on a northerly detour via La Gleize and Cheneux. Kampfgruppe Peiper was now stretched out in a column fifteen miles long reaching all the way back to Malmédy, and it made an easy target for one of the few air strikes launched by American aircraft in the early days of the Battle of the Bulge.

After the column had been badly shot up by marauding fighter-bombers in the vicinity of Cheneux, a group of thirty to forty unarmed American prisoners were collected together on the outskirts of the town, and while they stood with their hands clasped behind their heads four or five tanks and a half-track opened fire on them, killing them all. In a separate incident, an American jeep driver who had collided with a German armoured personnel carrier was shot to death only a few metres away from the vehicle in which Jochen Peiper himself was riding.

Leaving Cheneux, Peiper pressed forward due west, with only one bridge left to cross between him and his goal at Huy on the Meuse. With daylight fading, American engineers had only just finished wiring up the explosive charges under the bridge over the little Lienne river near Veucy when the lead tanks of the German column appeared in view. As one of Peiper's King Tigers opened fire, the Lieutenant in charge of the engineers' detail shouted the order 'Blow! Blow!' Peiper himself saw the bridge go up – and with it his final hopes of reaching his objective and completing his part in Hitler's master plan to turn the tide for Germany.

The bold offensive thrust of Kampfgruppe Peiper was over. Twist and turn as he would, Peiper could find no way forward. Increasingly embattled by a steadily strengthening enemy, cut off from his one line of retreat back to the main body of the German forces, fuel almost exhausted, ammunition running low – Peiper was in a desperate position. His only option was to await relief and reinforcements and fight off the closing American ring. For the next three days savage fighting took place in the area around Stoumont, La Gleize and Cheneux; and during that period more American prisoners and Belgian civilians were destined to lose their lives at the hands of their increasingly vexed and hard-pressed SS captors.

On the morning of 19 December, the Americans claimed, a number of units from Kampfgruppe Peiper arrived in Stoumont and in a long series of atrocities shot approximately 104 to 109 American prisoners of war. Seven were shot at the edge of a pasture by troopers of the 11th SS Panzer Company. Elements of the 3rd Panzer Pioneer Company shot four prisoners and a Belgian civilian in a chicken house and a nearby field, then murdered two unarmed American soldiers carrying a wounded German soldier, and rounded off a busy morning by shooting two Americans carrying a wounded American soldier on a litter. Fifteen to twenty Americans were gunned down by the crew of a Mark IV tank and at about the same time three American POWs were shot to death in the presence of the Kampfgruppe's Commander, Jochen Peiper.

Elements of the 2nd Panzer Company also took part in the unlawful killings at Stoumont. Fifteen to twenty-five POWs were standing in a field with their hands clasped behind their heads when they were fired upon by machine guns from several German tanks. At about 2 p.m. that afternoon tanks from the same Panzer Company reached a point about two kilometres west of Stoumont – the most westerly point attained during the offensive. Here some fifteen American prisoners with their hands above their heads were machine gunned by two of the tanks, and a little later ten more prisoners were murdered near the same spot after a machine gun and machine pistols were turned on them.

———

On 20 or 21 December an order was sent out from Mohnke's 1st SS Panzer Division headquarters, which a day or two previously had established itself in the small town of Wanne, to the effect that an enemy radio transmitter had been located in Wanne and that all male civilians in the town should be shot. Certain elements of Kampfgruppe Peiper – namely the 1st and the 7th SS Panzer Companies – were in Wanne at this time and pursuant to Mohnke's order a number of male civilians were taken from their homes and shot to death. In one recorded incident, Scharführer Valentin Bersin, a tank commander in the Second Platoon, First Company, First Battalion, First SS Panzer Regiment, ordered SS-Mann Georg Kotzur to shoot a civilian who was standing nearby, and added that he would bring more civilians for Kotzur to shoot. However, when another SS-Mann turned up, by the name of Hans Trettin, Kotzur said: 'You shoot the man, my pistol is jammed.' So Trettin went ahead and shot the man in the neck and then again in the head as he lay on the ground. Another civilian, perhaps wondering what the shooting was about, was then seen to emerge from one of the houses, whereupon Trettin asked Kotzur: 'You shoot this one.' But Kotzur said his pistol was still jammed, so Trettin took the second civilian to where the first one lay, and proceeded to shoot the second civilian to death as he had the first.

———

The Americans were to claim that between 19 and 23 December, when a large part of Kampfgruppe Peiper was concentrated in La Gleize, German troops shot a large number of American POWs, perhaps as many as 311, together with three Belgian civilians, in a whole series of atrocities committed in and around the village. Unlike those we have mentioned, these claims could never be substantiated, however, and neither surviving American prisoners nor local Belgian civilians could swear to having seen any American corpses around the town, other than a few who had obviously been killed in battle. On the contrary, prisoners claimed they had been well treated by Peiper's units and civilians testified that the wounded of both sides had been looked after with equal care. Peiper himself admitted that nine American prisoners of war had been shot while trying to escape from a work party, but if the circumstances were as he described them the shooting fell within the recognized 'laws and usages of war'. Just how many Americans died in La Gleize, if any, is a matter of conjecture, if not controversy, and the situation is confused by the fact that at the end of his occupation of the town Peiper released some 150 Americans to make their way back to their own lines – and by the unusual experience of one of Peiper's American prisoners, Major Hal D. McCown, CO of the 2nd Battalion of the US 119th Infantry Regiment. McCown was to state later that in the three days he spent as a prisoner of Peiper's troopers he came to respect the discipline and essential humanity of his German captors and above all of their commanding officer, Jochen Peiper. Given the circumstances, the old-fashioned comradeliness between the SS colonel and the American major was remarkable. It went so far that McCown was even summoned to spend a good part of the evening of 22 December in a cosy tête-à-tête at Peiper's command post listening to Peiper debate the Nazi world outlook and Germany's chances in the war.

At noon on 23 December a radio message came through from Mohnke stating that no relief could get through and ordering Peiper to break out as best he could. Before daybreak on the last Christmas Eve of the war, 800 men of what was left of Kampfgruppe Peiper crept out of La Gleize and began to make their way across country through deep snow to the safety of the German lines. They left behind them their useless, fuelless armour, the German and American wounded, and 150 able-bodied American prisoners who had been set free to return to their own lines. They kept only Hal McCown, whom Peiper had hoped to exchange as hostage for his own German wounded. But in a skirmish with an American outpost as Trois Ponts, McCown slipped away into the woods and made good his escape. It would be a year and a half before Peiper set eyes on him again – this time as a witness for the defence at Peiper's trial for murder.

On Christmas morning Peiper's weary soldiers at last established contact with their own side near Wanne. Peiper himself, who had not slept since the start of the offensive nine days previously, collapsed and had to be carried to the first aid station. But next day he was fit enough to set up his own command post in a château at Petit Thier not far from Wanne, and shortly afterwards was recommended for the Swords to his Knight's Cross by his Divisional Commander, Wilhelm Mohnke. Though Kampfgruppe Peiper had failed, as the entire German offensive in the Battle of the Bulge was to fail, it had been fought with immense tenacity and courage. It had also earned the bitter calumny of the Allies and was to damn Peiper himself as an arch war criminal for the rest of his days.

But even now the killing was not entirely over. No single act of violence counted more against Jochen Peiper personally than an incident that occurred on 10 or 13 January a little while after the German offensive had ground to a halt and Peiper's battle group had been broken up and dispersed to its component formations. Though the incident was short on numbers it was long on callous brutality. Peiper at this time was in his command post in the castle at Petit Thier, and on the day in question a lone soldier in a bedraggled and tattered American uniform was seen to stagger out of the neighbouring woods where he had been hiding for some time – possibly since the beginning of the German offensive several weeks before. The American was clearly in a bad way, for he had been without food or shelter for a considerable period of time in bitter winter weather. Half-starved and almost incoherent from exposure, the American stumbled towards the château, obviously hoping for succour from the Germans, since the only alternative was death alone in the winter woods. But he chose the wrong Germans. Two SS men, from Headquarters Company, a Sergeant Otto Wichmann and another, went out to help the American in, and half-guiding, half-carrying him, they brought him to Peiper's command post in a room inside the château.

They found Peiper in the company of the regimental surgeon, Major Kurt Sickel, and another officer. Peiper first inspected the American's pay book, then attempted to interrogate him. But the American was so far gone that he could only utter faint, unintelligible noises in reply. The regimental surgeon then examined the man and came to the conclusion that the poor wretch was suffering from third-degree frost-bite, especially on his hands. To Peiper the man looked like a mummy.

'Should I bring him up?' Sergeant Wichmann asked, referring to the first aid post which was upstairs on the second floor of the château.

Peiper and Sickel exchanged a meaningful glance, then the MO motioned towards the door with his thumb and said: 'Get the swine out and bump him off.'

Wichmann and the SS man who had helped him bring the American in in the first place then assisted the man out of the room and took him a short way up the road to a field. Here Wichmann lay him down in the snow and

261

with his Luger pistol shot him a number of times at point blank range in the back below the left shoulder. Later the SS men were to claim this was really meant as a mercy killing.

———

That many American prisoners had perished at the hands of Kampfgruppe Peiper over and above the multitude who had been shot down in cold blood at the Baugnez crossroads is beyond doubt. But *exactly* how many were killed in all the various incidents, and by *whom* precisely, it was not always possible to determine. Similarly there was no doubt whatsoever that Belgian civilians, including women and children, had lost their lives during Peiper's murderous advance through their towns and villages, but again the precise number and circumstances could not always be ascertained, still less the identity of the individuals responsible. With the help of the Stavelot Red Cross, American investigators produced a list of ninety-three civilians who were believed to have been killed by SS troops during the course of Peiper's lightning thrust. But it is possible that this list included civilians who had been killed accidentally during the fighting or had met their deaths in legitimate combat as members of the Belgian Resistance then active in the area. All this and more was to preoccupy the Americans throughout the rest of the war and for many months and years after the last shot had been fired. But the truth was to prove an elusive will-o'-the-wisp for all concerned.

INVESTIGATION

The Americans learned of the massacre at the Baugnez crossroads almost as soon as it had happened. On 18 December SHAEF received the following signal from the US First Army:

> SS troops . . . captured US soldier, traffic MP with about two hundred other US soldiers. American prisoners searched. When finished, Germans lined up Americans and shot them with machine-pistols and machine-guns. Wounded informant who escaped and more details follow later.

On 14 January 1945, after American troops had finally overrun the area of the massacre site, a First Army investigative team consisting of a graves registration unit, army photographers and a medic began their search of the field where the American POWs had been shot. Heavy snow had fallen shortly after the massacre and the field was still covered in a thick blanket of snow two to five feet deep, but the corpses, numbering seventy-two all told, were not difficult to locate. The bodies had remained frozen almost since death and were thus in an excellent state of preservation. Many, it was noted, were frozen with their hands above their head in the attitude of surrender in which they had been killed. After being photographed where they lay they were taken to Malmédy, where they were thawed out and medically examined.

From the post-mortem examination it was clear that most of the dead Americans had died as a result of bullet wounds in the face, chest and abdomen. Some, however, had died from a single bullet wound in the head, indicating that they were shot from very close range while still alive and unwounded. One had had the back of his head bashed in with a blunt instrument, presumably a rifle-butt. Others had been stabbed in the eyes, or had their eyes gouged out with a sharp implement, presumably a

263

bayonet, indicating that an element of sadism had accompanied the killings.

A fortnight later First Army inspectors completed their preliminary report. They had found out enough to establish a prima facie case that war crimes had been committed against US army troops and that a large number of American POWs had been murdered at the Baugnez crossroads. From captured documents and interrogation of German prisoners they had also identified Kampfgruppe Peiper as the German unit likely to have carried out the killings. But of all the soldiers who had been members of Kampfgruppe Peiper the actual name of only one individual who had been near the Baugnez crossroads at the time of the crime was known to the investigators. This was a German tank commander from the First SS Panzer Regiment who had fired a cannon shell through a farmhouse next to the massacre field and then handed the angry farmer a chit with his name and the field post number to which a claim for compensation for damages from the Nazi government could be sent.

At the end of January 1945 a SHAEF Court of Inquiry, which included Lt-Col. Bruce Macdonald, the Canadian investigator who was already investigating similar atrocities against Canadian soldiers in Normandy, began hearings on the Malmédy massacre at Harrogate, Yorkshire. The Court heard the testimony of thirty American survivors of the massacre, including a long and detailed statement from Sergeant Zack, together with information provided by German prisoners of war and Belgian civilians who had been in the area at the time of the atrocity. In March 1945 the SHAEF Court of Inquiry completed its final report. It concluded 'beyond question' that seventy-two American prisoners of war, who had done nothing to abrogate their rights as prisoners of war under the Geneva Convention, had been killed in an 'unprovoked, deliberate and brutal' way at the Baugnez crossroad, while thirty survivors of the massacre had been victims of assault with intent to commit murder.

Evidence had also been produced before the Court to suggest that American prisoners had been murdered at other points along Kampfgruppe Peiper's line of advance, which suggested that the shooting of prisoners of war was official German policy and that orders to shoot prisoners must have been issued at the start of the offensive. The SHAEF report recommended that members of Kampfgruppe Peiper already in Allied hands should be identified and interrogated about their actions during the offensive, and that efforts should be made to determine whether an order to shoot American prisoners had indeed been issued to German troops.

So long as the war went on, however, American investigators could achieve little more. The First SS Panzer Division, the *only* division to have killed prisoners on a systematic basis during the Battle of the Bulge, together with the rest of Sixth Panzer Army was transferred to the Eastern Front – minus its Commander, Wilhelm Mohnke, who had been summoned to Berlin for special duties – in a last-ditch effort to stem the Russian tide pouring through Hungary and into Austria. When the war ended the Division surrendered to the Americans and what was left of the old Kampfgruppe Peiper were corralled behind barbed wire in American POW camps.

But it was a much harder task to track down the Malmédy suspects than had been expected. Many had been killed in the last months of the war and the rest were lost among the millions of German POWs milling about in the chaotic network of POW compounds strung around Germany. Not until nearly four months after the end of the war was the American service newspaper *Stars and Stripes* able to reveal that the wanted war crimes suspect, Jochen Peiper, was in a POW camp near Munich. On 25 August Lt-Col. Martin H. Otto, Chief of the Investigation Section of the War Crimes Branch, United States Forces European Theatre, undertook his first interview with the commander of the SS formation which had carried out the Malmédy massacre.

In spite of this breakthrough, progress was painfully slow. By the end of October 1945 nearly a thousand former members of Kampfgruppe Peiper and the Leibstandarte had been rounded up and herded into a single internment barracks at Zuffenhausen near Ludwigsburg. Life was not comfortable for the internees there, as Otto Kumm, the last commander of the Leibstandarte, who had not taken part in the Ardennes offensive, recalled:

> It was entirely overcrowded. We hardly had any food. We were almost starving. We slept on wooden plank beds. Some of us were so undernourished that they could hardly get up. For months we had turnip soup for lunch and half a potato for dinner. Deliberately they collected heaps of food outside the fence, which was burnt once a month in front of our eyes.

But the inmates added little to what the investigators already knew. Many of the internees professed to know nothing of the killings, and a suspiciously large number of them pinned the blame for ordering the killings on SS-Sturmbannführer Walter Pringel, the Commander of the 1st Battalion, 1st SS Panzer Regiment, whom they knew to have been killed in the final fighting of the war. Fearing that the suspects had united in a conspiracy of collusion to obstruct the progress of the investigation, the investigation team arranged for the hard core of the suspects, the ones considered most likely to have been involved in the killings, to be transferred to a standard prison, where they could be segregated in individual cells, thereby putting

265

an end to collusion and starting the process of breaking them psychologically by means of solitary confinement. The prison chosen was a gloomy, nineteenth-century structure called Schwäbisch Hall, near Heilbronn.

Here at last the American investigators began to make progress. On 17 December 1945, a year after the Malmédy massacre, one of the inmates of Schwäbisch Hall, a former company commander of the First SS Panzer Grenadier Regiment, Heinz Reinhardt, made a significant statement to one of the interrogators, Lt William R. Perl:

> On the afternoon of the day before the attack – it was 15th December 1944 – a meeting of the company commanders was held at the CP of the armoured group. On this occasion Pringel stated that the impending battle would be the decisive battle. Amongst other things he said that we should behave toward the enemy in such a way that we create amongst them panic and terror, and that the reputation for spreading panic and terror through our behaviour should precede our troops so that the enemy should be frightened even to meet them. Amongst other things he also stated in connection with this that no prisoners should be taken ... On the same evening I repeated to my company in the Blankenheim Forest what Pringel told us.

Lieutenant Perl, who was to emerge as a controversial figure during the course of the Malmédy affair, described Reinhardt's admission as a major breakthrough. Over the next four months a flood of Peiper's men finally lowered their guard and one after the other made a series of sworn statements about atrocities committed by their Kampfgruppe during the Ardennes offensive. A former HQ Company Sergeant of the 1st SS Panzer Regiment gave a graphic description of shooting the half-starved American soldier at the château at Petit Thier (on the orders of the regimental surgeon, and with the cognizance of Peiper himself, as we have already described). A former gunner in a Panther tank, Sturmmann Georg Fleps, described his part in the actual Malmédy massacre – how he fired a shot at the American prisoners in the field at the Baugnez crossroads and how an armoured personnel carrier then opened up with its machine-gun and mowed all the prisoners down. A tank commander who had arrived at the crossroads after the massacre described how he found one of the Americans still alive and after relieving him of his watch and jacket shot him in the back of the neck, after which his tank gunner had fired a long burst into the bodies. Another SS man, a private soldier in the Third Panzer Pioneer Company, described in minute detail how he helped to machine-gun the prisoners at the Baugnez crossroads, then walked among the bodies shooting any who showed signs of life with his pistol. A comrade from the same unit described in similar detail the murder of a large group of prisoners at La Gleize.

As the piles of sworn statements from Peiper's men grew in volume and complexity it became clear to the investigators that the Malmédy massacre itself was only part of the picture, a minority of the killings that had taken place during Peiper's drive to the west. Groups of prisoners had been shot at various points along Peiper's route – and not just Americans, it seemed, but Belgian civilians, too. A tank commander stated that his gunner had fired his machine-gun at a group of Belgian women in Stavelot. A member of a penal unit attached to the 9th Panzer Pioneer Company admitted blowing out the brains of a Belgian woman as she stood in the kitchen of her house in Büllingen. The litany of gratuitous thuggery went on and on. The investigators were naturally delighted with the progress that was being made in the case. The suspects even named names, provided lists of comrades who had pulled the triggers of pistols, rifles, machine-guns, had happily, casually and unblinkingly gunned down unarmed Americans and defenceless Belgian men, women and children. The depth of detail in some of these affidavits was so remarkable that before long they began to be viewed in some quarters with a certain degree of suspicion. Even so, taken together these affidavits presented a common picture of frightfulness, and gave credence to the view that the order for Kampfgruppe Peiper to spread a wave of panic and fright had been carried out to its logical extreme.

The investigators were especially anxious to discover whether this order had specifically included the shooting of prisoners. Many of the statements provided by the inmates of Schwäbisch Hall seemed to indicate that it had. One SS private swore on oath that his company commander had said: 'There is an order not to take prisoners of war; also, civilians who show themselves on the streets or at windows will be shot without mercy.' A sergeant stated that *his* Company Commander had told his men: 'I am not giving you any orders to shoot prisoners of war, but you are well-trained SS soldiers, you know what you should do with prisoners without me telling you that.' Another Company Commander was alleged to have exhorted his men: 'Think of it, American gangsters have made our cities into a heap of rubble, millions of women and children have been killed. If you think of all that, you know what you as SS men have to do in case you capture American soldiers.'

On 11 March 1946 Peiper himself made a major statement on the question of pre-attack orders: how Mohnke had ordered him to fight 'fanatically' in the coming offensive; how Priess had ordered him to fight with brutality, as this was expressly desired by the Führer; how Dietrich's orders from the 6th Panzer Army spoke of a wave of terror and fright, and the need to break resistance by terror and to shoot prisoners of war where local conditions required it.

Under interrogation, the top three generals in the chain of command directly above Peiper – Sepp Dietrich, Fritz Kraemer and Hermann Priess – all denied that any order to shoot prisoners had been issued at Army or Corps level. Dietrich admitted he had incorporated Hitler's phrases about fighting 'hard and recklessly' and acting 'with brutality' and without 'humane inhibitions', but he was adamant that he had never suggested prisoners should be shot. Kraemer, his chief of staff, had emphasized the importance of speed and ruthlessness and the need to crush civilian resistance by terror – but he had never proposed prisoners should be shot, merely that they should not be the concern of the vanguard and should be left to the slower units following up behind. Priess, too, could recall nothing in the 6th Panzer Army orders about shooting prisoners.

The one key link in the chain of command who had nothing to say on the subject was the Division Commander, Oberführer Wilhelm Mohnke, who was not in American hands. Though it was Mohnke who gave Peiper his orders, no effort seems to have been made to find out exactly what it was Mohnke imparted to Peiper on the eve of the offensive, or whether he had made any reference to prisoners at their meeting. This was a gaping hole in American attempts to reconstruct the sequence of events and the chain of responsibility for the atrocities – the circuit breaker in the whole electrical system.

In the minds of the American interrogators, it made a neater, more logical, more comprehensible pattern of the inchoate mass of testimony if the war crimes committed by Kampfgruppe Peiper were seen as the ultimate and inevitable outcome of a general conspiracy which had its origins inside Adolf Hitler's head. This was to be the tack on which the prosecution would embark in the eventual trial. But some testimony seemed to suggest that the commander of Kampfgruppe Peiper was himself the instigator of orders to kill – or at any rate was more deeply involved in the killings than simply carrying out orders from above. According to the former commander of the Ninth Panzer Pioneer Company, at least a month before orders for the Ardennes offensive had been issued, Peiper had begun to talk about abandoning the relatively chivalrous combat ethic still employed in the fighting against the Western Allies in favour of the infinitely more barbarous code of conduct which had long been employed in the war against the Russians. 'A bad reputation,' Peiper had hinted, 'carries with it obligations.' Shortly before the offensive was due to begin, Peiper's officers read a secret regimental order which, after explaining that the mission of the Kampfgruppe was the deep penetration of the enemy's positions and that no dispersal of its forces would be possible, concluded with the statement: 'Therefore, the situation can arise when prisoners of war have to be shot.' According to the officer who volunteered this statement, all the officers who read these secret orders had

268

to sign a statement promising to keep their mouths shut. Peiper's former adjutant, Hans Gruhle, admitted the existence of such an order, while Josef Diefenthal, the CO of the 3rd Battalion of the 2nd Panzer Grenadier Regiment, admitted giving the order to shoot the prisoners at the Baugnez crossroads. It was testimony such as this which finally broke Peiper down.

By April 1946, the American investigating team, now headed by Lt-Col. Burton Ellis, had acquired sufficient evidence to warrant a prosecution against the seventy-four suspects in a military court. Some of this evidence had been obtained from American soldiers, Belgian civilians and German POWs not suspected of war crimes. But the great mass of evidence came from the sworn statements of the seventy-four suspects incarcerated in Schwäbisch Hall. This was to be the prosecution's strength – but also its weakness. Without it there could have been no trial. But because of it there could very likely be no justice either.

———

A great deal of controversy was to surround the evidence that emerged from Schwäbisch Hall, both as to its content and the way it was obtained. The German inmates of Schwäbisch Hall were to claim, and the American interrogators were naturally to deny, that most of the sworn statements used as evidence in the trial were extracted under duress so extreme as to constitute torture, and that many of the statements were the concoctions of the interrogators themselves. The truth behind the torture claims, like the truth behind the Malmédy killings, was never absolutely and finally determined. But the claims were universal and persistent, and they were backed up, moreover, by eye-witness testimony from Germans who were not war crimes suspects, and even by grudging admissions on the part of some of the interrogators, not a few of whom were Jewish refugees from Nazi Germany with a built-in antipathy to SS war criminals, both proved and suspected.

It seems, therefore, that many of the sworn statements which were to form the basis of the prosecution case were obtained as the result of pressure of one kind or another, though it is doubtful if this amounted to calculated torture as we normally understand the meaning of the word. Indeed, many of the interrogation techniques about which the SS suspects complained (infinitely less brutal than the techniques employed by the Nazis) formed part of the accepted repertoire employed in criminal investigation in America. They were cogent enough, however, to compel one of the suspects, Arvid Freimuth, to hang himself in his cell in March 1946 after having been heard to cry from his cell: 'I cannot utter another lie!'

Perhaps the commonest form of pressure used against the SS prisoners was solitary confinement. Jochen Peiper, who was one of the last to break, had been kept in solitary confinement for seven weeks at an American army interrogation centre at Oberursel, and on one occasion his cell had been heated to the almost unendurable temperature of 80°C for twenty-four hours. After his transfer to Zuffenhausen had been kept in a dark cellar for five weeks and was not allowed to wash or shave and for two days was given no food at all. Peiper wrote of these experiences later:

> The overnight change from being a member of a formation which had played the role of a family and the transition from being an honoured defender of the Fatherland to becoming a strictly isolated prisoner was so radical and the shock so deep that one's resistance was finished . . . and the atmosphere of a medieval court of the inquisition which controlled one's whole prison day added disgust and dull submission to the already present mood.

To solitary confinement, with all the strange contortions it worked on the human mind, were added what the investigators described as 'legitimate tricks, ruses and stratagems', including 'ceremonies' and 'mock trials'. Mock trials took place in a mock court consisting of a row of Americans, including a solemn, black-robed priest, seated at a table covered in a black cloth and ritually adorned with burning candles and a crucifix, very like a session of the Spanish Inquisition or a secret chapter of the Klu Klux Klan. Sometimes, as an added instrument of terror, there was a noose hanging from the ceiling as well. One young SS man, taken into a mock court with a hood over his head, fainted when the hood was removed when he saw the unnerving scene that confronted him. With one American investigator playing the prosecutor (or 'bad guy') and another playing the defence counsel (or 'good guy'), such 'trials' were intended to mislead the suspect into thinking that his last chance had come and that the more he divulged the better it would be for him.

Mock executions were sometimes an alternative to mock trials. One SS private by the name of Tomczak was told by his interrogator, 'If you don't confess, you'll be hanged at sunset.' After ten days in the 'death cell' Tomczak was told, 'Now you're finally going to be hanged.' He stated later:

> Someone pulled a black hood over my head so that I couldn't see anything. I was then taken out of my cell. By the changes in direction (I was guided by two men) I noted that I was being led hither and thither. When we finally stopped, I was told, 'You are now at the place of execution. There are several men hanging on the gallows.' Thereupon I was cross-examined

again, with the hood still over my head. All the same I couldn't confess about events in which I didn't participate or know anything about. Then Lieutenant Perl or Mr Thon (an American civilian interrogator) said, 'I'm going to count up to three. If you don't confess now, you're going up!' By 'going up' he meant hanging. A few moments later I was really hanging in the air and when I began to choke from lack of breath they let me down to ask me again whether I was ready to confess. The attempts at hanging, which were always signalled by the command, *'Hangman – up!'*, were repeated several times.

Sometimes stool pigeons were infiltrated into a suspect's cell. Sometimes prisoners were intimidated with threats of summary execution and secret liquidation if they did not tell the truth, or they were warned their families would have their ration books taken from them if they did not co-operate – a death sentence in itself in a nation now racked with hunger. They were confronted with the signed confessions of their comrades, or worse, with personal, on-the-spot denunciations by fellow SS men in whom they had once had trust.

These ploys were no doubt part and parcel of the interrogator's art. But it was over the question of physical violence that opinions grew most heated. Many of Peiper's men were later to claim that they had suffered extreme deprivation and sadistic beatings, including kicks to the genitals. Outsiders confirmed that physical assaults may have gone beyond heat-of-the-moment slaps and blows. A German dentist in the employ of the American army told how he had frequently been required to repair the dental injuries caused by the beatings inflicted on prisoners; their cries could even be heard in the town, he said. A German medical student told much the same story. If serious violence really was used against the prisoners – and it was never conclusively proved – it more probably came from the guards at Schwäbisch Hall, especially the vengeful Polish guards, rather than the investigative team. When the prisoners were moved from their cells they had to wear a hood over their heads, so that they could not communicate with other prisoners, and as they groped blindly along the prison corridors they were sometimes kicked and punched or pushed down a flight of stairs; even Sepp Dietrich was subject to this kind of gratuitous assault.

At the end of the day, the sworn statements that were to form the basis of much of the prosecution case were probably as much the product of the inner collapse of the SS men – the demoralization caused by total defeat and the destruction of everything for which they had fought and sacrificed – as the external pressure brought to bear by their interrogators. Be that as it may, however, it was the trial court and not the investigation team that would make the final judgement as to the guilt or innocence of the accused. By May 1946 the case was ready for trial.

271

TRIAL

The Malmédy Massacre trial opened at the former Nazi concentration camp at Dachau, near Munich, on 16 May 1946. Officially it was known as 'US v Valentin Bersin, et al.', Bersin being the name of the ex-SS tank commander who alphabetically headed the list of defendants. Eight serving officers of the American army sat on the bench, with Brigadier-General Josiah T. Dalbey, of the 3rd Infantry Division, presiding. A total of seventy-four officers and men of the Waffen-SS were collectively charged with 'violations of the laws and usages of war' in that they did 'wilfully, deliberately and wrongfully permit, encourage, aid, abet and participate in the killing, shooting, ill-treatment, abuse and torture of members of the Armed Forces of the United States of America, and of unarmed civilians.' Individual charges were listed separately.

The Malmédy trial was one of the outstanding war crimes trials of the post-war years, ranking second only to the trial of the major Nazi leaders at Nuremberg in the interest it aroused among the American public. For one thing, in terms of sheer numbers of accused it was a very big trial – in effect, a mass trial – which generated a huge volume of documentation. For another, it lasted a very long time – nearly two months in all, with three weeks devoted to the presentation of the prosecution case alone. It was also an extremely controversial trial, and ultimately an unsatisfactory one, for when it was all over and the dust had settled it was not at all clear whether justice had been done and the whole truth revealed.

There were two prongs to the prosecution thrust. The first had to do with the conspiratorial aspect of the case. The Malmédy massacre and all its associated atrocities, the prosecution charged, were the consequence of a criminal conspiracy on the part of all the accused. At the head of this conspiracy stood Adolf Hitler. At his conference in Bad Nauheim in December 1944 Hitler had given his senior commanders a general order to employ terror to smash enemy resistance in the coming Ardennes offen-

272

sive. Sepp Dietrich, it was alleged, had interpreted the Führer's order in a more concrete and specific way, and had given his commanders in the Sixth Panzer Army *carte blanche* to shoot prisoners of war as and when battlefield conditions warranted it. Dietrich's Order of the Day was passed down the chain of command, through corps and divisional levels to the companies and platoons that made up Kampfgruppe Peiper. The first prong of the prosecution case, therefore, was concerned with the issue of criminal orders through the chain of command. That is why three general officers – the Army Commander (Sepp Dietrich), the Army Chief-of-Staff (Fritz Kraemer), and the Corps Commander (Hermann Priess) – the only men in the courtroom who had not been members of Kampfgruppe Peiper, were having to stand trial now. Notably absent from the courtroom was the one crucial link in the chain of command – the Divisional Commander who actually passed on the orders to the Commander of Kampfgruppe Peiper, Wilhelm Mohnke.

The second prong of the prosecution attack had to do with the actual execution of the criminal orders passed down the chain of command, leading (according to the prosecution's figures) to the mass murder of between 538 and 749 American prisoners of war and over ninety Belgian civilians.

In the event it was difficult to prove that the atrocities which had been committed during the offensive actually added up to the total of 1,377 murder victims put forward by the prosecution. This was symptomatic of the difficulties of the prosecution's case. With the possible exception of the major atrocity at the Baugnez crossroads – the Malmédy massacre – the actual number of incidents and final total of killings resulting from Kampfgruppe Peiper's apocalyptic drive to the Meuse a year and a half before were approximate. In its opening address the prosecution itself was to admit that it was 'practically an impossibility to present to the Court the evidence on this mass of murders in a chronological sequence and in an understandable manner.' A subsequent revised figure of dead listed 308 American soldiers and 111 Belgian civilians, although the actual total was thought to be 300 higher. Whatever the final figure, it was obvious that an awful lot of prisoners of war and civilians had been murdered at the hands of Peiper's men, making it by far the worst military atrocity of the war in the West.

A mass of evidence was produced by the prosecution. Some of it consisted of testimony by German, Belgian and American witnesses, much of it vague as to the nature of the incidents or the identity of the individuals who had carried them out. Most of the prosecution evidence consisted of nearly a hundred sworn statements obtained from SS prisoners by the investigative team during the winter preceding the trial. These sworn statements formed the central core of the prosecution case and the prin-

273

cipal target of the defence attack. The question was: were these statements the confessions of guilt-ridden war criminals or the fabrications of their frustrated and unscrupulous interrogators? The defence claimed that they had been forced from the defendants under the pressure of physical and psychological duress. The prosecution rebutted this, only admitting that the investigators had employed the 'legitimate tricks, ruses and stratagems known to investigators' – chief of which was the stratagem known as the 'mock trial'. In the end, the Court refused to allow that the statements had been obtained by illegal means and did not take the matter into consideration when they came to passing final judgement. Nevertheless, the seed of doubt, planted in the mind of some Americans, especially that of the leading defence counsel, Colonel William Everett, was to sprout and take root, with unexpected consequences in the aftermath of the trial.

The defence called only a handful of witnesses – all but one of them ex-SS men, including Peiper himself, the exception being an American officer, Lt-Col. Hal D. McCown, who had recently been promoted. The purpose of these witnesses in the scheme of the defence case was to testify to the legality of the Germans' attitude to the treatment of prisoners of war. Fritz Kraemer, Sepp Dietrich's former chief of staff, denied that the Sixth Panzer Army's orders required the elimination of prisoners of war or civilians. On the contrary, he said, they went into considerable detail about the correct handling of prisoners. Far from murdering prisoners, Kraemer declared, the Sixth Panzer Army had taken 5,000 to 7,000 prisoners during the Ardennes offensive. His testimony was corroborated by Dietrich Ziemssen, who had been operations officer on Wilhelm Mohnke's staff with the 1st SS Panzer Division. Ziemssen was not on trial and offered his testimony voluntarily, even though the prosecution had threatened to charge him with war crimes offences if he testified for the defence. Ziemssen had personally set up two prisoner collection points and observed some 800 POWs making their way to them. The division had received no orders to carry out illegal acts, he said, nor issued any. Then it was Peiper's turn.

Before the former SS colonel took the witness stand, however, he was given a highly favourable character reference by the defence's star witness, Colonel Hal McCown. McCown had been Peiper's prisoner for four days during the Ardennes offensive and in the report he wrote after he had escaped from German captivity he described his captor in glowing terms. 'I have met few men,' recorded McCown, 'who have impressed me in as short a space of time as did this German officer.' The treatment he received from the Germans under Peiper's command was correct and fair, as was that meted out to other American POWs with whom he had come in contact. He had personally seen none of the scores or hundreds of American soldiers who were alleged to have been murdered in La Gleize. On the contrary, Kampfgruppe Peiper had treated a group of 150 American prisoners well in La Gleize and set them free when the formation was ordered to withdraw.

On the witness-stand, where he testified on his own behalf, Jochen Peiper cut an impressive figure. The defeat of the Fatherland, the annihilation of the Nazism, the long months of imprisonment, the rigours of interrogation, the loss of decorations and insignia, of everything he had lived and fought for – none of this had crushed the man's proud, even arrogant persona. In the Military Court, as in the war, he adhered to the principle that the best form of defence is attack. The sworn statements that had been used against him by the prosecution were lies, he declared. They had been forced from him by brutal and unscrupulous interrogators, notably the controversial Lieutenant Perl, using every kind of cruel and calculated psychological coercion. He had had to endure five weeks of solitary confinement in a darkened cell before being brought out for questioning. He had been told that the sons of an American senator and a great tycoon were among the prisoners who had been killed in the Malmédy massacre and that the outcry in America was so overwhelming that not even the President would be able to save him. He had been warned that the only thing he could do with what little remained of his life was to save his comrades by taking the guilt for the atrocities on to his own shoulders. All his superior officers – Dietrich, Kraemer, Priess (but not, of course, Mohnke) – had confessed to everything, Perl had informed him. He had even been confronted by former members of Kampfgruppe Peiper, who at Perl's prompting had boldly announced that it was he, Peiper, who had given the orders to shoot prisoners at the Baugnez crossroads, and at Stoumont and La Gleize. Demoralized by his comrades, despairing at the hopelessness of it all, the only thing he felt he could do was sign the statements Perl had prepared for him. And this, finally, he had done; and they were false, and he rejected them here and now.

Peiper claimed he had never issued any orders to shoot prisoners of war. When Mohnke had ordered him to fight fanatically, he had taken this to mean total commitment to the task in hand, stopping for nothing. The tactical orders he had received from the division had directed that prisoners should be disarmed and left where they were or sent to the rear and picked up by the Panzer Grenadier unit that was following up behind his own. He knew nothing of the shooting of prisoners at Stoumont and La Gleize, and the first he had heard of the Malmédy massacre was outside Trois Ponts on the following day.

But Peiper was not entirely successful in his efforts to establish his innocence. Though he denied having given any orders to shoot prisoners of war, he admitted having told Perl that there was no need to issue such orders, as it was obvious to experienced officers that prisoners had to be shot 'when local conditions of combat should require it'. Nor was Peiper able to give the Court any persuasive reason why the frost-bitten prisoner brought to his command post at Petit Thier should have been shot rather than taken to a medical aid post for treatment; nor why, after having told American investigators that between 200 and 250 American prisoners had been held at La Gleize, only 150 were still there to be released when Peiper pulled out. Under cross-examination, Peiper's grim realism about the nature of modern warfare, the fruit of six years of savage combat at the front, struck a chill note. When he again denied that his men had been ordered to shoot prisoners, the chief prosecutor, Colonel Burton Ellis, asked him sarcastically: 'Were all your men so undisciplined that they killed prisoners *without* orders?' To which Peiper replied: 'During combat sometimes there are situations about which one cannot talk on the green table.' When Peiper claimed that Belgian civilians had been shot because they had opened fire on his men, Ellis caustically demanded: 'Did you see any eighty-year-old women firing at you from the windows there in Büllingen? Did you see any one-year-old babies firing at you?' And Peiper had riposted: 'No, not even in Russia did I see any one-year-old babies firing.'

At the end of his long spell in the witness-stand, Jochen Peiper asked permission to make a final statement. What he had to say quite electrified the Court:

> Early in May, here, I had a personal conversation with Lt-Col. Ellis. This conversation occurred on a personal, human plane . . . I asked Colonel Ellis whether he, personally, believed all the things I am accused of here. I had told him that . . . all my testimony resulted only from my attitude, that I wanted to save my men. Upon that, Colonel Ellis said, 'I admire you, and I hardly know another soldier whom I estimate as highly as I do you, but you are sacrificing yourself on an ideal which no longer exists. The men whom you today think you have to cover up for are bums and criminals. I'll prove that to you in the course of the trial. We are now parting as friends, and when we see each other again before the Court we will be as enemies, and I'll have to paint you in the worst bloody colours, but you understand that I will only be doing my duty.'

So now we had two American colonels professing their personal affection and respect for their redoubtable SS counterpart, one on the defence side and one – the prosecutor himself no less – on the prosecution side. What the officers on the bench of the Court made of this odd state of affairs is not recorded. The prosecutor himself, clearly embarrassed by this startling revelation, did not try to deny it but asked for Peiper's statement to be struck from the records, a request which was refused. But it is doubtful if it weighed inordinately heavily in the Court's ultimate judgement, for at no point was it suggested that Colonel Ellis actually believed Peiper to be innocent of the charges against him.

Peiper's testimony was the high point of the defence case, but it was not the end of it. A procession of other witnesses took the stand, many of them defendants themselves. To defend seventy-four accused in one job lot was a complex task and grew even more complex when it was found that testimony offered in defence of one accused might well turn out to be useful as evidence against another. But some defence evidence was unequivocal. It had been alleged that between 175 and 311 POWs had been killed in La Gleize, for example, but the defence was able to produce the village priest and three other members of this small community, who all testified that, like Hal McCown, they had seen no trace of any American corpses, other than one charred body hanging half out of a Sherman tank. And so the evidence piled up and the trial documents multiplied and the confusion mounted until finally, on 9 July 1946, the submission of evidence in what was popularly known as the Malmédy Massacre trial was concluded.

There remained the closing addresses. The prosecutor, for his part, castigated the seventy-four accused as 'perpetrators of unrestrained Genghis Khan warfare' who would now have to pay the price of their misdeeds to the American people. The evidence of sworn statements, voluntarily uttered during the course of perfectly legitimate interrogation, were a sufficient proof of the guilt of the accused. Nor could the trigger men, the troopers who carried out the killings, escape the consequence of their crimes by claiming that they were only carrying out superior orders, for these orders were clearly illegal and should not have been obeyed. The law of the Allied occupation authorities regarding war crimes trials – Law No 10 of the Allied Control Council dated 20 December 1945 – stated unequivocally that superior orders did not exonerate a subordinate from responsibility for his deeds. Nor was the plea of military necessity a valid extenuation of the crimes committed by Kampfgruppe Peiper, for Peiper's men – all 'hardened and dangerous criminals' – had murdered often, spontaneously and 'with enthusiasm'. The prosecutor concluded with an impassioned appeal to the patriotic and humanitarian sentiments of the Court, and an admonition to the German people in the brave new post-war world:

> Today in America the survivors of these massacres, the mothers, fathers, sweethearts, wives and children of these comrades of ours who so needlessly fell, not on the field of battle, but from the tender mercies of the SS, are awaiting your

findings. These comrades would have been alive today if it had not been for the 1st SS Panzer Division, and they must not have died in vain. From their deaths let there come a clear understanding to our former enemies that they cannot wage warfare in a merciless and ruthless manner. They must learn that the end does not justify the means! It must be brought home to the German people that the principle of extermination which guided them in their last battle will not create for them a new and better world but will only bring disaster to their homeland and to themselves. Let their punishment be adequate for their crimes.

In reply, the defence did not attempt to deny that American prisoners of war had met their deaths at the hands of Kampfgruppe Peiper, but sought to justify them on the grounds of military necessity, as the prosecution had rightly predicted. Some of the killings, the defence maintained, were the product of 'injudicious conduct in the heat of battle' rather than a conspiracy to murder. In the total confusion which surrounded many of these incidents, it was not even certain that the Americans had even given themselves up as prisoners at the time of their deaths. The Malmédy massacre itself was the result of just such a 'mix-up'. Citing international law, the defence contended that a prisoner's right to be spared was not absolute. 'Victory would be hindered by stopping to give quarter, not to mention that during fighting it is often impracticable so to secure prisoners as to prevent their return to combat.' But this line of argument, quite apart from contravening Article 23(c) of the Hague Convention, was largely invalidated by the fact that it was not one which the defendants themselves had put forward, for the simple reason that to have done so would have admitted responsibility for the killings.

But in the end the defence tacitly *did* admit the guilt of the defendants, and sought to condone it as 'primitive impulses of vengeance and retaliation . . . called forth in the heat of battle or as the culmination of a war-weary last struggle against an overwhelming enemy . . . the inevitable by-product of man's resort to force and arms, whether he be enemy or ally.' Appealing to the Court for a fair and dispassionate judgement, Colonel Willis Everett ended the final address of the defence with a quotation from Tom Paine, the revolutionary 18th-century English political writer: 'He that would make his own liberty secure must guard even his enemy from oppression, for if he violates this duty, he establishes a precedent which will reach himself.'

The trial had taken a little less than two months to complete. The judgement was to take a little less than two hours. At around 4.30 p.m. on the afternoon of 11 July the President of the Court, Brigadier General Josiah T. Dalbey, addressing the seventy-three defendants – one had been released into French custody during the trial – pronounced the Court's findings: 'The Court in closed session, at least two-thirds of the members present at the time the vote was taken concurring in each finding of guilty, finds you of the particulars and the charge guilty.'

It had taken less than two minutes per person to reach this verdict. It was to take a good deal longer to decide the sentence. In the meantime forty of the defendants took the opportunity to make a plea of mitigation. Nearly two-thirds of those who did so were enlisted men and nearly a third of these denied having committed any war crime. One indeed claimed not to have fired a shot at anyone or anything throughout the entire offensive. The rest blamed the irresistible imperative of superior orders, or the stress and frenzy of battle conditions. Their average age was less than twenty-two. Their youth, however, belied their experience of war. One young NCO, for example, had fought for no less than 680 days at the front, had his tank knocked out eleven times and been wounded three times. The youthfulness of these battle-hardened SS warriors was a tragedy, no doubt, but not a mitigation. For the Americans who had been killed, abused and tortured during Kampfgruppe Peiper's lethal thrust through the Ardennes were no less youthful too. The Court did not forget this painful fact when they came to impose their sentences on the seventy-three guilty men.

On 16 July 1946 the Court reconvened to hand down the punishments. Grimly, Brigadier General Dalbey began with the SS man who alphabetically headed the list of defendants. 'Valentin Bersin,' he intoned, 'the Court in closed session, at least two-thirds of the members at the time the vote was taken concurring, sentences you to death by hanging at such time and place as higher authority directs.' For forty-five minutes the sentencing continued. By the end of it forty-three of the Malmédy convicts, Jochen Peiper included, had been sentenced to death; twenty-two had been sentenced to life imprisonment, among them Sepp Dietrich; the rest got terms of twenty, fifteen or ten years, including Priess, who got twenty years, and Kraemer, who got ten. The next day the prisoners were locked up in Landsberg fort, which was now an American army prison. In the early days of his career Adolf Hitler had been imprisoned in a cell here and composed his blueprint for the Third Reich, *Mein Kampf.* Now it was the place where the Americans hanged their war criminals.

———

But they did not hang. Colonel Everett, who had headed the defence team

279

during the trial, now looked back on the proceedings with grave misgivings. Increasingly, Everett felt that what had taken place amounted to a miscarriage of justice. His reasons for this were many and various; part personal, part professional. Though one part of his mind knew that Kampfgruppe Peiper had carried out atrocities, another part told him that there were especially extenuating circumstances. He believed, for example, that it had been impossible for the SS defendants to receive a fair hearing in a court in which so many of the principals were Jews. He also genuinely believed that confessions had been extorted from the defendants by illegal means and that the Court had deliberately chosen to overlook the fact. In short, he believed that the proceedings had been weighted against the defendants right from the outset. But what most troubled Everett was his gnawing fear that the American army had convicted former members of the German army for the kind of crimes he was sure the American army had also committed. Alarmingly, this fear was confirmed by none less than the President of the Court, Brigadier General Josiah Dalbey, shortly after the trial. Over a drink in the officers' club in Dachau, Dalbey confided to Everett that he had found the task of sentencing the defendants in the Malmédy case the most difficult of his life, because he knew that American troops had been guilty of the same offences.

With thoughts like these churning round in his troubled mind, it is not surprising that Everett became obsessed with the Malmédy case, and came to devote an inordinate proportion of his energy and personal resources to mounting a private campaign to modify the outcome of the trial. Everett was not without allies. When the case went for review at the War Crimes Branch of the Judge Advocate General's Department, an examination of fifteen of the seventy-three convictions concluded that three of them, which had resulted in one death sentence and two life imprisonments, had been based on insufficient evidence. Though this conclusion was rejected, hints of a growing unease about the conduct of the Malmédy investigation and trial began to surface in the American press. Early in 1947, for example, Ed Hartrich of the *New York Herald Tribune* filed a story to the effect that American interrogators had beaten up suspects in order to force confessions from them. Colonel Everett, meanwhile, threatened to take his appeal to the American Supreme Court and warned the War Crimes Branch in Washington that he intended to force a retrial.

At length, after the condemned men had languished in Landsberg Prison's version of 'Death Row' for more than a year, a fresh review of the Malmédy trial was submitted to the Theatre Judge Advocate in Germany by the office of the Deputy Judge Advocate General for War Crimes. This marked the beginning of a considerable shift away from the original trial sentences, though not the original verdicts. In this new review only twenty-five of the forty-three death sentences were confirmed, the remainder being commuted to varying longer terms of imprisonment. Of the twenty-two life sentences, only five were confirmed, the rest being reduced to ten to fifteen years' imprisonment, while shorter sentences were made shorter still. No question of a possible mis-trial was raised in this review. The commutations were based almost entirely on the youthfulness of the convicts in question at the time of the crime, or in a few cases on evidence of signs of contrition on the part of the men in question.

Not until February 1948 did the American army legal authorities in Germany square up to an investigation of the conduct of the trial proceedings in a report prepared at the next level up by the Theatre Judge Advocate's office. This report was drastically different from those that had preceded it and deeply critical of aspects of the Malmédy trial. In the first place, the report found substantial evidence that investigations had been improperly conducted before the trial, and that some so-called confessions were in fact fictional concoctions cobbled together by the investigators themselves. In the second place, the trial itself had been unfairly conducted in that a number of rulings from the bench had had the effect of constricting the defence's examination of witnesses, while allowing much greater latitude to the prosecution.

The War Crimes Board of Review came to the conclusion that there was insufficient evidence to convict twenty-nine of the seventy-three SS men who had been sentenced in the Malmédy trial – virtually two-fifths of all the cases. Sensationally, one of those who fell into this fortunate category was Sepp Dietrich, the Commander of the Sixth Panzer Army in the Battle of the Bulge, who had been sentenced to life imprisonment. In the trial the prosecution had alleged that Dietrich had been the man who had relayed Hitler's murderous orders to the army. But the review found no evidence that Dietrich had issued orders for prisoners or civilians to be shot, nor had he confessed to issuing such orders. The Board accordingly recommended disapproval of Sepp Dietrich's conviction, along with that of his former chief of staff, Fritz Kraemer. Thus the two senior officers at the top of the chain of command were exonerated from complicity in the atrocities committed by Kampfgruppe Peiper. Also exonerated was the third senior commander down the line, the corps commander, Hermann Priess. At the trial Priess had denied receiving any orders to kill prisoners and no evidence was produced to prove he had issued such orders himself. On the other hand, the Board upheld the conviction and death sentence passed on Jochen Peiper, who was held to be clearly guilty of passing on the lethal army order which resulted in the deaths of so many American prisoners and Belgian civilians. But where had such an order come from if it had not come from Dietrich, Kraemer or Priess? No mention was made in the War Crimes Board review of the missing link in the chain of command, the Divisional Commander, Wilhelm Mohnke, who was the officer who had briefed Peiper and given him his orders before the start of the offensive. The Board was content to note that even if there was no evidence of such an order having been given, Peiper demonstrated sufficient indifference to the fate of prisoners of war – the case of the half-starved American at Petit Thier was cited as an instance – to justify the verdict passed on him; and in any case, there was never any doubt that Peiper's unit had carried out major war crimes.

As a result of its findings, the War Crimes Board proposed swingeing cuts in the sentences. Nearly 75 per cent of the death sentences were disallowed, over 60 per cent of the life sentences reduced. Almost 40 per cent of the convictions were thrown out on the grounds of insufficient evidence. In addition, the Board declared that the conduct of the investigators before the trial had been either inept or unprincipled and that during the trial itself the Court had consistently favoured the prosecution. However, it was one thing for the Board to make its recommendations, it was another for the Theatre Advocate General or the Military Governor of the American Zone, General Clay, to accept them. In the end they only accepted some of them. Sepp Dietrich's life sentence was reconfirmed, as was Fritz Kraemer's ten-year term. Thirteen former convicts left Landsberg prison as free men. Twelve still faced the gallows.

Nearly two years had now passed since the start of the Malmédy trial in Dachau but still Everett had not finished with his private crusade to achieve out of court what he had failed to achieve in court. He petitioned the Supreme Court to file for a writ of habeas corpus which would lead to a retrial. He lobbied the Secretary of the Army, Kenneth C. Royall. The Supreme Court rejected Everett's petition but in July 1948 Royall set up a commission to review not just the Malmédy case but the sixty-six other trials at Dachau in which death sentences had been imposed. At the same time a Justice Review Board set up by Clay in Germany was asked to look into Everett's allegations about the Malmédy case. By February 1949 both investigative bodies had submitted their reports. Royall's commission recommended that all the death sentences should be commuted to life imprisonment. The Justice Review Board simply sat on the fence, content to note the many complaints about brutality by American investigators against their SS suspects during the pre-trial period. Many of these complaints came from German citizens who were neither SS men nor war crimes suspects, and had been collected by a confirmed anti-Nazi, the Archbishop of Cologne.

And so the Malmédy case dragged on, clouded in confusion and uncertainty, a running sore in the cause of American justice. The press, which had once brayed for Nazi blood, now thundered forth on the iniquities of military justice. In the States the affair ceased to be a purely judicial one, but became a burning political topic as well. In Germany

General Clay, though convinced the Malmédy convicts were guilty and that the twelve sentenced to death deserved to die, reduced the number due to hang to six. Meanwhile, a special investigative committee of the American Senate began to look into the affair, aided by a little-known, but opportunistic, unscrupulous, publicity-seeking Senator by the name of Joe McCarthy who was to use the Malmédy case as a useful *cause célèbre* with which to launch a notorious political career. From this point, the long, involved, tortuous re-examination of the Malmédy affair lies, perhaps, beyond the scope of this book. That there were grounds for reservations about the conduct of the investigation and the trial was established beyond reasonable doubt. But the exact truth as to what happened at Schwäbisch Hall – indeed, the exact truth as to what happened near Malmédy and elsewhere during the murderous advance of Kampfgruppe Peiper – never emerged, and doubtless never will.

And so, amid bitter squabbles and recriminations, the matter dragged on. The years passed, military government came to an end, West Germany became an autonomous state, and still the condemned men in Landsberg waited for news of their fate. Finally, in January 1951 the American military authorities bowed to the strongly flowing tide of public criticism. The death sentences on the six remaining condemned men were commuted to life imprisonment. From his cell Jochen Peiper wrote to Colonel Everett: 'Next to God it is to you from whom our blessings flow . . . In all the long and dark years you have been the beacon flame for the forlorn souls of the Malmédy boys, the voice and the conscience of the good America.' Three years later, Peiper's life sentence was reduced to thirty-five years, and just before Christmas 1956, twelve years after he had led his battle group on its catastrophic push to the Meuse, he set foot outside Landsberg prison, a free man at last.

INDICTMENT

Throughout the Malmédy trial one person had been notably absent – Wilhelm Mohnke. Notably is perhaps the wrong word, for Mohnke's name occurred relatively seldom in the course of the proceedings, and for the most part he was kept in low profile, almost as if he were a person who did not exist – as, to all intents and purposes, inside Lubyanka Prison, Moscow, he did not.

And yet Mohnke was a crucial figure in the trial, for without him half the prosecution case would have fallen to the ground. For as we have seen, that case rested on two planks. The first was the culpability of the majority of the accused in the actual killings. The second was the culpability of the senior officers in issuing and handing down illegal orders which permitted such killings to take place. The chain of command, the prosecution argued, began with the Commander of the Sixth Panzer Army, Sepp Dietrich, and proceeded via his Chief of Staff, Kraemer, to the Corps Commander, Priess, then to the Commander of the 1st SS Panzer Division (Leibstandarte), Wilhelm Mohnke, and thence to the Battle Group Commander, Jochen Peiper, and so on down to Battalion, Company and Platoon Commanders.

Clearly Mohnke was a key link in that chain, for without him there could have been no transference of higher orders to the man whose troops carried out the atrocities in the Ardennes, Jochen Peiper. Mohnke had attended Hitler's final briefing at Bad Nauheim and he knew exactly what the Führer had said and what he expected. He had also attended Sepp Dietrich's commanders' conference at Sixth Panzer Army Headquarters, where words like 'ruthlessness', 'brutality', 'a wave of terror and fright', were freely bandied about. It was at this conference that Dietrich, in response to a question about the disposition of prisoners, replied: 'Prisoners? You know what to do with them.' Mohnke was already a war criminal of long standing at this point. He had been responsible for the massacre of British prisoners

284

at Wormhoudt in 1940 and the massacre of Canadian prisoners in Normandy in 1944. He was a founder member of Hitler's own personal honour guard, the Leibstandarte, an élite SS formation with a savage record of brutality on the Russian Front. A fanatical Nazi, an utterly loyal servant of his Führer's will, Mohnke would have had no doubt as to Hitler's intentions at Bad Nauheim. All this he dutifully passed on to Peiper and his other commanders at his own briefing at 1st SS Panzer Division HQ on the eve of the Ardennes offensive – with the deadly consequences we have already described.

Mohnke therefore was an integral part of the chain of command which was tried and found guilty at Dachau and a punitive sentence would have been inescapable. What that sentence might have been we can only speculate. Of those in the chain of command above him, Sepp Dietrich received life imprisonment, Kraemer ten years, and Priess twenty years; while in the chain immediately below him Jochen Peiper, the commander who was personally briefed by Mohnke, was sentenced to death. On the basis of the trial as it was conducted in 1946 we would therefore estimate that Mohnke would have received life or twenty years and that he would have been released from prison at about the same time as he was eventually released from Soviet captivity. But if Mohnke had been present at the trial, if he had been subject to the same interrogation pressures that broke Dietrich and Peiper, would the prosecution have been able to build up a more substantial case against Mohnke, and would the court have found grounds for judging Mohnke guilty of greater culpability in the crimes, justifying a severer sentence – perhaps even death?

In an effort to produce an answer to this question – inevitably a speculative one – we can only draw attention to the obvious. In the first place, it is striking that of the two SS divisions which made up Priess's 1st SS Panzer Corps – or, for that matter, the four SS Panzer Divisions which formed part of the Sixth Panzer Army – only one carried out proven war crimes during the Battle of the Bulge. That division was, of course, Wilhelm Mohnke's 1st SS Panzer Division, which was responsible for the murder of hundreds of American prisoners and Belgian civilians in a period of little more than a week. The other division was guiltless of any known cases of conduct contrary to the laws and usages of war, even though it would have received exactly the same orders down the chain of command, apart from the orders handed out by Mohnke to the Leibstandarte. This fact is all the more remarkable when we consider that the other SS division in the 1st SS Panzer Corps was none other than the 12th SS Panzer Division (Hitler Jugend), which had enjoyed such a murderous reputation in Normandy when Mohnke was one of its regimental commanders only six months previously.

On the basis of the established and accepted principle that the commander is responsible for the conduct of his troops and the crimes committed by them, it is clear that in this respect Mohnke is infinitely more culpable for the crimes committed in the Ardennes than on account of the chain of command principle alone. But were there perhaps extenuating circumstances? After all, all the known murders and atrocities had been carried out by Kampfgruppe Peiper. Was it therefore not the case that Peiper and Peiper alone had taken it upon himself to wage war in this brutal and criminal way, either as a result of issuing illegal orders or failing to control the conduct of the troops under his command? Peiper had indeed been found guilty and sentenced to death for the war crimes committed by his battle group. But Peiper was a disciplined, efficient, responsible officer of the Waffen-SS. It is inconceivable that such an officer would have taken any actions, or permitted any of the officers and men under him to take any actions, which were in any way contrary to the orders that had been handed down to him. And who was it who handed those orders down to him?

The answer, as we know, is Wilhelm Mohnke. Moreover, Mohnke gave Peiper his orders in slightly unusual circumstances. Due to traffic jams on the roads, it will be recalled, Peiper arrived late at Mohnke's divisional conference and had to be briefed separately and in private. According to Peiper, it was Mohnke's Chief of Staff, Ziemssen, who gave him his written operational orders. So what was it that Mohnke imparted to Peiper orally during their short meeting at Mohnke's HQ? Sadly, we will never know for sure. Peiper made little reference to it in his trial testimony and the American investigators never pressed the point, perhaps because, with Mohnke in Moscow and not extraditable, there was little point. But given Hitler's oratory, Dietrich's Order of the Day, the desperate circumstances, and above all Mohnke's appalling past record in the matter of prisoners of war, it is unlikely that Mohnke exhorted Peiper to fight like a knight of old or spare much consideration for any enemy who fell alive into his hands.

This is brought powerfully home in the instance of the killings at Wanne, where members of the 1st and 7th SS Panzer Companies were accused of having taken Belgian civilians from their homes and shot them to death. As a result of these killings, the American Military Court at Dachau sentenced Valentin Bersin to death by hanging and Hans Trettin to life imprisonment. However, the Court had been told that the original order to shoot all the male civilian inhabitants of Wanne (over the age of sixteen) had come from the 1st SS Panzer Division headquarters. This division, as we know, was commanded by Wilhelm Mohnke, and therefore responsibility for the mass murder order must inevitably have rested with him and him alone – as the American Military Court would undoubtedly have insisted had Mohnke been among the accused at the trial. That being the case, it is difficult to envisage how Wilhelm Mohnke could have escaped the death sentence on that count alone.

286

There is one other factor to be taken into account in judging Mohnke's behaviour and the influence his state of mind might have had on his judgement and the orders he personally handed down to his subordinates. We have seen that both at Wormhoudt and in Normandy Mohnke was characteristically in a bad temper when he came to give orders regarding the disposition of prisoners of war. On this subject one of Mohnke's Regimental Commanders was later to write:

> I felt awfully sorry for my men, but I was to give them the most cruel orders. I couldn't possibly explain to them why I was to do so. The truth is that Oberführer Mohnke, my direct commander, seemed to be out of his mind at the time. Mohnke had been terribly wounded in Yugoslavia. Since that time he had become morphinomaniac, and during those troublesome days in the Ardennes he couldn't possibly get what he needed. So that great officer, but poor man in those days, wasn't very reliable at all. Imagine – Oberführer Mohnke threatening me with court martial and death if I didn't obey and pass on his orders!

PART VII

—

Berlin Citadel Command

APRIL–MAY 1945

The Ardennes offensive, Hitler's last gamble in the West, had failed. In February 1945 the huge Anglo-American army continued its great advance to the Rhine, the last real obstacle to the heartland of Nazi Germany. In March, with the river crossed, the Allied forces stood poised for a break out eastward across the Reich towards the Elbe and (so it was thought) Berlin.

The end of the war was now barely six weeks away. The Western Front was wide open. Henceforth the conquest of Germany became a mopping-up operation, accelerating to a headlong pursuit as Hitler's army in the west melted away under the sheer weight of the men and material under Eisenhower's command. Between Eisenhower and Berlin there was nothing that now need impede the drive to the capital – no natural barriers, field armies, or prepared defences, no lack of transport or supplies.

But it was not to be. At the end of March, Eisenhower announced a radical change of plans. The main Anglo-American effort was no longer to be a drive to Berlin but a broad thrust through the centre of Germany. Since the Russians, advancing in overwhelming strength across the Oder from the east, were now only thirty-five miles from the German capital, while the American spearheads still had 285 miles to go, Berlin was to be abandoned to the Red Army, now rolling towards the city like a storm.

By 20 April, Hitler's birthday, Russian spearheads were only fifteen miles from the city. By 21 April they were able to shell the city centre for the first time. Berlin was then the third largest city in the world and the biggest ever to be stormed by force of arms. 2,500,000 men and 6,250 tanks stood poised to encircle Berlin and fight their way through the streets to the most important objective in the capital – Target 106, the Reich Chancellery, where Adolf Hitler, decrepit in body and shattered in spirit, clung to the last vestiges of Nazi power and illusion in a concrete bunker deep beneath the Reich Chancellery garden.

The Führer had declared Berlin a fortress – the last of a whole string of fortresses. But the fortifications were derisory, and there were few troops, little artillery, and no planes. When General Weidling was put in command of the defence of Berlin, his first reaction was to declare: 'It would be much better to have me shot.' Hitler's plans for the defence of the capital struck Weidling as fantasy. By 22 April Hitler himself was forced to come to much the same brutal conclusion. When he learned that the German forces had failed to break the Russian ring round the north of the city, he finally broke down in an outburst the like of which none in Hitler's Bunker had ever seen before. 'The war is lost!' the Führer screamed. The Third Reich was finished; but he would defend the city to the end. And he told the generals of his staff: 'Either I win the battle for the Reich's capital or I shall fall as a symbol of the Reich.'

It was at this point, in despair and half-unhinged, that the Führer sent for the one trusted general on whom he felt he could rely in this dire and extreme predicament – Wilhelm Mohnke.

By now Mohnke had been promoted to the rank of SS-Brigadeführer and Major-General of the Waffen-SS, which made him, at thirty-four, the youngest general still serving in the Waffen-SS. He had also been transferred from the 1st SS Panzer Division Leibstandarte, which he had commanded in the Ardennes, to the Führer Reserve in the SS Führer Headquarters, where he took command of the Leibstandarte's Guard Regiment – a 1,200-strong detachment of combat veterans from the parent formation, the Leibstandarte Division – and awaited further orders. This meant that when the Leibstandarte Division marched off to fight its last campaign against the Russian hordes in Hungary, it did so without him. It also meant that Mohnke was now perfectly poised to carry out his last apocalyptic assignment as a faithful servant of his revered Commander-in-Chief, Adolf Hitler. So it was that on the fateful afternoon of 22 April 1945 General Mohnke was formally appointed commander of the central *Zitadelle* (or 'Citadel') area of Berlin.

The Citadel was the innermost keep of the Berlin defence system. In effect it was an island formed by the River Spree and the Landwehr Canal, with an eastern bastion around the Alexanderplatz, commanded by Lt-Col. Seifert, and a western bastion around the Knie, commanded by General Krukenberg. The Citadel encompassed the main government buildings in the centre of the capital, including, most importantly, the Reich Chancellery and the Bunker complex beneath it. In effect Mohnke had been given the task of guarding the Führer's person in the final defence of the Third Reich, an honour indeed. Only a Nazi and SS general and Leibstandarte veteran of proven and undoubted loyalty to his Führer and the cause could have been eligible for such a post. As General Chuikov, the Russian Commander who ran up against Mohnke's troops in the closing phase of the battle, was to comment later: 'The approaches to the Chancellery were defended by battalions from the special SS Leibstandarte Adolf Hitler. This formation was commanded by a faithful servant of the Führer, the hard-bitten Nazi, Mohnke.' Thus one of the founding members of Hitler's personal honour guard, the Leibstandarte, was to become Hitler's last general, for Mohnke reported only to Hitler and was the last commander in control of troops over whom the Führer maintained direct authority until the bitter end. To preserve the security of this last madhouse rump of the Third Reich, Mohnke at once threw a cordon around the entire perimeter, and no one was allowed through it in either direction without a special permit.

Mohnke's Kampfgruppe consisted of a variety of elements. The nucleus was his own Leibstandarte Regiment, and was made up of the Guard Battalion of the LAH at Lichterfelde, the Training and Replacement Battalion of the LAH brought in from Spreenhagen, and the FBK (Führer-Begleit-Kompanie), Hitler's personal SS honour guard, a small, select group of LAH soldiers. This nucleus of Leibstandarte troopers was reinforced by half of Himmler's own bodyguard battalion, and the 2,000-strong Freikorps Adolf Hitler, composed of volunteers from all over Germany who chose to rally to the final defence of their Führer. All these motley troops were organized by Mohnke into a Leibstandarte Brigade of nine battalions, and as the battle progressed the secretaries and other female staff of the government departments were encouraged to join his Kampfgruppe as female combatants known as Mohnke Girls.

Most of these troops were disposed along the southern perimeter of the Citadel area, forming a classic 'hedgehog' defensive position around the Potsdamerplatz, where they were supported by light tanks, mobile guns and anti-aircraft batteries. As Russian pressure increased, Mohnke deployed his howitzers to cover other key areas like the Unter den Linden and Belle Alliance Platz, but they were rationed to only twelve rounds per gun, and the gunners were under orders to fight as infantry once the twelve rounds were used up.

But Mohnke's role was not confined to the tactical direction of the troops at the barricades. As Hitler's last general he was also required to exercise a more personal, advisory function in his dealings with his Führer, with whom, in those last dire days, he came increasingly in contact. 'General Mohnke,' Hitler remarked when he advised Mohnke of his new appointment, 'you are a professional soldier, and you already wear the highest award a German soldier can win on the field of battle. My life is now in your hands. We have known each other since 1933. As soldier to soldier, I have one last request to make as I now give you command of the *Zitadelle*. Frankly, I had hoped to remain alive and in Berlin until 5 May. However, under no circumstances can I risk being captured alive. Whenever you feel that the military situation is such that you can no longer hold for more than

293

twenty-four hours, you must report this to me, in person. I shall take the consequences. This is a personal request. It is also an order.'

Mohnke, a man of few words, said nothing, but simply saluted. Hitler returned the salute, then shook his protector by the hand. Next day Mohnke marched his battle group of fighting troops, most of them Leibstandarte veterans, seven miles through the ruins of Berlin from the old Leibstandarte barracks at Lichterfelde to their stations in the cellars of the New Reich Chancellery, where he set up his command post for the last battle. It was here that a young cavalry officer, Gerhard Boldt, attached to Reinhard Gehlen's military intelligence staff in Berlin, first encountered Wilhelm Mohnke as he grappled with the frantic realities of his new task:

> Darkness had fallen; the streets were almost deserted; the thunder of the battle for Berlin had almost died entirely away. The deeper we got into the city, the more lifeless the gigantic metropolis appeared. We reached the Wilhelmplatz without incident and turned into the Voss-strasse. The long frontage of the Reich Chancellery rose up dark and massive against the clear night sky.
>
> As we approached the Reich Chancellery the dull burst of a shell shattered the illusion of peace. Everything appeared deserted. In front of the Party entrance lay a pile of rubble from a row of houses which had collapsed on the street. I ordered the car to stop near the Armed Forces entrances. There was no sign of the sentry who was usually on guard there. A hiss and roar shattered the eerie silence once again, and there was the bursting crash of a heavy shell, which must have landed near the Potsdamerplatz. Beyond the ruins, in the direction of the firing, a faint burning glow grew even brighter.
>
> The guards at the entrances had retreated into the protective darkness of the building. An SS man came up to me and asked me where I was going; then the NCO on guard duty had me conducted at once to the interior of the bunker under the Reich Chancellery. We used a dimly-lit side passage. Armed soldiers were leaning against the walls, some of them smoking, others talking, others crouching down asleep, with their heads lolling forwards. The sound of muffled talking mingled with the whirring of the ventilators.
>
> Eventually we reached the battle headquarters of SS Brigadeführer Mohnke, who until recently had been the commander of an SS division. Now he was the leader of the 'Adolf Hitler Volunteer Corps', which he had assembled a few days before in the Tiergarten, volunteers from all over what

remained of the Reich. Mohnke was speaking loudly to some SS officers, gesticulating all the time, and issuing orders. Despite the ventilators, the air in the small, bare room was stale and suffocating. Mohnke rang the Adjutant's office to check on my orders, and I was then escorted further into the interior of the bunker by two SS men.

The bunker rooms seemed more austere and uninviting than ever. The cold, grey, concrete walls exuded the damp, musty smell common to all new buildings. Our path took us through a maze of rooms, all of which were connected to each other by passages or thin steel doors. The musty smell, the confused sound of people talking, the humming of the ventilators pervaded everything like a nightmare. Several of the rooms were crammed, ceiling high, with bread, preserves and other supplies, so that it was difficult to get through. Other rooms and passages were full of soldiers, most of them leaning listlessly against the walls. Many of them were just lying or sitting on the bare concrete floor, gun in arm, asleep. They were all strong, young SS men. Their appearance did not exactly suggest that they were inspired by eagerness for battle: they seemed, rather, to be resigned to their fate.

The situation around Berlin was now critical. There is no more vivid description of the enveloping nightmare than that contained in a diary written by an officer of the Müncheberg Tank Division, which was then being pushed remorselessly back from Tempelhof towards the centre of the city:

April 24. The howling and explosions of the Stalin organs [multiple rocket launchers], the screaming of the wounded, the roaring of motors, and rattle of machine-guns. Clouds of smoke, and the stench of chlorine and fire. Dead women in the streets, killed while trying to get water. But also, here and there, women with bazookas, Silesian girls thirsting for revenge ... 8 p.m. Russian tanks carrying infantry are driving on the airport. Heavy fighting.
April 25. At 5.30 a.m. new, massive tank attacks. We are forced to retreat. Orders from the Chancellery: Our division is to move immediately to Alexanderplatz in the north. At 9 a.m. order cancelled. At 10 a.m. Russian drive on airport becomes irresistible. New defence line in the centre. Heavy street fighting – many civilian casualties. Dying animals. Women are fleeing from cellar to cellar. New order to go north, as before.

295

But the command situation is obviously in disorder, the Füh-rerbunker must have false information, the positions we are supposed to take over are already in Russian hands. We retreat, under heavy Russian air attacks. Inscriptions on the house walls: 'The hour before sunrise is the darkest' . . . Deserters hanged or shot. What we see on this march is unforgettable.

In the evening, proclamations of a new organization, Free Corps Mohnke: 'Bring your own weapons, equipment, rations. Every German man is needed.' Heavy fighting in the business district, inside the Stock Exchange. The first skirmishes in the subway tunnels, through which the Russians are trying to get behind our lines. The tunnels are packed with civilians.

April 26. The night is fiery red. Heavy shelling. Otherwise a terrible silence. We are sniped at from many houses – probably foreign labourers. About 5.30 a.m. another grinding artillery barrage. The Russians attack. We have to retreat again, fighting for street after street . . . New command post in the subway tunnels under Anhalt railway station. The station looks like an armed camp. Women and children huddling in niches and corners listening for the sounds of battle. Shells hit the roof, cement is crumbling from the ceiling. Powder smell and smoke in the tunnels . . . Late afternoon, we change position again. A terrible sight at the entrance of the subway station, one flight below street level: a heavy shell has pierced the roof, and men, women, soldiers, children are literally squashed against the walls.

As Russian pressure on the Citadel perimeter increased, Mohnke's plans for a last stand were put into action. Mohnke's orders were simple: dig in, take cover, don't draw the enemy's fire. In the Potzdamerplatz Mohnke's men took up their defensive positions. On 27 April the Russians launched a frontal assault with tanks. But the tanks were difficult to manoeuvre and in the narrow, rubble-blocked streets they were sitting ducks for the German Panzerfausts, the crude but deadly bazookas with which even women and children were armed in Berlin's final days. After losing a number of tanks, the Russians learnt their lesson, withdrew their armour, and blasted Mohnke's positions with their artillery. The Müncheberg diarist recorded the devastation in Mohnke's sector:

The whole large expanse of Potsdamerplatz is a waste of ruins. Masses of damaged vehicles, half-smashed trailers of the ambulances with the wounded still in them. Dead people every-where, many of them frightfully cut up by tanks and trucks . . .

The physical conditions were indescribable. There was no rest, no relief, no regular food, hardly any bread. Water had to be got from the tunnels and then filtered. There was another factor, the Müncheberg officer noted, which added greatly to the atmosphere of hellish delirium:

> The wounded that are not torn apart are hardly taken in anywhere. The civilians in their cellars are afraid of them. Too many of them have been hanged as deserters. And the flying courts-martial drive the civilians out of the cellars where they pick up deserters, because they are accessories to the crime.
>
> These courts-martial appear in our sector particularly often today. Most of them are very young SS officers. Hardly a medal or decoration on them. Blind and fanatical. The hope of relief and the fear of the courts-martial bring our men back to fighting pitch.
>
> General Mummert [commanding the LVII Infantry Corps, of which the Müncheberg Division was part] requests that no more courts-martial visit the sector. A division made up of the largest number of men with some of the highest decorations does not deserve to be persecuted by such babies. He is resolved to shoot down any courts-martial that takes action in our sector.

The courts-martial to which the Commander of the Müncheberg veterans took such violent objection were mostly fanatical young thugs from Wilhelm Mohnke's Leibstandarte Regiment. In deploying them in this repugnant manner Mohnke was actually carrying out the instructions of the Reichsführer-SS, Heinrich Himmler, who on 23 April, the day following Mohnke's assumption of command of the Citadel, had ordered the creation of 'flying field and station tribunals' – known in German as *Standgerichte*, or emergency courts – similar to those which had earlier terrorized the eastern German cities of Danzig, Königsberg and Breslau. The corpses of young German soldiers hanged by Mohnke's dreaded *Standgerichte* from the lamp-posts and shop-signs of the streets of Berlin like victims of a lynch mob in the American Deep South were one of the more sickening sights of this sick city. Often the bodies bore placards pinned to their clothes: 'Here I hang because I had no faith in the Führer!'; 'I am a deserter'; 'All traitors die like this one!' Sometimes more eloquent notices proclaimed not only the guilt of the dead man but the fatalistic fanaticism of those who had killed him. One such placard read:

Wer kämpft, kann sterben
Wer sein Vaterland verrät
müss sterben
WIR MUSSEN STERBEN

(Whoever fights, can die
Whoever betrays his Fatherland
must die
WE HAVE TO DIE)

(After the war, it should be said, the West German government decided that the executions carried out by the SS Standgerichte were criminal actions and that those responsible for them should be brought to justice. Several such cases were brought to court, including that of General Max Simon, the former Commander of the 16th SS Panzer-Grenadier Division, who carried out similar executions in the tiny village of Brettheim on 7 April 1945. Simon was first arraigned in October 1955, the same month in which Mohnke returned to Germany from captivity in the USSR. Though Mohnke could doubtless have been arraigned on similar charges, no such trial ever seems to have been contemplated.)

Meanwhile, Mohnke's battle group continued to hold out for the best part of a week against increasing Russian pressure. Almost every evening a pulverizing artillery barrage rained down on them. Virtually every hour the Russians drew the net tighter, and yard by yard fought their way closer to the heart of the city, the Bunker complex where the palsied and exhausted Führer still waited for a miracle to avert the inevitable end. But there would be no miracle. Then a sudden crisis sent a shudder through the Führer's inner court. The cause of this crisis was, to all intents and purposes, a member of his own family.

On the night of 27 April SS Lieutenant General Hermann Fegelein, the brother-in-law of Eva Braun and liaison man between Hitler and Himmler, was apprehended in his flat off the Kurfürstendamm and brought back to the Bunker. Fegelein had aroused Hitler's suspicion by not turning up to the Führer conferences for two days running, and sensing treachery the Führer had issued an order for the missing SS general to be found and brought in for questioning. When finally discovered it seems that Fegelein was on the point of decamping to the west with his foreign mistress and a bag full of Swiss francs and precious stones. Suspected of desertion, Fegelein was frog-marched by a group of four angry generals – Mohnke, Burgdorf, Krebs and Rattenhuber – to Mohnke's command post in the cellars in the New Reich Chancellery. At first Hitler had told Bormann to hand Fegelein over to Mohnke so that he could be stood at the front line in the battle for the Citadel. But Bormann pointed out that Fegelein would only run away again, so Hitler ordered him to be handed over to Mohnke to stand trial by court martial instead. Mohnke was thus saddled with the task of presiding over a military tribunal to try Eva Braun's brother-in-law on a life or death charge. Later he was to recall the extraordinary scene that ensued:

> We set up the court-martial tribunal in a room next to my command post. Someone located a green baize cloth and spread it over a long table. I was determined to carry out this distasteful assignment by the book. We military judges took our seats at the table with the standard German Army Manual of Courts-Martial before us. No sooner were we seated than defendant Fegelein began acting up in such an outrageous manner that the trial could not even commence.
>
> Roaring drunk, with wild, rolling eyes, Fegelein first brazenly challenged the competence of the Court. He kept blubbering that he was responsible to Himmler and Himmler alone, not Hitler. Fegelein had a right to defence counsel, but now rejected it. He refused to defend himself. The man was in wretched shape – bawling, whining, vomiting, shaking like an aspen leaf. Then he began urinating on the floor. He really was drunk; he was not acting. He tore off his épaulettes and threw them on the floor. He called us all a collection of German arseholes.

Even by the crazy standards of Bunker life, this was a surreal scene. For Mohnke, it seems, it was altogether too much. Though he believed there was ample evidence to prove that Fegelein was guilty of desertion in the face of the enemy, for which the penalty was death, he felt that the defendant was not in a fit condition to stand trial, as the German Army Manual required. When the other judges on the tribunal concurred, Mohnke promptly closed the proceedings and handed Fegelein over to the custody of General Rattenhuber, the Security Chief in the Reich Chancellery. The soused and hapless Fegelein was led away in handcuffs and Mohnke never saw him again. Suspected not only of desertion but of treason – the source of the leak of information from the Führer Headquarters to the enemy, perhaps via his foreign-born mistress, a possible British spy – Fegelein was passed on to General Heinrich Müller, the Chief of the Gestapo, for interrogation in the Gestapo cellar.

Fegelein's fate was sealed on the evening of 28 April when word reached Adolf Hitler that Fegelein's nominal boss, Heinrich Himmler, had been involved in clandestine and traitorous peace-feelers with the Western Allies. In a seething fury, Hitler ordered Fegelein to be executed immediately. An hour later, in the early hours of 29 April, after being

299

assured by Müller and Rattenhuber that Fegelein was truly dead and buried, Hitler coolly married the dead man's sister-in-law, Eva Braun, whose tears were tears of joy, not grief.

After a champagne wedding breakfast attended by ten or so intimates of the Bunker, Hitler retired to another room and dictated his last will and testament. He blamed the Jews for the war and the British for the invasion of Poland. He expelled Himmler and Goering from the Party, nominated Dönitz as President of the Reich and Goebbels as Chancellor, and called on the nation to continue to fight against international Jewry.

Later that morning he held his last war conference in the Bunker. The Commandant of Berlin, General Weidling, presented a bleak report. Ammunition had almost run out, no air drops could be expected, the two German armies on which Hitler pinned his hopes for the relief of the capital had been surrounded or stopped. Russian reinforcements were pouring into the city and their vanguard was only a few hundred yards from the Bunker. Within twenty-four hours, reported Weidling, 'the Russians will be able to spit in our windows.' Hitler then turned to Mohnke, who was present at the briefing, and asked him if he was in agreement with Weidling's assessment of the situation. Mohnke confirmed that he was. The Russians had reached the Weidendamm Bridge in the north, the Lustgarten in the east, the Potsdamer Strasse in the south and the Air Ministry and Tiergarten in the west.

The Führer was now finally forced to acknowledge that the situation was hopeless. Even so, he could not permit the surrender of Berlin. Wearily, he rose to leave. But Weidling, convinced that further resistance was madness, had one more question. What were his troops supposed to do, he queried, once they had run out of ammunition? In that case, Hitler conceded, the troops might be allowed to attempt to break out in small groups – a decision he was to confirm in writing in a letter sent to Weidling and Mohnke during the night. Only the previous day Weidling and Krebs had worked out an elaborate escape plan, in which Hitler and the rest of the Bunker denizens would be spirited out of Berlin by a force of forty tanks and two SS Regiments under the command of Wilhelm Mohnke. But Hitler would have none of it. He himself would remain in Berlin. He did not want to have to wait for the end 'somewhere under the open sky or in a farmhouse,' he told Weidling. He did not want to be caught wandering in the woods like a common criminal, or be put in a cage like an animal and exhibited to the public in Red Square. He would die in Berlin. General Mohnke would tell him when the time had come, when his suicide could be delayed no longer.

At 6 a.m. on the morning of 30 April, Mohnke was woken in his sleeping quarters in the cellars of the New Reich Chancellery by a phone call from Sergeant Rochus Misch, the Bunker switchboard operator. The Führer wished to see Mohnke alone in his quarters, Misch told the general.

300

Mohnke buttoned up his tunic and strode through the tunnel connecting the Chancellery and the Bunker. Misch ushered the general into Hitler's bedroom, then closed the door.

Hitler was sitting on the edge of his bed but rose when Mohnke entered, and sat down again in a chair, gesturing to Mohnke to sit on the bed. Mohnke then outlined the tactical situation in the streets up top. 'My Führer,' Mohnke told Hitler, 'as soldier to soldier, true to my oath to you, I no longer can guarantee that my exhausted, battle-weary troops can hold for more than one more day. I now expect a frontal, massed-tank attack at dawn, 1 May.'

In fact Stalin had already given the order for Berlin to be captured by May Day. The Führer now seemed fully aware that his life was at an end, and lapsed into a continuous monologue. For an hour the doomed leader of a Third Reich that had barely more than a week to run sat twitching in his dressing-gown and pouring out whatever was uppermost inside his head. This, it seemed, was failure and treachery. Years later Mohnke was to describe this weird episode to the former *Newsweek* bureau chief in Berlin, James O'Donnell in the only extended interview he ever gave to the press. Mohnke recalled:

> He reviewed his whole career, what he called the dream of National Socialism and why and how it failed. The German people had, in the end, proved unworthy, just not up to the supreme challenge. His spirit lifted when he reminded me of his old triumphs, like the tumultuous receptions in 1938 in Linz and Vienna. I, too, had participated as a member of the FBK [the SS honour bodyguard]. Then he spoke of the many exultant victory parades in which I had marched with the LAH. He was, so to speak, cheering himself up.

The war, Hitler told Mohnke, had been forced upon him by the Anglo-American plutocracy, the Marxist-Bolshevik world conspiracy, Jewish international finance, the Freemasons and the Jesuits. The only reason he had attacked the Soviet Union in 1941 was because he knew that the Soviet Union was about to attack Germany. He could have won, too, but for the abysmal incompetence of his general staff, that haven of reactionary aristocrats. Even inside his own inner circle treason was rife. Goering, Himmler and Speer had betrayed him and the Führer Headquarters leaked secrets like a sieve. 'As he said this,' Mohnke remembered, 'his voice rose, his fists clenched, his face turned white. It was obvious to me that the thought of treachery almost drove him mad.'

At length Hitler came to an end of it and Mohnke rose to leave. Hitler thanked him for his loyalty. 'Your troops have fought splendidly, I have no

301

complaints,' he told Mohnke. 'Would that all the others had fought as tenaciously.' But there was no medal for Mohnke, no parting present. Instead, Hitler handed Mohnke typed copies of his last will and testament, the gist of which he had already just related to the general in his bedroom monologue, and which he hoped Mohnke might carry safely out of the Russian encirclement. Then, as Mohnke returned to his command post to try and hold the Russians one last time, the Führer began to put in order the last day of his life.

Up in the streets, it was a morning worthy of the apocalypse. Berlin seemed to have regressed to an almost primordial state. Outside the old Gestapo headquarters in Albrechtstrasse an escaped lion had been seen loping by, and a zebra was reported to be grazing in one of the city's cemeteries. Elsewhere the shattered metropolis was like a vision of hell. Shellholes exposed corpses lying layers deep in the subways. In the lulls between the shell and rocket fire came the screams of women and young girls gang-raped by the Russian hordes. As Red Army assault squads fought their way room by room and floor by floor through the Reichstag, Herr and Frau Hitler bade a formal farewell to those members of the Bunker community who remained, then withdrew into their private subterranean apartment and closed the gas-proof, sound-proof steel door behind them.

At 3.40 p.m. Bormann, Goebbels, Hitler's senior adjutant, Günsche, and his valet, Linge, entered the room. Eva Braun had taken cyanide. Hitler had put a bullet through his right temple, simultaneously biting on a cyanide capsule to make doubly sure of his death. Then the bodies were carried up the four flights of stairs to the waste ground by the Bunker's emergency exit and soaked in petrol and set on fire. After a while, some SS men came and tossed the charred cadavers into a hole and perfunctorily covered them in rubble and dirt. The show was over.

When Günsche and Kempka clambered down the stairs into the Bunker after attending to the cremation of the bodies of Adolf and Eva Hitler, they found bedlam in the conference room, with people like Goebbels arguing hysterically and even tough front-line soldiers like Mohnke and Ratten-huber openly weeping. Eventually Goebbels regained control of himself and as his first act as the new Chancellor of Germany convened a meeting with Bormann, Mohnke, Burgdorf and Krebs to work out a plan of action for the immediate future, now that Hitler was dead. They were in agree-ment that their first step should be to try and negotiate an armistice with the Russians, and to obtain a ceasefire to enable Bormann to proceed through the enemy lines carrying instructions for Grand Admiral Dönitz, the new head of state. To this end, Mohnke was instructed to establish contact with the Russians through an emissary carrying a white flag, after which Krebs, who could speak Russian, would go through the enemy lines to parley with the Russian high command.

At midnight on 30 April, Krebs' small party, led by Mohnke, emerged from the Bunker and dashed across the road to the nearby subway, from which the group made their way to the command post of Lt-Col. Seifert, commanding the eastern sector of the Citadel. Seifert had organized Krebs' passage through the front line to Chuikov's HQ. After twelve hours of talks, however, Krebs' overtures were rejected on Stalin's orders. Bormann then volunteered to re-open negotiations by telephone, but as the line had been cut by shellfire he ordered Mohnke to have it restored. Mohnke protested that he would not send any of his soldiers to their deaths on that account. When Bormann began to rant and shout, Mohnke coldly retorted that he alone would decide where the men of his Kampfgruppe would be posted. Bormann had lost all authority since Hitler's death; and the officers in the Bunker had already agreed that if he ever tried to slip away they would arrest him.

That evening, 1 May 1945, it was the turn of Dr and Frau Goebbels to take their leave of the Bunker and the world. Only three people were there to watch their departure. One of them was Wilhelm Mohnke, who resolutely gave and received orders while all around him the very world itself dissolved in fire and ruin. Mohnke later related this description of the last minutes of the 'prophet' of the Nazi movement:

> Going over to the coat-rack in the small room that had served as his study, he donned his hat, his scarf, his long uniform overcoat. Slowly, he drew on his kid gloves, making each finger snug. Then, like a cavalier, he offered his right arm to his wife. They were wordless now. So were we three spectators. Slowly but steadily, leaning a bit on each other, they headed up the stairs to the courtyard.

Out in the Bunker back yard, in the troubled darkness of front-line Berlin, Frau Goebbels bit a cyanide capsule, and as she sank to her knees her husband blew her brains out. Then he, too, bit a capsule, squeezing the trigger of his pistol as he did so. It was 8.30 p.m. on 1 May 1945.

With Hitler and Goebbels dead, General Mohnke, the Bunker and Reich Chancellery Commandant, was left in effective charge. When Martin Bormann attempted to interfere and countermand one of Mohnke's orders, Mohnke – to the delight of the Bunker community – told him bluntly to 'get lost'. His first decision was to postpone the breakout attempt by the survivors in the Bunker from its original start-time, which had been scheduled for shortly after the death of the Goebbels couple. This was partly because the Russians had cut the proposed escape route, the East–West Axis, and a new route needed to be worked out; and partly because he felt that the would-be escapers needed a chance to catch up on their sleep during the following day. His second decision was to summon a meeting of all field-grade officers for the evening of that day to bring them up to date on the situation that now confronted them.

In shocked disbelief the assembled officers listened to Mohnke's version of the events of the last two days – of Hitler's wedding, the suicide of the bride and groom, followed by the deaths of the Goebbels family, the breakdown of armistice talks with the Russians in Berlin, and the failure of the German Ninth and Twelfth Armies to relieve the city. Those who listened to Mohnke realized that all hope had gone. The Third Reich was virtually at an end and the capital was doomed. Panic among the troops had to be avoided, Mohnke told the gathering, therefore news of the turn of events should not be broken until 10 p.m. General Weidling, the Commandant of Berlin, had ordered that front-line fighting should cease at 11 p.m., at which time all German troops should try and break out of the Russian ring as best they could, general direction north-west. 'This is a general order,' Mohnke concluded. 'There are no more specific details. I regret that I have no better information than some of you have about the battle situation in several of the outer boroughs of Berlin. Battle groups will simply have to play it by ear, probing to find their best march route. No provision can be made for any rearguard. We *are* the rearguard.'

The officers melted away into the dark of the doomed city. It was difficult to know how many fighting troops they still commanded. Of General Mohnke's own battle group of Leibstandarte veterans, less than a half, about 700 men, were still capable of bearing arms around the Reich Chancellery. But the brunt of the fighting had fallen on General Krukenberg's men in the Unter den Linden, half of whom were foreigners – the Danes, Swedes, Norwegians and Dutchmen of his SS Nordland Division, plus a battle group of Frenchmen from the Charlemagne Division and a battalion of Latvian SS men.

The conference over, Mohnke gave an order for the Bunker room in which Hitler had killed himself to be set on fire. Petrol was poured around the room and a flaming rag tossed into it. The fire burned hotly, pouring choking sulphurous smoke into the Bunker, then died for lack of oxygen. An uncanny silence descended on Hitler's last stronghold. All activity now was centred in the nearby Reich Chancellery cellars, where Mohnke was already deeply engrossed in planning the breakout of the Bunker and Chancellery survivors.

All through the afternoon of Tuesday, 1 May 1945, while others slept, General Mohnke had been methodically working out the logistics of the breakout – the groups, the timings, the route, the rendezvous point. When his escape plan was complete to his satisfaction he took it for formal approval to the general officers who, in the absence of his late Commander-in-Chief, Adolf Hitler, were now nominally his immediate military superiors – General Krebs and General Burgdorf in the Führerbunker, and General Weidling who was still negotiating the surrender of the city with the Russians from his command post a mile away.

Mohnke's plan envisaged a total of ten escape groups of varying sizes, each group under the command of a responsible leader. Mohnke was to lead the first group, General Rattenhuber the second and Werner Naumann the third, which was also to include the most senior serving member of the Nazi hierarchy, Martin Bormann. Originally Mohnke had suggested that Bormann should accompany him in the first group, but Bormann had declined and chosen the third instead. Mohnke took this as a sign of cowardice on Bormann's part, though it might have been a sign of cunning too, for if the first group succeeded in finding a way through, then the third could reasonably expect to make use of it without running the same risks. According to Mohnke's plan, each group was to leave the Reich Chancellery at twenty-minute intervals, so that the last group would not begin its escape bid until three hours after the first. As far as possible the escape route was to make use of the U-Bahn, the underground railway subway, to head north under the closing Russian ring. If all went well, the breakout groups would rendezvous in the woods near Schwerin, some eighty miles north-west of Berlin, and from there make their way with all possible speed to the headquarters of the new President of the Third Reich, Admiral Dönitz, in Schleswig-Holstein.

The mass breakout from the beleaguered city centre was like a step into a dark and very perilous void. The chances of success were less than even. No one knew for sure to what extent the Russians had penetrated Berlin's underground tunnel system. No one knew the exact state of the fighting front in the different parts of the city. But as Traudl Junge, an attractive young woman who had been one of Hitler's secretaries in the Bunker remarked: 'It was better than committing suicide in that hole.' Though Mohnke did not ever envisage fighting his way out, as a veteran front-line soldier he made a point of taking his service pistol and a machine-pistol just in case. He also carried slung round his neck a long waxed-paper packet containing a leather pouch full of Knight's Cross diamonds which Hitler had given him for safe keeping, and several important state documents, including copies of Hitler's two testaments of 30 April and Goebbels' protocol of 1 May, which he had been ordered to deliver to Dönitz. At a briefing of the field officers still under his command, Mohnke read Hitler's testaments aloud and enjoined them to memorize their contents as best they could in case the documents themselves never reached their destination.

Mohnke insisted that everybody else was properly dressed and equipped. Traudl Junge recalled:

> General Mohnke gave out weapons to everyone. Even the women were issued with pistols, but advised not to use them except in the direst emergencies. We were also supposed to be given more suitable clothes for our escape, for which purpose we had to go to a depot in a bunker beneath the Voss-strasse, some way away. To get there, we had to pass through the operating room of the medical centre. I had never seen a dead body, but that day I saw the horribly disfigured corpses of two soldiers lying on stretchers. Professor Haase [one of the Bunker medics] didn't even glance up as we passed him; he was busy amputating a foot.
>
> At the depot I was given a tin hat, a pair of trousers, a short jacket and a pair of heavy shoes. Then I quickly went back to our bunker. The strange new clothes seemed to hang off me, and I felt peculiar. Even the men had made changes to their clothing: many of them had taken off their medals and insignia of rank. Captain Hans Baur, Hitler's personal pilot, was rolling up the portrait of Frederick the Great which Hitler used to take everywhere with him and which he'd given Baur as a memento on the eve of his death.

The breakout was to begin an hour before midnight, the starting point being the underground fire brigade garage of the Reich Chancellery cellar complex facing the Wilhelmstrasse. Soon the time came for the first group to assemble. All the Bunker secretaries and Hitler's vegetarian cook were in that group. Traudl Junge remembered the final departure from the Führerbunker:

> 'We destroyed all our identity papers. I left behind money, food and clothes, taking only plenty of cigarettes, a few photographs, my pistol and the cyanide capsule. I was sure that I would never get through the Russian front line alive. The other women had bags and bundles . . .
>
> 'One after the other we left that horrifying place. For the last time I passed the door to Hitler's and Eva's apartments. His grey greatcoat was still hanging on a metal coat-rack; above it were his cap with the gold insignia and his leather gloves. The dog's lead was there, hanging like a noose from the gallows. For a second I thought of taking the gloves, or at least one of them, as a memento, but I gave up the idea before I'd even stretched out

my hand. I don't really know why. In Eva's bedroom the wardrobe doors stood open, and I caught sight of the silver fox fur coat she'd given me. But what could I have done with a coat like that in the hands of the enemy? I was more likely to need my poison capsule.

One of the Chancellery doctors, Professor Ernst-Guenther Schenk, later described the eerie scene as the actors in this grand finale began to file on to the cavernous, torch-lit stage:

> From the dark gangways they kept arriving, in small groups, both the fighting troops being pulled in from the outside, then the officers and men of the Reich Chancellery group. The troops, many of them very young, were already street fighting veterans. Other soldiers had stubble beards, blackened faces; they wore sweaty, torn, field-grey uniforms, which most had worn and slept in, without change, for almost a fortnight. The situation was heroic; the mood was not . . . There was little talk now of 'Führer, Folk and Fatherland.' To a man, each German soldier was silently calculating his own chances of survival.

At 10.50 p.m. Mohnke himself appeared on the scene. His group consisted mostly of the bits and bobs from the Führerbunker – the three female secretaries and the cook, Hitler's naval attaché and Hitler's former senior adjutant, Otto Günsche, who had now become General Mohnke's aide-de-camp following the Führer's suicide – a motley group of twenty men and four women all told. At 11 p.m. sharp, pistol in hand, Mohnke broke through the cellar window and led his party out into the threatening darkness of the Berlin night. Most of them had not set foot outside the Bunker for days. Few of them had expected such a conflagration as now consumed the city. All Berlin seemed to be blazing. The ruins of the Chancellery stood out gauntly against the flames, and everywhere there was the crashing of shells, cracking of rifle fire, the stuttering chatter of machine-guns. No enemy fire was coming in their direction, however, and the group made a dash for it down the street and across Wilhelmplatz, where dozens of starving Berliners had emerged from their shelters to cut up the carcase of a dead horse for food. In a short while Mohnke's group reached the relative safety of the Kaiserhof underground station. Too apprehensive to use their electric torches for fear the station was already in Russian hands, they crawled on hands and knees to the station platform, then elbowed their way through the throng of cowering Berliners who had sought refuge here from the street fighting above ground, and clambered on to the railway track for the next leg of the escape journey – eastward to

307

Stadtmitte station, then a sharp turn north along the tube line leading to Friedrichstrasse underground station.

So they went, groping and stumbling in the dark along the railway sleeper ties, strung out in a straggling line from which, one by one, the waifs and strays dropped out, lost somewhere in the labyrinth. By the time they left Friedrichstrasse station for the next underground lap under the River Spree to Stettiner Bahnhof subway station, the first group had been reduced to fifteen, and any hope of maintaining cohesion with the follow-up groups had long vanished. But Mohnke forged on, stomping resolutely along the track on his wooden foot, with the Russian artillery pounding the city above his head and the tunnel trembling under the impact as in an earthquake, until he came to a watertight steel bulkhead door that had been closed to shut off the tunnel.

It was here that Mohnke's ingrained life-long Prussian obedience to rules and orders proved his eventual undoing. Two employees of the Berlin Municipal Transport Company guarded the bulkhead door and they refused to open it, even for an SS general brandishing a pistol. The bulkhead was always kept closed after the last train had gone through, they protested, and they produced the company rule book to prove it. As far as they were concerned, it made no difference that the last train had gone through more than a week ago and another was not expected for an indefinite period, if at all. Mohnke might have felt justified in shooting these two staunch company servants on the spot. After all, he had had people shot for less. But as he later explained:

> Orders are to be obeyed, even if, as in this case, the order was no more than a Municipal Transport Company regulation, not even a military command. Even today, I harbour a lingering respect for this eccentric devotion to duty of those two stubborn, Cerberus-like guardians of the bulkhead. I suppose it was my own ingrained sense of duty that led me to respect theirs.

Mohnke's group had no alternative but to retrace their steps to the Friedrichstrasse underground station. With the planned escape route unexpectedly blocked, Mohnke had to cast about for an alternative way out. Clambering up through the twisted girders of the bombed-out S-Bahn (elevated railway) station at Friedrichstrasse, Mohnke peered about him in the dark. What he saw was like nothing he had ever set eyes on in his life before. Years later he was to recall:

> I now had a panoramic view of the Berlin night-time battle-field. It was unlike any previous one I had ever seen. It looked more like a painting, something apocalyptic by Hieronymus

Bosch. Even to a hardened soldier, it was most unreal, phantas-magoric. Most of the great city was pitch-dark; the moon was hiding; but flares, shell-bursts, the burning buildings, all these reflected on a low-lying, blackish-yellow cloud of sulphur-like smoke . . . This is one of the moments I still remember most clearly, for the reflections of the burning ruins were mirrored back from the water of the river, itself rippled by a steady night-time breeze. The Spree was now black, now red, very eerie. Again it was deathly quiet. Only the ghosts of shadows, sometimes real, sometimes imagined, lurked in the streets lead-ing to the stone quays on both sides of the river.

Mohnke could see nothing as clear-cut as a front-line, but he could tell that the Russians were already in possession of the upper end of the Fried-richstrasse, three or four blocks away, and that the tank trap on the Weidendamm bridge over the River Spree, which they would somehow have to cross in order to continue their way to the north of the city, was also in Russian hands. Fortunately, a narrow catwalk only two yards wide offered a precarious means of crossing the river, and Mohnke's group, now down to only twelve, scuttled across, their silhouettes presenting perfect targets against the glow of the fires behind them.

Three hours had now passed since they left the Reich Chancellery. It was cold and they were tired but it was imperative to keep moving and to make as much ground as possible under cover of what was left of the night. Their route now led them through an urban desert of ruined buildings, rubble mounds and crumbling cellars where terrified groups of Berliners huddled like bedouin nomads in a wan candle-lit glow. Everywhere there was evidence of Russian activity. In the Chausseestrasse a Russian tank blocked Mohnke's way and forced him to double back. From the city's famous Charité Hospital, only a block away from Mohnke's route, Russian soldiers, inflamed with ether alcohol, had run amok among the nurses and female patients, and one of the soldiers in Mohnke's party watched aghast as a naked woman was pursued across a rooftop by armed men and then leaped five or six stories to her death. The Russian artillery had opened up again and a tank battle was in progress by the Weidendamm bridge, where Martin Bormann's escape group had run into serious diffi-culties. As shells and rockets zoomed over their heads, one shell fell short and exploded in their midst, killing the former commander of the SS Nordland Division, General Ziegler.

So far it had taken them four hours to travel four miles. Shattered, and utterly weary, clothes soiled and tattered, faces smeared with the ash from the fires of Berlin, the surviving members of the group rested up in the freight yard of the Stettiner Bahnhof railway terminal. They were too tense to eat, too cold to sleep. But their halt lasted three hours and it was broad daylight before they set off again. Other stragglers, some 150 to 200 of them, had joined them in the freight yard, and it was a much longer column of would-be escapers that now trudged northwards beneath a great cloud of yellow dust that hung over the ruins like a mist over a mountain lake.

At 9 a.m. on the morning of 2 May 1945 Mohnke led his motley column into a municipal park called the Humboldthain in the heart of the working-class district of Wedding. And there, to their absolute amazement, they found assembled beneath the gigantic flak tower a spanking new German army formation drawn up, all stripped and bristling for action – Tiger tanks, heavy artillery, armoured weapons carriers with heavy machine-guns mounted, companies of infantry troops in clean battle dress. 'It was a fantastic apparition,' General Mohnke remembered, 'like a *fata morgana*. I had to rub my eyes. This otherwise unreal scene reminded me of pre-war manoeuvres in my days as a young troop officer, somewhere off on the Lüneburger or the Romintern Heath – the sunshine, the shining weapons, the distribution of field rations. There was no sign of serious battle fatigue. We who had been trudging all through the Berlin night were astounded. A crazy new hope dawned briefly.'

But not for long. Shortly after 10 a.m. someone with a radio picked up the news of General Weidling's capitulation of the city and of a general cease-fire. All plans for an armed breakout were abandoned. The tanks were immobilized, the guns spiked, grenades destroyed and rifle bolts tossed aside. To all intents the war was over. Feeling exposed and insecure in such a conspicuous place, Mohnke's party moved away at noon, and in a short while came to the cavernous premises of the Schultheiss-Patzenhofer brewery, where several hundred civilian and military refugees had already holed up to await the end. These people, in various stages of exhaustion, despair and hysteria, were passing the time in ways that befitted people who believed the end of the world was at hand, with heavy drinking parties on the first floor and group sex on the second.

Down in the cellars, amongst the brewery boilers, Mohnke's party took stock of the situation. Most of the breakout groups from the Reich Chancellery had survived this far, though there were notable absentees, including Hitler's Party Secretary, Martin Bormann. But it would not be long before the Russians stormed the brewery, it was thought, if only to lay their hands on the beer. Traudl Junge was still with Mohnke's escape group and remembered its final moments of liberty:

'Mohnke and Günsche sat down and started writing reports. Two soldiers entered carrying General Rattenhuber and they placed him on a makeshift bunk. He had been wounded in both legs, and was incoherent with fever; a doctor who was in the shelter took care of him. Rattenhuber took out his pistol and placed it at his side in readiness. He intended to kill himself rather than be taken prisoner.

A general came into the bunker [i.e. the brewery cellar] and spoke to the leader of our party [General Mohnke]. We learned that we were holed up in the last centre of resistance in Berlin. The Russians had just encircled the brewery and had ordered those inside to surrender.

Mohnke finished writing his report just one hour before the Russians' ultimatum expired. He turned to the women of the party and said: 'You must help us now. Since the men are all in uniform, we don't stand a chance of escaping, but you can try to get out of Berlin and go north to Admiral Dönitz's headquarters and give him this report.'

I didn't want to be part of this foolhardy scheme, but Frau Christian [another of Hitler's ex-secretaries] and the other two women persuaded me to go ahead. We took off our steel helmets, our pistols and our military jackets, shook hands with the men, and left.

From now on it was a case of *sauve qui peut*, every man and woman on his own. The oath of loyalty to the Führer, Mohnke told the officers and men, was binding only in his lifetime – and the Führer was now dead. A few, like Ambassador Hewel, chose suicide, but many that afternoon seized the opportunity to slip away to the north and west. For those who remained, including Wilhelm Mohnke, that afternoon was to prove the last that would be spent in liberty for many years.

At noon, Mohnke had left with Colonel Clausen to parley with a Red Army general, but had returned after an hour, leaving Clausen to continue the negotiations. There was little left to do but await the turn of events. In the early evening, as Red Army soldiers crept room by room towards Mohnke's position in the cellar, Colonel Clausen returned to the brewery. He said the Russians had told him that Berlin had surrendered and that Mohnke and his party would be treated honourably and allowed to keep their sidearms if they surrendered too. Mohnke's orderly officer, Otto Günsche, recalled what happened then:

> The generals replied that they wanted confirmation from authorized personnel, and the Russians suggested taking them to their command post. The generals agreed, including General Mohnke, who asked me to go with him. It was at the command post we learnt that General Weidling, commander of the city of Berlin, had signed a surrender for the troops in the capital – the

311

Berlin garrison, in other words – but not for the Wehrmacht as a whole. General Mohnke replied that, as we weren't part of the Berlin garrison, the capitulation didn't apply to us, and the Russians said, 'Show us where the rest of you are, or we'll shoot you now!'

Back at the brewery the officers in the cellar uncocked their pistols at a signal from Mohnke. There would be no last shoot-out, no second escape bid, no mass suicide. Mohnke had decided they would submit themselves to the mercy of their enemies as surrendered prisoners of war. At that moment, therefore, Mohnke for the first time found himself in the position of the many British, Canadian and American soldiers who had placed themselves in the hands of the Leibstandarte and SS Hitler Jugend units which he had commanded in Wormhoudt, Normandy and the Ardennes. Would the Russians behave as he had done?

312

PART VIII

—

Prisoner of the Russians

MAY 1945–OCTOBER 1955

At 8 p.m. three Russian jeeps arrived at the brewery and the twelve SS officers in Mohnke's group were bundled into them and driven off at great speed through the dark, deserted streets, heading back through the city centre in the direction of Tempelhof airport. The streets were still littered with the carnage of the battle, the cadavers of human beings, horses, dogs, burnt-out tanks, trucks and crashed planes. After twenty minutes the jeeps arrived at the Kommandatura of General Chuikov's Eighth Guards Army near the airport, and, after reporting briefly, drove on to a large building a few blocks away in the Belle Alliance Strasse. Here they all got out and the Germans were led under guard up four flights of stairs to the top floor.

Mohnke feared the worst. He remembered Hitler's order of March 1941 in the briefing for the invasion of Russia: 'German officers must free themselves of all conservative and conventional inhibitions. Such documents as the Geneva Convention do not apply in the East.' Later Mohnke was to comment: 'I believe most of us in the Waffen-SS fought bravely against the Russians, and that they as good soldiers respected that fact. Still, many cold-blooded crimes had been committed.'

But it was not a Russian military intelligence interrogation centre into which the SS officers were now led, but the officers' mess of the Eighth Guards Army, the crack tank army that had defeated the Germans at Stalingrad and headed the advance on Berlin. In this unlikely sanctuary a number of Red Army officers in smart dress uniforms with medals and ribbons waited to greet their defeated enemy. A small of cooking drifted through from the next room. It was a very odd and unexpected reception and the Germans remained highly puzzled and embarrassed. Then the principal host of the occasion arrived. He was Lieutenant General Belyavski, Chuikov's chief of staff, and with a bow to his guests he declared:

Gentlemen, we pride ourselves on having fought in the field against such valiant opponents. We congratulate you on the soldierly valour your troops often displayed. The battle for Berlin was a bitter encounter while it lasted, and this has been a long and cruel war . . . May I herewith invite you to be our guests for supper this evening, to enjoy what hospitality we can offer?

A door opened to reveal a dining-table laden to overflowing with luxuries such as Mohnke and his Nazi comrades had not set eyes on for months. There were hams and red caviar, capons, fish, fresh-baked bread and dairy butter – and a bottle of vodka before each place. Young Red Army girls in starched white pinafores served tea from a copper samovar. The Germans, who had eaten nothing but a few iron rations in the last twenty-fours hours, attacked the food with gusto, but made only a pretence at downing the endless toasts of vodka. The Russians impressed Mohnke as high-grade, courteous, smartly turned-out professionals. But as the evening wore on and the Russians grew drunker and jollier, the bizarre banquet turned into a *Uralfest*, a real Russian-style binge. At no point, however, could Mohnke and his fellows ever forget that they were now prisoners of the Red Army – 'which is why,' Mohnke was to recall, 'we were so stiff, so sober, so restrained.'

At 10.30 p.m. shortly after fresh supplies of vodka had been brought to the table, General Belyavski rose and brought the festivities peremptorily to an end. Without further ceremony a Red Army orderly roughly pushed Mohnke and his fellow SS officers into a bare attic room and bolted the door behind them. A single light bulb hung from the ceiling. A small window looked down to an enclosed courtyard full of stinking garbage four floors below. From other rooms came sounds of Russian revelry and radios blaring Red Army marches. Escape was impossible. The Germans had no alternative but to resign themselves to whatever fate had in store for them. Sitting on the floor, their backs to the wall, they dozed off. At dawn a guard brought the previous evening's copper samovar to serve as a communal chamber-pot. At 7 a.m. a platoon of thirty-six guards, three for each prisoner, arrived to take the German prisoners away. These men were not from the Red Army but the feared NKVD, or secret political police (later re-named the KGB). Realizing this, Mohnke felt even more despondent.

A truck drove Mohnke and his companions in a north-westerly direction through Berlin. The ruins of the capital of the Thousand Year Reich, the mountains of rubble, the shattered populace, the bewildered refugees – all this Mohnke had seen before. But he would never forget his first sight of the endless Russian supply columns moving into the city in the opposite direction that morning. 'Asia on this day was moving into the middle of Europe,' he recalled, 'a strange and exotic panorama.' Kalmuks, Uzbeks,

Azerbaijanis, Mongols from the wastes of Siberia and the steppes of Central Asia, many of them singing, many clothed in a startling variety of civilian garb, including the looted costumes of ransacked stage and opera wardrobes, passed by in an endless cavalcade of horse-drawn carts laden with plunder, with bicycles and beds, rugs and toilets, sinks and bureaux, chickens, ducks and geese, camp followers and gypsy women. 'What was here under way through the streets of Berlin,' Mohnke commented later, 'was something out of the great vastness of Russia beyond the Urals. We Germans knew it was a historical moment. We were fascinated – and speechless.'

Mohnke's party was now split up. At noon, Professor Schenk and six other officers were delivered to the NKVD headquarters at the edge of the city. General Mohnke, General Rattenhuber, Major Günsche (now Mohnke's adjutant) and Hans Baur (Hitler's pilot, who had the nominal rank of general), on the other hand, were driven a further twenty miles out of Berlin to Marshal Zhukov's former headquarters at a large estate near Strausberg, which the Russians had turned into a reception camp for captured German generals and their aides. Here Mohnke and his three companions were interrogated for six long days by Russian intelligence men, always on the same topic – the last days of Adolf Hitler in Berlin. It was Mohnke who first aroused the investigators' interest when he told them that he had heard that Hitler had killed himself as early as 30 April. Finally, on 9 May 1945 – the day after VE-Day in the West – Mohnke and Günsche, along with Generals Weidling, Rattenhuber and Baur, were driven out of the camp and bundled onto a Russian transport plane waiting at a nearby airfield.

It was at this point that Mohnke decided to take his own life while he still had the opportunity to do so. Unlike many other high-ranking Nazis he had no cyanide capsule. But he still had his service revolver and clip of ammunition concealed in his jock strap. 'Suddenly I decided to make use of the pistol,' Mohnke related, 'before it was taken away from me forever. The situation seemed hopeless. What had I now to live for? I confided my intention to Otto Günsche. It was he who really saved me.' As Mohnke took out the clip, Günsche snatched it from him and threw it away. 'General,' he told Mohnke, 'we survived the Führerbunker together; we lived through the breakout; perhaps we can pull through whatever now lies before us, too.' Mohnke had a wife and two children in his home town of Lübeck. At least it was the British and not the Russians who had taken the city, so perhaps they would be safe; but he was convinced he would never see his family again.

It was from the camp for high-ranking German officers at Strausberg that word was conveyed by inmates later repatriated to the West that Mohnke had survived the fighting in Berlin and was in Soviet hands. This news was noted by the British, Canadian and American investigators who were looking into the atrocities committed by the units under Mohnke's command in Wormhoudt, Normandy and the Ardennes; but thereafter the trail ran cold, and all requests submitted to the Soviet authorities for Mohnke's extradition to the West were met with silence or rebuttal. The prevailing view was that an SS general in Soviet hands was a non-person, as good as dead – particularly, perhaps, one who was so close to Adolf Hitler in the final days. So though Mohnke's name remained on the CROWCASS, United Nations and American Intelligence lists of wanted war criminals, interest in him faded away and little or no effort was made by the British, Canadians, Americans, or for that matter Belgians, who had lost several hundred civilians at the hands of Mohnke's 1st SS Panzer Division in December 1944, to develop a case against Mohnke for his part in these various crimes. Nor was any consideration given to the possibility of trying Mohnke *in absentia*, as for example Martin Bormann was tried *in absentia* at the Nuremberg trials and Klaus Barbie, the notorious chief of the Gestapo in Lyons, was tried *in absentia* by the French in 1949 – even though, in the Malmédy trial, Mohnke would automatically have been found guilty on the chain of command principle once the court had established the guilt of all those officers above and below him in that chain.

So what happened to Wilhelm Mohnke after he was bundled into a Russian plane at Strausberg? By his own account, he was flown to Moscow, a city in delirious mood, 9 May having been declared Victory Day in the USSR. There he was incarcerated initially in the giant Budirka prison, which also housed other generals from the final days in Berlin, including Generals Weidling and Rattenhuber. After being processed through Budirka into the vast Soviet prison system, which by then held several million other German prisoners of war as well as the millions of Soviet-born inmates, Mohnke was transferred to the NKVD's notorious central interrogation centre at Lubyanka in Moscow, where an out-of-favour Red Army artillery captain by the name of Alexander Solzhenitsyn was also a prisoner at that time, along with such top-ranking officers of the former Nazi Reich as Grand Admiral Raeder and Field Marshal Schörner.

At Lubyanka Mohnke now became a political prisoner rather than a simple prisoner of war. The Russians evidently believed Mohnke was a big catch, a high-ranking Nazi stalwart who had been close to the centre of things throughout the entire duration of the Hitler régime. There were many questions that Mohnke could help answer for them, not least the circumstances surrounding the death of Adolf Hitler himself. It was now that the real interrogation began. It was intensive, prolonged and much of it

318

was conducted at night. There were hours of endless questions, followed by long bouts when Mohnke and his comrades had to write down everything they knew or could remember on scores of sheets of paper. Though Stalin and a handful of senior army commanders and intelligence officers knew very well what had happened to Hitler, the Soviet leadership persisted in the charade of scorning the West's version of the last days of Hitler, suggesting instead that perhaps the erstwhile Führer had escaped and was still alive in hiding somewhere, and that it was a double whose body had been burned in Berlin. At any rate, for a long time Mohnke's interrogators remained suspicious and incredulous of the version of events presented to them by Mohnke and the other members of the so-called Reich Chancellery Group. Thus they accused Hitler's pilot, Hans Baur, of having flown the Führer away to safety and General Rattenhuber of having arranged his secret escape by U-boat to Argentina. They even accused Otto Günsche of deliberately allowing himself to be captured by the Russians so that he could put them on the wrong track about Hitler.

Baur later recalled the prison routine to which they were all subjected after being transferred back to Budirka from Lubyanka:

> We entered a new wave of interrogation: twenty-one nights from midnight to 5 a.m. When we went back to the cells, we were not allowed to sleep. They tried to play us off against each other . . . It was an insane time. Always the same questions, the same threats, the same promises, no sleep, less and less to eat, and always the same cold and malicious faces of the interrogators.

There is little doubt that the Russians would have made good use of the fact that the Canadians had been asking for Mohnke to be handed over to them to stand trial for war crimes committed against Canadian troops in Normandy. Mohnke had never set foot in the USSR during the war and therefore had no specific war crimes charges to answer in that country. But the threat of extradition to the West, and the ultimate threat of a Canadian noose, would have been a powerful instrument of persuasion in the NKVD's hands.

According to the Canadian journalist, William Stevenson, Mohnke thereby became a pawn in the Cold War game against the West. He told the Russians everything he knew, and what he did not know he invented. He fed Stalin's suspicions about a secret rapport between the Anglo-Americans and the Germans, and spoke at length of Nazi plans for a Fourth Reich, of the transfer of gold and currency to neutral countries, of Alpine hideaways and underground escape routes. Though the Russians would not admit that Mohnke was in their hands – to do so would be to devalue Mohnke's usefulness in their long-term stratagem – they used his information, leaked out through Soviet intelligence sources, to discredit

319

the West. Mohnke was also valuable as a means of checking the accuracy of relevant disclosures by the Western Allies. The luckless Wilhelm was thus stranded in much the same hapless situation as the tragic hero of Evelyn Waugh's black comedy, *A Handful of Dust* – confined to a mud hut in a village of savages, so to speak, and forced to read endless stories to a tribal bully who would never ever let him go.

When the Canadian war crimes investigators tried yet again to enlist Soviet help in locating the wanted Mohnke, the Soviet authorities again used the occasion to stir the Cold War brew. Charging that Mohnke's accomplice in the murder of Canadian prisoners of war in Normandy – the convicted war criminal, Kurt Meyer – had been appointed to a post with NATO, the Soviet authorities quipped: 'These forces, as is well known, are directed against the democratic [i.e. Communist] republics . . . Imperialist warmongers have permitted Nazis to return to their former military and civic positions.' The implication was that even if the Russians did hold Mohnke, they would never stoop so low as the Western Powers and let a Nazi war criminal loose on the world again.

After a year of prolonged interrogation, the NKVD investigators seemed to become rather more convinced about the veracity of their German prisoners' version of the last days of the Third Reich. In the summer of 1946 Mohnke and some of the other Bunker folk – Baur, Linge, Klingemeier, Rattenhuber, Günsche, Misch and several others – were given a brief respite from their dreary confinement in Soviet camps and prisons and taken secretly to Berlin to re-enact the final Bunker scenes of a year before for the benefit of the Soviet investigators. According to Baur, they were taken in a prison train which took nine days to complete the journey.*

> 'Each day we were given some dirty brown water from the locomotive,' Baur remembered, 'half of a salted herring, and about a pound of bread. Half-starved, we arrived in Berlin. If we thought we had known bad prisons before, we found out differently in Berlin's Lichtenberg. It was a crazy place in which sailors held sway . . . Lichtenberg was pervaded by the sound of screaming and crying.'

The cells in this hell-hole contained only one object, a bucket that had to be used for every purpose – for washing in, for putting food in, and for relieving the call of nature.

* Some other members of the Reich Chancellery Group may have been taken to Berlin by air on a lightning visit lasting only twenty-four hours. It is not clear why Baur should have been taken by train or stayed so long – unless, perhaps, as a former pilot he was viewed as a potential hijack risk.

Late one evening Mohnke and his fellow captives were taken back to the Führerbunker. It was a spooky experience to revisit the scene of the historic melodrama of a year ago. At dead of night, under the glare of arc lamps and the probing lenses of film cameras, Mohnke and the others, all dressed in their prison drabs, were forced to re-enact Hitler's death, burial and cremation *in situ* in the Bunker and the Reich Chancellery garden. Then they were taken back to the USSR, to camps in the Urals, the Arctic and elsewhere, for the years of confinement that stretched endlessly before them.

For several years the captives received no letters or news from home. Then in 1949 a wave of brief summary trials followed. Most of the high-ranking German prisoners received a standard sentence of twenty-five years' imprisonment. By decree of the Soviet government, generals were exempt from forced labour, which was the fate of most of the multitude of lower-ranking German prisoners. But they were not exempt from all the grinding daily ghastliness of life in the Soviet camp and prison system; and when, in due course, they were transferred to the generals' camp at Woikowo, 300 kilometres to the east of Moscow, there was no one else to do the chores but the generals themselves. Eventually there were 186 German generals in the small, overcrowded camp at Woikowa, one of them being Wilhelm Mohnke. Upon Mohnke and his fellow generals fell the tasks of peeling potatoes, tending the garden, feeding the rabbits, bringing in the harvest from the surrounding fields. Though life was menial and mundane for such eminent henchmen of Hitler's Reich, it was almost positively pleasant compared with their less fortunate comrades of lower rank who were locked in a grim battle for survival in other camps. Moreover, a glimmer of hope had begun to dawn.

In 1953 Stalin died. Not long afterwards, as part of a political rapprochement between the Soviet Union and West Germany, the West German Chancellor, Konrad Adenauer, paid an official visit to Moscow, during which the fate of the many German prisoners inside the USSR was discussed. A little while later, three Russian generals appeared in the camp at Woikowo and announced spectacular tidings – the prisoners were now free men, they declared, and soon they would be on their way home. For Mohnke, unimaginably, his long, weary years of Russian captivity ended as they had begun, with a surprise banquet given by their Russian captors. From the hotel of the nearby town of Ivanovo lorries arrived bringing cooks, utensils and provisions. In the dining-hall of the generals' camp the tables were laden with all the luxuries of a truly festive occasion, with rows of bottles of beer, wine, champagne and vodka, soup, cooked meats, puddings and pies, coffee and cake. There were speeches and toasts, and suits, coats, hats, shirts and other civilian clothing to be issued, and travel plans to be detailed. Then the great day came. A train was waiting in

321

Ivanovo station to take the prisoners to Moscow on the first stage of their joyous, long dreamed-of journey back to their homeland.

In Moscow the prisoners were transferred to sleeping cars hitched on to the back of the Moscow–Berlin express. Then they were travelling back across the flat plains of European Russia, across the very terrain where all those years ago Hitler's invading armies had marched on the Soviet capital – triumphant, ruthless, criminal, and seemingly unstoppable. For the crime of that invasion, for the barbarity of Operation Barbarossa, the emaciated Nazi generals on the Moscow–Berlin express had paid a heavy price during those inhuman years in the prison camps. And because of the heaviness of that price, the inhumanity of those years, they were now received not as international war criminals, which some of them were, but as national heroes when close on midnight the train brought them back at last to Herlehausen station and the bosom of the Fatherland. On the bus ride from the station to the reception centre for repatriated prisoners of war at Friedland, run by the German Red Cross and the Organization of Returning Veterans, the homecomers were treated to emotionally unnerving scenes of welcome. Though it was late and dark, there were waving crowds in towns and villages lit by lanterns and children bearing lighted candles; everywhere there were cheers and smiles and gifts and church bells ringing out; and crowds of reporters and film and TV cameras, a ceaseless, bewildering, overwhelming excitement. At Friedland there was an official reception and a speech of welcome by the West German Vice-Chancellor. The Hitler years, the war, the crushing years of captivity in the Soviet Union were behind them. They were home, and they were free.

Wilhelm Mohnke returned to a greatly transformed Germany on 10 October 1955. Long afterwards he was to allow himself a brief public comment on his years in Russian imprisonment:

> Let me here make a personal, private remark. I was in Soviet captivity for more than ten years. I spent seven long years in interrogation. But I was never tortured or threatened. I am not a Communist in any sense of the word. Yet I certainly have no antipathy towards the Russians as a people. The racist part of the National Socialist creed never appealed to me.

It could be argued that Mohnke had served a long sentence for the crimes of the Nazi conspiracy in which he had played such a notable part. But he had served that sentence in the hands of a nation against which he had barely lifted a finger except in self-defence; and not as a punishment for war crimes but as a common fate shared by millions of other German soldiers who had had the misfortune to become prisoners of war of the

322

Russians. Where, then, did that leave him in relation to those nations who had once vainly sought his arrest for crimes against their people for which he was plainly and personally culpable? Had Mohnke expiated his crimes in Russia? Or was he truly at a new beginning?

Many of the Reich Chancellery Group who returned to Germany with Mohnke – former members of Hitler's entourage like Baur, Linge, Kempka and Günsche – adopted a high profile, gave press interviews, and took the earliest opportunity to burst into print about their sensational experiences at Hitler's court. The notable exception was Mohnke. Hitler's last general slipped away almost as soon as his wooden foot touched the miraculously re-paved soil of his West German Fatherland, and he went to ground and disappeared from view so effectively that not even old chums from the Leibstandarte, the Bunker and the Russian camps, such as Misch and Schenk, were able to discover his whereabouts.

It has been suggested that Mohnke was greatly helped by the protection afforded by the new West German secret intelligence organization, 'The Org', which was based at Dahlem and directed by Reinhard Gehlen, with undercover backing from the American CIA. Gehlen's organization went to great pains to debrief every single repatriated German prisoner in order to help develop a detailed panoramic intelligence profile of the Soviet Union as seen through their eyes. Mohnke, it was said, did a tit for tat deal with Gehlen on his return: he would give the low-down on the Russians in return for protection from the Canadians, the British, and the Americans. Whatever the facts of the matter, for Mohnke release from Russian captivity did not mark the end of the battle for survival. The trick now was to dodge the arrows of retribution aimed by his country's erstwhile enemies in the West.

Fortunately for Mohnke, those arrows took a long time coming.

323

PART IX

—

'A Nice Quiet Friendly Old Man'

1955–88

After his return to West Germany in 1955, Wilhelm Mohnke went to ground. Next to nothing was heard of him and his whereabouts were not known. His closest comrades never saw him and he did not even show up at the annual reunions of the old comrades association of the regiment he had helped to found and lived to command, the SS Leibstandarte. For years, hoping to evade any effort to investigate him for war crimes, he simply disappeared. When scholars and historians tried to make contact with him they met with a wall of silence. Thus Charles Messenger, a scrupulously objective English military historian who was writing a biography of Mohnke's one-time commanding officer, Sepp Dietrich, met with no response when he tried to approach Mohnke via the Leibstandarte Division's last commander, Otto Kumm. It is known that at some point Mohnke and his wife went to live in the vicinity of Hamburg. It is also known that he eventually rose to own a successful dealership in trailers and small trucks. But seventeen years were to pass before any foreigner picked up Mohnke's spoor again.

Then, in May 1972, an English clergyman, the Reverend Leslie Aitken, National Chaplain to the Dunkirk Veterans' Association, paid a visit to the village of Le Paradis, in northern France, in order to dedicate a memorial to the men of the Royal Norfolk Regiment who had been murdered there by the SS-Totenkopf in May 1940. It happened that at the time Aitken was visiting Le Paradis, two other Englishmen were visiting nearby Wormhoudt, where a large number of men of the Royal Warwickshire Regiment had been massacred by the SS Leibstandarte on the day after the atrocity at Le Paradis. One of these was William Cordrey, formerly of the Royal Warwicks, who had been taken prisoner by the SS at Wormhoudt in 1940 and lived to tell the tale. The other was his nephew, Douglas Cordrey, a London bus driver who had been collecting information on the Wormhoudt massacre for some while. It was from Douglas Cordrey, on his return from France, that Leslie Aitken first heard of the dreadful events at Wormhoudt. And it was then that the unmasking of Wilhelm Mohnke really began.

Douglas Cordrey gave Aitken the names of the handful of men known to have survived the massacre in the barn at Wormhoudt. Aitken then embarked on the painstaking task of tracing the men and putting together the pieces of the story. Charles Daley, John Lavelle and Alf Tombs were the first to be found during the early months of the search, and on 28 May 1973 – the thirty-third anniversary of the Wormhoudt massacre – all four were able to attend the unveiling of a memorial stone erected halfway along the road from Wormhoudt to Esquelbecq in memory of the men who died in the barn that had once stood a few fields away from the spot. Two thousand people attended the dedication conducted by the Reverend Aitken, including the Mayor of Esquelbecq and many of the citizens of Wormhoudt, and a large British contingent made up of members of branches of the Dunkirk Veterans' Association from all over the world, who were in France for the Annual Pilgrimage to Dunkirk. Thus the men who had fought and died in a rearguard action that helped ensure the safe evacuation of an entire army at last had a fitting memorial. The inscription read:

To the Glory of God
and in memory
of the men
of
The Royal Warwickshire Regiment
The Cheshire Regiment
and
The Royal Artillery
who, on 28 May 1940, were massacred
in a barn near this spot,
also of the men who were murdered as they were
being marched to the barn
'We will remember them'

Not long afterwards, Aitken found Reginald West and George Hall. With some difficulty he then tracked down Richard Parry, a retired vet living in the Lake District, and later George Hopper, and finally Jim Dutton, whose reward for his part in the rearguard battle to save the British Expeditionary Force, and for the traumas he suffered as a survivor of a mass murder, was abject poverty and homelessness. Most of these men bore the physical scars of their ordeal and all had to live every day with the unbearable memory of it. Bert Evans only had one arm and was scarred by bullet and shrapnel wounds. Charles Daley had an artificial leg, and he also bore, as Leslie Aitken put it, 'other scars'. Richard Parry still bore the scars of the bullet wound inflicted when an SS guard shot him through the face at point-blank range outside the barn. Alf Tombs and John Lavelle were in constant pain from their wounds. Many of the survivors had suffered for years from recurring nightmares about the horror in the barn atrocity. Because of their disabilities some of the men had difficulty finding suitable employment. Yet their disability pensions were derisory, and one of them had actually had his pension withdrawn. All were bemused at the fact that the crime of which they had been victims had been overlooked and forgotten by history and their country. Some of them found they were simply not believed, not even by their families, when they tried to tell the story of the barn murder. Most of the men were not looking for revenge, but they still hoped that one day justice would be done. This hardly seemed possible when there was not even a proper acknowledgement that a crime had been committed.

All this the Reverend Aitken valiantly set out to put right. He assisted with the welfare of the survivors and helped put a roof over Jim Dutton's head. He took down their stories and pieced them together with other material which he finally published as a book, *Massacre on the Road to Dunkirk*, in 1977. By this time it was fairly clear to Aitken, as it had been to the British war crimes investigators at the end of the war, that Wilhelm Mohnke held the clue to the cause of the massacre at Wormhoudt. But as far as Aitken could make out, Mohnke was generally believed to be either dead or living beyond the reach of British justice in East Germany. It was not until he attended a dinner at which several former Wehrmacht personnel were also present that Aitken discovered the truth. When he asked a former high-ranking German officer whether he had known Sepp Dietrich, the following revealing conversation took place:

> 'Yes,' the German officer replied, 'he was a remarkable man.'
> 'Did you ever meet Wilhelm Mohnke?' Aitken asked.
> 'I have only heard stories,' the officer said, 'but that is all.'
> 'I have heard and read,' Aitken went on, 'that he is in East Germany, or even dead.'
> 'Yes, that would be so,' the German commented, 'and I have heard that he is alive, and living in Lübeck – but that is quiet gossip!'

Aitken was intrigued and embarked on a prolonged correspondence with the State Prosecutor in Lübeck. If Mohnke was indeed alive, he asked, would it not be possible for him to be questioned about his alleged complicity in the massacre? In reply the State Prosecutor confirmed that Mohnke was alive, and even provided Aitken with his address near Hamburg; but he could not be persuaded that Mohnke had any case to answer. 'Your description of Mohnke as a suspected war criminal has not been proved,' the Prosecutor wrote in one letter. 'I can see no possibility of this complex question being further explained.' When Aitken pressed, the Prosecutor wrote again: 'Extensive investigations have been instituted. The accused Mohnke has denied the deed . . . Should it not be possible for you to name persons can make statements to the events in question, I have to discontinue the proceedings, because the existing means of proof are not enough.'

Having drawn a blank with the Germans, Aitken changed tack and loosed off a letter to the Canadians, whom he knew had at one time been interested in Mohnke's complicity in the murder of Canadian soldiers in Normandy in 1944. The letter, addressed to the famous 'Mounties' (Royal Canadian Mounted Police), sent the Canadian Judge Advocate General's office rummaging through its archives and gradually it determined that at the end of the war the Canadian war crimes investigators had indeed named Mohnke as a prime suspect in the murder of at least fifty-two Canadian soldiers in Normandy and had prepared a charge sheet against him on the basis of four separate incidents. However, when the No 1 Canadian War Crimes Investigation Unit was disbanded in June 1946, the Mohnke case was handed over to the British, who inadvertently allowed the key witness, a Polish SS man called Withold Stangenberg, to be repatriated to Poland. An internal memo dated June 1976 ended on a hopeful note. 'In 1946,' it read, 'the No 1 Canadian War Crimes Investigation Unit was prepared to bring Mohnke to trial if he and the Polish witness could be found. With the co-operation of the present Polish and German authorities, this might yet be done.'

This was perfectly true. Both Mohnke, the suspect, and Stangenberg, the witness, were at this time still alive; Mohnke's address was already known and Stangenberg's could easily have been found. But at a higher level of the Canadian government a more cautious note was sounded. The Deputy Minister for National Defence advised the Under-Secretary of State for External Affairs that 'there may be reasons why Canada may not wish at this point in time to be involved directly in the prosecution of war crimes.' Nevertheless, the Deputy Minister felt it would be remiss not to make the Canadian investigative documents available to the State Prosecutor in West Germany if he wished to make use of them. 'If it transpires that he does not wish to receive the documents,' the Deputy Defence Minister concluded, 'then a policy decision will have to be faced as to whether to press the German authorities to make a fuller investigation and to proceed to a prosecution.'*

To the Reverend Aitken the Department of National Defence wrote on 16 September 1976: 'The report of our investigation has been passed to the authorities concerned for any action that may be necessary.' For a long time Aitken heard nothing more. Then the outcome was unofficially leaked to him by the Canadian authorities: 'It is now almost two years since I handed in my report, and I know that it was forwarded to the appropriate authorities for action. Consequently, I assume that no action can be taken now for lack of witnesses.'

It seemed it was the end of the road in Canada too. To add insult to injury, the British authorities had also displayed a stunning degree of circumspection in their response to Leslie Aitken's endeavours to see justice done. When Aitken submitted the manuscript of his book to the Ministry of Defence for vetting, he was informed that while the Ministry had no objection to his describing the movements of the CO of the SS-Leibstandarte at Wormhoudt on the day of the massacre, they would rather no mention was made of the fact that he had spent the day hiding in a ditch, as this 'could cause resultant embarrassment to the individual, if he is still alive, or to his family.' Similarly, the Ministry had no objection to mentioning the name of one of the SS guards who had helped round up the prisoners, 'provided the name is not used in any derogatory sense.' This was freedom of information writ large, for the SS man in question had been killed in Russia all of thirty years ago. If the Ministry of Defence could entertain such delicate scruples over the feelings of an SS war criminal like Dietrich, who had been convicted by the Americans for the Malmédy massacre and by the West Germans for the Roehm murders, and had in any case been dead for ten years, there seemed little chance they would be inclined to endure the slightest impertinence regarding an unconvicted war criminal like Wilhelm Mohnke, who was still alive and kicking. At any rate, Aitken decided to remove the chapter from his book which indicted Mohnke for war crimes against British and Canadian prisoners of war, and in its place inserted a sentence implying that there was no proof that Mohnke had had anything to do with any of them.

* The West German Prosecutor never followed up the Canadian approach, never spoke to the Wormhoudt survivors whose identities had been made known by Aitken, never attempted to locate the Polish witnesses, never sought the British war crimes files, and, as far as we know, never interrogated any other SS men involved. This poses the question: if they did none of these things what *did* they do, and why were they so confident of their position when they dismissed Aitken's enquiry out of hand? As we shall see, this is a typical outcome. In many instances involving war crimes cases the West Germans have shown they lack the will, and also the legal facility, to proceed further.

As time passed, the Wormhoudt survivors – among them Jim Dutton, George Hall, John Lavelle, and Richard Parry – began to pass away; while Wilhelm Mohnke, confident perhaps that no evidence would ever be brought against him, began to appear more openly in society, albeit mainly old Nazi society. Though Mohnke had been wary of the Press as a result of some unfortunate post-war experiences, he surfaced in the early seventies to give an interview to the *Newsweek* Bureau Chief in Berlin, James O'Donnell, after a friend of O'Donnell, the Hamburg-based British journalist, Tom Agoston, had found Mohnke's name in a new issue of the Hamburg telephone directory. The interview was later incorporated into O'Donnell's account of the last days of Hitler, first published in Germany as *Die Katakombe* (*The Berlin Bunker*) in 1976.

Meanwhile Mohnke had made the acquaintance of another journalist, Gerd Heidemann, an obsessive and unscrupulous reporter from the German picture magazine *Stern*, which had its offices in Hamburg. In 1973 Heidemann had purchased a yacht, *Carin II*, which had once belonged to Reich Marshal Hermann Goering and for ten years after the war to the British Royal Family. Not long after Heidemann bought the boat he started an affair with Goering's daughter, Edda, who gave him much of the Goering memorabilia with which the yacht was furnished – Goering's dinner service, his drinking goblets, tea cups and ashtrays. Gradually, the possession of Goering's yacht and Goering's daughter drew the *Stern* reporter into a circle of former Nazis that included former SS General Karl Wolff, who had been Himmler's liaison officer with Hitler and the man who had negotiated the surrender of the German forces in Italy to the Allies, and – former SS General Wilhelm Mohnke. Mohnke had been introduced to Heidemann by another *Stern* reporter, and soon established a very friendly relationship with Heidemann. Mohnke was then about sixty-three years old, silver-haired, but still lithe and powerfully built, and looking (as someone who knew him at this time described him) 'as if he had just stepped out of a Hollywood war film.'

Before long Heidemann began to throw regular Third Reich parties on board his yacht, where Mohnke and Wolff were guests of honour and Goering's attractive daughter poured whisky for all the various friends and Nazis who came on board, including Hitler's ex-valet, Heinz Linge, and his favourite woman test pilot, Hanna Reitsch. 'We started to have long drinking evenings on board,' Heidemann recalled, 'with different people of quite different opinions talking to each other. I have always been a passionate reader of thrillers. Suddenly I was living a thriller.' Heidemann began reading all the books on the Third Reich he could lay his hands on. 'I wanted to be part of the conversation,' he said, 'not just sit and drink whisky.'

It was not long before he began taping the interesting conversations he was having with Mohnke, Wolff and the other Nazis about the old days, and especially about the supposed Odessa escape network to South America. In 1976 he signed a hefty contract for a book based on these taped reminiscences to be called *Bord Gespräche* (*Deck Conversations*) and sub-titled, 'Personalities from History Meet on Goering's Former Yacht *Carin II*'. Heidemann took to taking Mohnke and the others on sailing excursions up the Elbe or out to the North Sea island of Sylt. The champagne and caviar flowed, the tape recorder ran endlessly on, but the practical results of these sessions were for the most part worthless, just hours of rudderless tipsy ramblings about the old days. Moreover, after massive overdoses of the company of Hitler's former bunker retinue and SS generals like Mohnke and Wolff, it seemed that Heidemann was slowly turning into a Nazi himself. When he married for the third time in 1979 – not Edda Goering, but her best friend – SS Generals Mohnke and Wolff were the two witnesses at the wedding. When he went off with his new bride to look for Nazi fugitives in the South American jungle, it was General Wolff who accompanied the couple on their working honeymoon. Heidemann had hoped to find Martin Bormann and the Auschwitz doctor, Josef Mengele. Instead he found Walter Rauff, wanted for the murder of 97,000 Jewish women and children, and Klaus Barbie, the former Gestapo chief and 'Butcher of Lyons', with whom he quickly established friendly relations.

By this time Heidemann was disastrously deep in debt. The costs of keeping Goering's yacht cost him two-thirds of his monthly salary and he had lost a fortune purchasing a collection of letters between Churchill and Mussolini which turned out to be fakes. It was Mohnke who now intervened to help Heidemann. His intervention was to lead directly to the bizarre and sensational episode known as the 'Hitler Diaries Affair'. Mohnke suggested that Heidemann should get in touch with an ex-SS acquaintance of his, Jakob Tiefenthaeler, who had an extensive network of old Nazi contacts and Nazi memorabilia collectors and might be able to help sell his yacht for him. Following Mohnke's tip, Heidemann rang Tiefenthaeler, who worked on an American air base near Augsburg in Bavaria. Tiefenthaeler recalled:

> I'd known Mohnke for a long time. Heidemann said in his telephone conversation that Mohnke had told him that I might be able to find buyers for his yacht. I asked Heidemann to send me technical details and pictures of the ship and I said that I'd try to find somebody.

Tiefenthaeler worked hard at his task. He advertised the yacht for more than a million marks in the States and approached an Australian millionaire, a Persian Gulf oil sheikh, and an African tyrant, Idi Amin, who wanted the yacht to cruise around Lake Victoria. While the Bavarian SS man was following up these leads, Heidemann himself paid a visit to a wealthy German collector of Nazi memorabilia whom Tiefenthaeler thought might be interested in buying some of the Goering pieces that were kept on board the yacht. This man was Fritz Stiefel, of Waiblingen, near Stuttgart. Stiefel owned a fine collection of Nazi memorabilia which he housed on display in a large, windowless room protected by thick steel doors which bore the sign: BEWARE. HIGH VOLTAGE. DANGER TO LIFE. On 6 January 1980, as Heidemann was shown round this large private collection of Third Reich souvenirs, Stiefel handed him a black notebook with the initials AH inscribed on one corner of the cover. This, explained Stiefel, was a secret diary of Adolf Hitler. There were twenty-six other volumes like this one, he said. All of them had been retrieved from the wreckage of a plane that had crashed in East Germany while on a flight from Berlin in the last days of the war.

Heidemann was fatally hooked. He began to make enquiries. He visited the site of the plane crash and the graves of the crew. He contacted the source of the diaries, an East German-born con man, forger and collector of Nazi memorabilia by the name of Konrad Kujau (alias Konrad Fischer), who lived in Stuttgart and claimed the diaries were smuggled out to him by high-placed relatives in East Germany who had acquired them from villagers living near the plane crash site. And before long he had done a deal: in return for paying part of the proceeds to Kujau, he would sell the diaries to *Stern* in the scoop of the century.

A year to the day after he had first set eyes on the single Hitler diary, Heidemann met Wilhelm Mohnke again at the interment of Grand Admiral Karl Dönitz, Hitler's successor as leader of the Third Reich, then went back to Mohnke's house not far away to attend a small party Mohnke was giving to honour the passing of the late Nazi submariner and head of state. 'It was on this occasion,' Mohnke recalled, 'that Herr Heidemann told us for the first time that there were supposed to be Hitler diaries. That was thought by the people there to be impossible.' Two of Hitler's former adjutants who were at Mohnke's party – Richard Schulze-Kossens and Otto Günsche, who had accompanied Mohnke into Soviet captivity after the war – were highly sceptical that Hitler would ever have had the time to keep a personal diary. But Heidemann was not to be put off. Three weeks later he sold the twenty-seven Hitler diaries to *Stern*'s publishers for the mighty sum of 85,000 DM each, or 2,295,000 DM the lot (worth £733,226 at the present rate of exchange of 3.13 DM to the sterling pound). This marked the formal beginning of the process by which the publishing scoop of the decade was to become the hoax of the century.

Mohnke continued to doubt the veracity of the Hitler diaries, however. In the spring of 1981, when Heidemann had acquired the first three diaries, he rang up Mohnke to tell him that he had found references to the SS Leibstandarte Adolf Hitler in them, and even things about Mohnke himself. When Mohnke arrived at Heidemann's flat, he was shown the relevant entries but could not decipher the crabbed, old-fashioned handwriting, so Heidemann read them out loud to him:

15 March 1933: Visit of the specially chosen men, and the plans for the new *Standarte* of the SS in Lichterfelde. These SS *Standarte* carry my name.

17 March 1933: From today an SS *Standarte* is in place in Lichterfelde. As from now all the relevant security measures will be taken by these people. These people are particularly good National Socialists. The *Standarte* are now carrying my name and are sworn in to me.

18 March 1933: Visit to the Leibstandarte. They are very fine men. Stayed up talking to members of the Cabinet until very late at night.

Apart from being very banal, these entries were also very wrong, as Mohnke bluntly informed Heidemann, Mohnke recalled:

I said to Herr Heidemann that several things in these diaries were simply not true. First, the SS *Standarte* never had their barracks in Lichterfelde. I belonged to that troop and in March and April we were in the Friesenstrasse, in the police barracks. Secondly, at that time this troop of men did not have the name *Leibstandarte*. Thirdly, the entry for 18 March 1933 was false: Adolf Hitler never visited the troop in the Friesenstrasse.

But Heidemann was as a man possessed. 'Perhaps,' he told Mohnke, 'Adolf Hitler *planned* all that and was putting his thoughts down on paper.' So the circus went on, and Heidemann, now charging 100,000 DM per diary, had gone from beggar to rich man. He talked of buying Hitler's boyhood house in Leonding, Austria. He began to purchase vast quantities of Nazi memorabilia from the same person who was actually dispensing the Hitler diaries in instalments – Konrad Kujau. One of the items was a palpable fake – a Belgian FN pistol with which it was claimed Hitler had shot himself in the Bunker. When Heidemann showed the pistol to Mohnke and Günsche they were aghast, for they both knew that the pistol Hitler had used was a much bigger calibre Walther 7.65 mm. Günsche was especially well qualified to pass judgement, for it was he who had picked the weapon up from the floor after it had fallen from the dead Führer's hands. But his censure was in vain.

By the spring of 1983, when the complete set of Hitler diaries – now numbering more than sixty volumes – were launched on the world, the affair had become a sensation. On 25 April *Stern* published the first instalment in a massive two and a quarter million edition. All seemed to be going to plan. But all was not. At a press conference to launch the diaries in the *Stern* canteen that morning grave doubts were expressed by expert witnesses as to the authenticity of the diaries. An eminent British historian, Lord Dacre – better known as Hugh Trevor-Roper, the man who first revealed Hitler's fate to the world in his book *The Last Days of Hitler* – withdrew the authentication of the diaries he had given in a blaze of publicity only a week before. Another British historian of the Hitler period, the author David Irving, seized the microphone and yelled: 'I know the collection where these diaries come from. It is an old collection, full of forgeries.' Had anyone thought of having the ink tested for age, Irving asked before his microphone was switched off by *Stern* executives. 'Ink! Ink!' cried the assembled journalists. 'Torpedo running,' Irving muttered as he resumed his seat. The publishing coup had turned into a publishing disaster almost at the very moment of its launch. It was the height of irony that two men who sat not far away from each other at the chaotic press conference, but failed to recognize each other, were General Wilhelm Mohnke and Antony Terry of the London *Sunday Times*, a former British war crimes interrogator from the London Cage who thirty-seven years ago had helped investigate Mohnke's part in the Wormhoudt massacre.

Within a fortnight the hoax – the biggest fraud in publishing history – was blown. Government forensic tests proved conclusively that the diaries were fakes. Kujau, who had committed the forgeries, fled. Heidemann, still naïvely believing to the very end that at least some of the diaries were genuine, was fired by his magazine and his yacht was impounded. In August 1984 the two men were put on trial. Heidemann was accused of stealing 1.7 of the 9.3 million DM handed over by *Stern* for the diaries; Kujau of stealing 1.5 million DM. Both were found guilty and sentenced to more than four years imprisonment each. 5 million DM of *Stern*'s money – worth £1,597,444 in English money – was unaccounted for. It still is.

———

This spectacular fraud in West Germany had left Mohnke exposed to public view but, though he was in a sense a fugitive war criminal, it had left him unharmed. It required a far more minor affair in Great Britain, barely a storm in a teacup by comparison, to leave the former SS general in grave peril. This was the affair of the Regimental POW Fund.

The matter began when one of the survivors of the Wormhoudt massacre, Reginald West, got to hear of a benevolent fund set up towards the end of the war to help ex-POWs of the Royal Warwickshire Regiment who were in financial need. West was an ex-POW and an old age pensioner with hardly a penny to bless his name and therefore felt he qualified for a little assistance from his old Regiment. But the Regimental Association which administered the POW Fund did not agree. Perplexed, West wrote back to ask whether anyone was receiving benefits from the Fund, for he knew of many ex-soldiers in need who received nothing, and most had never even heard of the Fund. In September 1975 the Regimental Association wrote back to West to say that in fact they had paid out £1,000 in grants in the previous year – and also £850 'for other Association activities'. West rightly smelled a rat. Who had been the beneficiaries of the £1,000? And what were those other activities which had benefited almost as much? He went to his local solicitors who fired off a letter demanding an explanation from the Regimental Association. The reply, from the Association's solicitors, was less than forthcoming. Information as to who benefited from the £1,000 was confidential and so could not be revealed. The £850 went towards some of the costs of running the Association and paying for its reunions and other functions. West's solicitors commented indignantly:

> Frankly, I can find no justification for this expenditure [i.e. the £850] in the terms of the Charity Commission scheme . . . I am prepared to say that it is disgraceful that such a trickle of benefit should be applied out of a fund which has grown to such proportions while those for whom it was originally set up receive virtually nothing.

An enquiry as to the terms of the Charity Commission scheme revealed further dismal news. In 1956, for some reason, the trustees had seen fit to extend the parameters for the Fund, and under the existing conditions of benefit it seemed very likely that the Fund would be kept going for many more years to come, with a small trickle of benefit going to the old soldiers of the 1939–45 war, who may or may not have been prisoners of war, and the greater part going to officers and men who may never have served during the Second World War or have been prisoners of war at all. West's solicitor rightly commented: 'I cannot think this was the intention of those who contributed to the original funds for the benefit of prisoners of war.'

In May 1976 the Regimental Association informed Reg West that he was not considered to be in need of financial assistance and that a grant could not be approved. Outraged, West next wrote to his MP, Jeff Rooker, who was the Labour parliamentary representative for Perry Barr, Birmingham. West pointed out that as a former POW from the 2nd Battalion The Royal Warwickshire Regiment, seventy years of age and living on an old age pension of £21.78 with his wife, he imagined he would have been entitled to a grant from the POW Fund to subsidize his income. But though the credit balance of the POW Fund now stood at £33,333, he had been turned down.

'Surely, sir,' West wrote, 'if the money was contributed by individuals for the purpose of distribution to ex-POWs and had risen to the aforesaid total, it is entirely wrong for the Committee to hold on to this money, especially as the Regiment has been disbanded. The matter affects not only myself but a number of men I know who have also been POWs and members of the 2nd Battalion The Royal Warwickshire Regiment and are badly in need of financial assistance.'

Jeff Rooker at once took up cudgels on his constituent's behalf. He found that the capital of the POW Fund was actually increasing because the income was not being fully spent, and that the Regimental Association had made little or no effort to find old soldiers in need who could benefit from the Fund. One of these old soldiers was Jim Dutton, a survivor of the barn massacre, who was homeless and had to spend his nights in derelict buildings. Dutton had not received a penny from the Fund. It was beginning to seem that the administrators of the POW Fund were more concerned about keeping the Fund intact than distributing it to ex-POWs who were entitled to benefits. In May 1977 the *Birmingham Post* took up the cause, followed by the *Birmingham Evening Mail* with a news story headed 'WAR VETERANS' FUND LYING IDLE'. The POW Fund now stood at £41,000, the paper reported, but no effort had been made to trace ex-POWs and pay them. The paper quoted Reg West as saying: 'The money should be shared out among the few ex-POWs who are still alive.' Another Wormhoudt massacre survivor, George Hall, was quoted as saying: 'I didn't know about the Fund till a few months ago. I am not asking for charity but we must be entitled to this money.' As a result of the publicity provided by this article, Jeff Rooker was able to send Lt-Col. M. Ryan, OBE, the then Regimental Secretary of the Royal Warwickshire Regimental Association, a list of twenty-one people who felt they were entitled to claim on the Fund. Another ex-POW spoke for them all when he wrote:

> I consider that anyone who has suffered the indignity of being a prisoner of war for (in my case) four and a half years has suffered sufficiently to justify payment from these Funds. It makes me sad to think that after all these years many of my comrades will most probably never benefit from this fund. Many will have passed away not knowing about this matter. How one can hold on for so many years to a Fund that was meant to help

338

us POWs when we returned home (and believe me 4,000 of us were in need especially then) is beyond my understanding.

The Fund continued to behave in a way that was beyond everybody's understanding. Alf Tombs, a survivor of the barn massacre who was in constant pain from his wounds, applied for a grant and was told that he did not qualify as being in financial need. Of the twenty-one people whose names had been forwarded to the Regimental Association by Jeff Rooker, only seven qualified for grants amounting to an average of £31 each – or £220 *in toto* out of a kitty with £41,000 in it at that time. In 1980, when the Fund appreciated by £25,000, as well as providing an income of £3,500, all the ex-soldiers and widows received as the year's handout was a princely £10 at Christmas. It was small consolation when the Charity Commission, after a long and complex inquiry, concluded that the Regimental Association had wrongly used the POW Fund of £2,631 to pay for such general purpose expenses as regimental reunions, Christmas parties, wreaths for the dead and a donation towards Lord Montgomery's funeral. But according to one of Jeff Rooker's informants, who had fought with the 2nd Royal Warwicks at Wormhoudt and in Burma, and whose family had seen service in the Regiment since 1896, the misdirection of funds was on an even wider scale. In November 1981 he wrote to Rooker:

> The Regiment has a very busy annual calendar comprising Normandy Day, Officers' Reunion Dinner, Other Ranks' Reunion Dinner, Colour Day, Armistice Sunday, Albert Hall, etc. These get-togethers are endless. . . . It is time to halt this lunacy and send the money where it is needed most – men crippled by war, unemployed, with lost homes, lost wives. Men like Nicholls, whose sister had no money to bury him with when he died; Sawyer, eighteen years of service, no pension: Trevis, no job and no home; Evans, survivor from the barn murders, arm blown off; Lavelle, Tombs, Daley, all survivors from the barn murders . . . I am a pensioner, aged seventy-one years. My wife passed away in September 1980 with terminal cancer. The cost of the cremation was £400 and my pension dropped immediately to £40. I sent the relevant papers to the Regimental Association in Warwick in the hope of some reimbursement for my very slender saving account – I have yet to bury myself. All I received from Warwick was a very polite brush-off and told to go somewhere else. My return reply takes no stretch of the imagination

339

– I told them that I had hung their letter up in an Irish bricklayer's bog.

By now the POW Fund had doubled in five years and stood at over £100,000. Jeff Rooker, frustrated by the downright incongruity of it all, was almost helpless. He had asked a question in the House. He had badgered the Minister of Defence. He had got the London *Sunday Express* to take up the story. But he was helpless to do more. As the years went by the Fund increased by leaps and bounds while death took its toll of the ageing people who were most eligible to benefit from it. By the beginning of 1988 the Fund was worth £234,000, but it still played hard to get. Reg West, Wormhoudt massacre survivor, now aged eighty-two and living on a pittance, was turned down yet again, though the Regimental Association relented a little later and finally agreed to meet the costs of the veteran POW's coal bill. No doubt this change of heart had nothing to do with all the Press publicity the Regimental Association was receiving at the time.

How could this curious state of affairs be allowed to continue? Unfortunately, due to the vagaries of the regulations governing charities in the United Kingdom, organizations like the Warwicks' POW Fund are able to operate without public scrutiny and without proper accountability, for all the world like a left-over relic from the Victorian age. The Warwicks' POW Fund is not the only Fund of this kind that has failed to meet the purposes for which it was set up. A more painful example is that of the Far Eastern Prisoners of War Fund, which at one time totalled £4,816,473, and from which British citizens who had been POWs in Japanese hands received a princely compensation of £76.50 each, or £48.50 if they had been civilian internees.

———

While one of the dwindling band of Wormhoudt massacre survivors was managing, more than forty years after the end of the war, to screw the price of a few bags of domestic coal out of a regimental benevolent fund with nearly a quarter of a million pounds in its kitty, the perpetrator of the Wormhoudt massacre was enjoying a life of comfort and ease on a Waffen-SS veteran's pension of £20,000 a year. But the injustice of the relative life situations of Reginald West and Wilhelm Mohnke, and the outrageous treatment meted out to British war veterans – wounded former front-line fighters, ex-POWs and victims of Nazi atrocities at that – is not the only point to this sorry tale of the Royal Warwickshire Regimental Association POW Fund. For it was the POW Fund which was to lead, by a series of coincidences, to the beginning of a new British initiative in the implemen-

340

tation of justice in the Mohnke case, and eventually to this present book. This is what happened.

Early in 1988, Ian Sayer, a life-long student of Nazi history and the Second World War, launched a new magazine called *World War II Investigator*, which was intended as a vehicle for little-known aspects of the war and for some of the remarkable wartime stories contained in Sayer's own extensive documents archive. While researching one of these stories – the Albanian gold mystery – Sayer had occasion to visit the Westminster office of Jeff Rooker, MP, who took the opportunity to show Sayer the file on the nagging and unsatisfactory matter of the Warwicks' POW Fund. Leafing through the file, Sayer came across a press clipping about an SS officer involved in a massacre of Royal Warwickshire POWs. He asked Rooker to send him a copy of the file, but when it came the clipping was missing, and it did not finally reach him until March 1988.

Sayer was now able to read the clipping, from *Weekend* magazine, with closer attention, and quickly realized that the SS officer who was mentioned in it was the same SS officer that Tom Agoston, the Hamburg-based journalist, had told him in 1981 he had introduced to James O'Donnell when he was writing his book *Die Katakombe*. Sayer immediately rang Agoston, who told him that Mohnke had moved house but was able to provide his new address and telephone number. Sayer then conducted preliminary research into Mohnke's wartime activities. He looked out documents. He tracked down Wormhoudt survivors like Reginald West and war crimes investigators like Bunny Pantcheff. Soon he discovered that Mohnke had been implicated in three major massacres of unarmed POWs and civilians – the first time anyone had connected Mohnke with all three atrocities. It seemed extraordinary that a major war criminal, wanted for war crimes by the British, Canadian and American governments, and listed as wanted by the United Nations War Crimes Commission, should still be at large in West Germany. At the very least the British government ought to be stirred into action over the case.

At the press launch of the new magazine at London's Savoy Hotel on 24 March 1988, Sayer spoke to Gary Curtis of TV-AM about the Mohnke affair. TV-AM were to remain closely interested in developments from that point forward. The investigative TV programme, *World in Action*, sent one of their producers to check out Mohnke's whereabouts in the Hamburg area, and on his return he confirmed that Mohnke was indeed living at the address Sayer had given him. Armed with that confirmation, Sayer then arranged with Jeff Rooker for a question about the Wormhoudt massacre to be asked in the House of Commons and for Mohnke to be specifically named for his part in the murder of British POWs in France in 1940. At 2.54 p.m. on Thursday, 21 April 1988, Rooker got to his feet and put his question to Douglas Hurd, the Home

341

Secretary – the first top-level acknowledgement that Mohnke had a case to answer in Britain.

Moments after raising the question in the House, a secret investigative file on the Wormhoudt case prepared by the British War Crimes Interrogation Unit was handed to Jeff Rooker. This had been obtained through Peter Mitchell, of the *Coventry Evening Telegraph*, who had been keenly interested in the Wormhoudt case and continued to be so as the story developed. This was a major step in unravelling the Wormhoudt atrocity, for strictly speaking the file was still classified and unavailable for public scrutiny until the year 2021; but in the interests of justice this copy had been forwarded by a former member of the original war crimes investigative team at the London Cage, Richard Richter. Rooker and Sayer agreed that in the public interest the file should be published immediately, and that a Trust Fund for the Wormhoudt massacre survivors should be set up into which a portion of any profits from any publications relating to the Mohnke case should be paid.

By now the press campaign had begun to steamroll. The London *Daily Express* had led the pack by splashing the story on its front page for two days running, together with a major feature inside. 'NAZI KILLER NAMED BY MP,' proclaimed the *Express*'s banner headlines. 'FACE TO FACE WITH HITLER HENCHMAN.' On 24 April the London *Sunday Times* ran a major story on the Mohnke case and the secret Wormhoudt file on their front page, for which they made a four-figure contribution to the Survivors' Fund. The London *Star* did not mince its words or stint its headlines: 'SECRET OF THE NAZI BUTCHER', ran one; 'NAZI SWINE', ran another; 'I'D SHOOT THE BASTARD', ran a third. Every British national newspaper – *The Times*, *Telegraph*, *Independent*, *Mirror*, *Standard* – printed major stories about the affair and both BBC TV News and Independent Television News ran the story as a major news item. Meanwhile, TV-AM ran a question-and-answer feature on their breakfast programme, in which Ian Sayer took part, and Central TV produced a 30-minute documentary on the Wormhoudt massacre in a series called *The Cook Report*, which in spite of some inaccuracies brought the horror home to an even wider audience. Before long the Wormhoudt survivors received their first cheques from the newly founded Survivors' Trust Fund – for sums already forty or fifty times greater than the typical annual hand-out to eligible recipients of the Royal Warwickshires' POW Fund.

The ripples from the affair were spreading wider. All the wire services and the provincial press took up the case. The media began their own enquiries. So heavy were their demands on the services of the Public Record Office at Kew that the Press Office was forced to telephone Ian Sayer and ask him for help in locating the relevant records. TV-AM, in a brilliant 24-hour sleuthing stint, discovered the whereabouts in Poland of the missing witness in the Canadian POW murder case, Withold Stangenberg, thus proving that if the Canadian and British war crimes investigators had been more wholehearted about the case they too could have located the same key witness, thereby helping to reinforce his original statement and identify Mohnke. Sadly, however, Stangenberg had died only a few years previously.

By now the German Press had picked up the scent from the British papers, and, no doubt to Wilhelm Mohnke's extreme discomfiture, advised their German readership that Hitler's last general was wanted by the British to answer war crimes charges. On 21 April Mohnke told the *Hamburger-Abendblatt*: 'We were in combat and of course we took prisoners. But when they had laid down their arms, then the fighting was over for them. We live with an easy conscience.' On 22 April Wilhelm Mohnke pleaded innocence in the mass-circulation Hamburg newspaper, *Bild*, in an interview headlined: 'THE ENGLISH HUNT DOWN HITLER'S LAST GENERAL.' 'I have never concealed a thing,' he told the paper, 'unlike Waldheim. I was in Dunkirk, it's true. But what kind of beasts must they have been to slaughter prisoners of war with bayonets and so on? That is an appalling crime.' Mohnke's sixty-three-year-old wife told the *Bild-Zeitung*: 'Infamous lies. My husband wants to to be left in peace. He is seventy-seven years old.' And a neighbour commented: 'A nice quiet friendly old man. Why can't he be left in peace?' On 2 May *Die Welt* published extracts from a letter from Reginald West couriered to the Public Prosecutor in Lübeck requesting that he re-open their investigation into Mohnke's involvement in the Wormhoudt massacre.

On the other side of the Atlantic, both the Canadians and the Americans were made aware of their countries' interests in Mohnke's wartime activities. The *Ottawa Citizen* in Canada and the *Washington Times* in the States gave the story a new airing and on 12 May a question on the Normandy killings was tabled in the Canadian Parliament by MP Robert Kaplan – though the Canadian Justice Minister appeared to duck the issue by replying that Canada would be willing to co-operate with the British authorities in the pursuit of justice, rather than initiate an investigation of their own.

The campaign to re-open the Mohnke case, led by Jeff Rooker, MP, and Ian Sayer, now had the united support of the House of Commons, the entire British media, the powerful All-Party War Crimes Group, the Association of Jewish Ex-Service Men and Women (AJEX), the British Legion, the American Legion (the US servicemen's veterans organization) and the distinguished London lawyer, Sir David Napley, who agreed to assist with free legal advice. But there were strange lapses of interest, and neither the Americans nor the Belgians, who had both lost several hundred

343

of their citizens as a result of the actions taken by SS units under Wilhelm Mohnke's command, showed much inclination to set the process of justice in motion. But a major step forward was taken in Britain when Roger Freeman, Parliamentary Under-Secretary of State at the Ministry of Defence, made an important reply to a second question tabled in the House by Jeff Rooker on 28 June 1988. Freeman's reply was a model of its kind – well-researched, balanced and eloquent – and after a résumé of the case based on an examination of the investigative papers held by the Judge Advocate General, he concluded with these memorable words, which we have quoted once already in this book and will quote again:

> The Wormhoudt massacre was a sordid, brutal and dishonourable event in a bloody war, and the British government will do their part to facilitate justice.

Though there were certain aspects of Freeman's statement with which we would now cavil – for example, that there did not appear to be any firm evidence with which to indict Mohnke, which we would contend is simply not true – it did commit the British government to taking the matter to a further stage. In practice, this meant leaning on the West German authorities to re-open the case and look long and hard at the evidence so far developed. This is what the Germans did indeed do, and what, at the time of writing, they are still doing now. In the course of their enquiries they naturally required Mohnke himself to present himself before them, a shock to his system so great that in the autumn of 1988 he suffered a mild heart attack and had to be taken away to hospital. From an American government agency it was also learnt that Mohnke had been placed on the American Watch List, which meant that he was barred from entering the United States of America, like another suspect figure from the Nazi period, the Austrian President, Kurt Waldheim.

The net was certainly closing in on Mohnke. As this book has shown, he has a great deal to answer for. But *will* he be bought to trial? *Can* he be brought to trial? Indeed, some people will ask, *should* he be brought to trial?

344

PART X

Hitler's Last General – The Summing Up

1989

We have gone to considerable pains to chronicle the wartime activities of SS General Wilhelm Mohnke and to show that a number of prima facie war crimes cases are still outstanding against him. Briefly summarized, the charges are:

Complicity as Battalion Commander in the SS Leibstandarte Regiment Adolf Hitler in the murder of between 80 and 90 unarmed British POWs at Wormhoudt, France, on 28 May 1940.

Complicity as Regimental Commander in the 12th SS Panzer Division Hitler Jugend in the murder of 35 unarmed Canadian POWs near Fontenay-Le-Pesnil, Normandy, on 8 June 1944 (the 'Canadian massacre'); the murder of 6 Canadian POWs at Le Mesnil-Patry, Normandy, on 7–11 June 1944 (the 'First Aid Post killings'); the murder of 5 Canadian POWs at Les Saullets, Normandy, on 11 June 1944; the murder of 3 Canadian POWs near Haut du Bosq, Normandy, on 11 June 1944 on Mohnke's direct orders (the 'Stangenberg case').

Complicity as Divisional Commander of the SS Leibstandarte Division Adolf Hitler in the murder of several hundred unarmed American POWs and defenceless Belgian civilians in the Ardennes, Belgium, between 19 December 1944 and early January 1945, and specifically the issuing of a direct order to execute all male civilians over the age of 16 at Wanne on 20–21 December 1944.

Suspected complicity in the deaths of fellow Germans as a result of the *Standgerichte* (flying courts) set up on his orders in the final stages of the battle for Berlin in April–May 1945.

As a result of these crimes, Mohnke is still on the wanted lists of the British,

Canadian and American governments and of the United Nations War Crimes Commission. But it is one thing being on a wanted list; it is an entirely different matter being the subject of an on-going prosecution. When Mohnke returned from Soviet captivity in 1955 the Allies appeared to have lost interest in war crimes cases such as his. In recent years, however, the Allied governments with the greatest residual involvement in Mohnke's wartime activities have set up new machinery for the processing of war crimes cases.

In March 1979 the Americans established a special unit within the Justice Department whose only function was to investigate war crimes. This was the OSI, or Office of Special Investigations, the present director of which is Neal Sher. The OSI is a dedicated team, and will continue its job, as Sher put it recently, 'as long as anyone accused of Nazi war crimes is alive and living in the United States.' The OSI's determination to settle old scores with Nazi butchers who had immigrated into the United States resulted in its most publicized scalp to date when in 1986 a Ukrainian-born naturalized American by the name of John Demjanjuk was deported to Israel as a war criminal suspected of being the sadistic guard known as 'Ivan the Terrible' who ran the gas ovens at Treblinka extermination camp. At his highly sensational but controversial trial in 1988, Demjanjuk was found guilty of atrocious crimes in the extermination camps and sentenced to death.

All this was in great contrast to the war crimes record of the Canadian authorities who in the first forty years following the end of the Second World War demonstrated a notably half-hearted attitude towards war criminals who had immigrated to their country, and for reasons of political expediency actually obstructed investigations into their Nazi past. Even former Prime Ministers came down on the war criminals' side, by helping one of the most vicious of them to get away, and by blocking all attempts to bring proceedings against suspects.

Recently, however, the Canadians have put their house in better order by establishing the Federal War Crimes Unit under a Deputy Justice Minister and enacting legislation to prosecute war criminals and perpetrators of crimes against humanity. Theoretically at least, the Canadians can now try and imprison war criminals found on Canadian soil – though in practice it is doubtful, given the expected filibustering in the courts, that any tangible results will be seen within the next five years, if ever.

As far as Wilhelm Mohnke is concerned, however, the new look in Canada and the United States is unlikely to lead directly to investigation or prosecution. The Americans can only *deport* war criminals and have no authority to prosecute any foreign Nazi war criminal if the crimes were not committed in the USA. The Canadians can only try war criminals found in Canadian territory. Neither can *extradite* a war criminal from West Germany for trial in either the United States or Canada. The most they could

348

do to expedite Mohnke's prosecution would be to exert pressure on the West German prosecutor and offer to make documentary evidence available to him should he wish to receive it.

The British are in much the same position as their North American allies. No possibility currently exists of bringing Mohnke to Britain to stand trial. In fact, after the phasing out of the War Crimes Interrogation Unit at the London Cage in 1948, the British never had an organization specifically tailored to investigate Nazi war criminals, either in Britain or abroad, and British law contains no provision for the prosecution of a crime committed outside territory under British jurisdiction. However, events began to move quickly when in 1986 it was discovered that a number of ex-Nazis suspected of appalling crimes had found asylum in the United Kingdom after the war. The All-Party War Crimes Group was formed later in the year with the purpose of bringing war criminals in Britain to justice, and in 1987 the Home Secretary indicated that the government might be prepared to consider changing the law to enable the prosecution in Britain of crimes committed outside of Britain during the Second World War – more specifically by former SS men who had become naturalized Britons. Theoretically, such a new law could have a bearing on the Mohnke case. But in practice the chances of the West Germans agreeing to the extradition of Mohnke to Britain are virtually nil. In this case, as in so many others, the West Germans hold virtually all the cards.

Since 1949 the West German courts have been the principal place to which those seeking to bring war criminals to justice have had to turn. Germany's record for bringing such criminals to trial has not proved an impressive one, however. The country's legal system is complicated and legal matters are conducted with an unusual adherence to the letter of the law. A leading American war crimes prosecutor described his sense of frustration when dealing with the West Germans in these terms:

> The West Germans are our friends, and the State Department frowns on anything negative we have to say about them. And we have to work closely with them quite often in developing information on cases and in running investigations, and they have been and continue to be very helpful in that area. But you have to believe *they will go to almost any length to avoid directly prosecuting a war criminal*. They desperately want to put all this behind them, and every time they prosecute it opens old wounds. You have to believe they all but designed their legal system to avoid the problem.

An analysis of the statistics shows the extent of the problem. Since the end of the Second World War, 91,160 suspected war criminals have been investigated by the West German authorities. A relatively small proportion of these suspects were actually brought to trial, of whom 6,482 were convicted, 12 being sentenced to death, 160 to life imprisonment, and the remainder to shorter sentences, the average time served being less than four years. West Germany's post-war record looks even less satisfactory when one considers that 75 per cent of trials resulted from indictments brought when the courts were under the control of the Allied Occupation, and even at that time only a hundred or so involved serious crimes such as murder, and only fifteen involved concentration camp killings. Reviewing these figures, the head of the German-based Association of Victims of Nazi Persecution, Karl Eerlebeck, commented: 'It just points up an extraordinarily indifferent attitude towards old Nazis.' And Simon Wiesenthal went on record as saying: 'We have just scratched the surface. The majority of former Nazis who committed serious crimes are still free.' One of them, of course, being Wilhelm Mohnke.

The fact remains that the West Germans have persistently failed to convict the most barbarous war criminals, even when the evidence against them, by the legal standards of any other civilized nation, was overwhelming. They have also persistently failed to prosecute suspected war criminals on the grounds of insufficient documentary and other evidence, even when such evidence could be readily made available to them. And they have persistently failed to take action against war criminals deported from other countries, who have thus been gratified to find that the country which had been the very fountain-head of Nazism and the Holocaust was a Valhalla on earth where even monsters and murderers could rest their bones in peace and ease. We have to ask: *is this the nation to which the British, Canadian and American governments propose to direct their requests for justice to be done against persons who have committed terrible crimes against the citizens of their own countries?*

It is not simply the legal system and the State Prosecutors that make such heavy weather of war crimes cases. The West German public and the West German government, all the way up to the Chancellor, Helmut Kohl, display an equal distaste for bringing old Nazis to justice. Today an increasing number of West Germans, especially the younger ones, evince a desire to turn their back on the past and put the Nazi era behind them. This prevailing mood was dramatically expressed at the forty-fourth session of the United Nations Commission on Human Rights in March 1988, when Helmut Kohl and the West German government bitterly opposed a motion entitled 'Prosecution and Punishment of All War Criminals and Persons Who Have Committed Crimes Against Humanity.' The resolution was adopted by an overwhelming majority vote which served notice on the Germans that if they intended to banish Nazi atrocities and the Holocaust to the wastebin of history they would bring on themselves worldwide condemnation. The resolution condemned recent attempts to deny the facts of Nazi genocide, commended those countries which had prosecuted war criminals with vigour, pointed out that most war criminals were still at large in UN member nations, and urged all nations to take measures to ensure full co-operation 'for the purpose of securing, preferably in the place where they committed the deed, the prosecution and just punishment of those who had committed war crimes and crimes against humanity.'

Although the complex legal mechanism in West Germany is admirably tooled to snarl up the process of war criminal prosecutions, if so desired, the wheels do sometimes turn and a war criminal is sometimes convicted by the courts where the blaze of international publicity makes it politically inadvisable to sabotage the justice process. Notable instances of war criminals deported to Germany and successfully convicted include Fritz Stangl, the commandant of the Treblinka death camp, who was extradited to West Germany and sentenced to life imprisonment in 1973; and Hermine Braunstein, a singularly sadistic female guard at several of the death camps in Poland. In 1973 Braunstein was deported from the United States, where she had married an American citizen and become a naturalized American, and after a trial lasting all of six years she was sentenced to life imprisonment. Recently a former Auschwitz guard caused a sensation in Germany by escaping from the court where he was on trial for multiple murder. At the time of writing he is still at large, pursued by a posse of police in a manhunt such as the Federal Republic has not seen for many a year. But if the Germans can pursue a suspect guard with such zeal, why, we must ask, could they not have shown a little more dedication in the case of Wilhelm Mohnke?

So how could the British, Canadian or American governments get round the West German problem, if they had a mind to? One stab at a solution came from Sir David Napley, the Wormhoudt survivors' legal representative, who in June 1988 expressed the view that it might be possible to extradite Mohnke out of West German hands by reconvening the Nuremberg Tribunal in Berlin. However, this view was scotched somewhat by a former prosecutor on the UN War Crimes Commission Colonel Professor Gerald Draper, who wrote in a letter to the London *Times*:

> The International Military Tribunal which sat at Nuremberg was set up and constituted by the four-Power London agreement of 8 August 1945. A 'reconvening' of that tribunal would require the consent of the four Powers concerned, namely France, the United Kingdom, the United States of America and Russia. Further, it is more than possible that such rights and responsibilities as those four Powers have retained are so ves-

tigial and nominal that they would not support the exercise of any war crimes jurisdiction by those Powers in Berlin . . .

By the London agreement of 1945 the four signatories agreed to establish an international military tribunal for one purpose only, namely, to try the major war criminals of the European Axis whose offences have no peculiar geographical location. The crimes alleged against the former SS officer Mohnke have very specific locations, namely, Wormhoudt, in 1940, and Malmédy, in 1944.

The SS Leibstandarte Adolf Hitler Division, in which Mohnke served as a commander, had a very odious reputation on both the eastern and western fronts and the specific locations of its gross crimes have been written in the annals of infamy.

I do not think that Sir David's views will stand up to legal challenge. The German Federal Republic has jurisdiction – and the suspect.

In fact, the idea of setting up some kind of international tribunal to try war crimes cases where judicial proceedings are restricted by the laws of the nation involved is still being bandied about in the United Nations. But though a tribunal would solve many problems – not least, perhaps, the stranglehold which the West Germans exercise over the majority of war crimes cases still pending – it seems unlikely that it could be constituted before the last crop of Nazi barbarians went the way of all flesh. A few years ago the most vicious of the war criminals known to be alive and to have escaped punishment – Eichmann's number two, Aloïs Brunner – told German reporters that he would be prepared to 'stand trial before an international tribunal, but not go to Israel.' He was on safe ground here, for as he knew, no such tribunal exists and probably it never will.

We have attempted to address ourselves to the questions: *can* Mohnke be prosecuted, and *will* Mohnke be prosecuted? We now turn to the question: *should* Mohnke be prosecuted? A broad spectrum of man-in-the-street opinion believes that, whatever war crimes Mohnke may have committed, he should now be left alone to live out what is left of his old age in peace. The main reason for this compassionate point of view is that the crimes in question were committed a very long time ago and Mohnke is a nice, neighbourly, harmless old man who could not hurt a fly. For time is the enemy for those seeking justice against ageing Nazi war criminals like Mohnke. The older the dwindling ranks of surviving Nazis become, the feebler they seem on the public's television screens, then the harder it is to persuade those who were not alive in the heyday of Nazi bestiality that such men should still be brought to account. Because a seventy-eight-year-old

352

man with a wooden foot and a limp does not look remotely capable of ordering the murder of hundreds of defenceless prisoners in cold blood, it is assumed that this was always so. The failure to comprehend the nature of the crime on the part of the multitudes of the innocent and the young of the late 1980s is in part a failure of the imagination to intuitively grasp the full reality of the violence and horror of Nazi evil. How else could this concerned and compassionate section of the public conclude that it is wrong to seek justice for mass murder simply because of the passage of time and the ageing of the perpetrators? As Neal Sher, Director of the Office of Special Investigations in the United States Justice Department, remarked in Hong Kong in April 1988 on the subject of these killer-pensioners: 'They look very grandfatherly. They don't walk around in black uniforms carrying whips.' But, he concluded: 'We must show mass murderers that the passage of time will not allow them to escape.'

Elsewhere Sher has declared:

> If a person has persecuted others ... I will pursue them whether it can be shown that the persecution was committed against thousands or a single individual. I believe justice demands an accounting, no matter the passage of time, and it is not the kind of thing that can or should be quantified.

A second reason why some people oppose the prosecution of Nazi war criminals is that similar crimes were committed by Allied troops against the Germans. There is some truth in this. Indeed, it seems a fact of life of almost every major conflict that 'our' side may on occasion mete out to the enemy what it is claimed 'they' mete out all too frequently to 'us'. The English writer Robert Graves, for example, has described how on the battlefields of the Western Front in the First World War, British Tommies were sometimes known to have placed hand grenades (with the safety pins pulled out) in the greatcoat pockets of German prisoners whom they could not be bothered to escort to the rear. And as recently as the Vietnam War dreadful incidents have been attributed to both sides in the conflict, including the American side, the most notorious being the My Lai massacre.

In March 1968, at the village of My Lai in South Vietnam, nearly 500 unarmed and peaceful Vietnamese villagers were slaughtered by an American infantry company in circumstances every bit as barbaric and horrific as the worst kind of comparable SS atrocity in the Second World War. As one American participant described it in a recent interview:

> I started killing: old men, women, children, water buffaloes, everything. We were told to leave nothing standing. I killed

353

another twenty to twenty-five, cut their throats, cut off their hands, cut out their tongues, their hair, scalped 'em, I did it. I didn't know I had it in me. I lined up fifty people, women, old men, children, everybody, and just mowed 'em down. It was just like the gas chambers – what Hitler did.

But the GIs went a good deal further than the Waffen-SS had normally ever done, and to the universal carnage added a horrifying catalogue of acts of sexual sadism, including the raping, sodomizing, bayoneting and butchering of women and young girls (a fact deeply covered up by the American authorities). Only one man was found guilty of the crimes committed at My Lai – a platoon commander, Lieutenant William Calley, who had been charged with the murder of 109 civilians, was found guilty of the murder of 20, and sentenced to life imprisonment, though in the end he never served a day in prison for his part in one of the most notorious war crimes in recent history.

In the Second World War, as we have seen, the killing of prisoners of war was almost routine on both sides on the Russian Front. On the Western Front such atrocities were less frequent, but they did occur, particularly in units in which Wilhelm Mohnke held command. But the Germans were not alone to blame. There were persistent rumours in Normandy that SS troops would not be taken prisoner, and it is a fact that Kurt Meyer's death sentence was commuted by the C-in-C of the Canadian Occupation Forces because he knew that Canadian troops had also been guilty of killing prisoners of war. At the trial of one of Mohnke's battalion commanders in Normandy, furthermore, it was alleged that a British armoured car regiment, the Inns of Court, had been involved in a dubious action against the Hitler Jugend Division in which German prisoners had been shot.

The murder of prisoners of war was not confined to the land. It was alleged that in July 1942, for example, Britain's most decorated submarine commander, Commander Anthony Miers (later Rear Admiral Sir Anthony Miers VC, KBE, CB, DSO and Bar), intercepted a German freighter off Crete, sank her, and then machine-gunned seven German survivors, members of a German Alpine Regiment in Crete, who had surrendered and were therefore prisoners of war, after they had been cast adrift in a rubber dinghy. Three weeks after the alleged killings Commander Miers received the Victoria Cross from King George VI. A German submarine commander, Lieutenant Commander Eck, who also machine-gunned survivors from the Greek merchant ship *Peleus* after the ship had been sunk off the West African coast, was tried for war crimes by the British in 1945 and executed by firing squad along with two of his officers.

The most notorious example of brutality against Axis prisoners, however, involved one of America's greatest combat leaders, General Patton. This is what happened.

After the Malmédy massacre trial was over, one of the trial judges, in a confidential, off-the-record aside, intimated to the chief defence counsel, Willis Everett, that he had been a little unhappy about the trial because he knew that on various occasions American troops had done precisely what the Malmédy SS men had been accused of doing. This was true. Worse, it could be argued that American's most adulated army commander, the bold and dashing General George Patton, could himself have been put on trial for the very same reason that SS-Oberstgruppenführer Sepp Dietrich, commander of the Sixth Panzer Army in the Battle of the Bulge, had been put on trial at Dachau. In Patton's case, the incident in question was known as the Biscari massacre.

Like the Malmédy massacre, the Biscari massacre involved more than one set of mass murders, but all seemed to stem from a common cause – Patton's blood-curdling exhortation to his troops on the eve of the invasion of Sicily in July 1943. According to a junior officer who took what Patton said very much to heart, the general's speech went like this:

> When we land against the enemy, don't forget to hit him and hit him hard. When we meet the enemy we will kill him. We will show him no mercy. He has killed thousands of your comrades and he must die. If you company officers in leading your men against the enemy find him shooting at you and when you get within two hundred yards of him he wishes to surrender – oh no! That bastard will die! You will kill him. Stick him between the third and fourth ribs. You will tell your men that. They must have the killer instinct. Tell them to stick him. Stick him in the liver. We will get the name of killers and killers are immortal. When word reaches him that he is being faced by a killer battalion he will fight less. We must build up that name as killers.

What Patton was trying to do in his own inimitable and terrifyingly blunt way was to instil the fighting spirit in an element of his Seventh Army – the 45th Infantry Division commanded by Major General Troy H. Middleton – that was to form a spearhead of the invasion but had not yet seen any action in the war. In its emphasis on ruthlessness and implacable hatred of the enemy Patton's speech resembled Kurt Meyer's address to his troops of the 12 SS Hitler Youth Division on the eve of the Normandy invasion and Sepp Dietrich's Order of the Day to the Sixth Panzer Army at the start of the Ardennes offensive. That it got through to the fighting men is evident from a recollection of one of them, a private soldier who took part in the ensuing battle and later recalled: 'We were told that General Patton said that if they don't surrender until you get up close to them, then look for their third and fourth ribs and stick it in there. Fuck them – no prisoners!'

On the assault ship heading for the invasion beaches one of the battalion commanders told his men over the ship's loudspeakers that no enemy soldiers were to be taken prisoner unless they came down the beaches with their hands in the air. It was kill or be killed, he told his men – 'so for God's sake kill!' And in a perfect echo of Kurt Meyer's words at the Abbaye Ardenne after D-Day, an officer in the 45th Division remembered that Patton had said: 'The more prisoners we took, the more we'd have to feed, and not to fool with prisoners.'

Most alarmingly, Patton's general line of argument was rapidly turned into concrete action as the invasion proceeded. On 14 July Patton's fiery words came back to haunt him. That evening he recorded in his diary that his Corps Commander, General Omar Bradley, had reported 'in great excitement that a captain had been responsible for the murder of perhaps as many as seventy prisoners.' Patton's instinctive reaction to this news was disturbingly ambivalent. The prisoners had not only been shot in cold blood, which was bad enough, but they had been shot in ranks, 'an even greater error,' Patton noted – presumably because corpses in neat rows could hardly be made to look like battlefield casualties. Patton continued: 'I told Bradley that it was probably an exaggeration but in any case to tell the officer to certify that the dead men were snipers or had attempted to escape or something, as it would make a stink in the Press, and also would drive the civilians mad. Anyhow, they are dead, so nothing can be done about it.'

The next morning the 45th Division Chaplain, Lt-Col. William E. King, went out to inspect a group of bodies in an olive grove along the road between Biscari and the nearby airfield. Altogether thirty-four Italian and two German soldiers had been shot after first having had to take off their boots and shirts to deter escape. At the airfield the chaplain saw another group of bodies lying in a line as if they had been mowed down by a machine gun. Further on, near the command post of the 2nd Battalion, 180th Infantry Regiment, there was another group of bodies. At the battalion command post several angry American soldiers, sickened by what they had seen the previous day, remonstrated with the chaplain. The prisoners had been shot with their hands up while being taken to the rear, they complained bitterly. They had gone into the war to fight that sort of brutality.

Near the command post the chaplain came upon another group of prisoners who were still alive – if only by the skin of their teeth. When the chaplain went into the compound where the prisoners had been herded, one of the American guards asked him whether he had come to bury the prisoners. 'Here they are,' the guard told him, 'and here I am with this tommy-gun, and here you are, and we have been told not to take any prisoners.'

On General Bradley's orders an investigation began immediately. It was soon determined that all the killings had been carried out by elements of the 180th Infantry Regiment, commanded by Colonel E. Cookson, who claimed to have repeated Patton's speech word for word to his men. Two cases were brought to trial by general court martial, though it is likely that more than two incidents had occurred. At the first trial in September Sergeant Horace T. West of the 180th Infantry Regiment, 45th Division, was charged with violation of the 92nd Article of War in that he had 'with malice aforethought, wilfully, deliberately, feloniously, unlawfully and with premeditation . . . murdered thirty-seven Axis prisoners of war.'

West admitted that he had killed the prisoners, nearly all of them with his own gun. But he claimed that he had done so under the belief that he was acting under orders and while the balance of his mind was disturbed. Instructed by his battalion commander to take the prisoners to the rear, West merely marched them a few hundred yards down the road to the airfield, warned his comrades to look the other way if they did not want to watch, then gunned down all but half a dozen or so of the prisoners with a Thompson sub-machine gun he had borrowed from another guard.

Sergeant West was found guilty of multiple murder and sentenced to life imprisonment; but little more than a year later the sentence was commuted and West was returned to the ranks as a private soldier.

The second case, also involving the 180th Infantry Regiment, was not dissimilar from the first. During the battle for the airfield near Biscari, forty Italian soldiers surrendered to men of C Company commanded by Captain John C. Compton. Asked by a company sergeant what should be done with the prisoners, Compton ordered them to be shot, and a firing squad of a score or more of American soldiers promptly carried out the executions. In his defence, Compton was in no doubt that he was carrying out superior orders – before long a favourite Nazi plea in the post-war war crimes trials – and he cited Patton's inflammatory invasion speech quoted above. 'I ordered them shot,' claimed Compton, 'because I thought it came under the General's instructions. Right or wrong, a three star general's advice is good enough for me and I took him at his word.' Unlike the luckless, but profoundly culpable Sergeant West, Captain Compton was found not guilty of murder and was acquitted – only to be killed in combat a short while later.

Grave doubts were raised about the legal safeness of Compton's acquittal and about Patton's role in the war crimes committed by American troops in Sicily. There was consternation when word of Patton's pre-invasion speech reached Washington and had it not been for the overriding military requirements of the impending Normandy invasion it is likely that

Eisenhower would have relieved Patton of his command on account of the Biscari killings and other transgressions of one kind or another. Both the atrocities and the trials were, of course, kept a close secret at the time, partly for fear of giving the Germans a stunning propaganda coup and partly to deny a section of the American public a chance to air their anti-war, if not pro-Fascist, sentiments. Thus the Biscari massacre was never raised as a formal defence or extenuation in German war crimes trials like the Mal-médy trial, and as far as can be ascertained it was not until Liddell Hart raised the matter informally and out of court at the time of the Siebken trial in Hamburg that the Biscari affair came to the ears of interested parties in Germany.

But had the Biscari case been handled in the same way as the Malmédy trial, along the lines laid down by the Occupation authorities at the time, the following interesting sentences would have been handed down to the chain-of-command officers responsible: Army Commander, General Patton – life imprisonment; Corps Commander, General Bradley – 10 years; Regimental Commander, Colonel Cookson – death. What sentence the Divisional Commander, General Middleton, would have received we can only guess, for his German opposite number, Oberführer Wilhelm Mohnke, was not available for judgement and sentence in the Malmédy trial.

It cannot be denied that war crimes have indeed been committed by the Allies in the Second World War, and in other conflicts both before and after. But we have two points to make in this respect. The first is that as far as the Second World War is concerned there were considerable differences between the Allies and the Germans with regard to the scale, frequency and premeditation of the war crimes committed (specifically, prisoner of war murders) and that no wrong-doing which Allied soldiers might have perpetrated on occasion can measure up to the sheer vastness of the overall picture of German violence and brutality in the European War. Even so, there is nothing to prevent anyone from investigating Allied war crimes, just as we have investigated German ones; indeed, it would seem perfectly fair and proper to do so.*

The second point is that the fact that one side committed a war crime does not exonerate anyone who committed exactly the same crime on the other side. The fact that Mohnke is now in his sere and yellow years, the fact that on occasion the British, Canadians and Americans committed the

---

* One school of thought still continues to argue that the Allied aerial bombing campaign against German cities, in which many hundreds of thousands of German civilians lost their lives, is an Allied war crime commensurate in scale to Nazi atrocities against non-Jewish civilians in Nazi-occupied Europe.

same sort of crime of which Mohnke is accused, does not in our opinion invalidate the charges against him or provide a valid reason why a prosecution should not be brought against him.

We have now reached a position where in our view the governments of the combatant nations of the Second World War should get off the fence and come to one of two decisions:

1 Either bring all outstanding war crimes cases to trial

2 Or abandon all war crimes prosecutions for ever more, stating their reasons for so doing.

If, in the best interests of justice, the British, Canadian and American governments elect for the first alteranative, then it will be incumbent on them, if they wish to see justice prevail in the Mohnke case, to put all due and reasonable pressure on the West German authorities to persuade them to set the wheels of justice in motion. The determination and decisiveness shown by France in bringing Klaus Barbie to trial and demanding the extradition of Aloïs Brunner from Syria shows what can be done when there is a will to do it. The British, the Canadians and the Americans should take heed of this. For as Simon Wiesenthal, the renowned Holocaust survivor and Nazi hunter, has declared: 'When history looks back, I want people to know the Nazis were not able to kill eleven million people and get away with it.'

SOURCE NOTES

PART I

p. 3 *et seq*. Mohnke's final session with Hitler is based on Mohnke's own account given in an interview with James O'Donnell and published in O'Donnell's *The Berlin Bunker*, (London, 1979).

PART II

pp. 11–12. Mohnke's early career is based on the biographical entry in *Die Generale der Waffen-SS* by Nikolaus von Preradovich, (Berg am See, 1985), which is in turn based on Mohnke's official SS cvs in the Berlin Document Centre.

p. 12 *et seq*. For the early years of the Leibstandarte see *inter alia The Leibstandarte* by Rudolf Lehmann, vol 1, (J. J. Federwicz Publishing, Winnipeg, 1987); *Die Leibstandarte im Bild* by Rudolf Lehmann, (Osnabrück, 1983); *Hitler's Guard – The Story of the Leibstandarte SS Adolf Hitler 1933–45* by James J. Weingartner, (Southern Illinois University Press, 1975); *Hitler's Elite – Leibstandarte SS* by James Lucas and Matthew Cooper, (London, 1975); *History of the SS* by G. S. Graber, (London, 1978); *Hitler's Gladiator* by Charles Messenger, (London, 1988).

p. 14. For the Roehm purge see *The Knight of the Long Knives* by James Gallo, (New York, 1972).

p. 18. 'These men revealed. . . .' Quotation from Lucas and Cooper, op. cit.

p. 18. 'After a time we got to a point. . . .' *idem*.

p. 19 *et seq*. For the Leibstandarte in the Polish campaign see Lehmann, op. cit. and Weingartner, op. cit.

p. 20. War crimes alleged to have been committed by the 2nd Battalion Leibstandarte in Poland are listed by the United Nations War Crimes Commission under file reference number 284/P/G/29.

361

p. 21 *et seq*. For the Leibstandarte after Poland, including Hitler's visit to Bad Ems, see Lehmann, *The Leibstandarte*.

p. 22–3. The original of Jodl's unpublished letter to Ley is in the Sayer Archives, Wentworth.

PART III

p. 27 *et seq*. There are many general accounts of the British retreat to Dunkirk. For the overall picture see *The War in France and Flanders 1939–40* by Major L. F. Ellis, (HMSO, 1953) and *Destination Dunkirk* by Gregory Blaxland, (London, 1973). The account of the retreat of the 2nd Royal Warwicks to Wormhoudt is based on *History of the Royal Warwickshire Regiment 1919–55* by Marcus Cunliffe, (London, 1956), the Battalion War Diary and Personal Diary of Captain L. T. Tomes, Battalion Adjutant, extracts of which have been published in *Massacre on the Road to Dunkirk* by Leslie Aitken, 2nd edition, (London, 1988).

p. 34. 'I think this was the worst experince. . . .' Tomes, op. cit.

p. 35. 'British soldiers, Germans surround! . . .' Tomes, op. cit.

p. 37 *et seq*. The overall account of the Battle for Wormhoudt is based on the Royal Warwicks regimental history and Battalion War Diary, plus the Intelligence Summary of the 2nd Battalion 28–9 May 1940.

p. 38. 'Hello, boys! We're here. . . .' Intelligence Summary, op. cit.

P. 39. 'When we drove along. . . .' Max Wünsche quoted in *Hitler's Gladiator* by Charles Messenger, (London, 1988).

pp. 40–5, Arthur Baxter's account is from a letter by Arthur R. Baxter, Pershore, Worcs, to Tom H. Nicholls, Leamington Spa, dated 14 December 1979 and forwarded to Jeff Rooker, MP, by T. H. Nicholls on 23 May 1988. Also on a letter from Arthur Baxter to Jeff Rooker, MP, dated 21 April 1988.

p. 46. 'We entered the square in Wormhoudt. . . .' Corporal Oxley quoted in the official history of the Cheshire Regiment pp. 182–4.

p. 48. 'Sure enough, there they were. . . .' Bill Cordrey quoted by Aitken, op. cit.

p. 49. XIX War Diary quoted in Warwicks regimental history, op. cit.

p. 49. 'It became obvious that. . . .' Tomes, op. cit.

p. 50 *et seq*. The capture of British personnel at Wormhoudt is based on three sets of testimony by survivors, including Bill Cordrey, Charles Daley, Bert Evans, George Merry, Richard Parry, Alf Tombs, Reginald West. The first set is contained in the debriefing statements collected by the War Crimes Interrogation Unit shortly after the war. The second set is contained in interviews made by Leonard Aitken in the 1970s. The third set is based on telephone interviews with a dwindling number of survivors by the authors in 1989. The principal source for the events at Wormhoudt are the two reports prepared by the War Crimes Interrogation Unit at the London District Cage in 1947 – WCIV/LDC/1500 and WCIV/LDC/1650.

p. 54. 'We were told to get out of the carrier. . . .' Cordrey quoted by Aitken, op. cit.

p. 55. 'I saw a man with an anti-tank rifle. . . .' Tomes diary, op. cit.

p. 56. Movements of Battalion HQ etc. described in the regimental history and battalion war diary, op. cit.

p. 57. 'After coming to I saw some Germans. . . .' Oxley in Cheshire regimental history, op. cit.

pp. 58–9. 'I did not abandon my gun. . . .' Letter from Tom H. Nicholls, Leamington Spa, to Jeff Rooker, MP, dated 22 April 1988.

p. 59. Shooting of men of Worcester Regimet from anonymous letter from Malvern, Worcs, to Jeff Rooker, MP, 21 April 1988, by survivor. Also article in Worcestershire Regiment magazine, October 1987 regarding murder of men of 8th Battalion The Worcestershire Regiment in the barn at Wormhoudt, p. 60. The account of the massacre uses the same body of testimony cited for the capture (*see* source notes for p. 50 *et seq.*)

p. 61. 'There were bodies of our lads. . . ' Tombs in a written statement to the Royal Warwickshire Regiment after his repatriation to Britain from German POW camp (no date).

p. 61. 'As they stood there. . . .' Evans quoted in Aitken, op. cit, p. 73.

pp. 62–3. For the incident at the LAH Battalion HQ see Senf's testimony in the second Wormhoudt Report, also Parry's statement to the WCIU, and interview material in Aitken, op. cit.

p. 64. 'In the far left-hand corner of the barn. . . .' Letter from J. A. Borland, Chelmsley Wood, to Jeff Rooker, MP, June 1988.

p. 66. Details of SS guards from second Wormhoudt Report.

p. 66. Lynn-Allen incident based on Evans' testimony to WCIU and Aitken, also statement by Lt Kenneth Keene, Royal Warwicks, to Royal Warwicks HQ, Warwick on 16 December 1943.

p. 66. Corporal Gill's version of this incident is in his statement for the WCIU in the Wormhoudt Report.

p. 67. Kramer's evidence about 6.35mm pistols is from his statement to the WCIU in the second Wormhoudt Report.

p. 69. Identity of soldier who survived the firing squad is in statements to WCIU by Lavelle and Daley included in Wormhoudt Report, also Keene, op. cit.

p. 70. Fahey incident in Brian Fahey's unpublished manuscript account entitled *Wormhoudt* sent to the authors in December 1988.

p. 71. For the scene in the barn when the shooting was over see Aitken, op. cit.

p. 71. Wildsmith's version is in *Meeting of Generals* by Tony Foster, (Toronto, 1986).

p. 72. The shooting of Parry is in the Wormhoudt Report and Aitken. The Merry incident is also in Aitken.

p. 74. 'I'd just got into the grounds of this farm. . . .' Evans in written statement to The Royal Warwickshire Regiment, Warwick, on repatriation from German POW camp.

pp. 75–6. Escape attempts in Wormhoudt Report (statement by Corporal Gill), and Aitken, also Tombs statement to Royal Warwicks HQ.

pp. 76–8. Hall and West escape attempts in Aitken, op, cit.

p. 78. General Guderian quote for his *Panzer Leader*, (London, 1952).

pp. 79–80. Account of treatment of second batch of POWs based on Albert Montague's statement to WCIU in Wormhoudt Report, plus telephone interview with Montague by authors, Tomes' diary and Aitken, op. cit.

p. 81. 'Sometime before midnight. . . .' Beutler in statement to WCIU in second Wormhoudt Report.

p. 81. LAH inventory of captured British soldiers and equipment in Lehmann, vol. 1, *The Leibstandarte*.

p. 81. Rodenbücher in statement to WCIU in second Wormhoudt Report.

pp. 82–4. Survivors' final moments at barn from Wormhoudt Report, Aitken and Keene, op. cit.

p. 83. 'Fortunately they saw me. . . .' Parry quoted in Aitken, op. cit.

p. 83. 'The swines.' Lavelle to WCIU in Wormhoudt Report.

p. 86. 'They never returned. . . .' Jeff Rooker, MP, to the House of Commons (*Hansard*, 25 May 1988).

p. 87. 'I shall be grateful if you will come to London. . . .' Urgent memorandum from J. A. G. to Daley, 3 June 1947.

pp. 87 *et seq*. Colonel Scotland profile from *The London Cage* by Lt-Col. A. P. Scotland, (London, 1957).

p. 90. Details of London Cage and personnel from unpublished manuscript entitled *Escape to Murder* by T. X. H. Pantcheff, (no date).

pp. 91–2. For the Le Paradis case see Scotland, op. cit., an account of the massacre in *After the Battle* magazine, and *The Vengeance of Private Pooley* by Cyril Jolly, (London, 1956).

p. 92. Tom Field-Fisher's comments on authors' first draft of Le Paradis account, 1989.

p. 94. 'None of them broke down. . . .' T. X. H. Pantcheff in telephone interview with authors, 1988–9.

p. 94. 'After he had shown me how he had lain. . . .' Pantcheff, ibid.

p. 95. Otto Baum on the London Cage in letter to authors from Jost W. Schneider, Wuppertal, dated 21 August 1988.

p. 95. 'As for our methods at the Cage. . . .' Scotland, op. cit.

p. 97. 'The deed of which the Leibstandarte is accused. . . .' Dietrich's statement to the WCIU in Wormhoudt Report.

p. 98. For the power of the SS oath see Scotland, op. cit.

p. 99. 'One man we were never able to trace. . . .' Scotland, op. cit.

p. 99. 'As in similar investigations. . . .' Wormhoudt Report, (WCIU/LDC/1500).

p. 99. 'It has thus only been possible to trace one man. . . .' Wormhoudt Report, ibid.

p. 100. Richter on Senf in letter from Richard Richter to Ministry of Defence dated 14 October 1988, copy sent to Jeff Rooker, MP.

p. 101. 'There was no point in going on and on for nothing. . . .' Pantcheff in telephone interview with the authors, op. cit.

p. 102. 'I'd have said there was a prima facie case against Mohnke. . . .' Pantcheff, ibid.

p. 103. 'When I was interrogated. . . .' Beutler to WCIU in Wormhoudt Report.

p. 103. 'I was asked during my oral interrogation. . . .' Mass to WCIU in Wormhoudt Report.

p. 104. 'I've met Mr Otto Baum. . . .' Letter to authors from Jost W. Schneider, Wuppertal, West Germany, 27 October 1988.

p. 105. 'The bodies of the victims. . . .' Second Wormhoudt Report.

p. 105. Gautier quoted in article by David Nicholson-Lord entitled Pressure grows to make SS officer stand trial in *The Times*, London, 25 June 1988.

p. 105. Army Graves records in letter from Imperial War Graves Commission to W. J. Kelly, Huddersfield, dated 10 December 1952, re: grave of Pte B. P. Kelly.

p. 106. 'There can be no doubt. . . .' Freeman's speech in *Hansard*, 28 June 1940.

p. 107. 'The attitude of the local French was hostile. . . .' Letter from George Amos, Takely, Herts, to Jeff Rooker, MP, 29 April 1988.

p. 108. Le Fort Rose information in second Wormhoudt Report.

p. 108. Some details of the 'paroxysm of violence' in Wormhoudt were given by Tom Nicholls in telephone interview with authors and by French eyewitnesses in *The Cook Report*, (Roger Cook, Central TV, Birmingham, 7 June 1988 and 14 June 1988).

p. 111. Parry's information (and quotes) from statements to WCIU in first and second Wormhoudt Reports.

p. 112. Rules of evidence in military courts explained in *Crossroads of Death* by James J. Weingartner, (London, 1979). *See also The Trial of Kurt Meyer* by Lt-Col. B. J. S. Macdonald, QC. Field-Fisher's comment on evidence in marginal note to author's first draft of manuscript 1989.

p. 112–13. Statistical analysis based on review of all German evidence to WCIU in both Wormhoudt Reports.

p. 114. German Ten Commandments quoted in *The Scourge of the Swastika* by Lord Russell of Liverpool, (London, 1955).

p. 114–15. 'Before the start of a big operation. . . .' Maas in Wormhoudt Report, Hasewinkel, op. cit.

p. 118. Descriptions and quotes by SS men in Wormhoudt Reports.

p. 119–20. 'When I asked him whether he suspected anything. . . .' Kummert to WCIU in Wormhoudt Report. Quotes from Hasewinkel, Rofallski, Wachowiak, ibid.

p. 121. Revolver incident from Beutler, ibid.

p. 123–4. Senf quotes from second Wormhoudt Report, p. 126, ibid.

p. 128–30. SS statements from Wormhoudt Reports.

p. 132. The allegation against the DLI is contained in *Dunkirk – The Necessary Myth* by Nicholas Harman (London, 1982). The inquiry refuting the allegation is outlined in a letter to *World War II Investigator* magazine from P. J. Jeffreys and I. R. English dated 23 November 1988.

p. 132. 'There was good reason for assuming. . . .' Scotland, op. cit.

p. 133. 'The truth of the matter is that the men of the Waffen-SS were bad losers.' We are indebted for this assessment to an appraisal by Phil Buss, quoted in a letter to Ian Sayer from Hugh Page Taylor dated 26 June 1988.

p. 133. 'Everyone talked of revenge.' Aitken, op. cit.

p. 134. Jeff Rooker's question to the House in *Hansard*, 25 May 1988.

p. 135. 'The Wormhoudt massacre was a sordid event. . . .' Freeman in *Hansard*, 28 June 1988.

PART IV

p. 139. Hitler quote and LAH after French campaign in Lehmann, *The Leibstandarte*, op. cit.

p. 139–40. 'It was a warm spring evening in March 1941. . . .' Lehmann, op. cit.

p. 141. 'The Yugoslavian air force. . . .' Lehmann, op. cit. Mohnke's wounding, idem.

p. 141. '*Das Bein bleibt dran.* . . .' Information relayed by Gerd Cuppens, s-Gravenwezel, Belgium.

p. 141. Mohnke's career, April 1941 to March 1942, in Preradovich, *Die Generale der Waffen-SS* (Berg Am See, 1985).

p. 142. LAH brutality in Russia (including quotes) from Lucas and Cooper, op. cit.

PART V

p. 149–50. 12th SS Panzer Division recce battalion views D-Day invasion. See *Blood and Honour – The History of the 12th SS Panzer Division* by Craig W. H. Luther (San José, Calif., 1987).

p. 150. 'Hundreds of enemy ships sighted. . . .' Luther, op. cit.

p. 151 *et seq*. For the formation and training of the 12th SS Panzers see Luther, op. cit.

p. 154. 'SS troops shall take no prisoners. . . .' Evidence given to SHAEF Court of Inquiry, Chartres, 1944 (PRO ref. no. TS 26/856/XP 0/80). Following quotes on p. 155, idem.

p. 155. The Murder Division, Macdonald, op. cit. p. 15.

p. 155. Seventh Army orders quoted by Luther, op. cit., from Telephone Log of Seventh Army.

p. 156. Murders at Authie and Buron. In Part IV of Proceedings of SHAEF Court of Inquiry, France, 20 August 1944. *See also* Macdonald, op. cit.

p. 158. Argentan incident. SHAEF inquiry, op. cit. Captain Brown incident in Macdonald, op. cit.

p. 159. Abbaye Ardenne. Evidence placed before the Military Court at the trial of Kurt Meyer. See Macdonald, op. cit. Jesionek, quote pp. 158–9, idem.

p. 160. The Bretteville L'Orgeuilleuse incident. SHAEF Inquiry and Macdonald, op. cit.

p. 160. Bremer and the Château d'Audrieu incident. SHAEF Inquiry, op. cit.

p. 161. Engineering Battalion incident. SHAEF and Macdonald, op. cit.

p. 163 *et seq*. Fontenay-Le-Mesnil incident. Macdonald, op. cit. and United Nations War Crimes Commission charge sheet no 67/CRO/ 12SS/2.

p. 165. Le Mesnil-Patry case. SHAEF Inquiry, Record of Trial of Siebken and Schnabel, Macdonald, op. cit., and United Nations op. cit. p. 166. Les Saullets incident, SHAEF, Macdonald, op. cit.

p. 166. Les Saullets murders, United Nations op. cit. p. 167, Stangenberg case, SHAEF, Macdonald, op. cit. and United Nations.

p. 170. Reaction to news of murders of Canadian POWs summarized in Macdonalds, op. cit. ('Introduction').

p. 177. Recovery of bodies at Haut du Bosq in Macdonald and United Nations, op. cit.

p. 179. Assessment of Mohnke in Macdonald, pp. 29–30.

p. 180. 'I have here during these proceedings. . . .' Meyer quoted in Macdonald, op. cit. See also Tony Foster *Meeting of Generals* (Ontario, 1986).

p. 181. 'If murders repeatedly took place. . . .' Macdonald, op. cit.

p. 182. Eberbach's assessment of Mohnke and other SS officers cited by Macdonald.

p. 182. For Vokes various reasons for commuting Meyer's death sentence see Luther, op. cit. p. 193, citing *Vokes, My Story* by Major-General Vokes (Ottawa). See also Luther op. cit. for summary of Meyer's subsequent life.

p. 183. Index of War Crimes listed by Canadian Government as FD No. 1, folio 26, RG 24, vol. 2906 File HQS 8959–9–5 vol. 1.

p. 184. 'Confirmation of Mohnke's complicity. . . .' Macdonald, pp. 30–1.

p. 184. '"The Canadian Government," railed Macdonald. . . .' From letter to D. A. A. G. London from Lt-Col. Macdonald dated 27 February 1946.

p. 185. 'This is a case which should certainly be proceeded with . . . .' Letter to Judge Advocate General, London, dated 22 May 1946.

p. 186. 'Two French civilians. . . .' From Macdonald, op. cit., p. 187.

p. 187. Schnabel's deposition of 18 June 1948 is included in the papers of the Record of Trial of Siebken and Schnabel, (PRO WO 235/796).

p. 188. Schnabel's second statement in Record of Trial, op. cit.

p. 190. Albers' deposition in Record of Trial, op. cit.

p. 191. Siebken's deposition in Record of Trial, op. cit.

pp. 194–228. The section entitled 'Trial' is based on the Record of Trial (Military Courts for the Trial of War Criminals) of Bernhard Siebken, Dietrich Schnabel, Heinrich Albers and Fritz Gunther Bundschuh before a British Military Court in Hamburg on 28 August and 21 October to 9 November 1948. The trial records and related documents are contained in the Public Records Office at Kew, file reference no WO 235/796. Unless otherwise stated all quotations in this section, together with much ancillary matter, come from the papers in this file. The source notes that follow relate only to material of different origin.

p. 197. Footnote, Macdonald's version is contained in his *Trial of Kurt Meyer* p. 24.

p. 207. Meyer's confirmation was in a letter sent to Charles Messenger from Leverkusen, West Germany, July 1988.

p. 213. The Inns of Court War Diary from which this quote is taken is in the PRO ref. WO 171/854. The diary account of this action is also printed in Hubert Meyer's *Kriegsgeschichte der 12–SS Panzer Division Hitler Jugend*, (Osnabrück, 1982). Meyer's comment on the Siebke trial is on pp. 588–9 vol. II.

p. 226. Liddel Hart's letter to Meitzel copied in Meyer's letter to Messenger, op. cit.

p. 228. For Albert Pierrepoint see *Pierrepoint* by Albert Pierrepoint (London, 1974).

p. 233. Mohnke's UN War Crimes Commissin charge no. for the Normandy killings is 67/CNO/12SS/2 and his Wanted List no. is 169 (murder).

p. 236. 'A lot of prisoners of war were captured in Normandy. . . .' Quoted in *The Citizen*, Toronto, 1988.

PART VI

Among the many works written about the Ardennes offensive, the following were especially useful for background to Peiper's attempted thrust to the Meuse: *Battle of the Bulge – Then and Now* by Jean Paul Pallud, (London, 1984); *The Battle of the Bulge – The Definitive Account* by Charles B. Macdonald, (London, 1984); *The Bitter Woods* by John S. D. Eisenhower, (London, 1969); *The Ardennes – Battle of the Bulge* by Hugh M. Cole, (United States Army in World War II, Washington DC, 1965).

For the Malmédy massacre and trial, the most analytical and scholarly published source is *Crossroads of Death* by James J. Weingartner, (University of California Press, 1979), to which we have referred on a number of occasions. The primary source for the trial is, of course, the trial records (United States versus Bersin et al). The Malmédy trial records (338 6–24) are contained in 75 boxes in Suitland (boxes 4–9 labelled Exhibit 1–6; boxes 71–75 labelled Testimony 1–5; boxes 22–28 labelled Evidence 1–7).

p. 242. 'Prisoners? You know what to do with them. . . .' In *Hitler's Last Gamble* by Jacques Nobécourt, (London, 1967).

p. 242. Footnote. Operation Black orders cited in *The Nazi Hunters* by Charles Ashman and Robert Wagman, (New York, 1988).

p. 245. 'The battle will decide whether Germany. . . .' From *SS Peiper* by Leo Kessler, (London, 1986), citing Skorzeny.

p. 245. 'I did not read the material given to me. . . .' Peiper in a statement made to the Court (from the Malmédy Trial Records).

p. 247. 'About midnight a group of officers. . . .' Bouck in a letter to Peiper after the war, quoted by Kessler op. cit. p. 50.

p. 248 *et seq*. This account of the massacre at the Baugnez crossroads is based on testimony in the Malmédy Trial records, Weingartner op. cit., Pallud op. cit.

p. 259. The circumstances of the shooting of civilians in Wanne is summarized on pp. 21–2 of the Review and Recommendations by the Deputy Judge Advocate, 7708 War Crimes Group, European Command, Germany, 20 October 1947 in the Malmédy Trial Records, and described in greater detail on p. 201 of the same, in an outline of the Evidence for the Prosecution against Hans Trettin.

p. 263. 'SS troops captured US soldier. . . .' Weingartner op. cit. quoting SHAEF Inquiry into Malmédy massacre.

p. 266. 'On the afternoon of the day before the attack. . . .' Weingartner, p. 77–8, citing Proecutin Exhibit P–15–A.

p. 270. 'Someone pulled a black hood. . . .' Statement made by Tomczak at Landsberg on 22 January 1948, quoted in Whiting op. cit.

pp. 272 *et seq*. Sources for the 'Trial' section include the Malmédy trial records, also the helpful analysis in Weingartner *Crossroads of Death* op. cit., particularly with regard to the aftermath and judicial reviews of the case.

p. 287. 'I felt awfully sorry for my men. . . .' Quotation from regimental commander (name withheld) contributed by Gerd Cuppens, s-Gravenwezel, Belgium.

PART VII

p. 292. The main source for Mohnke in Berlin is James O'Donnell's unique interview with Mohnke, included in his *The Berlin Bunker* (London, 1979), to which we are indebted.

p. 292. Chuikov quote from *The End of the Third Reich* by Vasili I. Chuikov, (London, 1967).

p. 293. Hitler's remarks to Mohnke from O'Donnell, op. cit.

p. 294. 'Darkness had fallen. . . .' from *Hitler's Last Days* by Gerhard Boldt, (London, 1973).

p. 295. Müncheberg diary entries from *Flight in the Winter* by Jürgen Thorwald, (London, 1953).

pp. 296–7 Müncheberg diary from Thorwald, op. cit.

p. 298. '*Wer kämphft, kann sterben . . . .*' From *The Decline and Fall of Nazi Germany and Imperial Japan* by Hans Dollinger, (London, 1968).

p. 299. 'We set up the court-martial tribunal . . . .' O'Donnell, op. cit.

pp. 300–2, Hitler's session with Mohnke in O'Donnell, op. cit.

p. 303. 'Going over to the coat-rack. . . .' O'Donnell, op. cit.

p. 305. For the situation in the Bunker on the eve of the breakout, in addition to O'Donnell, see also accounts by Traudl Junge and Otto Günsche in *Last Witnesses in the Bunker* by Pierre Galante and Eugene Silianoff, (London, 1989).

p. 306. 'General Mohnke gave out weapons. . . .' Junge in Galante and Silianoff, op. cit. 'We detroyed all out identity papers. . . .' ibid.

p. 307. 'From the dark gangways. . . .' Schenk quoted in O'Donnell, op. cit.

p. 308. 'Orders are to be obeyed. . . .' O'Donnell, op. cit. 'I now had a panoramic view . . . .' ibid.

p. 310. 'It was a fantastic apparition. . . .' O'Donnell, op. cit.

p. 310. 'Mohnke and Günsche sat down. . . .' Junge in Galante and Silianoff, op. cit.

p. 311. 'The generals replied. . . .' Günsche in Galante and Silianoff, op. cit.

PART VIII

p. 315–18. For Mohnke's account of his capture and treatment by the Russians in Berlin see O'Donnell, op. cit.

p. 319 *et seq*. Mohnke has provided no account of his experiences in the

Soviet Union, but from accounts by other Nazi generals, especially that of Hans Baur, it is possible to recontruct his probable curriculum vitae up to 1955.

p. 319. 'We entered a new wave. . . .' From *Hitler at my Side* by Hans Baur, (Houston, 1986).

p. 320. For Mohnke in the Cold War see *The Bormann Brotherhood* by William Stevenson (New York, 1973).

p. 320. 'These forces, as is well known. . . .' Stevenson, op. cit.

p. 321. 'Each day we were given. . . .' Baur, op. cit.

p. 321. The return to the Berlin Bunker is described in Baur and O'Donnell, op. cit.

p. 321 *et seq*. For the German generals' life in the camps and repatriation to Germany see Baur, op. cit.

p. 322. 'Let me make a personal, private remark. . . .' Mohnke quoted in O'Donnell, op. cit.

p. 323. The possibility that Mohnke did a deal with German and American intelligence was mentioned by Jeff Rooker, MP, in a speech of the House of Commons, London, in 1988.

PART IX

p. 327. For an account of the re-discovery of Mohnke in the early 1970s, see Aitken, op. cit.

p. 329. Conversation ith German officer based on Aitken, op. cit.

p. 330. Correspondence from West German State Prosecutor in Aitken, pp. 162–6.

p. 330. Canadian internal memo from Memorandum 1325–1 (DHIST), 4 June 1976, Directorate of History, Department of National Defence, Ottawa.

p. 330. Letter from C. R. Nixon, Deputy Minister for National Defence, to H. B. Robinson, Under-Secretary of State for External Affairs, Ottawa, 8 July 1976.

p. 331. 'The report of our investigation. . . .' Letter to L. R. Aitken from W. A. B. Douglas, Directorate of History, Department of National Defence, Ottawa, 16 Sept 1976.

p. 331. 'It is now almost two years. . . .' Aitken, op. cit. p. 167.

p. 331. Ministry of Defence vetting from letter to L. R. Aitken from Ministry of Defence, Whitehall, dated 27 November 1973.

p. 332 *et seq*. For a full account of Mohnke, Heidemann and Hitler Diaries see *Selling Hitler – The Story of the Hitler Diaries* by Robert Harris, (London, 1986).

p. 333. 'I'd known Mohnke for a long time. . . .' Harris, op. cit.

p. 335. Extracts from Hitler's diary in Harris, op. cit.

p. 335. 'I said to Herr Heidemann. . . .' Harris, op. cit.

p. 337. 'They had paid out £1,000 in grants. . . .' Regimental Secretary, The Royal Warwickshire Association, Warwick, to R. West, 29 Sept 1975.

p. 337. 'Frankly, I can find no justification. . . .' W. Douglas Clark, Brookes & Co, West Bromwich, to R. West, 2 March 1976.

p. 338. 'Surely, sir. . . .' R. West, Great Barr, Birmingham, to Jeff Rooker, MP, 6 June 1976.

p. 338. 'The money should be shared out. . . .' Survivors' quotes from *Birmingham Post*, 25 May 1977.

p. 338. 'I consider that anyone. . . .' F. Stevens, Monyhull, Birmingham, to *Birmingham Evening Mail*, 12 June 1977.

p. 339. 'Grants amounting to an average of £31 each. . . .' Based on information sent to Jeff Rooker, MP, by The Royal Warwickshire Association, 24 November 1977.

p. 339. 'had wrongly used the POW Fund of £2,631. . . .' Charity Competition to Jeff Rooker, MP, 12 December 1977.

p. 339. 'The Regiment has a very busy annual calendar. . . .' From letter to Jeff Rooker, MP, from a member of his constituency (name withheld), 17 November 1981.

p. 343. Question tabled in the Canadian Parliament. See House of Commons Debates (Hansard), Ottawa, 12 May 1988.

p. 344. Mohnke on the American Watch List. Information from District Attorney of King's County, Brooklyn, New York to Ian Sayer, 29 July 1988.

PART X

p. 349. 'The West Germans are our friends. . . .' Quoted from *The Nazi Hunters* by Charles Ashman and Robert J. Wagman (New York, 1988).

p. 350. Eerlebeck and Wiesenthal quotes from Ashman and Wagman, op. cit.

p. 351. Professor Draper letter from correspondence page of *The Times*, London, 1988.

p. 353. 'They look very grandfatherly. . . .' Reuters press release, 27 April 1988.

p. 353. 'If a person has persecuted others. . . .' Ashman and Wagman, op. cit. p. 16.

p. 353. 'I started killing. . . .' Quoted from My Lai: A Hal-Told Story by Michael Bilton and Kevin Sim, *Sunday Times Magazine*, London, 23 April 1989.

p. 354. For an account of the Commander Miers episode see the *Sunday Telegraph*, London, 5 February 1989, ('Was Royal Navy VC Submariner a War Criminal?').

p. 355. 'When we land against the enemy. . . .' From *Record of Trial of Compton, John T., 0–406922, Captain, Infantry*, 23 October 1943, USAJ.

p. 356. Patton diary entry from *The Patton Papers 1940–45*, (Boston, 1974).

p. 357. 'I ordered them shot. . . .' Compton Record of Trial, op. cit.

For a detailed account of the Biscari incident, see *Massacre at Biscari: Patton and an American War Crime* by James J. Weingartner, Southern Illinois University at Edwardsville, (1988).

p. 359. 'When history looks back. . . .' Ashman and Wagman, op. cit.

INDEX

375

Bild-Zeitung, 343
Birmingham Evening Mail, 338
Birmingham Post, 338
Biscari, 355, 358
Bizerta, 227
Blankenheim forest, 246, 266
Blitzkrieg, 139
Blood and Honor (Luther), 213n
Bodarwé, Adèle, 251
Boldt, Gerhard, 294–5
Bollezeele, 117
Bolt, K.J., 159n
Boraston, J.H., 171
Bord Gesprache (Heidemann), 333
Boris, Czar, 140
Borland, John, 64–5
Bormann, Martin: Night of the
    Long Knives, 15; and Fegelein,
    298; Hitler's suicide, 302;
    escape from Berlin, 303, 305,
    309, 310, 333; trial, 318
Botting, Douglas, 43n
Bouck, Lyle, 247
Boulogne, 32, 75
Bowes, A., 165
Box, Lance-Corporal, 74, 75
Bradley, Omar, 356, 357, 358
Brauchitsch, Heinrich von, 226
Braun, Eva, 291–312
Braunstein, Hermann, 351
Brazil, 89
Bremer, Gerhard: LAH, 12;
    character, 153, 182; Château
    d'Audrieu, 160–1, 235;
    SHAEF indictment, 173, 175;
    imprisonment, 183
Breslau, 17, 297
Bresseville-sur-Laize, 178n
Bretteville l'Orgueilleuse, 183,
    184
Britain: All-Party War Crimes
    Group, 343, 349; Anti-Tank
    Regiment, 36, 40, 45, 58, 59,

Britain – contd
    64, 115; Army Graves Service,
    105–6; British Expeditionary
    Force, 22–3, 27–36; Cheshire
    Regiment, 35, 36, 37–49, 54,
    56, 62, 64, 66n, 74, 96, 115,
    116, 133, 195n; Durham Light
    Infantry, 132; Essex Scottish
    Regiment, 171; Glosters, 30,
    34, 36; Hussars, 162, 166; Inns
    of Court Regiment, 213, 354;
    MI19, 90; Military Court, 91,
    194–228, 230, 234; Ministry of
    Defence, 331; Ministry of War,
    86; 50th Northumbrian
    Division, 132, 150; Oxfordshire
    and Buckinghamshire Light
    Infantry, 30; prisoners of war,
    40, 60–72, 120; Royal Air
    Force, 28, 90–1; Royal
    Artillery, 45, 51, 62, 64, 70, 74,
    109, 165, 195n; Royal Norfolk
    Regiment, 35, 91, 132, 133,
    327; Royal Scots Greys, 195n;
    Royal Warwickshire Regiment,
    23, 27–36, 37–49, 50–9, 62,
    64, 68, 70, 71n, 74, 79, 84, 87,
    106n, 109, 115, 125, 131, 133,
    171n, 327, 336–40, 341, 342;
    Second British Army, 150;
    Sherbrooke Fusiliers, 157n,
    158; Stormont, Dundas and
    Glengarry Highlanders, 159n;
    Third British Division, 150;
    21st Army Group, 170; War
    Crimes Interrogation Unit,
    90–102, 103, 104, 112n, 117,
    118, 342; War Office, 109; 8th
    Worcestershire Regiment, 59,
    64, 116; Worcestershire
    Yeomanry, 36, 39
British Legion, 343
Brown, W.L., 158

377

386

389